Introduction to Middle Level Education

Fourth Edition

Introduction to Middle Level Education

Sara Davis Powell

Belmont Abbey College

Pearson

Director and Publisher: Kevin Davis
Portfolio Manager: Drew Bennett
Managing Content Producer: Megan Moffo
Content Producer: Yagnesh Jani
Portfolio Management Assistant: Maria Feliberty
Executive Field Marketing Manager: Krista Clark
Procurement Specialist: Deidra Headlee
Cover Design: Pearson CSC, Jerilyn Bockorick
Cover Art: Hill Street Studios/Blend Images/Getty Images
Full Service Vendor: Pearson CSC
Full Service Project Management: Pearson CSC, Mohamed Hameed
Editorial Project Manager: Pearson CSC, Gheron Lising
Printer-Binder: LSC Communications
Cover Printer: LSC Communications
Text Font: PalatinoLTPro-Roman

Credits and acknowledgments borrowed from other sources and reproduced, with permission, in this textbook appear on appropriate page within text (or on page iv).

Photo Credits: Photo on page 3 courtesy of John Lounsbury; photo on pages 55 and 177 courtesy of Rhonda VanPelt; photo on pages 163, 193 and 215 courtesy of Jon Theiss/Pearson Education, Inc; photo on page 232 courtesy of Molly Morrison; photo on page 276 courtesy of Nancy Ruppert. All the other photos taken by the author, Sara Davis Powell.

Library of Congress Cataloging-in-Publication Data

Will be provided upon Request

10 9 8 7 6 5 4 3 2 1 RRD-VA 14 13 12 11 10

ISBN-13: 978-0-13-498680-7
ISBN-10: 0-13-498680-6

To my husband, Rus, who makes all aspects of our life together a delightful partnership.

To my sons, Jesse, Cody, Travis, and Noah, and their families, who continually give me so much pleasure and many reasons to be proud.

To middle level kids and teachers, who grow and learn together every day.

Brief Contents

Contents

About the Author

SARA DAVIS POWELL is a teacher—from the middle school classroom to teacher preparation as a professor—and chair of education at Belmont Abbey College in North Carolina. She is a young adolescent advocate who writes about middle level teacher preparation, emphasizing a balance of developmentally appropriate and academically rigorous practice. Actively involved in local classrooms and the middle school community through the facilitation of professional development, supervision of clinical interns, and research and writing about middle level issues, she is also a frequent speaker at regional and national conferences, where her enthusiasm for middle level education is contagious. Powell's most recent books include *Your Introduction to Education: Explorations in Teaching*, third edition (Pearson, 2019) and *Wayside Teaching: Connecting with Students to Support Learning* (Corwin, 2010).

Married with four sons, four daughters-in-laws, and three grandchildren, she enjoys watching lakeside sunsets at home with her husband, Rus, and spending time with her sons and their families. When not on her dock, with her family, or writing at home, chances are she can be reached at Belmont Abbey College, 100 Belmont-Mt. Holly Road, Belmont, North Carolina 28012; (704) 461–5059; sarapowell@bac.edu.

Preface

New to This Edition

Introduction to Middle Level Education offers a comprehensive and contemporary body of knowledge that speaks directly to teacher candidates in a voice that invites them into today's middle level classrooms. The fourth edition is a compelling look at a variety of current issues and topics affecting young adolescents, their teachers, and their schools, including discussions of 21st century knowledge and skill requirements such as global awareness, civic engagement, information literacy, and ethical responsibility.

Yet, despite all the changes both students and teachers face, the developmental needs of young adolescents remain predictable. Relevant and challenging curriculum, engaging instruction, ongoing assessment that is growth-promoting, developmental responsiveness, and strategies for creating and maintaining a positive and productive learning environment—all of these and other vital components of middle level education must be firmly in place.

New Chapter

Chapter 11, "Citizenship and Civility in the Middle Grades," is completely new and extremely timely. Our nation is faced with increasing levels of violence, divisiveness, and rancor never before experienced by the majority of today's population. Now is the time to promote citizenship and civility among young adolescents who encapsulate the future of our republic. Topics in this new chapter include:

- Civic knowledge across the curriculum
- Current events
- Elections
- Civic skills across the curriculum
- Global citizenship skills
- Civic skills related to the Common Core
- Digital citizenship
- Civic dispositions
- Civic engagement
- Social consciousness and responsibility
- Service learning
- Civility.

An extensive list of resources available to help teach citizenship, civic engagement, and civility in our classrooms is provided.

New Features

Making the Teaching and Learning Connection consists of personal letters written directly to readers by outstanding teachers and middle level leaders. All include a photo of the letter writer and most include a video. The topics are pertinent to our relationships with young adolescents. It's coincidental, yet worth noting, that *Making the Teaching and Learning Connection* includes the initials *TLC*, often recognized as standing for *Tender Loving Care*. This is what middle level teachers must provide for young adolescents as we help them grow and become healthy, happy, altruistic, and productive citizens.

- Chapter 1 *TLC*: John Lounsbury, a legend in middle level circles, and one of the finest gentlemen and teachers I have ever known, tells us about his philosophy of teaching that includes spiritual aspects of our profession.

- Chapter 2 *TLC*: Dani Ramsey tells us how she uses bio poems as an outlet for young adolescents to explore who they are and how their emotions and social experiences impact them.

- Chapter 3 *TLC*: Amy Goodwin understands that she teaches the whole child. She tells us how she addresses bullying through literature and class discussion.

- Chapter 4 *TLC*: Charlie Bull's devotion to kids raised in poverty is evident as he describes his students and his teaching style.

- Chapter 5 *TLC*: Traci Peters tells us she thrives within structure and organization and that her middle level students do as well.

- Chapter 6 *TLC*: Derek Boucher writes about his commitment to teaching students to read with fluency and comprehension.

- Chapter 7 *TLC*: Macy Ingle tells us that she realized what she had missed in her own science education when she started using the 5E lesson plan—engage, explore, explain, elaborate, and evaluate.

- Chapter 8 *TLC*: Dee Lanier explains his school's emphasis on solving real-world challenges and how he continually assesses student learning.

- Chapter 9 *TLC*: Kurt Hansen, an admitted science geek, tells us active engagement in the classroom is vital, as is linking lessons to curricular standards through careful planning.

- Chapter 10 *TLC*: Kadean Maddix writes about his journey toward the middle level math classroom and his devotion to his students.

- Chapter 11 *TLC*: Former Supreme Court Justice Sandra Day O'Connor's dedication to civic knowledge and skills shines through in this chapter's *TLC*.

- Chapter 12 *TLC*: Nancy Ruppert, a true leader of middle level education and former president of the Association for Middle Level Education, gives heartfelt advice about the value and power of relationships.

New Concepts and Emphases

- In Chapter 1, increased emphasis is placed on middle level education philosophy as expressed by the founders of the middle school concept. Their legacy remains a driving force in how we interact with, and educate, young adolescents today.

- In Chapter 2, the concept of social-emotional learning (SEL) is examined. Executive skills, or executive function, comprise a set of mental qualities that help us get things done. These skills are applied to middle level classrooms.

- In Chapter 3, we explore issues revolving around gender and gender identity, including dilemmas involved with childhood gender nonconformity and transgender youth.

- In Chapter 4, statistics concerning young adolescent substance abuse are both updated and enhanced. Sleep, essential to productivity, is a new topic in the societal context of middle level education.

- In Chapter 5, emphasis is placed on common planning time as vital to effective teaching and learning in a middle level setting.

- In Chapter 6, strategies for helping young adolescents increase their memory capacity are included.

- In Chapter 7, an extensive section has been added addressing neuroscience research and implications for middle level teaching and learning. A section addressing the importance of choice and how to include it in the classroom is added.
- In Chapter 8, additional emphasis is provided on formative assessment, common assessments, and response patterns.
- In Chapter 9, the gradual release model has been added, along with the concept of academic language, a component of edTPA. In addition, SIOP: Sheltered Instruction Observation Protocol is addressed not only as beneficial for English learners, but for all learners.
- In Chapter 10, de-escalation strategies of the Crisis Prevention Institute are applied to middle level classrooms to help prevent behavior issues.
- Chapter 11 is entirely new.
- In Chapter 12, a major section addressing professionalism is added, including becoming a reflective practitioner, balancing professional and personal life, and maintaining positive dispositions.

New Accountability

Each chapter consists of three to six major topic sections. Each topic section is followed by four multiple choice items with explanations for each answer choice. Students can use the self-checks to make sure they are grasping the knowledge in the chapters.

New Videos

This fourth edition includes 10 videos from the third edition and 22 *new* videos illustrating concepts throughout the text. The Instructor's Manual includes accountability questions for every video that may be used as study guides or as quizzes to make sure students are watching the videos when assigned.

Included in This Edition

To help prepare teachers who will consistently make the teaching and learning connection, the following features from the third edition are retained in this new edition:

- *eText Access:* As a Pearson eText this edition includes embedded access to websites and video features that invite readers to explore the personal stories of middle level teachers and students, as well as numerous resources that are valuable to teaching and learning.
- *Association for Middle Level Education Teacher Preparation Standards:* The 2012 AMLE teacher preparation standards are linked to chapter content throughout the text.
- *This We Believe:*   The 16 tenets of effective schools for young adolescents are emphasized throughout the text.
- *Goals for Young Adolescent Development (This We Believe):* The 13 goals for young adolescent development as stated in *This We Believe* are prominent in each chapter as the content addresses them.
- *Common Core State Standards:*   An emphasis on the Common Core State Standards that influence teaching and learning in middle level schools is prominent throughout and includes a valuable Q&A feature addressing the development and implementation of the standards.
- *The Bully, the Bullied, and the Bystander:*   Extensive coverage of bullying, those affected by it, and ways to both prevent and respond to it are included in Chapter 4 as we address the societal context of middle level education.

- *Social Media:*   Each chapter contains references to the ever-burgeoning technology for teaching and learning, with increased emphasis on cybercitizenship and the avoidance of cyberbullying and sexting.
- *Virtual Field Experiences:*   Throughout the fourth edition Pearson eText readers view videos of teacher interviews and room tours, student interviews, classroom lessons, a middle school tour, a principal discussing what she looks for in teachers, and a variety of stories about teachers making a difference.
- *PowerPoint Presentations:*   In the Instructor's Manual, each chapter is detailed in PowerPoint slides for classroom use.

The fourth edition of *Introduction to Middle Level Education* also includes:

Activities. Following each chapter are a variety of activities. Group activities require readers to work cooperatively to accomplish particular tasks. Individual activities give readers opportunities to explore middle level concepts on their own. The personal journal section asks readers to reflect on their own experiences.

Glossary. An evolving common vocabulary among educators allows us to talk about our profession with mutual understanding. Some words and phrases have specialized meanings and nuances when used within a middle level education context. Many of these terms are explained in the glossary.

For instructors. The following are provided electronically: a comprehensive Instructor's Manual including author suggestions for exploration of text content, PowerPoint slide presentations for each chapter, and a chapter-by-chapter test bank.

Organization

Introduction to Middle Level Education includes 12 chapters. Separating the body of knowledge of middle level education into discrete chapters seems arbitrary, but it is efficient to do so. Given the limits of the written word, I have chosen to organize this book in a traditional way. Chapter 1 focuses on the philosophy and history of middle level education and the elements that have given it legitimacy and theoretical grounding. Chapter 2 is an overview of student physical, intellectual, emotional, social, and character development. Chapter 3 looks at the diversity among our students from cultural, to socioeconomic, to learning styles, and more. Chapter 4 addresses the societal context of middle level education. Chapter 5 delves into the structures of people, time, and place, including teaming, advisory, flexible schedules, and classroom/school facilities. Chapters 6, 7, and 8 discuss curriculum, instruction, and assessment at the middle level, and Chapter 9 details all levels of planning for instruction. Chapter 10 deals with the important topic of creating and maintaining a positive and productive learning environment. Chapter 11 addresses citizenship responsibilities and ways to promote civic engagement and civility. Chapter 12 explores some of the realities of teaching young adolescents, the relationships that are so crucial to successful teaching and learning, elements of professionalism, and the critical issues of transitioning into and out of middle grades.

Author's Note

Introduction to Middle Level Education models the ideals of middle level education in that it is both academically rigorous and developmentally responsive—academically rigorous because it includes a comprehensive body of knowledge, and developmentally responsive because it approaches these topics without intimidating or boring the reader. I am an experienced middle level teacher speaking to other teachers whether they are teacher candidates completing bachelor or master's degrees; career changers preparing to take their skills and backgrounds into the middle level classroom; elementary or high school teachers getting ready for the challenges and joys of spending their days with young adolescents; or teachers who desire to dig deeper into their profession, seeking insights and encouragement. Writing a book allows me only to speak, not actually converse. My hope is that readers will talk to each other about middle level education, prompted by my side of the "conversation."

Teachers are my heroes. They make the minute-by-minute decisions on which student success and well-being depend. If knowledge is power, and I believe it is, the more we understand about the nature of early adolescence, with both its documented predictability and its absurd volatility, the more prepared we are to make the relatively insignificant, as well as life-changing, decisions. Yes, experience is the best teacher. However, opportunities to read, reflect, discuss, and speculate will sharpen our focus on, and widen our peripheral vision of, middle level education and all that is involved in teaching young adolescents. This book provides such opportunities.

The tenets of *Turning Points* (Carnegie Corporation, 1989), *Turning Points 2000* (*Jackson & Davis, 2000*), and *This We Believe (NMSA, 2010)*; the underpinnings of the Association for Middle Level Education; and the AMLE teacher preparation standards permeate every page. This strong conceptual foundation focuses us squarely on students and learning. As a unique phase of human development, early adolescence deserves continued concentrated research and study that will further deepen our understanding of how best to meet the needs of the students in our charge. The fourth edition of *Introduction to Middle Level Education* addresses the issues of teaching and learning with young adolescents in commonsense ways that infuse practicality with theory.

This book is a work of non-traditional scholarship—scholarly by way of knowledge base and non-traditional by way of personalization. I believe I best serve teachers, in whatever career stage, by speaking in first person from both a research base and my own and others' experiences in the classroom. I welcome all readers to the adventure of exploring the landscape of middle level education!

Acknowledgments

I want to thank the teachers, students, and principals who allowed me to wander the halls of their schools, interview the people involved in middle level education, and take pictures of teachers and young adolescents in action.

Special thanks go to my editor Drew Bennett, production manager Yagnesh Jani, and Gheron Lising and Mohamed Hameed of Pearson CSC for their guidance and prompt responses to my questions and requests. I appreciate the time and suggestions given by four reviewers:

Chapter 1
Middle Level Education Philosophy and History

Sara Davis Powell

Vision has been viewed as an acute sense of the possible. Research and exemplary practice over the past four decades have provided middle level educators with a strong sense of what is, indeed, possible in the education of young adolescents. Idealistic and uplifting, the resulting vision reflects our best knowledge and lights the way toward achieving a truly successful middle level school for every young adolescent.

THIS WE BELIEVE, 2010, P. 27.

 ## Learning Outcomes

After studying this chapter, you will have knowledge and skills to:

1.1 Define the basic elements of middle level education philosophy.

1.2 Describe the history of middle level education.

1.3 Explain the function and value of organizations and publications focusing on middle level education.

1.4 Summarize middle level teacher preparation standards and teacher candidate assessments.

1.5 Recognize that while characteristics may vary, effective teachers make the teaching and learning connection.

Dear Future Middle Level Teacher,

Teaching middle level learners is a career filled with exhilaration, challenge, day-to-day (and sometimes life-altering) decisions that affect young adolescents, and a complete absence of boredom. Sound intriguing? If so, this may be your destiny!

Middle level education is referred to in a variety of ways—middle level settings, middle grades education, **middle school**, schools in the middle, and so on. By whatever name, we are referring to a philosophy of educating young adolescents that is different from elementary philosophy, high school philosophy, or **junior high** philosophy. This philosophy calls for us to recognize the unique needs of young adolescents and meet them in developmentally appropriate ways.

Young adolescents are eager to grow up, but often frightened by the process. They sense that their bodies are changing due to puberty, and they experience confusing and sometimes conflicting emotions. One minute they may be playing with action figures or Barbie dolls, and the next crying over what a girlfriend or boyfriend supposedly said at lunch. One minute they may appear totally self-absorbed, and the next give away all of their allowance to a worthy cause. The unique set of contradictions displayed by kids in the middle—their curiosity, their quirky ways of expressing themselves, and their determination that life should be fair—both intrigue and inspire middle level teachers.

Middle level education is not for everyone. In fact, your friends may not understand the appeal of spending your days with young adolescents; they may cringe when they recall this stage of life. But that's exactly the point. Kids 10 to 15 years old need us to remember the difficult times, as well as the good times, and determine to make this puberty-driven roller coaster of emotions and social exploration safe and productive . . . and don't forget about fun!

Middle level learners, their school settings, the vistas they discover, the depth and breadth of what they know and can do, and the physical, cognitive, emotional, social, and moral growth they experience are influenced by the teachers who choose to spend their days in the middle. Welcome to the adventure!

SDP

LO 1.1 Philosophy of Middle Level Education

Before considering the history of middle level education, it's imperative to explore the philosophy that guides and gives life to successful education of young adolescents, often referred to as middle level/school concept. A philosophy is a system of thought and principles that guide practice. Middle level philosophy is composed of principles based on the needs of young adolescents and our best thinking about how to meet those needs through effective practice. Throughout this text we examine these principles.

Developmental responsiveness requires that we understand the unique nature of young adolescents and continually consider how we can use that knowledge to build a supportive learning environment. All our interactions with, and decisions that affect, young adolescents must be built on our unambiguous determination to be developmentally responsive. The school organization or structure, policies, curriculum, instruction, assessment, and teacher-student relationships must focus on the attributes of young adolescents. Developmental responsiveness is not a "warm and fuzzy" concept as some may perceive it, but rather a research-based component of effective teaching and learning. You will see the word *relationships* repeatedly in any information discussing young adolescents and middle level schools. There's no way to overstate the value of healthy, trusting relationships among students and the adults who serve them.

Making the Teaching and Learning Connection is a feature in every chapter. It's a wonderful coincidence that the title of the feature contains the letters TLC which once stood most prominently in pop culture for Tender Loving Care. This is descriptive of the overall approach that brings the most positive and productive results when teaching middle level kids in ways that lead to their learning. It's not soft or permissive, but involves the determination to do everything possible to care for the growing young adolescents in our classrooms. In this chapter's TLC we have words of Dr. John Lounsbury, a name you will read throughout this book. Young adolescents and middle level education have no better or wiser friend than Dr. Lounsbury; he has a history of promoting teaching and learning for more than 70 years. He is the man I consider my most valuable mentor through what he has written, the words he has spoken at meetings and conferences, his leadership of the Association for Middle Level Education, and our personal friendship. Read his words once, and then again, and then again. They are rich and meaningful.

Making the Teaching and Learning Connection

 Dr. John Lounsbury continues to positively impact the ways we make the teaching and learning connection with young adolescents. Here he shares his belief that teaching is a moral endeavor with a spiritual dimension. Read his words carefully and internalize them.

"In real estate, the three factors that are tied to success are: location, location, location. While in teaching, the three factors that spell success are: *relationships, relationships, relationships.*

Teaching is a very human experience—and a moral matter. What teachers inevitably teach is who they are. The content falls to second place. Rudyard Kipling, long ago, penned these lines, my favorites:

"No printed word nor spoken plea can teach young minds what they should be.

Not all the books on all the shelves, but what the teachers are themselves."

These words are sobering, to say the least, for what teachers teach are who they are as persons—their values, behaviors, and mannerisms—all come across with certainty in a student-teacher relationship, completely independent of any stated material or instructional technique used.

Teacher preparation, then, should give some attention to helping teacher candidates become better persons and sensitive to the enduring impact they have on students, as well as mastering the traditional materials of planning for instruction, assessing student progress, and exploring new approaches.

I believe that teaching includes a spiritual dimension, one seldom openly acknowledged, but which is of enduring importance, especially in the middle

> school level. There is in teaching an ethical impulse which calls for teaching to go beyond the head and touch the heart and soul. A full education has to involve heart as well as head, attitude as well as information, spirit as well as scholarship, and conscience as well as competence".
>
> With gratitude to all who care for young adolescents,
>
> John

Educational experiences for young adolescents must be challenging, with appropriately high expectations for each individual student. We often hear middle level educators say that the mantra of our work is that we believe in **developmental appropriateness** and **academic rigor**. These two concepts are not at all mutually exclusive, but rather completely compatible and complementary. The ability of young adolescents to grasp more complex and abstract ideas increases throughout their middle school years. Because students' intellectual capacity matures at varying rates, teachers must know students well, continually recognize them as unique individuals, and understand when and how to challenge them based on what Vygotsky calls the **zone of proximal development**, or the level at which a student can almost, but not completely, grasp a concept or perform a skill. Teachers use **scaffolding** to support student learning as they progress needing help to independently grasping a concept or performing a skill.

Middle level philosophy promotes **empowerment** of all students, or teaching the knowledge and skills they need to take responsibility for their lives. "Early adolescence is a time of uncertainty with respect to self-confidence, peer relationships, and independence. To counteract this uncertainty, teachers provide students with a sense of empowerment over their own learning" (Levin & Mee, 2016). Young adolescents are exploring their independence and encountering opportunities to take responsibility for themselves. They are social beings who are learning more about themselves and others as relationships become more complex. Empowerment involves helping them learn how to "address life's challenges, to function successfully at all levels of society, and to be creators of knowledge" (National Middle School Association, 2010, p.13).

Carolyn Gomez, a sixth grade teacher in Stillwater, Oklahoma, believes that part of forming relationships with students involves letting students get to know us. She reveals to them her interests and family news, as well as what she enjoys about teaching and what challenges her most.

As a part of fulfilling a moral imperative, middle level philosophy insists on **equity**, or the quality of being fair and impartial. In middle level philosophy, bias does not exist; we advocate for all students and ensure their rights to learn. When the philosophy is applied, all students matter, and matter equally. We honor individuals and their potential and provide engaging instruction and support for each young adolescent.

Remember the definition of philosophy? A philosophy is a system of thought and principles that guide practice. Particular practices closely align with middle level philosophy and "put legs" on the principles, including teaming, **interdisciplinary instruction,** common planning time, exploratory courses, and advisory. We will discuss these practices and more throughout this book.

By whatever name—middle level philosophy, middle school concept, *This We Believe*—teachers dedicated to meeting the physical, cognitive, emotional, social, and moral needs of young adolescents provide education that is developmentally responsive, challenging, empowering, and equitable.

Enhanced eText

Video Example 1. 1

Teacher Carolyn Gomez tells us how she forms and maintains healthy, productive relationships with kids.

Self-Check 1.1

LO 1.2 Brief History of Middle Level Education

The years involved in the history of middle level education are relatively few, just over a century. The first separate school organization established to bridge the gap between elementary and high school began in 1909. These new schools were aptly named *junior highs* and were established to be preparatory schools for students going on to high school, where they would enter one of two defined tracks. The tracks had two broad purposes: to provide enriched curriculum for college-bound students, or to provide vocational training for those preparing to enter the workforce.

Elementary schools consisting of self-contained grade level classes were, and basically still are, intended to provide consistency and security for children, as experienced ideally in a family setting. As they are today, high schools at the beginning of the 20th century were basically departmentalized by subject area, with students changing classes four to eight times a day. The junior high resembled the high school in structure in 1909 but generally was smaller to allow for a greater sense of personalization, while still functioning in a departmentalized fashion. Even though there was little written research about the early adolescence stage of life, the junior high concept met a recognized need that made it a widespread and rapidly growing part of public education.

As early as 1945, some educators were troubled by what they observed in junior highs. An early advocate for junior high wrote about what he perceived as persistent problems. His list included the following (Anfara & Waks, 2000):

- Curriculum that was too subject-centered
- Teachers who were inadequately prepared to teach young adolescents
- Classrooms that were teacher-centered and textbook-centered
- Students who were tracked. (p. 47)

By 1960, approximately four out of five high school graduates attended junior high as part of a 6–3–3 grade configuration—six years of elementary, three years of junior high, and three years of high school. By the mid-1960s, variations began to emerge, resulting in middle level schools consisting of grades 5–8 or grades 6–8 (McEwin & Greene, 2010).

In the summer of 1963, William Alexander broke ground for the establishment of what are now middle schools when he presented a "philosophy" of the characteristics needed in a transitional school at the Cornell University Junior High School Conference. Alexander urged the maintenance of the positive contributions of junior highs such as core curriculum, guidance programs, exploratory education, and vocational/home arts, and the elimination of high school practices such as competitive sports and subject matter orientation. He conducted a survey of junior highs whose grade configurations had evolved into grades 5–8 or grades 6–8 from original 6–3–3, 6–2–4, and 6–6 grade structures. The results of this study were published in *The Emergent Middle School* by Alexander in 1969. This book described middle school as a new concept, not merely a rearrangement of junior high. A brief overview of some of the differences between traditional junior highs and middle level schools based on concepts proposed by Alexander and others is in Figure 1.1. All of the concepts presented in the middle school column are discussed in detail in this text. Although it may seem out-of-date to even discuss junior high and compare its basic concepts to middle school concepts, it's still relevant to consider why middle level philosophy was developed.

FIGURE 1.1 Differences between junior high and middle school

Junior High	Middle School
1. Subject-centered	Student-oriented
2. Emphasis is on cognitive development	Emphasis is on both cognitive and affective development
3. Organizes teachers in subject-based departments	Organizes teachers and students in interdisciplinary teams
4. Traditional instruction dominates	Experiential approaches to instruction
5. Six to eight class periods per day	Allows for block and flexible scheduling
6. Provides academic classes	Provides exploratory, academic, and nonacademic classes
7. Offers study hall and/or homeroom	Offers advisor/advisee, teacher/student opportunities
8. Classrooms arranged randomly or by subject or grade level	Team classrooms in close proximity

An excellent resource for delving more deeply into the history of middle level education is a research study published by Research in Middle Level Education in 2016 titled *An Historical Overview of the Middle School Movement, 1963–2015* by Schaefer, Malu, and Yoon. The authors examined more than 2,000 documents, research studies, and articles chronicling the development of middle level education beginning with William Alexander's 1963 speech at Cornell University. They tell us 1963–1979 was a time of beginning the search for identity for what has become the Middle School Movement. In 1968, there were about 1,000 schools labeled as middle schools; by 1980 there were more than 5,000. This tremendous growth spurred advancement and progress in the 1980s, with some of the most important practices recognized including teaming, interdisciplinary curriculum and advisory. As middle level education became more established in the 1990s, some outside the movement began questioning and challenging beliefs and practices of those who embraced middle level philosophy, including advisory, cooperative learning, and teaming. Recognizing the need to validate the middle level philosophy as described for more than 50 years by those close to young adolescents and their education, the first decade of the 21st century saw an impressive increase in research studies, both small- and large-scale. This emphasis on research to support and inform practices both in the U.S. and internationally continues into the second decade of the century.

In 1988, a second major research study following up on Alexander's 1969 *The Emergent Middle School* was conducted, with a third study in 1993, and a fourth in 2001. The most recent study was conducted in 2009, the results of which will be referred to numerous times in this text. Conducted by professors emeritus Ken McEwin and Melanie Greene of Appalachian State University, this latest study published in 2011 provides valuable comparisons of the practices of middle level schools that excel in teaching and learning.

A ground-breaking study is underway, with results to be revealed in 2020. The study, Middle Grades Longitudinal Study of 2017–18 (MGLS:2017), is sponsored by the National Center for Education Statistics (NCES), part of the U.S. Department of Education. It is the first nationally representative study that examines the educational experiences and outcomes of students in 6th grade as they progress through 8th grade. MGLS:2017 attempts to determine factors that predict success for students in grades 6, 7, and 8 while discovering more about student development and influences both inside and outside school. A unique feature of the study is that information will be gathered from multiple sources: students, their parents, school administrators, and mathematics and special education teachers. The study will assess students' mathematics and reading skills, socioemotional development, and executive functions such as working memory, attention, and impulse control. To learn more about this study and explore findings as they are published, simply access the NCES site and enter MGLS:2017 in the search bar.

There are more than 15,000 middle level schools in the United States, serving students ages 10-15. The most prevalent grade configuration for middle schools is 6–8, but configurations of grades 5–8 and grades 7–8 also exist (McEwin & Greene, 2011). Because early adolescence includes ages 10–15, some schools serving grades 7–9 may also qualify as middle schools. The **Association for Middle Level Education (AMLE)** continues to set high expectations for what an effective middle level school setting that is developmentally responsive, challenging, empowering, and equitable should "look like."

Not all young adolescents attend middle schools. Some districts serve 10- to 15-year-olds in K–8 schools, while others utilize 7–12 grade bands, or even K–12. AMLE strongly endorses the idea of a unique school in the middle (between elementary and high schools), staffed by adults who understand and appreciate young adolescents. However, the organization acknowledges that developmental appropriateness and academic rigor can be accomplished in a school regardless of the name out front or the grade level configuration within. Specific grade configurations and practices may always be controversial. This fact keeps us fresh and on our toes. Controversy stretches us. But remember, it's all about the kids and our responsibility to do what's best for them.

Seventh grade focus teacher **Traci Peters** tells us that she prepared to teach elementary students, but found that her college education prepared her to cross the grade-level divide and be successful in middle school. She now loves spending her days with young adolescents and attending to their developmental and academic needs.

Middle level education is not without its critics. There are those who say public education is failing to meet the needs of young adolescents, especially those who attend middle schools. When middle school national and international test results are weak, the critics' case is bolstered. Middle level philosophy as espoused by AMLE is blamed. But it's not the philosophy. Every aspect of middle level philosophy is developed distinctly for the unique stage of early adolescence. It's not the philosophy . . . it's the lack of conscientious implementation in many schools that serve young adolescents.

When we consider that most of the educators who invested their careers in the establishment and proliferation of middle level schools are still with us, and are still inspiring our efforts, the history of middle level education comes alive as an ongoing progression of events. The pioneers of middle level education have made, and continue to impact, significant progress. Smith and McEwin (2011) published *The Legacy of Middle School Leaders: In Their Own Words*. This historical account focuses on contributions of leaders who have shaped the American middle level movement. Included are synopses of the impact of William Alexander and Donald Eichhorn, both of whom died before the legacy project, along with edited transcripts of extensive interviews with 18 influential individuals who, together, encompass the essence of middle level philosophy: John Arnold, Al Arth, James Beane, Sherrel Bergmann, Thomas Dickinson, Nancy Doda, Thomas Erb, Thomas Gatewood, Paul George, Howard Johnston, Joan Lipsitz, John Lounsbury, Ken McEwin, Chris Stevenson, John Swaim, Sue Swaim, Conrad Toepfer, and Gordon Vars. As you learn more about middle level philosophy and practices, you are sure to see these names over and over. Pay attention to what they have to say and what is said about them. They continue to guide and inspire the work of middle level educators.

Enhanced eText

Video Example 1.2

Teacher Traci Peters talks about her path to middle level education and how she views her students.

Self-Check 1.2

LO 1.3 Organizations and Publications Focusing on Middle Level Education

Teachers and administrators whose careers focus on young adolescents are fortunate to have national and state organizations to support their work, including the Association for Middle Level Education and the **National Forum to Accelerate Middle-Grades**

Reform. In addition, three publications established middle level education mission and philosophy: *Turning Points* (1989), *Turning Points 2000* (2000), and *This We Believe* (2010). The latter is the position statement of the Association for Middle Level Education. Many more publications have been written to give us guidance on how best to meet the needs of young adolescents, but these three have been seminal in guiding middle level decision making.

Association for Middle Level Education

The Association for Middle Level Education (AMLE), formerly the **National Middle School Association**, was founded in 1973. This organization is dedicated exclusively to the education, development, and growth of young adolescents. AMLE provides a voice and a professional structure for middle level educators and has grown to include members in all states and dozens of countries. More than 50 affiliate organizations of AMLE sponsor local, regional, and state activities focused on middle level education. The AMLE website is an excellent resource featuring ways to advocate for young adolescents, professional development opportunities, professional teacher standards, the latest research on middle level education, and a publications shopping bonanza for all who are interested in early adolescence.

One very important affiliate of AMLE is the **Collegiate Middle Level Association (CMLA)**, a university student organization with student officers and activities. Each CMLA chapter promotes middle level teacher preparation through group meetings featuring professional development, involvement of CMLA members in local schools above and beyond field experiences, and fundraising to support attendance at state and national conferences. I have been privileged to be a faculty sponsor of a CMLA and can personally attest to what wonderful organizations they can be.

The largest selection of books written specifically for middle level practitioners is available through AMLE catalogs, at middle level conferences, and on the AMLE website by selecting *AMLE Store*. Five times a year AMLE publishes the *Middle School Journal*, a refreshing and informative compilation of articles that is highly regarded for both its topical and scholarly content. The *AMLE Magazine*, a very practical journal featuring reader-friendly articles, is published nine times a year. Membership in the Association for Middle Level Education is accompanied by subscriptions to both the *Middle School Journal* and the *AMLE Magazine*. AMLE also publishes *Research in Middle Level Education Online*, several online newsletters, and videos. In addition, the website contains AMLE position statements, along with the latest in news items and legislation affecting middle level education. You will also find membership information. College students can join AMLE and enjoy all the benefits of membership, including monthly journals, for only $25 a year.

One of the highlights provided by the Association for Middle Level Education is the widely acclaimed AMLE annual fall conference. This conference draws thousands of teachers, future teachers, principals, central office personnel, university faculty, state department officials, parents, and community members, all vitally interested in the promotion of developmentally appropriate practices. It's an exciting conference that all middle level teachers should have the opportunity to attend. Lasting three days, the main events include keynote speakers, concurrent sessions on topics of interest to adults who work with young adolescents, and

Used with permission from the Association for Middle Level Education www.amle.org

site visits to local schools to view exemplary practices. Perhaps the major inspiration provided by this annual conference comes from the realization that we are not alone, the knowledge that hundreds of thousands of adults concerned with young adolescent development and education are represented by those who attend. State **affiliates** of AMLE also sponsor annual conferences that are perhaps more accessible to you than the national conference.

The National Forum to Accelerate Middle-Grades Reform

The **National Forum to Accelerate Middle-Grades Reform** is an organization of researchers, educators, leaders, and officers of professional organizations, all invited to join and committed to advocating for young adolescents to improve academic performance and health. The National Forum is working diligently to promote best practices for young adolescents. In 1999, the National Forum launched the **Schools to Watch** initiative, with middle schools across the country identified because they meet, or are making significant progress toward meeting, specific criteria for high performance including academic excellence, developmental responsiveness, social equity, and organizational structures and processes. Schools apply to be part of the Schools to Watch Project anticipating the multi-layered guidance and support opportunities will lead to needed improvements and, ultimately, designation as a School to Watch. A recent four-year study of the impact of implementation on school and student outcomes found that middle level schools with the highest levels of implementation of the Schools to Watch criteria achieved higher levels of success (Flowers, Begum, Carpenter, & Mulhall, 2017). For more information on Schools to Watch, see the National Forum to Accelerate Middle-Grades Reform website.

Turning Points

Turning Points: Preparing American Youth for the 21st Century was published in 1989 by the Carnegie Council on Adolescent Development. Yes, 1989 was a long time ago. So why include words this old in a 21st century textbook? It's simple. The philosophy is still relevant. The Carnegie Council's research showed that substantial numbers of America's young adolescents were at risk of reaching adulthood inadequately prepared to function productively. As a result of this finding, the Council developed a research-based document that has shaped middle school philosophy. This study continues to lead the way in both describing characteristics of young adolescents and prescribing ways to meet their needs within the school setting.

More than 100,000 copies of the full report, as well as more than 200,000 copies of the abridged version, have been disseminated. The eight tenets of *Turning Points* summarized in Table 1.1 provide a model of what a middle school can be. The tenets are interrelated elements that, when taken as a whole, provide a vision for teaching and learning appropriate for young adolescents.

Turning Points 2000

The original **Turning Points** (1989) provided a framework for middle grades education, whereas **Turning Points 2000** (2000) gives us in-depth insights into how to improve middle grades education. Strong emphasis is placed on curriculum, instruction, and assessment. The point is made that organizational changes (teaming, flexible scheduling, schools-within-schools, etc.) may be necessary, but not sufficient, for significant improvement in academic achievement.

TABLE 1.1 Turning Points

Turning Points: Preparing American Youth for the 21st Century Carnegie Council on Adolescent Development, 1989	
Creating a community for learning	Schools should be places where close, trusting relationships with adults and peers create a climate for students' personal growth and intellectual development.
Teaching a core of common knowledge	Every student in the middle grades should learn to think critically through mastery of an appropriate body of knowledge, lead a healthy life, behave ethically and lawfully, and assume the responsibilities of citizenship in a pluralistic society.
Ensuring success for all students	All young adolescents should have the opportunity to succeed in every aspect of the middle grade program, regardless of previous achievement or the pace at which they learn.
Empowering teachers and administrators	Decisions concerning the experiences of middle grade students should be made by the adults who know them best.
Preparing teachers for the middle grades	Teachers in middle grade schools should be selected and specially educated to teach young adolescents.
Improving academic performance through better health and fitness	Young adolescents must be healthy in order to learn.
Reengaging families in the education of young adolescents	Families and middle grade schools must be allied through trust and respect if young adolescents are to succeed in school.
Connecting schools with communities	Responsibility for each middle grade student's success should be shared by schools and community organizations.

Based on: *Turning Points: Preparing American Youth for the 21st Century* (pp. 37–70), by Carnegie Council on Adolescent Development, 1989, Washington, DC: Author.

Turning Points 2000, written by Anthony Jackson and Gayle Davis, traces the progress of middle schools, and the degrees of implementation of middle level philosophy, since publication of the original *Turning Points* in 1989. *Turning Points 2000* reports that as schools implemented more of the tenets of *Turning Points*, and with greater fidelity, their students' standardized test scores in mathematics, language arts, and reading rose significantly. These results occurred at both the low and high ends of proficiency scales. The report also states that still to be reached are the schools that need improvement most—the ones in high-poverty urban and rural communities where lack of achievement is rampant and pockets of excellence are few and far between. Middle school philosophy has achieved its greatest level of acceptance and success primarily in suburban and upper-income areas (Jackson & Davis, 2000). *Turning Points 2000* provides useful applications for implementing what research tells us is best practice for young adolescents. In doing so, the authors altered the original eight tenets. The newer document contains seven recommendations listed in Figure 1.2 that have at their core the goal of ensuring success for every student, reflecting the centrality of teaching and learning.

FIGURE 1.2 Turning Points 2000

Turning Points 2000 calls for schools that

- Base their curriculum on established standards.
- Incorporate a variety of instructional strategies that help students learn the knowledge and skills of the standards.
- Support teachers in their professional growth as they increase their skills in teaching young adolescents.
- Emphasize the importance of relationships in establishing environments that foster intellectual development.
- Encourage teachers to be involved in governance decisions, acknowledging that they know students best.
- Teach the whole child in an environment that emphasizes academic performance, dispositions of care, and the development of ethical citizens.
- Include family and community in efforts to support learning and positive development.

Based on: *Turning Points 2000: Educating Adolescents in the 21st Century* by A.W. Jackson and G.A. Davis, 2000. New York, NY: Carnegie Corporation of New York.

This We Believe

Contributing to our understanding of why middle level settings are unique and necessary is the Association for Middle Level Education position paper, ***This We Believe***. First published in 1982 and then revised in 1995 and 2003, and again in 2010 as *This We Believe: Keys to Educating Young Adolescents*, the document seeks to isolate and quantify the unique aspects of young adolescents and identify the appropriate support, responses, and environment of an effective middle level setting. In doing so, *This We Believe* provides both a mission statement and benchmarks for what the effective school for young adolescents should be and has contributed a framework within which decisions about programs can be made. Sixteen general characteristics of successful schools for young adolescents are outlined, summarized in Figure 1.3. Throughout this text we explore schools that have at least some of these characteristics and ways to embed them in middle level settings.

Standard 3

Middle Level Philosophy and School Organization

Element a. Middle Level Philosophical Foundations: Middle level teacher candidates demonstrate an understanding of the philosophical foundations of developmentally responsive middle level programs and schools.

Self-Check 1.3

FIGURE 1.3 This We Believe

National Middle School Association (now AMLE) believes successful schools for young adolescents include the following characteristics:

Curriculum, Instruction, and Assessment

- Educators value young adolescents and are prepared to teach them.
- Students and teachers are engaged in active, purposeful learning.
- Curriculum is challenging, exploratory, integrative, and relevant.
- Educators use multiple learning and teaching approaches.
- Varied and ongoing assessments advance learning as well as measure it.

Leadership and Organization

- A shared vision developed by all stakeholders guides every decision.
- Leaders are committed to and knowledgeable about this age group, educational research, and best practices.
- Leaders demonstrate courage and collaboration.
- Ongoing professional development reflects best educational practices.
- Organizational structures foster purposeful learning and meaningful relationships.

Culture and Community

- The school environment is inviting, safe, inclusive, and supportive of all.
- Every student's academic and personal development is guided by an adult advocate.
- Comprehensive guidance and support services meet the needs of young adolescents.
- Health and wellness are supported in curricula, schoolwide programs, and related policies.
- The school actively involves families in the education of their children.
- The school includes community and business partners.

Based on: *This We Believe* by the Association of Middle Level Education. Westerville, OH: Author.

LO 1.4 Middle Level Teacher Preparation Standards and Assessments

In 1995, the National Council for the Accreditation of Teacher Education (NCATE) recognized the need for the establishment of **standards** for the preparation of middle level teachers. Most schools of education are either accredited, or are seeking accreditation, through the Council for the Accreditation of Educator Preparation (CAEP), the reconfigured and renamed national accreditation organization. In 2000, the National Middle School Association (now AMLE) and NCATE (now CAEP) jointly established seven standards for middle level teacher preparation. In 2012, the Association for Middle Level Education revised these **standards**, with the major tenets in Figure 1.4. Each of the five standards includes two to four elements, an explanation, references, and a rubric indicating target, acceptable, and unacceptable performance. For instance, Standard 1: Young Adolescent Development includes the following four elements:

- Knowledge of Young Adolescent Development
- Knowledge of the Implications of Diversity on Young Adolescent Development
- Implications of Young Adolescent Development for Middle Level Curriculum and Instruction
- Implications of Young Adolescent Development for Middle Level Programs and Practices.

Each standard, with specific elements, is addressed within this book. Familiarize yourself with the standards and recognize that many of the elements are addressed numerous times and in a variety of ways, chapter after chapter.

FIGURE 1.4 Middle level teacher preparation standards

Association for Middle Level Education Middle Level Teacher Preparation Standards

All Young Adolescents: The middle level standards interpret "all young adolescents" to be inclusive, comprising students of diverse ethnicity, race, language, religion, socioeconomic status, gender, sexual orientation, regional or geographic origin, and those with exceptional learning needs.

Middle Level: The grade levels included in "middle level" are determined by middle level teacher licensure regulations in each state, for example grades 4–9, 5–8, 6–9.

Standard 1: Young Adolescent Development

Middle level teacher candidates understand the major concepts, principles, theories, and research related to young adolescent development, and they provide opportunities that support student development and learning.

Standard 2: Middle Level Curriculum

Middle level teacher candidates understand and use the central concepts, tools of inquiry, standards, research and structures of content to plan and implement curriculum that develops all young adolescents' competence in subject matter.

Standard 3: Middle Level Philosophy and School Organization

Middle level teacher candidates understand the major concepts, principles, theories, and research underlying the philosophical foundations of developmentally responsive middle level programs and schools, and they work successfully within these organizational components.

Standard 4: Middle Level Instruction and Assessment

Middle level teacher candidates understand, use, and reflect on the major concepts, principles, theories, and research related to data-informed instruction and assessment, and they employ a variety of strategies for a developmentally appropriate climate to meet the varying abilities and learning styles of all young adolescents.

Standard 5: Middle Level Professional Roles

Middle level teacher candidates understand the complexity of teaching young adolescents, and they engage in practices and behaviors that develop their competence as professionals.

Based on: Association for Middle Level Education (AMLE), 4151 Executive Parkway, Suite 300, Westerville, OH 43081, 1-800-528-6672, www.amle.org.

The **Educational Testing Service (ETS)** has developed a series of assessments designed to test teacher candidates according to the standards established by most states in the areas of basic academic skills, subject knowledge, knowledge of teaching methods, and classroom performance. These assessments form the **Praxis** series. ETS tells us that there are three basic uses for the Praxis results: universities may use them to assess the knowledge of teacher candidates; states may use them for granting initial licensure; and professional organizations may require their successful completion as part of the criteria for certification.

You may have taken Praxis I or Praxis Core in conjunction with entry requirements for your teacher education program. The exams assess basic knowledge in reading, writing, and math. The Praxis II series is designed to assess specific knowledge and skills aligning with your chosen level of teaching and/or subject area: mathematics, science, literature and language studies, and history/social studies. Exactly which tests are required varies from state to state. One of the most widely used tests in the Praxis series is the Principles of Learning and Teaching (PLT). This assessment is divided into grade levels, with middle level defined as grades 5–9. Success on the test requires knowledge of young adolescent development, curriculum, instruction, assessment, and maintenance of an appropriate learning environment. The Praxis series exams are not the only ones required of teacher candidates. In an increasing number of states other tests are required, like the Massachusetts Test for Educator Licensure and the North Carolina Test for Educator Licensure. These tests tend to be more comprehensive and difficult concerning content knowledge than the Praxis exams.

Many states now require **edTPA**, an in-depth performance-based, subject-specific assessment that measures and supports the skills and knowledge of teaching.

Self-Check 1.4

LO 1.5 Effective Middle Level Teachers

For centuries attempts have been made to list the characteristics of effective teachers. This is a healthy endeavor because it involves observation and reflection, and then articulation about teaching and learning. What we know for sure is that teachers who positively influence student learning may have only that characteristic in common. Making the teaching and learning connection is both the goal and the reality of effective teachers. The ways they go about engaging students in learning, their personalities, and their teaching styles may widely vary. An interesting site all about young adolescents and their teachers is **Middle Web**. Dedicated to increasing achievement for all middle level students, the site features numerous articles and dozens of links to help increase teacher knowledge and skills.

Although researched and written at the end of the 20th century, a list of positive characteristics of middle level teachers is still quite relevant. In their book, *Middle Level Teachers: Portraits of Excellence* (1995), four major contributors to our knowledge of middle level education provide us with 16 research-based traits of effective middle level teachers. Al Arth, John Lounsbury, Ken McEwin, and John Swaim tell us that effective middle level teachers should strive to possess the characteristics listed in Figure 1.5. The wisdom in this list is sound, aligning with AMLE teacher preparation standards. Recognize the authors' names?

Now let's get to know nine teachers. They are real teachers, but some of their circumstances have been altered in these profiles. Their backgrounds, personal attributes, education, teaching styles, and attitudes mirror teachers I have known. We will meet the teachers now and learn from their experiences in the Professional Practice sections to come. They will interact with one another, with other teachers, and with students, as

FIGURE 1.5   The effective middle level teacher

1. Is sensitive to the individual differences, cultural backgrounds, and exceptionalities of young adolescents, treats them with respect, and celebrates their special nature.

2. Understands and welcomes the role of advocate, adult role model, and advisor.

3. Is self-confident and personally secure—can take student challenges while teaching.

4. Makes decisions about teaching based on a thorough understanding of the physical, social, intellectual, and emotional development of young adolescents.

5. Is dedicated to improving the welfare and education of young adolescents.

6. Works collaboratively and professionally to initiate needed changes.

7. Establishes and maintains a disciplined learning environment that is safe and respects the dignity of young adolescents.

8. Ensures that all young adolescents will succeed in learning.

9. Has a broad, interdisciplinary knowledge of the subjects in the middle level curriculum and depth of content knowledge in one or more areas.

10. Is committed to integrating curriculum.

11. Uses varied evaluation techniques that both teach and assess the broad goals of middle level education and provide for student self-evaluation.

12. Recognizes that major goals of middle level education include the development of humane values, respect for self, and positive attitudes toward learning.

13. Seeks out positive and constructive relationships and communicates with young adolescents in a variety of environments.

14. Works closely with families to form partnerships to help young adolescents be successful at school.

15. Utilizes a wide variety of developmentally appropriate instructional strategies.

16. Acquires, creates, and utilizes a wide variety of resources to improve the learning experiences of young adolescents.

Based on: Arth, A., Lounsbury, J.H., McEwin, C.K., & Swaim, J.H. *Middle Level Teachers: Portraits of Excellence* (1995).

well as administrators, community members, and parents. Pictures of the teachers are provided so you will feel even better acquainted with them. Throughout the text they talk directly to you in a feature called "Teachers Speak." Here are our focus teachers:

- Jermaine Joyner, 6th, 7th, 8th grade technology, African American, age 31

- Sadie Fox, 8th grade science, Caucasian American, age 26

- Keith Richardson, 6th grade language arts, Caucasian American, age 40

- Carmen Esparza, 6th, 7th, 8th grade bilingual language arts and social studies, Hispanic American, age 34

- Jesse White, 8th grade social studies, Caucasian American, age 29

- Traci Peters, 7th grade math, Caucasian American, age 36

- Deirdre McGrew, 6th, 7th, 8th grade remedial language arts and social studies, African American, age 48

- Joey Huber, 7th grade student teacher, Caucasian American, age 22

- Sarah Gardner, 6th grade student teacher, Caucasian American, age 21

Jermaine Joyner

This is my fourth year working in a public school. Right after I got my degree in computer science, I went to work for a large chain store and made house calls with *Geek* on my name badge. After a year or so, I was unhappy with my job and decided to teach computer classes at a private school. After qualifying for state certification, I took a position at Jefferson Middle School, an inner-city school that was converted to a magnet

school in the mid-1990s. I am almost finished with my master's degree in administration, and I would really like to be an assistant principal here in a few years.

Jefferson's magnet status is based on technology. We have laptop carts, 30 tablets, 30 iPods, and 30 video cameras. We also have SMART technology in each classroom. Students apply to Jefferson and are chosen by lottery. Those who apply must have at least a C average and a good attendance record. We have been able to attract quite a few kids from the suburbs. Those from the neighborhood around the school qualify for free lunch. The kids from the suburbs are wealthy enough to have private transportation to get here from outside the city. Actually, I think the mix works.

I am the computer teacher, and I teach six 45-minute periods a day, two for each grade level. Computer science is a related arts course, and all the kids take it for one semester a year. I'm able to build on what they know and can do from 6th to 7th to 8th grade. My job at Jefferson gives me lots of room to be creative. Two years ago, I took a back room in the library and turned it into a TV station. It fits right in with our technology focus. I wrote grants and checked with the district and other schools trying to obtain all the equipment we would need to do daily student broadcasts. Now I have a small group of kids who come to me before and after school as the *Broadcast Club*. We tape a brief daily program shown each morning. Makes my day!

Sadie Fox

You know, I had a lot of careers from which to choose. In college I thought about law school and pre-med. I know I could have been an attorney or a medical doctor, but I'm not. I chose, instead, to spend my days with kids, and I love it! They are quirky and unpredictable. Watching them grow is a delight.

I translated my love of science into teaching the subject to kids who often don't seem to care very much. My challenge is to catch them enjoying some aspect of a lesson and then get them hooked by doing something just a little off the wall. Some of them get so interested that they begin to ask questions. My standard answer is, "Hey, when you find out, share it with us." That sends them to the Internet or to the library. It's great.

I guess I've always been pretty competitive. I began a science club at Valley View four years ago when I first started teaching. It grew quickly as we entered a Science Olympiad competition, and we won! We continued to win and made it to the national level. Each year since, we have excelled. For a rural area with people scattered over more than 1,500 square miles with only a few places to shop and eat, having a team of 8th graders win national science competitions . . . well, let's just say that the kids enjoy near rock star status.

Since I started teaching at Valley View, I have finished a master's degree in science education and achieved National Board Certification. It's been a lot of work, but totally worth it. One of these days I plan to go back to graduate school and get a PhD. I think I would enjoy teaching at the university level.

Keith Richardson

Right out of high school I went to a community college and, as I worked in a local restaurant, completed an associate degree. That qualified me for a job in a textile mill where my dad and his dad worked for years. I got the job I wanted and got married at age 20. I received

several promotions and had two kids. The problem was that I wasn't very satisfied with how I was spending my days. I left the house at 7 a.m. and often didn't get home until 6:00 in the evening. I was often asked to work swing shifts when someone called in sick. With two weeks of vacation a year and my sons growing quickly, I started reconsidering my choices.

I decided to go back to college and get a four-year degree so I could teach middle or high school language arts. This decision wasn't really based on the time constraints of my job at the mill. I was always an avid reader and often wrote short stories for fun. I have taught Sunday School since I was a teenager and was often told I was a natural for getting people to understand things. As a teacher, the dilemma of not enough time with my family was solved. This was a decision I could live with!

I think I fit middle school. I'm patient, I can laugh at myself, and kids seem to like my easygoing style. I get restless with traditional instruction, and I know the students do too. I try to keep them hopping by doing active things. They read anything they want during DEAR (Drop Everything And Read). The catch is that they have to tell the class about what they are reading twice every nine weeks, and they can't do regular book reports. They come up with some pretty crazy stuff, but the bottom line is, *they read*!

Carmen Esparza

I'm a second generation American. My parents came to the United States when they were teenagers. They made a lot of sacrifices so my three brothers and I could have all the opportunities we enjoy today. We were born in Colorado and, therefore, are U.S. citizens. My oldest brother and I went to Colorado State. He's an engineer, and I majored in Spanish and minored in secondary education. After teaching high school Spanish for a few years near Denver, I went back to school and got a master's degree in English. I read a lot about bilingual education and made the decision to pursue a position in a middle school. I guess there aren't many of us around with degrees in both Spanish and English, and I got a job right away. About that time I became pregnant. When my baby girl was born, I decided to be a stay-at-home mom for a while. Three babies later, I am back!

Teaching whole classes of English language learners is exhausting. I teach both language arts and social studies, about half in Spanish and half in English. I teach all the kids who need bilingual education in grades 6–8, each grade level in a separate class. The trick is to engage the students in their own learning and use lots of visuals.

The longer I teach, the more the reality sinks in that I can't "save" kids by myself. I can influence them and maybe help a few stay in school, but it's an uphill battle when I consider the strikes against them. Many aren't citizens and live in fear of being sent back to Mexico or Central America. I try to stay positive and help my kids get to the place where they have choices in life.

(Continued)

Jesse White

I've been teaching for six years, all of them at Lincoln Middle School. I taught 7th grade science the first two years, and then a social studies position opened on the 8th grade Wildcats team. I jumped at the chance to be on a team with a couple of teachers I not only admired but who stepped in and served as informal mentors to me. I've been here ever since, and I'm quite happy with what I do.

Lincoln is a Title I school. We have mostly black and Hispanic students, and most get free breakfast and lunch. They almost all live within walking distance of the school. Funny thing . . . they're never really anxious to leave campus. During the day they often act like school is the last place they want to be, but then they stick around after school. I made a commitment my first year to be a teacher who's always accessible, so I stick around too. If I'm going to be here anyway, I figure I might as well help with the football and soccer teams. So, I help coach and find that I get to talk with kids on the field who rarely participate in class. It's a good outreach for me. I rarely get home before 6:00, but, if I worked in business or industry, I would have about the same length of workday. The difference is that once I get home, sometimes I'm not really finished with my work.

One thing I really appreciate about teaching on a team is team planning time. We teach three 90-minute blocks, with one block for planning, 45 minutes for individual planning, and 45 minutes with my team. As the social studies teacher, I find that I can integrate all kinds of things into American history. When we talk about our teaching plans for the week, I can often support what's happening in language arts by emphasizing what's being taught. For instance, if they are learning about poetry, I find poems written in the period of history we're studying. If I can find something about an invention that goes along with the science curriculum, I throw it in. I like making connections. We still haven't done a true interdisciplinary unit. That's one of my goals for next year.

Traci Peters

I'm a 7th grade math teacher, and I can't imagine doing anything else. I loved math as a student, but planned to teach elementary school. Well, I ended up in a middle school math classroom, and I'm so glad because it suits me. I enjoy organization and being prepared. These two qualities serve me well with my two algebra classes and two pre-algebra classes. I have a super team to work with. We all like each other, and that makes going to work fun! And, of course, the kids make it fun too, and also sometimes very frustrating. But that's OK. Overall, it's the best job anywhere. I have National Board Certification and that has added to my income and my sense of professionalism.

I'm married to a wonderful man who supports me in my career. I have a beautiful son who isn't in school yet. That's

the one negative thing about teaching, but my mom takes care of Robbie for me and probably would throw a fit if I hinted at staying at home. I'm very fortunate.

Most of my students do really well on standardized tests. It's hard to show a lot of progress in three of my classes because their scores are already good. The students I have in 7th grade algebra and pre-algebra are the ones who achieve at math. My fourth class is a mix of students who have never excelled in math and those who have recently come to the United States.

Our school is in a fairly well-to-do suburb, and most of the parents of my algebra and pre-algebra students are college educated. All the technology gadgets out there are likely in the hands of my students. They take to graphing calculators naturally. But when it comes to basic math concepts, I still rely on a whiteboard and an overhead projector. I use as many manipulatives as possible, like pattern blocks and paper folding. My philosophy is that experiencing math is the way to go.

Deirdre McGrew

Teaching is my fourth career. I started out as a journalist. Then I went to work for a publishing house, and then I became an associate minister at my church. Along the way I got two master's degrees, a husband, and five children! Quite a life, don't you think?

I've taught elementary school and both language arts and social studies in middle school. When my principal heard about what some schools were doing to meet the needs of kids at risk for failing, she started thinking about how we could adapt the plan at Cario. We don't have a real large population of kids at risk, but we are always looking for new ways to reach them. Because my principal knows what a soft spot I have for kids who struggle, she suggested that we think about starting CARE, Cario Academic Recovery and Enrichment. I have a group of 12–15 students in grades 6–8 for half a day for language arts and social studies, and a colleague has 12–15 students in grades 6–8 for half a day for math and science. We switch kids at lunch.

Through CARE we can make instruction very personalized. I have eight computers to use with the Scholastic Read 180 program. I do whole group instruction on basic skills for just a little while each day. Then the kids read and work on projects that combine the language arts and social studies standards. I am able to spend individual time with each student each day. I can see regular progress. Makes it worth the planning and effort!

Will I teach for the rest of my career? I honestly don't know. Life is full of surprises, and I'm always open to them.

Joey Huber

I'm a student teacher. I have to keep saying it to believe it! I'm a student teacher. Most of my friends are business majors and have no idea what they'll do when we graduate. They're thinking maybe they'll need to go to graduate school to get a job in their field. They've done internships, and most dreaded getting up in the morning to go. But not me! I love being a teacher! To be in my school all day every day for 16 weeks I had to give up playing college baseball. I had a partial scholarship for the first seven semesters of college but gave it up for one semester to be in the classroom. No regrets!

When I did some fieldwork at my school, I figured I needed to befriend my students. I wanted to be their buddy, and I accomplished it. But that wasn't smart, as I soon found out. There's a line teachers can't cross and still be the *teacher*. I'll tell you more about this later.

At my school the 6th graders are divided into teams with just two teachers. The 7th and 8th grade teams have three teachers on them. We have a math teacher, a language arts teacher, and a teacher who teaches science and social studies on a rotating basis. There are 86 kids on the Starfish team. Our classes are heterogeneous, with some really high achievers, some with IEPs, and lots in between. My cooperating teachers are different from each other, but they each seem to reach the kids in unique ways.

After school I am an assistant coach of the baseball team. This is one of the best experiences I have ever had and more than makes up for not playing the game myself. I can teach them all I know and demonstrate how to play. I know that when I teach I want to coach as well.

Sarah Gardner

I always knew I wanted to be a teacher. I was in Teacher Cadets in high school and went to college knowing that teaching was in my future. I loved the classes and now I am crazy about student teaching! I am assigned to a 6th grade team with two wonderful cooperating teachers. They are very responsive to the students, and I know I will learn so much from them. Half the students on our team are in the Academically and Intellectually Gifted (AIG) program for academically and intellectually gifted students. The other half are considered regular learners, most of whom make adequate progress but aren't designated AIG.

I'll teach math and social studies for eight weeks, and then language arts and science for eight weeks. Math is really my favorite subject, but, because my certification will be in all the subjects for K–6, I need to experience all the areas. My plan is to teach middle school next year, though. I understand that I can take the Praxis II exams in math and maybe language arts and then be able to teach 7th and 8th grade in these subjects.

Something that bothers me a lot is that when we have the AIG classes we have mostly white students. When we have the other students, we have diversity. Everything I learned in my classes in college tells me that this is a problem. I remember learning about what's called the *soft bigotry of low expectations*. My question is "How has this happened?" When I ask my cooperating teachers, they say it seems to have been this way for their whole careers. By the time students get to middle school, they have been labeled as AIG or not. I don't mean to say that average achievers are not succeeding. If they are working hard and making progress, then they are succeeding. But did these students' elementary teachers not expect them to be really bright? Would I have done any better? I'm starting to think about going to graduate school to learn more about gifted education. I'm interested in figuring out some answers to my questions.

Why It Matters

Middle level philosophy is grounded in two areas—our understanding of the unique nature of young adolescents and how we choose to respond to their needs. It's a philosophy, an attitude, and a belief in possibilities that shape curriculum, instruction, and assessment, and all the ways we interact with our students. It's not necessarily quantifiable. It requires reflection and the renewal of resources, both physical and psychological. Middle level philosophy asks the adults who touch the lives of young adolescents to stretch and grow right along with their students.

With ongoing growth comes the ability to balance what we know and understand about young adolescents with how we respond to their needs. To maintain balance is to continually weigh what we know against what we do. Sound and reasoned judgment, along with an eye for appropriateness, will maintain this sensitive equilibrium. As you read this text, you will develop a grasp of the enormity of the task for middle level teachers and the challenges that make middle level education rewarding.

Group Activities

1. Obtain a wall map of your city and/or county. Locate and mark each middle school in your surrounding area as found on school and district websites. This will help put your future discussions of local middle schools in context.

2. As a class, begin an electronic or paper file to which you all have access. This file should have a section designated for each local (city or county) middle school. As data and observations are collected, add them to the file.

3. Assign each class member a middle school in your area to research by going online to get the approximate number of students. Record the number of students and the published mission statement in your class file.

Individual Activities

1. Establish an electronic portfolio in which you collect your own work concerning middle level education. Include group activities, individual activities, your personal journal, observation and interview notes, helpful resources, media coverage of middle level education, and so on.

2. Choose a mission statement from a local middle school. Write a brief assessment of the statement as you examine it for elements of *This We Believe.*

Personal Journal

At the end of each chapter, there are questions and/or prompts that require you to draw on your own experiences. Feel free to react to any portion of the chapter beyond the items asked for. The part of your electronic file established in Individual Activity 1 should be for your eyes only, shared at your own discretion or at the request of your instructor.

1. What was the grade structure of your K–12 school experience? Was any part of it called *Middle School*?

Briefly describe aspect(s) of your middle level school you experienced or remember.

2. What do you recall about the facility you attended during the middle level years? How was it different from your elementary and high schools?

3. Do you identify with or "see yourself" in one focus teacher more than the others? Briefly describe what traits led you to choose the teacher.

Professional Practice

This is the first of the Professional Practice features you will find at the end of each chapter. Please copy this file in your electronic portfolio and complete the items. You may print and share as requested by your instructor. The scenarios, multiple choice questions, and constructed response items ask you to apply the knowledge in this text and from your course discussions to classroom and school situations. The items are designed to provide practice for a variety of the Praxis II exams that may be required for licensure/certification. Most of the scenarios involve teachers you met in this chapter and the students you will meet in Chapter 2. For some items, more than one choice may be defensible. The purpose of the items is to stimulate thought and discussion.

When Lake Park Junior High changed the sign out front to Lake Park Middle School, it joined all the other middle level schools in the district whose signs changed at the same time. Yes, they were way behind the national trend, but the community was growing and the decision was finally made to move 6th graders from elementary schools to newly formed middle schools. Ninth grade was moved to the high schools where additions had been built to accommodate more students.

Lake Park principal Mr. Hammond was given the task by the district superintendent of exploring middle level philosophy and arranging for an August staff day where junior high teachers would learn about how middle schools are different from junior highs and, more important, what to do with 6th graders in schools used to 7th, 8th, and 9th graders. He had read about the Association for Middle Level Education in the National Association of Secondary School Principals (NASSP) journals and recognized AMLE as the best source for direction. He went online and joined AMLE in order to receive publications. He ordered books on middle level philosophy and checked with the state to see if they could recommend middle schools for him to visit. It was June and he had little time to prepare for August.

1. In his efforts to explore middle level philosophy, which combination of sources of information might be most helpful?

   a. state education newsletters designed to share information on what's happening in local areas; *Middle School Journal*; NASSP Bulletin

   b. *Turning Points* from the Carnegie Corporation; NASSP Bulletin

   c. *Middle School Journal*; *Turning Points* from the Carnegie Corporation

   d. *This We Believe* and *Middle School Journal*

2. What will likely be the most significant barrier for Mr. Hammond as he moves forward and envisions the August staff development day?

   a. principals who are resistant to change

   b. parental concerns about the districtwide change

   c. teachers who have not been specifically prepared for middle level education

   d. lack of viable role model schools in the area

3. From what you know about Mr. Hammond's efforts, what is the most important element he is missing?

   a. attendance at a middle level education conference

   b. collaborative planning with teacher leaders at his school

   c. research about why the district now wants to incorporate middle level schools

   d. meeting with rising 6th graders to listen to their concerns about changing schools

4. Return to the 16 characteristics of successful schools for young adolescents in Figure 1.3. Choose one characteristic in each of the three categories. What are the necessary factors for making each statement true about a school?

Chapter 2
Development of Middle Level Learners

Sara Davis Powell

Young people undergo more rapid and profound personal changes between the ages of 10 and 15 than at any other time in their lives. . . . Early adolescence is also a period of tremendous variability among youngsters of the same gender and chronological age in all areas of their development.

THIS WE BELIEVE, P. 5.

 ## Learning Outcomes

After studying this chapter, you will have knowledge and skills to:

2.1 Describe aspects of physical development including varying growth rates and puberty.

2.2 Summarize characteristics of intellectual development, including variability among middle level learners.

2.3 Analyze how emotional development is manifested and interrelated to other areas of development.

2.4 Explore social development involving adult and peer relationships.

2.5 Examine young adolescent character traits and ways to enhance healthy development.

2.6 Articulate *This We Believe* goals for young adolescent development.

Dear Future Middle Level Teacher,

Now let's think about young adolescents and their development. The middle school years represent a unique and significant period of human development. Young adolescents are in a world of their own and yet are keenly aware of their surroundings—the places, people, and things that make up their world. By middle school, students have begun to develop diversified views of themselves. Often these views seem to conflict. Consider the following statements based on the work of Donna San Antonio (2006). In what ways do they apply to your own development?

- Young adolescents may be fiercely independent, yet need and seek meaningful relationships with adults.
- Young adolescents may reveal emotional vulnerability, yet be deeply self-protective.
- Young adolescents may be capable of complex critical thinking, yet be disorganized and excessively forgetful.
- Young adolescents may be compassionate in their desire to make the world a better place, yet display a high level of self-centeredness and even cruelty toward a classmate.

In this chapter, we discuss five broad developmental perspectives—physical, intellectual, emotional, social, and character. Each of these perspectives interacts with, and influences, all of the others. In the ever-changing world of early adolescence, it is artificial to separate these areas of development. Exploring them separately must be considered only an organizing tool. Let the perspectives flow in and out of one another as you read and reflect.

One thing you can count on is that, in your middle level classroom, no two students will be at the same stage of development in all the areas at once—nor will an individual student develop uniformly across all areas. That physically mature boy may be painfully shy. The tiny girl who looks more like a third-grader may be ready to tackle the quadratic equation. It's a fascinating world when you spend your days with 10- to 15-year-olds!

SDP

Standard 1
Young Adolescent Development

Element a. Knowledge of Young Adolescent Development: Middle level teacher candidates demonstrate a comprehensive knowledge of young adolescent development. They use this understanding of the intellectual, physical, social, emotional, and moral characteristics, needs, and interests of young adolescents to create healthy, respectful, supportive, and challenging learning environments for all young adolescents, including those whose language and cultures are different from their own.

LO 2.1 Physical Development

Remember the days when self-consciousness took priority over everything else? Maybe you were one of the lucky ones with looks and self-esteem that gave you the confidence to be relatively free of trauma when it came to your physical appearance. But let's face it, even the cheerleaders and the coolest guy around had their moments of doubt. Perhaps the physical burden was never feeling quite good-looking enough. This desire to be physically attractive is part of the human condition and needs to be put in perspective. Easy to say as adults! Young adolescents, however, often lack perspective.

In the inconsistent world of early adolescence, there is one predictable factor: physical development influences every other type of development middle level students experience—emotional, social, intellectual, and character.

If we held up a bag of male body parts and asked a blindfolded 12-year-old boy to reach inside, grab parts randomly, and become the young adolescent that is the composite of those parts, the result would be a middle level student in 6th or 7th grade. There is no such thing as typical because these newly double-digit-aged kids so often appear to be "Mister Potato Heads" in this awkward stage of life. Ears too big, arms too long, voices too squeaky. Girls, too, often resemble creatures of mismatched parts. Their hips may widen before their breasts develop, their noses may be too big for their faces.

Growth spurts usually occur for boys between the ages of 12 and 15, but, for some boys, rapid physical growth may be delayed well into high school. Growth is seldom even or gradual for young adolescents. Bones tend to grow more rapidly than muscles. Although weight gain generally accompanies bone growth, without equivalent development of muscle, awkwardness and clumsiness are inevitable. Joint pain, leg aches, restlessness, and fatigue may accompany these uneven periods of growth. Outer extremities, such as hands and feet, grow before arms and legs. Have you ever heard someone say that you can predict the adult size of a puppy by looking at the size of its paws? Well, chances are if a boy needs a size 13 sneaker by age 12, 30 × 28 jeans will be history by age 14! So, in his new 32 × 34 jeans, he walks into middle school to greet his 8th grade year as a remarkably different-looking young adolescent than his 6th and 7th grade teachers experienced. As a middle school teacher, I never tire of gasping (to the delight of many a boy), "This can't be the same Cody who sat by the window in my third period class last year!"

Girls generally experience rapid growth a year or two before boys. Remember middle school dances? The tall, gangly girls giggled in one corner while shorter, "cutie-pie" boys taunted each other to ask for a dance—only to find that their faces often matched up with developing breasts.

Each of these three boys is 11 years old. Although we may think the boy in the center is the most mature, his teacher tells us he is actually less emotionally mature than his two much smaller classmates.

Sara Davis Powell

Puberty

Outward growth spurts indicate big changes on the inside. Between childhood and the beginning of young adulthood is the transition period known as **puberty**. The word *puberty* often causes parent and teacher alike to shudder. If we think it's scary as adults to spend time around kids experiencing puberty, let's try to recall what it was like to have puberty actually taking place inside us. During puberty, biological changes that make us taller, heavier, and more muscular are accompanied by hormonal changes that forever alter our bodies in equally significant ways. Although testosterone, the male hormone, and estrogen, the female hormone, are present in all of us, the balance of the hormones is broken during puberty so that one hormone takes over to influence sexual development. All of this is happening for some at the same time as those mismatched parts are appearing almost overnight. At this point, if you are thinking, "I'm supposed to teach these creatures subject-verb agreement and the Pythagorean theorem?" you are beginning to get the picture of some of the challenges (and the joys) of middle level education.

Many changes occur during puberty. Hair growth develops under arms, on legs, in pubic areas, and on the face. The voice changes as the larynx grows larger. Girls' voices may become mellow, and boys' voices may go through those embarrassing falsetto-crack-bass-crack-falsetto moments. Oil and sweat glands may begin to function, resulting in all kinds of potentially embarrassing situations. Acne medication, shampoo, and deodorant appear on shopping lists, and longer, more frequent showers become (or should become) part of a daily routine.

Sexual Maturity

With puberty comes sexual maturation. Yes, these wonderful, awkward, funny-sounding, often aromatic configurations we call young adolescents have all the parts necessary to reproduce themselves. Because the body often matures before mental and emotional decision-making skills, developing middle level students are at high risk for either poor decisions or not thinking at all before acting. Ill-timed sexual experimentation can easily lead to multiple unfortunate consequences, only two of which are sexually transmitted diseases and pregnancy.

Timing

Perhaps at no other stage of life does timing play such an important role. Rapid physical changes, puberty, and sexual maturation generally take place, in starts and stops, between the ages of 10 and 14. Puberty, with all its miraculous changes, is a challenging period of life for many young adolescents.

Sara Davis Powell

Young adolescents experience sexual maturation and begin developing more mature relationships.

The changes experienced by growing children happen sporadically, predictable only in the sense that there are growth patterns. These patterns happen rapidly and early for some, and slowly and haltingly for others. The early bloomers may be boastful, but are often embarrassed. The late bloomers are almost always self-conscious. There are emotional consequences associated with physical changes that can lead to long-lasting and very memorable scars on the psyche that haunt for a lifetime. Let's look at some issues that may accompany physical development and explore some ways we, as teachers, might make the child-to-adolescent passage a bit less chaotic.

Physical Development Issues

Physical development issues are many and are often uncomfortable for both teachers and students. Here are some issues, along with suggestions for how we can make a difference, both as individual teachers and on school and district levels.

1. Middle level students need information on physical development. Not only do middle level students have a tough time finding answers, they can rarely define the question or problem when it comes to physical growth and changes. A comprehensive health education curriculum is invaluable. National and state standards are available that outline what 10- to 14-year-olds need to know about wellness, puberty, and sexual maturation. A health educator is needed in every school—someone who is honest, straightforward, trustworthy from a student perspective, and accessible. Boys and girls should be separated at times to allow for more honest and detailed questions and answers.

2. Physical changes affect behavior. Teachers serve students well when they recognize and accept a variety of behaviors that may result directly from the turmoil caused and/or aggravated by the biological aspects of puberty. When opportunities arise to address the unspoken questions and resulting behaviors, teachers should reassure students that their anxieties are normal, and even expected. Middle level students are restless and uncomfortable much of the time. Because of varying growth rates and the excess energy that may accompany these periods of rapid change, regulation desks arranged in rows do not always provide the physical setting students need. Providing a classroom with a variety of seating possibilities can prove very beneficial. Perhaps a couple of tables with chairs, desks of varying sizes, a few comfortable chairs, and a couch will provide ample choices. I realize that this gives students a lot of freedom, and many teachers are hesitant to build their classroom environments in this way. However, I have found that most middle level students respond positively when their needs are taken into consideration and when teachers do things that show respect for them. The legitimate restlessness resulting from growing bodies may be exacerbated by long periods of sitting, regardless of the variety of chairs provided. It's no secret that active learning is more effective than passive learning. Movement stimulates the learning process. Find ways to get students up and moving as part of instruction.

3. Rapid growth requires increased and balanced nutrition. There are two problems when it comes to young adolescents increasing what they eat in a balanced way. Body image worries scream "thin" to many middle level students. And then, when they're hungry, their taste buds, along with peer pressure, often lead them to less nutritional food choices.

   A comprehensive health program will include lessons on good nutrition. But the health educator can't do it alone. All of us need to emphasize healthy eating. When we have a snack, let's make it something nutritional like an apple or carrot. When we eat in the cafeteria, let's model healthy eating habits. Middle level kids are often hungry. If, as a faculty, a decision can be made to allow eating during the day other than at lunchtime, then find a way to let kids have snacks, perhaps mid-morning or mid-afternoon, provided the snacks follow healthy eating guidelines you and your team and administration have established.

4. Young adolescents should not be stereotyped according to physical characteristics. Many growth issues factor into physical ability. Some middle level students experience athletic success as they mature. Others find themselves lacking the coordination and stamina they may have had in elementary school. Let's give middle level students the opportunity to explore athletics and find their talents and interests according to their own timing. Tall boys are not automatically talented at, or even interested in, basketball. Petite girls are not all destined to be gymnasts. Physical development sometimes leads to a child's interest in a particular activity or sport, but mental development also influences activity choices.

   Plan ways to incorporate a variety of intramural opportunities that allow less physically skilled students to participate in team and individual activities. Offer classes in exploratory time or after-school that help students learn skills such as dancing, tennis, martial arts, and so on.

   The quality of a middle level chorus depends on vocal cord development. Some activities in home economics, home arts, and shop arts require dexterity, and some art forms require coordination and spatial sense. Although we would like all middle level students to experience success in all areas, we need to understand that while the brain may be willing, biological development may not have caught up. Let's make sure that exploratory courses and intramural activities are opportunities to experience and experiment in broad areas that allow for, and accommodate, differences in development and natural abilities.

5. Many girls will experience the first signs of a menstrual period during the school day. This development alone will cause most girls to be upset and anxious, depending on the amount of information they have or the level of openness they have experienced among friends and family. A common cause of absenteeism among young adolescent girls is menstrual pain. Teachers need to be very sensitive to girls' requests to leave the classroom suddenly, as well as to girls who are late to class or stay in the restroom longer than expected. Of course, the key to knowing the legitimacy of these events is knowing our students. Not every tardy girl is menstruating. Just be aware that questioning tardiness or restroom requests in front of other students is never appropriate. Make sure your school clinic has feminine hygiene products available. Menstrual discomfort is real, not psychosomatic, and can't simply be willed away. As with other physical aspects of life, some will use cramping as an excuse to miss activities in class when perhaps it's not necessary. We should try to err on the side of belief, however, rather than punishing sincere girls who need our understanding.

6. Some middle level students (and I'm not just talking about girls!) feel a compulsion to check themselves out visually on a regular basis. I found that having a full-length mirror in an out-of-the-way place in the classroom served a positive purpose. I also placed a smaller mirror on the wall by the pencil sharpener, so it was never obvious who needed visual reassurance and who simply had a dull pencil. These mirrors were up in August and were a natural part of the classroom setting. As a result, I had very few problems related to them.

7. Overactive glands may cause difficulties. Because glands of all kinds may be newly activated or overactive in young adolescents, by mid-morning a student may realize that he forgot to use deodorant, or perhaps he feels the need for just a touch of something that smells good. Consider having a brown paper bag in a supply closet with spray deodorant and an inexpensive bottle of aftershave, along with a very light fragrance for girls. As with the mirrors, this may be an extra that some teachers may not be comfortable providing. Very few students will ever use these items, but you may save some 12-year-old a world of embarrassment. It's worth the effort.

If comfortable with both the issue and the students, we may have occasions to initiate a personal hygiene discussion with students who, for whatever reason, need our brown bags of smell-good items. A trusted guidance counselor may be a better choice than the classroom teacher for this kind of heart-to-heart. It all depends on the individuals involved.

The physical development of young adolescents may come in sudden spurts or with gradual subtlety. The changes accompanying physical development may be met with emotional turmoil or casual acceptance. In fact, all four of these descriptors may be manifested in one student. Regardless of student responses to physical changes, they are sure to affect the other areas of development. Let's look next at intellectual development.

Self-Check 2.1

LO 2.2 Intellectual Development

Middle level students experience a transitional state between childlike thinking and adult thinking. Childlike thinking is characterized as **concrete thinking**. This means that children organize information and experiences around things that are visible and familiar. They have difficulty visualizing concepts that they cannot see or touch. In the concrete stage, children have rigid patterns of thinking. Middle grades students who are concrete thinkers learn concepts much more readily when they are taught using manipulatives and hands-on activities that help bridge the transition from concrete to more adult **abstract thinking** and learning.

The intellectual, or cognitive, transition that occurs in puberty opens whole new worlds for children progressing to the teen years. They begin to think in more general terms and to visualize events without having to see them. They can form mental connections, put things in perspective, and predict in more complex ways.

Becoming

We must not lose sight of a very important word—*becoming*. As vital as it is to understand how the terms *concrete* and *abstract* apply to the thinking process, it is just as vital to understand the transition between the two distinct stages. Middle level learners are generally concrete thinkers at age 10, and some may remain basically concrete through age 14. However, they may be concrete at age 10 and well on their way to abstract thinking capabilities by age 11. One thing is certain: they are *becoming*. Some researchers tell us that the complete transition into abstract thinking may not take place until the age of 17 or 18. In fact, according to The University of Rochester Medical Center Health Encyclopedia (2017), adult brains and teen brains function quite differently. Adults think with the **prefrontal cortex**, the brain's rational part, while teens process information with the emotional part of the brain, the **amygdala**. Research evidence now shows that some parts of the brain do not fully develop until the mid-20s. This may mean that *your* brain is still developing, that you are still becoming. Pretty exciting, right?

Although we may be able to identify and characterize stages of intellectual/cognitive growth, we must remember that the process of moving from concrete to abstract thinking is completely individual. In other words, *becoming* is **idiosyncratic**, or happening at different rates and at different times for all of us. To complicate matters even further, the other areas of development influence this intellectual growth. By itself, intellectual development is variable, but just think about how physical, emotional, social, and character development figure into the mix of progressing from childhood to adolescence and subsequently to adulthood. It's a complex period of development, to say the least.

Intellectual Development Issues

We should be aware of the variety of intellectual development in the classroom and of the issues this variability presents to the teacher. This awareness leads us to seek ways to assist in this important growth process.

1. The attention span of young adolescents may not be as great as it was in late elementary school or will be in high school. This issue has profound implications for instruction. Expecting a middle level learner to sit through a 20-minute lecture, much less a 45-minute one, and gain a great deal of knowledge is often unrealistic. Attention will wander and learning will be hit or miss at times. Breaking up blocks of time into manageable segments is a technique that should be mastered by middle level teachers.

2. Middle level students often have very vivid imaginations that can be linked to concepts as abstract thinking develops. Purposefully channelling imagination into learning experiences conjures up creativity that has not been possible before. Encouraging students to use their imaginations and creativity to discover nuances and possibilities, rather than simply feeding them information, helps them take advantage of this imagination-meets-abstract-thinking stage of life.

3. Because intellectual development is so variable among young adolescents, a group of 25 seventh-graders may represent a whole spectrum of developmental levels. This is one of the biggest challenges of middle level education. The question is, "How do we facilitate the learning of a prescribed curriculum, that is, state and national standards, in a classroom filled with students who are at very different places in development?" As teachers, we must be observers, constantly monitoring what's working and what isn't, and for which students at which times. We must fill our "instructional toolboxes" to the brim with ways of teaching concepts and skills to students at variable levels of readiness. One size does not fit all!

   As the shift from concrete to abstract thinking is ongoing, it is possible to lose opportunities to challenge middle level students. We must adjust and readjust our lesson components; we must watch closely and listen carefully to our students. We need to vary our instructional approaches to make the most of learning opportunities.

4. Physical development and intellectual development happen concurrently. Active learning should take precedence over passive learning. Let's get middle level students up and moving. They have a need to experience learning—to move, to touch, to manipulate, to search for meaning and understanding. The concept of inquiry, or discovery, learning should pervade what we do in the classroom.

5. A major shift in the intellectual development of middle level students is their newly acquired ability to think about their own thinking, or to experience **metacognition**. We "miss the boat" when it comes to helping students take charge of their own learning if we fail to ask them to reflect on their learning processes. We can help them explore how their thinking takes place and what happens inside and outside the classroom that increases comprehension and makes learning specific skills easier and faster.

6. Middle level students begin to understand what is meaningful and useful, with application to their lives. This intellectual development issue has major implications for what we teach, the **curriculum**. Framing our lessons in the context of real life makes learning a more natural process of satisfying intellectual curiosity that arises from this sense of purpose and usefulness. However, there are times when young adolescent intellectual development appears to be at the mercy of emotions.

Self-Check 2.2

LO 2.3 Emotional Development

Parents, teachers, and even young adolescents themselves often refer to the roller-coaster emotions that accompany the middle level years as difficult to understand and impossible to predict. Recall from the last section that teens process in the emotional part of the brain. If you have ridden a roller-coaster, you can no doubt close your eyes and recall the exhilaration of anticipation, the sheer terror of the actual descents, and brief moments of calm during levelling-off sections. But even in those "catch your breath" phases of the ride, there is an anticipation that keeps the adrenaline flowing and a sense of peace at bay. That's how early adolescence can be characterized.

Dan Goleman, author of *Emotional Intelligence* (1995), says that emotional intelligence, or EQ, determines about 80 percent of a person's success in life. The work of Goleman has been continued by **Six Seconds**, a nonprofit organization that helps individuals, parents, and educators navigate emotional issues in ways that increase emotional intelligence. Goleman and others who continue to research the concept of EQ tell us we need to include five dimensions of emotional intelligence into what we do in schools. These five dimensions are self-awareness, handling emotions, motivation, empathy, and social skills. They believe it is possible to raise the emotional intelligence of students by, among other things, being available to them with an empathetic ear.

You likely noticed that the Dan Goleman reference dates back to 1995. Even so, his theory lives on today. In 2018, Joel Garfinkle wrote about emotional intelligence and its impact on leadership in "5 Qualities of Emotionally Intelligent Leaders." Garfinkle emphasizes the benefits of leaders in all sectors being empathetic, self-aware, positive, considerate, and authentic. Emotional intelligence and related practices matter. You will be the leader of your classroom, helping motivate and form future leaders!

Variety of Emotions

Numerous descriptors are used when referring to the emotional states of early adolescence. Young adolescents may have emotions that are unpredictable, extreme, and unstable. They may be moody, anxious, angry, and embarrassed by things that we don't see as important. Of course, not every 10- to 15-year-old experiences all these characteristics and, when compared to the student next to him at lunch, none to the identical extent. Although these descriptors seem to be negative in nature, my experience leads me to add hopeful, optimistic, and excited to the list. I see these positive emotions exhibited every day by young adolescents. The message here is that variability makes for a wide emotional spectrum of middle level students. All of the descriptors are tied into the concept of self. The development of positive **self-concept** is crucial but often elusive. A young adolescent's self-concept is the sum total of what he knows about himself, including gender, name, personality, physical characteristics, likes and dislikes, beliefs, and family. If asked, "Who are you?" he will use his self-concept to answer. Helping students explore their self-concepts and recognize their strengths should be a goal of every middle level teacher.

When a young adolescent senses a loss of control over the environment, as in the sheer terror roller-coaster moments, the result may a loss of **self-esteem**, or how one values or sees worth of self-concept traits. The myriad changes of the 10- to 15-year-old experience may seem overwhelming. Developing positive self-concept, challenging for many young adolescents, may prove to be especially difficult for minority students. As teachers we must create learning environments that account for cultural, ethnic, and racial differences. This helps foster young adolescents' *empowerment* as they acquire the knowledge and skills needed to take responsibility for their lives. This foundational principle of middle level philosophy should be consistently reinforced with a sense of urgency.

There's a new concept emerging that deserves some consideration. In his book, *Barking Up the Wrong Tree* (2016), Eric Barker proposes the value of **self-compassion**, basing his premise on research that looks at the keys to success. He states that the value of self-confidence and self-esteem are overrated. Self-compassion encourages us to face our flaws and our weaknesses and view ourselves realistically. Barker says that we should treat ourselves with the same kindness and understanding we show others. Hard to argue with that, right? As with most issues in middle level education, and in life as a whole, finding balance is the best idea. We want young adolescents to be confident, yet realistic. Perhaps self-compassion has a real place in our philosophy.

In this chapter's *Making the Teaching and Learning Connection*, we meet Dani Ramsey, an ELA teacher at a Title I school. She understands that the emotional stability of her students impacts every aspect of their lives. Among many strategies, she tells us about writing bio poems and how they allow her students to use self-expression to explore their lives. The bio poems are revealing in all cases and heart-wrenching in many.

Enhanced eText
Video Example 2.1

Teacher Dani Ramsey shows us how to use bio poems to increase academic skill as they provide a personalized outlet for emotion and self-expression. Some of her students read their bio poems.

Making the Teaching and Learning Connection

Dear future teachers,
My name is Dani Ramsey. I teach 6th grade English language arts (ELA) in a Title I middle school.
I can't honestly say that being a teacher was my dream job in high school, or even in college. But once I entered my classroom, I was hooked! I fell in love with the possibility of changing the direction of kids' lives through my teaching.

The kids I work with five days a week mostly live in homes at or near the poverty line. But that doesn't at all define who they are or who they may become. Many lack structure at home and I provide that. I often call them Miss and Mr. I thank them for their responses. I respect them and expect respect in return. I am consistent. They can count on me to treat them the same today and tomorrow.

Every day I see my students driven by their emotions and social relationships. Sometimes they don't know how to react in certain situations and they simply withdraw. Other times they say and do things that I know they don't mean, things that can hurt others. They're finding their way.

One of my favorite activities in ELA is having students write bio poems. These special poems require them to use many of the elements of the standards: brainstorming, biography, metaphor, simile, alliteration, and more. Bio poems are not fillers or meaningless activities. They combine academic practice with an outlet for young adolescents to explore who they are. They evoke emotions. The first thing I do is show students several examples of bio poems because in order to create their own, they need to see a finished product and understand where they're heading with the task. Then I have them brainstorm answers to specific questions, without the added step of making their responses into poems. Once they have explored their responses I ask them to put their answers in poem format.

Middle level teachers need to use a variety of instructional strategies to engage learners. Give bio poems a try in your classroom!

Best wishes to you!
Dani

Sara Davis Powell

Many factors contribute to the development of self-concept in young adolescents. The emotional roller-coaster ride often includes dips that lead to periods of sadness. The alliances formed in early adolescence are often very strong.

Interrelatedness

Emotional development is interrelated with both physical and intellectual development. The physical changes described in this chapter are enough to cause emotions to occasionally go haywire. Imagine growing from 4 feet 11 inches to 5 feet 4 inches in the three short summer months between 7th and 8th grade. Or consider the creamy, smooth complexion that becomes embarrassingly blemished during the first semester of 7th grade. How about the unpredictable erections that occur while finding the surface area of a cylinder or discussing the merits of the Panama Canal? The list of physical changes that can provoke emotional responses could go on and on, with each of us adding our own personal traumas. Be keenly aware that each time you are in a classroom of 25 middle grades students in the process of *becoming*, there are potentially 25 cases of moodiness and insecurity and emotional distress in there with you. Dealing with the physical changes taking place in their bodies is a persistent emotional challenge for young adolescents.

Emotional development is also entangled with intellectual development in ways we are just now beginning to understand and document. Brain researchers tell us that emotions strongly influence our ability to pay attention and retain information. The implications of this regarding the way we approach teaching and learning are tremendous. Emotional concerns can impede academics unless middle level teachers know how to work with these factors and channel concerns into productive results by understanding the context of the student's world.

Worry

Middle grades students worry about almost everything. Their fears have changed from those of childhood to concerns about social and appearance issues. "Do I fit in? Do my jeans look like everybody else's? Is my hair right? Will they want me to sit with them at lunch? Did he notice my braces? Will I be in the 'right' group on the field trip?" Worry, fear, and anxiety are common emotions of early adolescence. From an adult perspective, the sources of these negative emotions may seem trivial, but remember that our perceptions become our realities. To middle grades students, their worries are legitimate and quite real. To try to convince them otherwise is futile and potentially harmful. If we denigrate their concerns, we are, in students' minds, denigrating them and adding to their anxieties and uncertainties. Our responses should be tempered with understanding and the absence of judgmental attitudes. When a 12-year-old girl is crying because she found uncomplimentary notes written about her by kids she considered friends, the last thing she wants to hear is "It's no big deal, you'll find new friends." Instead, we should acknowledge that she is hurt. The gift of an understanding ear will allow her to express her feelings and know that someone cares. It won't take away the hurt, but it will legitimize her emotions and give her the opportunity to work through the grief of the moment.

Emotional Development Issues

Our goal regarding emotional development should be to help our students find their way toward emotional maturity. This task is compounded by the challenge of teaching socially acceptable ways of both controlling and expressing emotions. Along with displaying emotions in socially acceptable ways, emotional maturity must include dealing with personal emotions in mentally healthy ways. Middle level schools must provide opportunities for students to see that a wide range of emotions is normal. Creating an environment that says "It's OK to feel the way you do" will enhance self-acceptance and allow emotional maturity to progress.

1. Because emotions may occur suddenly and without warning, self-regulation is very difficult. Sensitivity to the emotions of our students should make us acutely aware of the volatility they are experiencing. When an outburst of emotion or some sort of personal affront is aimed at us, we have the perfect opportunity to model self-regulation. The sage advice of "take a deep breath and count to 10" has a lot of validity in a middle-grades setting. Show how it's done and encourage students to do likewise.

2. Because of emotional variability, young adolescents may be at high risk of making poor decisions. We can help students recognize that many emotions are fleeting; what they feel at one moment may change quickly and unexpectedly. By thinking out loud when a decision needs to be made, we can model the difference between reacting and responding. Reactions are emotionally triggered, whereas responses are the result of thinking through those emotions. We want our students to make decisions based more on rational thought than on emotions.

3. Some incidences and events trigger emotions to the point of disruption of the learning process. As individual teachers, but preferably as a team of teachers, we have a very beneficial tool for dealing with emotions—providing a psychologically safe environment in which concerns may be aired. This environment may include appropriate readings and videos that present possible solutions to emotionally charged dilemmas and situations. Encouraging students to role-play and involve themselves in simulations may be a vehicle for venting worries, anxieties, and emotional distress and preventing the disruption of the learning process.

Not only can the learning process be affected by emotions, but social relationships and growth are often impacted as well. Closely linked to emotional development is social development, which, in turn, affects overall development of easily influenced and socially self-conscious young adolescents.

> **Self-Check 2.3**

LO 2.4 Social Development

As young adolescents become aware of the unique aspects of themselves, they also become acutely aware of others around them—most specifically their peers. They may develop an exaggerated view of themselves, often thinking that everyone's attention is on them. This perception can lead to uneasiness in social settings. The emotion-laden search for personal identity integrates experiences with developing bodies, biological drive, new thinking capacities, and expanding social roles. Although it may be uncomfortable, socialization plays a major role in the psychological growth process, as it is influenced by, and interrelated with, physical, intellectual, and emotional development. Look for students who don't seem to fit in. They need our attention. As a 12-year-old, David McBeath's 6-foot stature puts his physical development far ahead of his emotional, social, and cognitive development.

The need for socialization is especially strong during early adolescence. As we explored in Chapter 1, middle level philosophy originated partially from the belief that the school can and should play a major role in both the cognitive and **affective dimensions** of the development of the whole child, including aspects of socialization.

Enhanced eText
Video Example 2.2

Student David McBeath is an example of a young adolescent whose physical development has gotten ahead of other areas. David needs our understanding, and perhaps our help with socialization.

Adult Relationships

Young adolescents often find themselves caught between their desire to be safe and secure (as in childhood) and their desire for freedom and independence. Because adults generally represent security, the struggle for change often revolves around relationships with them. Although affirmation of parental love and teacher approval are secretly sought, young adolescents may act out in argumentative and rebellious ways against adults closest to them—parents, guardians, and teachers. This rebellion, in its many forms, is normal and even necessary, as attempts are made to demonstrate that they have minds of their own. Considering the options, perhaps rebellion during early adolescence is preferable to rebellion at other times in life when even more dangerous options become available.

Peer and Group Relationships

As young adolescents begin to discover that it is unlikely that they can always please the adults with authority over them as well as the kids they hang around with, a loyalty shift usually takes place. Friends generally take on greater significance. Fear of being different, and therefore not accepted by peers, is a drive that for most is unavoidable. They adopt personalities and appearances that will win them placement in a group. I remember distinctly the groups that existed during my middle level years, and I'm certain you remember yours too. Natural selection played a role in group formation. There were certain groups with which I knew I could not align. The cheerleader, for instance, was not a possibility for me because I didn't look the part, regardless of how I tried. I recognized the choices that were realistic and found my way into a group that was comfortable. Being part of a group provides security and is a source of feedback when experimentation and dilemmas occur. It seems that simply being part of a group is more important than which group. Most of us don't choose our families or teachers, so choosing friends and a peer group takes on importance as a factor in establishing identity and independence. It's a decision-making opportunity.

Group alignment creates peer pressure, the driving force created by the need or desire to conform. Giving in to peer pressure is absolutely normal at any age. Peer pressure can have a positive or negative influence. If peer pressure dictates that good grades, church attendance, and politeness are the norm, then most adults cheer the influence. However, if peer pressure leads to smoking, drinking, drugs, vandalism, or early sex, then it is viewed as negative. Most peer pressure is somewhere in between and varies according to circumstances and timing. Like it or not, the influence of peers is a phenomenon that is inevitable. Adults can and should attempt to influence the choices of friends and peer groups, but the truth is that young adolescents will assert their need for independence and make choices that only locking them in their rooms until age 21 could prevent.

In the beginning of early adolescence, around ages 10 to 12, same-sex friendships are the most vital. The need for a "best friend" to whom there is uncompromising loyalty and from whom the same is expected is a driving force. Once best friend status is achieved, relegation to "second best friend" is a devastating prospect. This appears to be much more pronounced in girls than boys. Girls will bare their souls to best friends, whereas boys are often content to be in a group where they laugh at the same things and are physically active in the same interest areas. When and with whom opposite-sex attractions occur occupies a place in young adolescent variability that exceeds most other aspects of the age. Some "puppy love" experiences heavily influence 11-year-olds, but for others opposite-sex attractions do not wield a great deal of influence until age 16 or so.

The social development of early adolescence includes some notable paradoxes. In their quest for independence, adolescents will freely conform to fit in. They rebel against adult authority while doing what they can to become adultlike. Social development implies relationships with other people, and yet this is an age

Enhanced eText
Video Example 2.3

Young adolescent boys often have simplistic ideas of friendship. They are friends with other boys that like to do what they do. They may argue, but quickly get over it.

of egocentricity and perhaps selfishness. These paradoxes take place simultaneously with expanding possibilities for violence, bullying, aggression, and a variety of abusive scenarios.

Social Development Issues

There are many issues involved in the social development of young adolescents. Our own memories of the preteen and early teen years serve as acute reminders of just how significant social issues can be during this period of life.

Sara Davis Powell

The alliances formed in early adolescence are often very strong.

1. Young adolescents have a very strong need to be part of a social group. Students who are part of **advisory** groups—small groups who form close relationships with each other and an adult in the school—often feel a bond of trust, or at least a sense that they know the others in the group. Clubs give students chances to get to know others with similar interests. At a minimum, we should adhere to the *Turning Points* tenet that calls for us to create small learning communities. This translates into teams, the basic organizational foundation of middle level education. In addition, giving students free time during the school day allows for informal socialization.

   If we do not allow for socialization time, we are depriving our students of growth opportunities. Kids are going to talk, pass notes, send text messages, gather in groups, and so on. If we don't give them time for such activities, they will take the time from us. Showing that we understand socialization needs should be part of our visible attitude toward our students. Social validation is important.

2. Some young adolescents are targets. Kids often pick on others as a way of diverting attention from themselves, their differences, or their insecurities. Regardless of the reasons, it happens. As educators, we need to do what we can to stifle this activity. Be sensitive to the kids who seem to be the outcasts, and never say things like "stop picking on Sam" in front of Sam or other kids who aren't involved. This will just make things worse for unfortunate Sam as students tease him because the teacher has come to his rescue. Instead, we need to find interests and activities that Sam does well and capitalize on them. Identify kids with similar interests/skills and arrange for Sam to get together with them. We should also encourage Sam not to react to teasing. Then it will no longer be fun for the perpetrators and it will lessen the occurrences. As strange as it may seem, some kids who become targets actually thrive on it in a perverse way. Attention, even though it's negative, gives a sense of identity. These students would benefit from multiple visits with the school counselor.

3. Early adolescence is a prime time for shyness, given the self-consciousness of the age. Young adolescents may experience symptoms such as blushing, sweating, and increased heart rate. The need to conform to group norms may cause them to hide the symptoms and appear to be confident. Whether shyness is obvious, or not, it can be painful and viewed as a negative trait by peers and adults. Providing a variety of outlets for socialization will help ease shyness. Offering activity opportunities that vary enough to appeal to a variety of students may help shy students find their talents and interests, and find other students who share them.

4. Teachers' social backgrounds may be different from their students' backgrounds; our realities may be unlike those of our students. This is a very common phenomenon. Student learning will be more meaningful if teachers understand the young adolescent. Knowing student social realities will assist us in relating to them and connecting them more fully to school experiences.

Social-Emotional Learning

The concept of **social-emotional learning (SEL)** has been researched, written about, and is responsible for programs and initiatives in many schools. Every day teachers witness the ways learning is intertwined with emotional and social development. While we don't need hard research by scientists to prove the relationships among emotional, social, and cognitive development, it's validating to know it exists. New understanding of the nature of biology, emotions, and intelligence and how they relate to happiness and success continue to gain attention among both social and natural scientists. In a report published in 2017, a group of 28 scientists agreed on a number of statements concerning social-emotional learning. The statements include assurances that emotional, social, and cognitive capabilities are interdependent; that emotional, social and cognitive competencies can be taught; and that teaching emotional, social, and cognitive competencies will lead to desirable results such as academic excellence, empathy, collaboration, creativity, and respect, all of which fit perfectly into middle level philosophy (Jones & Kahn, 2017).

To neglect young adolescents' emotional and social growth has negative consequences on cognitive growth. But this is not new information for middle level teachers. Addressing the needs of the whole child has always been in the forefront of effective middle level teaching and learning. Linking social and emotional development with cognitive learning weaves throughout all our major documents; pick up *This We Believe, Turning Points*, or *Turning Points 2000* and read all about the concept. On the Collaborative for Academic, Social, and Emotional Learning (CASEL) website we read, "Successful SEL is not a standalone program or an add-on. It is central to how schools, communities, and families value and support the social, emotional, and academic development of their children." The competencies promoted by the organization include self-awareness, self-management, social awareness, responsible decision-making, and relationship skills. Could have come right out of a middle school playbook! SEL is not new, but the recent emphasis is a reminder that middle level philosophy is alive and well.

Self-Check 2.4

LO 2.5 Character Development

The discussion of character development has the potential to become value-laden as we deal with morals and ethics. Rather than steering clear of the topic because of possible controversy, or embedding it in discussions of emotional and social development, let's take a look at the characteristics of early adolescence in terms of character development and explore how what they do and what happens to them may be dealt with in healthy ways within our middle level schools. Time spent in school accounts for a major chunk of early adolescence. The school is an influential part of the context for character development.

Young Adolescent Character Traits

Many generalizations can be made about typical character traits of young adolescents. Here are a few to consider. Young adolescents:

- are often concerned about fairness.

    Telling a teacher "you're not fair" is a terrible rebuke. Middle grades students have definite ideas about what adults should be and should do in regard to treating students fairly. When adults disappoint them, students are not quick to forgive or forget.

- sometimes ask unanswerable questions.

Middle grades students want to know answers to major questions, such as the meaning of life and what their roles should be in society. They usually realize that adults don't have all these answers, but they at least want adults to treat their questions seriously.

- need support, but seldom ask for it.

To make wise decisions about moral issues, young adolescents need us to be positive role models to help them with issues of right and wrong.

- often make poor decisions as a result of their strong need for peer acceptance.

During the middle level years, students often value social approval over moral convictions. This may lead to decisions that have harmful, often life-changing consequences.

School Programs

Understanding that young adolescents are continually struggling with character development, we naturally ask ourselves how we can help them. Over the years, schools have institutionalized many character-development programs delivered to students in a variety of ways. Classes and occasional meetings devoted to character development are often plagued with controversy over exactly what values and aspects of character should be promoted in public schools. Even with the controversy, there is a renewed call for schools to address character issues, perhaps due to the increase in violent incidents in our schools beginning at the end of the 20th century and increasing in this century with devasting intensity and frequency.

Groups of citizens and educators often debate which character traits to emphasize. From Aristotle's universal values of wisdom, courage, temperance, and justice, to C. S. Lewis's list that includes respect, responsibility, honesty, compassion, and fairness, we struggle to impart a sense of right and wrong that will not conflict with religious values or be perceived as politically incorrect. Communities attempt to come up with what they consider universally (or at least locally) acceptable values.

Most character-building curricula specify qualities of good character. Following are some of the most commonly used terms for the desired characteristics of many programs:

- Trustworthiness
- Respect for others
- Responsibility
- Fairness
- Caring
- Citizenship

Character Education Partnership is a nonpartisan, nonsectarian, coalition of organizations and individuals committed to fostering effective character education in U.S. schools, serving as a resource for people and organizations that are integrating character education into their schools and communities.

As teachers we have the capacity to actually *be* the character-building program. In a practical sense, we have no choice. Whether students acknowledge it or not, they watch us and count on us to model exemplary character. So even if your district or school doesn't have an organized character-development program, your students are observing, and to some degree internalizing, the morals and values you exemplify.

Character Development Issues

The issues involved in character development tend to be more dependent on the context of home and community than those in other developmental areas.

1. Some students grow up in homes that emphasize a very strict moral code, and others live in homes in which there are few moral guidelines or restrictions. We need to understand that home life heavily influences the behaviors and attitudes of the kids in our classes. Through conscientiously being positive role models, understanding home influences, and finding ways to gently prod students toward what our communities consider good character, we will be teachers who make a difference. We cannot lose sight of the variability of influences outside the school. Individualizing our approach to character development is essential.

2. Students are continually faced with contradictions concerning character; we can't erase or deny them. Creating a forum that allows students to candidly discuss their disappointments in adults, in their personal lives, or in the media will help them understand that they are not alone in their feelings. Through discussion comes opportunity for growth. We need to remember, however, that when kids come to us to talk about character, emotional, or social issues, sometimes they simply want to talk and need someone who will listen rather than give advice.

3. Middle grades students are especially vulnerable to falling in with the wrong crowd. Before values are established, being accepted by a group may take precedence. As we've discussed, socialization is a major force during the middle grades years. When socialization leads to the acceptance of values, morals, or ethics that result in undesirable behavior, we have a problem. As teachers of young adolescents, we have the responsibility to expose kids to all kinds of relationships and groups. We can, in fact, act as engineers in our own classrooms as we build experiences that give our students social and value choices in a context that allows them to question and to change their minds.

Self-Check 2.5

LO 2.6 Goals of Middle Level Education

What does student learning and positive growth look like? *This We Believe* (2010, pp. 11–12) explicitly lists student characteristics that signal learning and growth, the purposes of effective teaching and learning. I have numbered the characteristics for convenience as they are listed, but the list is not hierarchical. Each statement stands alone as a distinct goal for helping each young adolescent "become a fully functioning, self-actualized person" (p. 11). Each young adolescent should:

> *TWB* Goal 1. Become actively aware of the larger world, asking significant and relevant questions about the world and wrestling with big ideas and questions for which there may not be one right answer.
>
> *TWB* Goal 2. Be able to think rationally and critically and express thought clearly.
>
> *TWB* Goal 3. Read deeply to independently gather, assess, and interpret information from a variety of sources and read avidly for enjoyment and lifelong learning.

TWB **Goal 4.** Use digital tools to explore, communicate, and collaborate with the world and learn from the rich and varied resources available.

TWB **Goal 5.** Be a good steward of the earth and its resources and a wise and intelligent consumer of the wide array of goods and services available.

TWB **Goal 6.** Understand and use the major concepts, skills, and tools of inquiry in the areas of health and physical education, language arts, world languages, mathematics, natural and physical sciences, and the social sciences.

TWB **Goal 7.** Explore music, art, and careers, and recognize their importance to personal growth and learning.

TWB **Goal 8.** Develop his or her strengths, particular skills, talents, or interests and have an emerging understanding of his or her potential contributions to society and to personal fulfillment.

TWB **Goal 9.** Recognize, articulate, and make responsible, ethical decisions concerning his or her own health and wellness needs.

TWB **Goal 10.** Respect and value the diverse ways people look, speak, think, and act within the immediate community and around the world.

TWB **Goal 11.** Develop the interpersonal and social skills needed to learn, work, and play with others harmoniously and confidently.

TWB **Goal 12.** Assume responsibility for his or her own actions and be cognizant of and ready to accept obligations for the welfare of others.

TWB **Goal 13.** Understand local, national, and global civic responsibilities and demonstrate active citizenship through participation in endeavors that serve and benefit those larger communities.

Quite a list, isn't it? They aren't just words; in each statement we find a lens through which we should view every student in our middle level classrooms. Throughout this book these statements will appear when we discuss attitudes, approaches, and actions that promote student learning and positive growth in one or more of the 13 specific areas. The temptation will be to just look past these important goals because you've read them before, but please resist. These desirable characteristics need to be ingrained in us. They need to be our vision for every young adolescent we serve. In these statements we find the results that define our effectiveness.

Executive Skills

Now that we have thought about young adolescent development, let's look at some skills that will be very valuable as young adolescents grow toward the 13 goals articulated in *This We Believe*. **Executive skills**, or **executive function** as the concept is also referred to, comprise a set of mental qualities that help us get things done. We all have many to lesser or greater degrees, with some skills perhaps still weak even for adults.

Executive skills are the same for adults and young adolescents. Adults have the advantage of thinking in the prefrontal cortex, the brain's rational part, as we've discussed, while teens process information with the emotional part of the brain, the amygdala. Researchers tell us executive skills most readily reside in the brain's rational area. This means that most of the skills, and their development to optimal levels, don't come naturally to most young adolescents. Because we know the skills are beneficial makes it important for us to present them to students as something to work toward, helping them grow the skills as rapidly as possible within their individual development.

In *Smart but Scattered Teens* (2013), the authors present 11 executive skills that are in the process of being developed during adolescence.

- Response inhibition
- Working memory
- Emotional control
- Flexibility
- Sustained attention
- Task initiation
- Planning/prioritizing
- Organization
- Time management
- Goal-directed persistence
- Metacognition.

Just looking at the list seems to describe young adolescents, provided we preface it with "skills that are part of the process of *becoming*." These are skills most well-adjusted adults appear to have much of the time, but that kids in middle school often lack. They are brain-based skills that come from neurosciences literature (Guare, Dawson, & Guare, 2013). Almost all the issues we've looked at in each of the five areas of development can be linked to the 11 skills. The authors of *Smart but Scattered Teens* believe that isolating the specific skills makes teaching them, and then intervening when success is elusive, easier because we can come up with strategies that actually solve problems that arise from weak or lacking skill implementation.

As you continue reading this text, look for strategies that relate to the executive skills or functions. Awareness of them will help you recognize opportunities to teach and reinforce the skills in your future classroom. Rick Wormeli (2013) cautions us to not hold a lack of executive skills against our students, as he quips that we all get there!

Self-Check 2.6

Meet the Students

We've established that young adolescent development is, diosyncratic meaning it occurs in stops and starts, is seldom predictable, and no two students develop in the same ways at the same time. Reading about student development and diversity serves as foundational knowledge. When we see the concepts through real kids, we internalize them. That's why including focus students is a vital part of this textbook. Here you meet our nine focus students in 6th grade. They represent only a portion of the elements of diversity among young adolescents. These kids are included in the Professional Practice exercises at the end of each chapter, as well as in a feature called See How They Grow as we watch them grow from 6th to 7th to 8th grade. Get to know these students, and think about how you might use what you read in subsequent chapters to be an effective teacher for them.

Zach 6th grade, Lincoln Middle School
Zach is basically a good kid. He experienced his own bouts of trouble in elementary school but is doing fine so far in 6th grade. Zach's mom, Melinda, teaches at Lincoln Middle School where Zach is now a student. She lives near the Title I school because, as a single mom with responsibility for her aging parents and her son, the house they all share is less expensive. Her concern is that Zach is one of the few Caucasian kids at Lincoln. She knows as a teacher that skin color shouldn't be an issue, that it's really socioeconomic, but she still worries. There are discipline and motivational issues at Lincoln that other schools, primarily in the suburbs, don't face as frequently. She hopes that Zach is growing up to be well-rounded and culturally sensitive and that those qualities will serve him well.

Zach was diagnosed with ADHD in 3rd grade. Mom and his teachers watched him carefully for two years before going to his pediatrician with their concerns. Melinda didn't want Zach "labeled" unless there was a significant problem and a promise of help through either behavior modifications or medication, or both. Zach began taking Ritalin in the beginning of 4th grade, and the medicine appears to be helping him concentrate and learn. It also assists him with behavioral issues he faced earlier.

DeVante 6th grade, Jefferson Middle School
DeVante is surviving as a beginning 6th grader at Jefferson Middle School, but life wasn't always so good for him. After failing both kindergarten and 3rd grade, DeVante is considerably taller and more socially street-wise than others about to enter middle school. His granny and sole guardian was at her wit's end. She didn't like the neighborhood school but didn't know what else to do. She needed help and managed to get DeVante into the Boys and Girls Club near their downtown apartment the summer after 5th grade. It was difficult to convince him to try it because he only wanted to hang out with kids his age (13) rather than the 11-year-olds who just completed 5th grade with him. One of the volunteers at the Boys and Girls Club told DeVante's grandmother about Jefferson, a magnet school not far away. DeVante reluctantly applied and was accepted.

DeVante's granny gets by on food stamps and other government assistance. This means, as a 6th grader, he rarely has spending money. When he hangs out with the older kids, they buy him things—food, shoes, an occasional beer. They like DeVante, and that's a problem. The 13- to 15-year-olds in the neighborhood are being groomed by a local gang. Most will do whatever gang members say and actually idolize the older boys who have dropped out of high school. No wonder Granny is concerned.

Emily 6th grade, Madison Middle School
Emily is shy and immature. Her mom worries that she is too young for middle school. She was allowed to start kindergarten at age 4, and it's quite obvious that another year in elementary school would have been good from a social standpoint. Mom divorced when Emily and her older brother were quite young. Emily spends one weekend a month with Dad and his second wife. Her mom remarried two years ago, and, in the bargain, Emily got three young stepsiblings.

Emily has a speech impediment that accounts for some of her shyness. If she just says a few words, it's not obvious. More than that, and it's easy to pick up on. In elementary school she spent time each day with a speech therapist and dreads doing the same thing in middle school. Now that she's in 6th grade, she's just waiting for the first day when someone comes to the door and asks for her. She's quite nervous about being singled out.

Kim 6th grade, Jefferson Middle School
Kim's dad is a doctor and her mom is a bank executive. She has an older brother and a younger sister. Life for three generations on both sides of the family has been good, with lots of successful careers and lifestyles to match. Kim is a good student, but not particularly interested in math, science, or social studies. She likes to write and begged her parents to let her attend Jefferson Middle School, an inner-city magnet school focusing on technology and communications. They were reluctant but decided to give the school a chance. Kim has wanted to be a television news anchor ever since her aunt became a successful broadcaster in Atlanta.

Kim is very visual. She learns best when she sees what's supposed to be learned, and graphic representations appeal to her. Just hearing something often goes right past her. Kim's elementary school teachers understood this. Mom and Dad are a little concerned about her transition to Jefferson. Kim's visual learning style is accompanied by a seemingly nonstop need to talk.

Gabe 6th grade, Valley View Middle School
Gabe is a quiet, small-for-his-age Hispanic boy who was born in the United States. His mom, dad, and two younger sisters speak Spanish at home. Dad works as a farmhand 10–12 hours a day to provide a meager living for the family. For three months a year the family moves across the Kansas border so Dad can work in a restaurant when he's not needed on the farm. This poses a problem for Gabe now that he is a 6th grader at Valley View Middle School. He seems pretty happy at school, but doesn't stand out, either in a positive way or as a behavioral problem.

The fact that Gabe is a U.S. citizen makes his parents happy. They know their three children will have more opportunities than they had. They adore Gabe and his sisters but have found that helping Gabe with homework is a thing of the past. In the middle of 4th grade they were at a loss to help, and Gabe's teacher assumed it was because of language difficulties. But that's not the whole reason. Gabe's parents completed only the equivalent of 6th grade in Mexico.

Janie 6th grade, Cario Middle School
Janie has always liked school and done well. Her circle of girlfriends has been together since kindergarten. They go to the mall and the movies and talk on the phone incessantly. She has lived in the same neighborhood since she was 2 years old. Her dad is a successful realtor; her mom cares for Janie and her 7-year-old brother full-time in their home. As she happily enters 6th grade, Mom and Dad are confident that Janie will be fine at Cario Middle School. Their only concern about her actually has a possible positive side. The summer after

(Continued)

5th grade Janie became conscious of her weight and started cutting back on sweets and spent more time riding her bike. She wanted to lose weight for middle school.

Janie loves to read. She was a Judy Blume fan in elementary school and read some of the books three times. She anxiously awaited each Harry Potter book even before she could read them with comprehension. She knew her parents would read them to her. Now she has discovered Jodi Picoult. Mom thinks the books are a little old for her, but she's just glad Janie's love of reading continues.

Andy 6th grade, Hamilton Middle School
Andy lives in a trailer on the outskirts of a small southern town. He's an only child whose mom died of cancer two years ago. Andy and his dad hunt and fish every weekend during the school year. He's not at all out of place in his rural community where there are definite social strata. The two quite distinct groups of people get along as groups, but a look at the children in the school gym shows that some of their lifestyle priorities and resources are quite different.

Andy has been heavy all his life. When he was a baby, everyone thought he was adorable. Now that he's in 6th grade, he has become more conscious of his size but still doesn't care very much. Unfortunately, he has started using chewing tobacco. He is often distracted in class and sometimes makes inappropriate remarks to other students. He's always been an average student who does much better when he experiences a concept rather than reading about it or doing paper and pencil work.

Darma 6th grade, Lake Park Middle School
Darma, his parents, and younger brother emigrated from Indonesia when he was 6 years old. He is a very interesting boy who enjoys playing chess and collecting comic books. He has a close group of friends and doesn't really care to socialize with other kids outside this circle. He's fine with going to middle school and knows he will continue to be in an academically gifted class where he is very comfortable. Darma's last name is Superman, a common surname in his native country. His friends, of course, call him "Superman," a nickname he actually likes.

In Indonesia many people speak both Indonesian and English. Darma has grown up speaking English outside his home, so language is not a problem for him. Although he does well in all his classes, Darma is fascinated with patterns and sequences, making math a favorite subject. He is meticulously organized and has trouble relating to kids who don't share his passion for order. Teachers, of course, look forward to having Darma in class because he consistently meets or exceeds their expectations.

Maria 6th grade, MLK Middle School
Maria was born in Mexico and came to the United States when she was 7 years old. Her dad took her brothers back to Mexico to help care for his parents, and she hasn't seen them in three years. Her mom is a housekeeper at a downtown hotel and works evenings and weekends. Since she was in 4th grade, Maria has been staying by herself after school until Mom returns after midnight. On weekends she watches TV and mostly sits around, locked in her apartment. Her mom wants her to have all the advantages she didn't have, but Maria is sad most of the time. Her mom hasn't learned much English, and neither has Maria.

Each year Maria barely passes to the next grade. Teachers have suspected a learning disability, but, because she's an English language learner, it's been hard to pinpoint. In middle school she may fall even further behind. Emotionally and socially Maria is growing more and more restless. She doesn't want to stay inside anymore now that she's in middle school. This worries Mom, but she doesn't know what to do about it. She wants Maria to be successful in school and to have nice friends.

Why It Matters

There are as many possible combinations of developmental traits as there are middle level students. All our students are evolving and becoming—they are not finished products. Our challenge as teachers is to accept them as they are and do what we can to help them grow in healthy ways physically, intellectually, emotionally, socially, and with positive and productive character traits.

Now that we have briefly considered the development of young adolescents, you may be thinking, "What does all this have to do with teaching them how to factor binomials?" The answer is *everything*. Or perhaps you are thinking that your future students will be enamored with the American Revolution and will leave their prepubescent/pubescent selves behind when you grab their imaginations with your detailed lecture. *Think again.* The jolt of *becoming* is often so staggering that learning is not a given but mind-wandering likely is. Case in point . . . I read this years ago in a journal, the name of which I can't recall. The timing may not be scientifically derived, but the point is valid. "An 8th grade boy likely thinks of sex every 20 seconds." Binomials and the

American Revolution have some significant competition. Better have a plan for really engaging instruction!

As middle level teachers, we contend with much more than content. Skillfully, we find ways to capture attention and keep it long enough to engage young adolescents in their own learning. The more we understand about what affects our kids, the better we are at helping make early adolescence a period of positive development for young adolescents.

Group Activities

1. In small groups, make bulleted lists of possible characteristics or descriptors of middle level students for each of the five developmental areas discussed in this chapter. Feel free to add to what this text covers. It would take volumes to be comprehensive! Share your lists with other groups.

2. How do movies and television shows portray middle level students? As a class, brainstorm about all the 10- to 15-year-olds we see on TV and in movies. What characteristics from your lists do these fictional kids exemplify?

Individual Activities

1. Interview at least three of your friends and ask them to describe themselves as young adolescents in the five developmental areas. Write brief sketches of them using your interview notes. Would you have predicted them to be as they are today given their self-described young adolescent personas?

2. Go to a place where you are likely to see groups of young adolescents. Try the mall, a fast food restaurant, a sporting event, or another afterschool hangout. Describe what you observe during a 10- or 15-minute period. Include their physical size/shape, clothing, accessories, hairstyles, socialization patterns, and so on. This exercise may bring back memories! Be prepared to share your observations with your class.

Personal Journal

1. Write an honest appraisal of yourself during early adolescence. Try to think about the span of 6th, 7th, and 8th grade rather than one particular time frame. Consider all five areas of development at each grade level.

2. Call at least two family members, if possible, to ask them to recall what you were like as a young adolescent. Assure them that you can remain objective about their comments because you are now a mature teacher candidate. Try the "if you'll be honest with me, I'll be honest with you" ploy. Compare your family members' observations to your own self-assessment.

Professional Practice

Jermaine Joyner

Jermaine Joyner has so much energy and is filled with ideas he wants to implement at Jefferson Middle School, a technology and communication magnet school in an urban area. Magnet status was given to Jefferson in 1998 in an effort to draw students from the suburbs to downtown to achieve both racial and socioeconomic integration. **Magnet schools** encourage students from across an entire school district to attend them based on a theme or special emphasis. The

plan had worked. About half the Jefferson kids were from the immediate neighborhood and half from various areas in the district.

Mr. Joyner is the school's computer guru. He teaches all three grade levels and has been able to build a program that allows students to start at a basic computer literacy level and steadily progress to more advanced computer applications. One of his pet initiatives is the development of a television studio where five-minute daily programs are taped and broadcast to the whole student body. The Broadcast Club meets before and after school.

(Continued)

DeVante 6th grade

DeVante is one of the new 6th graders at Jefferson. The school is not in his immediate neighborhood, but he gave in to Granny's urging, reluctantly applied, and won a spot at the school through lottery selection. DeVante has a troubled past. He has failed twice and prefers to hang around with older kids, many of whom have gang ties. He's unhappy about having to leave his own neighborhood for school. *Keep in mind that there may be more than one appropriate response to the items, leading to discussion among classmates.*

1. Which barrier is most significant for Mr. Joyner to overcome in his sponsorship of the Broadcast Club?

   a. getting kids interested in spending extra time the club requires

   b. finding ways to encourage kids from across a wide spectrum of lifestyles to work together

   c. convincing other teachers that the five minutes required for the broadcast is worth the time

   d. maintaining equipment and the expense required to do so

2. Which circumstance will likely have the most positive impact on DeVante?

   a. being in classes with a variety of students

   b. learning computer skills in Mr. Joyner's class

   c. being older and physically larger than other kids, which will help keep him from being a target

   d. joining the Broadcast Club at the insistence of Mr. Joyner

3. During his first few months at Jefferson, DeVante is hesitant to even crack a smile. He is attending the school begrudgingly. It wasn't his idea. About the first week in December Mr. Joyner sees a spark of interest as DeVante actually starts a conversation with him. What is the most likely reason DeVante shows signs of interest in the Broadcast Club?

   a. Having Mr. Joyner as a role model of a successful African American man is having an impact.

   b. He sees broadcasting as a possible career interest.

   c. He has made close friends with kids in the school.

   d. He has reconciled himself to the fact that Jefferson is his school and he might as well make the most of it.

4. Explain the meaning of this Donna San Antonio quote: "I believe that we cannot accomplish our academic goals without a purposeful and thoughtful focus on social development." How does this statement relate to middle level philosophy? Why is it a significant statement to consider when thinking about the challenges posed by DeVante's move to Jefferson Middle School?

Chapter 3
Diversity among Middle Level Learners

Sara Davis Powell

Everyone in an inviting school works proactively to eliminate harassment, verbal abuse, bullying, and name-calling. Students and teachers understand that they are part of a community in which differences are respected and celebrated. . . . Every student—no matter what creed, color, or uniqueness—is a genuine and contributing member of the school community.

THIS WE BELIEVE, P. 34.

 ## Learning Outcomes

3.1 Explore sex and gender differences and related classroom approaches.

3.2 Examine student differences based on culture, ethnicity, race, and linguistics.

3.3 Explore the ramifications of student socioeconomic diversity.

3.4 Recognize family differences and ways to involve families in the life of the school.

3.5 Analyze academic diversity including learning differences, ability, and effort.

3.6 Categorize exceptionalities among learners and possible ways to meet their needs.

Dear Future Middle Level Teacher,

Young adolescents display diversity in some obvious physical ways through attributes such as gender, skin color, height, and weight. Less obvious is their diversity in academic ability/achievement and motivation. Diversity in family makeup, socioeconomic status, and the presence of disabilities challenge teachers as they work to provide opportunities for optimal growth during the middle school years. In this chapter we explore some of the differences among middle level learners, not to place labels on them, but to understand them.

As you read, reflect on the characteristics of diverse populations as generalities rather than stereotypical images. **Generalizations** are supported by data. **Stereotyping** involves making sweeping statements that are often misperceptions and negative. For instance, to say that girls *tend to* prefer pink and purple does not mean that *all* girls prefer pink and purple. This is a generalization. To say that the favorite colors of all girls are pink and purple becomes a stereotype. So be open to generalizations, not offended by them. Remember there are always exceptions.

Also keep in mind that everything about young adolescents screams diversity. Not only are no two alike, within an individual student we may see several personalities over the course of a day. They are *becoming* in fits and starts, trying on new emotions, social behaviors, and attitudes round the clock, searching for the person they will mature to be. It's wonderful to witness!

SDP

Standard 1
Young Adolescent Development

Element b. Knowledge of the Implications of Diversity on Young Adolescent Development: Middle level teacher candidates demonstrate their understanding of the implications of diversity on the development of young adolescents. They implement curriculum and instruction that is responsive to young adolescents' local, national, and international histories, language/dialects, and individual identities (e.g., race, ethnicity, culture, age, appearance, ability, sexual orientation, socioeconomic status, family composition). They participate successfully in middle level practices that consider and celebrate the diversity of all young adolescents.

LO 3.1 Sex and Gender

There was a time not long ago when the word gender simply called for a discussion of girls and boys—straightforward and simple. Although this discussion is still appropriate, it's hardly the last word. In addition, if we were discussing young children, the conversation would be different from what you are reading. Young adolescents have already been thoroughly indoctrinated in what femininity and masculinity look and act like, or at least in generalities.

At birth, nature bestows both males and females with about equal amounts of testosterone and estrogen. Because of this, their development is much the same through early elementary school. In puberty, the balance of the two hormones ends. Some researchers tell us there's little evidence that male and female brains are that different by nature, while other researchers disagree. The sexes share 99.8% of their genes (Elliot, 2012). Yet, that two tenths of one percent makes a world of difference when compared to the shared 99.8. Boys and girls look different, dress differently, choose different activities, group by sex, and talk about different things. The question debated now—and perhaps forever: Are the behaviors learned or innate? Michael Gurian is considered a contemporary expert on gender differences and is an author of many books and articles including *The Wonder of Boys, The Wonder of Girls* and, most recently, *Saving Our Sons* (2017). Gurian tells us the differences between boys and girls are evident from birth. While the discussion of when and how the differences between the sexes emerge, our concern as teachers is to learn as much as we can about both sexes and then find ways to make the teaching and learning connection.

Nurture, or the environment, is everything that affects a person other than gene make-up. In other words, it's the other 99.8%. Most of nurture reinforces traditional male roles and female roles; they're inescapable. Parental attitudes, clothing and toy manufacturers, media, and more dictate what boys and girls think about, enjoy, wear, play with . . . you see where this is going. Societal and cultural expectations set the scene for stereotypical boy and girl behaviors.

Let's take a look at some statistics that will affect your middle level classroom and school. The statistics were compiled by Michael Gurian (2017) to exemplify how girls and boys fare in school settings. Please remember that the issues leading to the discrepancies are complex.

- For every 100 girls suspended in public elementary and secondary, 215 boys are suspended.

- For every 100 girls expelled in public elementary and secondary, 297 boys are expelled.

- For every 100 girls diagnosed with a special education disability, 217 boys are diagnosed.

- For every 100 girls 6- to 14-years-old who have difficulty getting along with others, 183 boys have difficulty getting along with others.

- For every 100 women enrolled in college in the United States, there are 78 men enrolled.

- For every 100 American women who earn bachelor degrees, 75 American men earn bachelor degrees.

- For every 100 American women who earn master's degrees, 66 American men earn master's degrees.

- For every 100 American women who earn doctoral degrees, 91 American men earn doctoral degrees.

Sara Davis Powell

Girls and boys often have playful relationships in middle school, as we see with focus student Emily.

Sex and Gender Identity

According to the American Academy of Pediatrics (2015a), being a boy or a girl, for most children, is something that feels very natural. The **sex** of a child is assigned at birth; babies are male or female based on physical characteristics. When children are able to express themselves, they will declare themselves to be a boy or a girl; this is their **gender identity** based on the role of a male and a female in society. Gender identity is complex and can be controversial because it is an individual's concept of self (Newman, 2016).

Most children's gender identities align with their biological sex. Gender identity becomes a "basic anchor in the personality and forms a core part of one's self-identity" (Gollnick & Chinn, 2017, p. 88). By the time kids start school they have clear ideas about gender roles; most strive to fulfill the roles and are reminded that they should. However, for some children, the match between biological sex and gender identity is not so clear.

A phenomenon called **childhood gender nonconformity** affects 2–7% of children, most under the age of 12 (Padawer, 2012). Because middle level education serves students ages 10–15, students exhibiting gender nonconformity may be in your 5th, 6th, or even 7th grade classes. Children with gender nonconformity often dress like the opposite sex; girls prefer to participate in activities society views as boy activities and boys prefer to participate in activities society views as girl activities. The children have a preference for what we typically think of as the opposite sex's preferences. Children with gender nonconformity often exhibit it less and less with time, either because psychologically they become more comfortable with their biological sex or from peer pressure. Some persist and, by adolescence, are homosexual or **transgender** (American Academy of Pediatrics, 2015b).

Discussion about people who are transgender has become more and more common. When Bruce Jenner, Olympic gold medal-winning athlete, revealed that he was transgender and would become Caitlyn Jenner, media was abuzz with the news. Jenner brought transgender discussions into the open in 2015. Transgender refers to people who persistently identify with a gender that is different from their birth sex. Research suggests that children who are persistent, consistent, and insistent about their gender identity are the ones who are most likely to become transgender adults. When it comes to acceptance in a school setting, we can follow the lead of the U.S. military, an organization that typically follows conservative traditions. Transgender individuals may serve in all branches of the military with impunity (Caputo, 2017). As educators, we can do no less.

Sexual Orientation

There is research leading to identification of brain differences between males and females and between **heterosexual** and **homosexual** individuals. (Wlassoff, 2015). **Sexual orientation** is the sex to which one is sexually and romantically attracted—typically referred to as heterosexuality, bisexuality, and homosexuality. Some dismiss this research, so the field remains controversial, but the research continues. Some estimates say that about 10% of the population is homosexual, or *gay*. There are gay people of every race, age, and family background. We can't tell if a male or female is gay just by appearance. Because a boy has some feminine qualities or a girl acts masculine at times does not mean that he or she is gay. The word gay is typically used for males, while **lesbian** is used for females who are homosexual. People who have sexual or romantic feelings for both men and women are called **bisexual**. All of the major medical organizations state that homosexuality is a form of sexual expression, not a mental disorder or illness. According to The American Psychiatric Association, The American Psychological Association, and the American Academy of Pediatrics, there are both biological and psychological factors involved in homosexuality (American Academy of Pediatrics, 2016).

LGBTQ is a common way of referring to those who identify as lesbian, gay, bisexual, transgender, or questioning. Wondering about sex and gender is a normal part of life and many adolescents ask themselves the question (American Academy of Pediatrics, 2015a). Our students may be questioning their levels of masculinity or femininity, wondering if they are "normal," conflicted about whether they are possibly homosexual, hiding their sense that their brains and bodies are not in sync—and all this during your lesson on the industrial revolution. This complicates your role as teacher, doesn't it?

Enhanced eText
Video Example 3.1

Teacher Amy Goodwin talks with us about her teaching philosophy and style. We then see a portion of her lesson where she addresses issues of acceptance within an English language arts lesson.

Making the Teaching and Learning Connection

Hello, future teachers!

My name is Amy. I vividly remember my first experiences in classrooms as I prepared to teach. I know you are excited and nervous at the same time. You are not alone!

I thought I wanted to teach high school English when I was in college. After observing [students] in a middle school classroom, I knew I wanted to spend my days with them. Now, six years later, there's no place I'd rather be!

We hear a lot about bullying and, yes, it's pretty widespread among young adolescents who don't understand the physical and emotional changes happening to them. They are insecure and sometimes say and do things they don't really mean. I try to use the sensitivity they have deep inside to teach them to stop and think before speaking words that can hurt. For kids at this age, issues concerning sexual orientation both fascinate them and make them uncomfortable. I chose to address these issues in a class setting to let them explore and talk about their beliefs, misunderstandings, and even their fears in a safe environment. But to do this, they have to trust me. The most important responsibility I have is build healthy relationships with my students who are exploring all sorts of things and finding their way toward adulthood.

In this lesson I'm emphasizing reading comprehension and vocabulary while hopefully teaching valuable lessons. We don't do any one activity for very long. Kids are easily distracted, so short bursts of different teaching strategies work best. I get them involved and give them time to talk with each other. I think through the questions I want to ask before teaching the lesson. The right questions are so important. Remember that it's vital to tie lessons together so students get the big picture. I remember my professors emphasizing activating prior knowledge. They were right!

Using humor can help ease tension and let the students see I identify with them. My reference to Gina and the softball game tells the kids that I know what they do outside my classroom. Humor plus personalization: win–win!

My best advice is to love your students and show it. We teach the whole student, not just their intellect. Relationships matter. You've chosen a great profession!

Amy

Our Approach

Let's think about how we can help all students feel safe in our classrooms. The concept of "safety"—academic, emotional, social, physical—in the classroom is absolutely necessary for making the teaching and learning connection (Sadowski, 2016).

- Increasingly, middle level schools are experimenting with single-gender settings. Some schools are dividing boys and girls for particular classes. For instance, science may be taught as a single-gender subject while all the other classes are coeducational. In other schools, the whole core (language arts, math, science, social studies) may be taught in single-gender classes, while the noncore classes are coeducational. Still other schools are totally single-gender. Whether girls and boys are together or separated in the classroom, employing a variety of engaging instructional practices is imperative. Hands-on learning sometimes appeals more to physical activity-oriented boys. Anything that gets boys (and many girls!) moving, rather than sitting still with paper and pencil, will be beneficial. Let students choose topics that interest them for reading and writing assignments. Girls appear to be more willing to complete assignments for the sake of completion, but boys tend to need to be interested in a topic to want to complete it. Try to make learning relevant and purposeful.

- Acknowledging gender differences is not the same as perpetuating stereotypes that may result in unfair treatment. Print and electronic media often portray gender differences in exaggerated ways. In selling products and/or services, the media will shamelessly capitalize on commonly assumed gender differences. A proactive way to approach gender differences, while giving students a sense of perspective on the subject, is to acquaint young adolescents with the impact that magazines, television, movies, social media, and advertisements have on our society. Frank discussions of how we are influenced in terms of gender stereotyping provide a valuable service to developing young adolescents.

- **Sexism** is the belief that one sex is superior to another, most often expressed as male superiority to females. For most of the 20th century, the prevalent opinion was that boys were simply smarter and higher achieving than girls. However, the most recent data refutes this notion. Since the 1990s girls have steadily approached the overall academic achievements of boys and in some case outperformed them. In math and science girls' scores have almost caught up with boys'. Yet in reading and writing the gap between boys and girls has widened, with girls continuing to excel in these areas (Bennett, 2015).

- When it comes to unequal treatment of girls and boys in educational settings, we need to find ways to avoid what many of us do naturally as a result of social conditioning. We are often unaware of how we interact with students. Unintentionally treating boys and girls differently often leads to allowing boys to interrupt girls, and then at times going so far as to praise girls for their patience. Avoiding such discrimination may be difficult even when we are aware of it. I don't think educators would intentionally create unequal opportunities for learning between girls and boys, but many, myself included, have unintentionally treated them differently when it comes to expectations and classroom question/answer sessions. I became aware that I called on boys more frequently than girls when a college student completing a field experience in my 8th grade math classroom kept a tally without my knowledge. She presented the results to me, and I have worked toward balance for two decades. Colleagues can help each other detect how they approach gender, or we can keep track of our own questioning using a seating chart on a clipboard. When we direct discussions, we can keep track of boy and girl talk time and encourage gender balance.

- **Sexual harassment** is a form of sex discrimination involving unwanted and unwelcome sexual behavior. The perpetrator in many cases is in a position of power. It happens in schools and is reported by both girls and boys. Harassment can be verbal (insults, jokes, rumors), visual (sharing photos, obscene gestures), or physical (fondling, flashing, touching). If actions by another student or adult are unwelcome by the victim and make him or her uncomfortable, scared, or confused, it's sexual harassment.

- It's important that lesbian, gay, bisexual, transgender, and questioning students experience a school environment that is supportive. These students often find that the two places where they spend the most time and encounter adults most frequently—home and school—are the places where they are most misunderstood. Make it clear that slurs or jokes based on gender, gender identity, or sexual orientation are not tolerated. "That's so gay" or "You're so gay" are phrases often heard in middle schools. The kids that use these expressions rarely mean that an assignment to which they respond "That's so gay" has anything to do with homosexuality. It's a phrase commonly used to mean undesirable. But what if you're gay, lesbian, or bisexual? It becomes a hurtful slur. Norma Bailey, a respected outspoken advocate for young adolescents who are LGBTQ, tells us that teachers must step up and change the school's culture into one that accepts differences of gender preferences. She says we must work to give "clear signals to *all* students, regardless of sexual orientation or gender identity or gender expression, that they are valuable and valued members of our school community" (Bailey, 2011, p. 15). Young adolescent LGBTQ students are more likely to be verbally and physically attacked, to be threatened, to skip school, to drop out of school, and to attempt suicide. According to the Gay, Lesbian, and Straight Education Network's National School Climate Survey released in 2016, U.S. middle and high schools are hostile environments for many LGBTQ students. The guarded good news is that the survey shows signs of improvement since 2001 (Gay, Lesbian, and Straight Education Network, 2016). As educators committed to meeting the needs of all students in developmentally responsive ways, we must not ignore or sidestep the needs of these students.

- If you sense a young adolescent is confused or worried about anything, it's important that they talk about their feelings. Be sure all students know they can confide in and trust the school's guidance counselors. Never deny a student who asks to see the counselor. Remember, as middle level educators, we teach the whole child.

Self-Check 3.1

LO 3.2 Culture, Ethnicity, Race, and Language Diversity

In discussions concerning cultural similarities and differences, often certain phraseology is used. As commonly used as the words *culture, ethnicity*, and *race* are, scholars define them in a variety of ways. Let's settle on what appear to be widely accepted definitions. **Culture** refers to specific shared values, beliefs, and attitudes. **Ethnicity** simply refers to an individual's country of origin. **Race** categorizes individuals into groups (such as white, black, Asian) based on certain outward physical characteristics. It is not a precise way to categorize people, but remains a term frequently used in our society (Gollnick & Chinn, 2017). Race is more obvious than culture and is often assumed before even asking about ethnicity. *Culture* involves many variables, often encompasses both race and ethnicity, and may be the most difficult to grasp. *Ethnicity* tells us much more than *race* about our students. Just knowing, for instance, that a student is Hispanic doesn't reveal much about culture. However, if a student is Hispanic from Mexico, his culture may be quite different compared to a student from Puerto Rico.

There is tremendous variability in the number of nonwhite students in individual regions of the United States, as illustrated in Table 3.1. Nonwhite individuals comprise black, Hispanic, Asian, Asian/Pacific Islander, and American Indian/Alaska Native races, or combinations of races. According to the 2010 census, more than 10 million

TABLE 3.1 Percentage distribution of enrollment in public elementary and secondary schools, by race/ethnicity and region: 2013 and U.S. predictions for 2020, 2025

Region	Total		White		Black		Hispanic		Asian/Pacific Islander		American Indian/Alaskan Native		Two or More Races	
	#	%	#	%	#	%	#	%	#	%	#	%	#	%
U.S.	50,045	100	25,160	50	7,805	16	12,452	25	2,593	5	523	1	1,511	3
U.S. Prediction for 2020	50,477	100	23,882	47	7,756	15	14,142	28	2,892	6	463	1	1,638	3
U.S. Prediction for 2025	51,420	100	23,465	46	7,863	15	14,677	29	3,139	6	439	1	1,863	4
Northeast	7,961	100	4,593	58	1,158	15	1,492	19	533	0.7	28	0.3	1,582	2
Midwest	10,573	100	7,111	67	1,464	14	1,212	12	341	3	87	0.8	358	3
South	19,299	100	8,722	45	4,561	24	4,671	24	614	3	185	1	546	3
West	12,212	100	4,733	39	623	5	5,077	42	1,105	9	224	2	49	4

Based on: U.S. Department of Education, National Center for Education Statistics, Common Core of Data (CCD), "State Nonfiscal Survey of Public Elementary and Secondary Education," 1995–96 through 2013–14; and National Elementary and Secondary Enrollment by Race/Ethnicity Projection Model, 1972 through 2025.

people indicated they were multiracial by marking more than one of the five races listed. Between 2016 and 2017, Hispanics accounted for over half the U.S. population growth at 51%. Asian growth accounted for 24%, black growth accounted for 16%, and the white population actually decreased by almost 10,000. Of the over 325 million U.S. residents in 2017, about 60% were white, about 18% were Hispanic, about 13% were black, and about 6% were Asian. The others are multiracial. It's interesting to note that while Hispanic growth increased in the early part of the century, between 2016 and 2017 it leveled off with no increase, a trend that began during the recession of 2008. (Pew Hispanic Center, 2017).

Numerous books and articles address differences in culture, ethnicity, and race. This topic permeates most teacher education and staff development programs. I encourage you to take advantage of growth opportunities for addressing this vital topic.

Racial diversity adds richness to academics and relationships.

Sara Davis Powell

Understanding Differences

First, we need to recognize our own prejudices. When these prejudices stem from components of race, they amount to racism. **Racism** is prejudice based on the belief that one race is superior to another (Gollnick & Chinn, 2017). To avoid racism, we need to examine our own deeply held beliefs, whether consciously or unconsciously manifested. For many, this is a lifelong endeavor. The sooner we begin, the more effectively we will meet the diverse needs of our students.

It's easy to misinterpret the behaviors of those from whom we differ. Because statistically most teachers in the United States are white and were raised in predominantly white communities, knowledge of other races is often limited. Here's where generalizations may be helpful. Please remember that a generalization is not a stereotype and does not label all students in a group, but it can help us understand characteristics if they appear.

Teachers need to be particularly aware of the unique concerns presented when adolescents of mixed race or mixed ethnic backgrounds are present in the classroom or school. The number of biracial, multiracial/biethnic, or multiethnic children is increasing, and these children populate our schools in statistically significant numbers. Because much of a child's self-identity and self-esteem are tied to a sense of pride in cultural or racial background, children of mixed heritage can experience pressure to identify with only one of their ethnic or racial backgrounds (usually the one of color). At the same time, society often makes them feel alienated, belittled, and insignificant as they experience insensitivity from both mainstream and minority groups. Identity issues may intensify during the middle level years as a facet of the young adolescent's search for self-awareness.

Cultural Pluralism

Cultural pluralism is the recognition that our country's people consist of varying cultures, ethnicities, and races that all contribute to a common goal of freedom and productivity. It is the maintenance of other cultures as parallel and equal with the dominant culture. **Assimilation** is the process of bringing all races and ethnicities into the mainstream by encouraging them to behave in ways that align with the dominant culture (Gollnick & Chinn, 2017). Some assimilation is inevitable, but it becomes detrimental when individual or group culture is destroyed or devalued. Expecting everyone to look, act, and think alike is unhealthy for a country that values individualism and human rights.

Promoting cultural pluralism in a middle level school involves teaching a curriculum that includes the history and contributions of a variety of cultures. But it goes beyond social studies curriculum to an attitude that says, "We value every aspect of your life and traditions." In this crucial time of development, we must make sure no student is excluded from full participation in the life of the school.

Language Diversity

So far we've talked about culture, ethnicity, and race. Now let's consider linguistics. There's little dispute that language assimilation is valuable. That's why we do what we can to help English learners become fluent readers, writers, and speakers of English. People whose first language is not English are referred to as **English learners (ELs)** or English language leaners **(ELLs)**. As our nation becomes more and more diverse, the number of languages spoken in the homes of students increases.

In 2015, more than 5 million students in U.S. schools were English learners (ELs), or 9.4% of our total school population. In California the percentage skyrocketed to 22.4%. In cities, or urban settings, ELs comprised an average of 14% of the student population. Spanish was the more prominent language spoken in student homes, accounting for

Sara Davis Powell

In her bilingual history class, Ynez benefits from writing notes in both Spanish and English, as well as illustrating events and concepts.

78% of EL students. The other 22% was dominated by Arabic, Chinese, and Vietnamese (National Center for Education Statistics, 2015a). We're talking about a significant number of students.

These kids are all around us, in suburban, urban, and rural settings. Not long ago EL students were primarily living in California, Texas, and New York. Now rural areas in the Midwest, medium-sized towns in the Northwest, and cities along the Southeast coast have large populations of these students, many of whom are at risk for academic failure for multiple reasons, not just language differences.

Standard 3

Middle Level Philosophy and School Organization

Element b. Middle Level Organization and Best Practices: Middle level teacher candidates utilize their knowledge of the effective components of middle level programs and schools to foster equitable educational practices and to enhance learning for all students (e.g., race, ethnicity, culture, age, appearance, ability, sexual orientation, socioeconomic status, family composition). They demonstrate their ability to apply this knowledge and to function successfully within a variety of school organizational settings (e.g., grades K–8, 6–8, 7–12).

Multicultural Education

Addressing cultural diversity and emphasizing how elements including race, ethnicity, class, and gender interact and affect the lives of our students is commonly referred to as **multicultural education**. To be **culturally responsive** teachers, we must respect diversity, view diversity as strength, and reflect cultures in teaching and learning experiences (Gollnick & Chinn, 2017). We must have high expectations for all students, make sure materials in classrooms reflect a wide array of contributions and perspectives, and use different teaching strategies as needed by the young adolescents we serve. Too often what passes for multicultural education is a poster or two depicting Martin Luther King or César Chávez. Teachers may give lip service to Cinco de Mayo, Kwanza, or the Chinese New Year. This is not multicultural education. The sense that differences are not only accepted but celebrated is needed. Respect and appreciation for differences should permeate our classrooms and interactions. Please remember that we won't always address varying cultures in the best, or even most accurate, light due to misinformation or lack of knowledge. Our students will forgive our mistakes and help us correct them as long as they sense our desire is sincere.

> *TWB* Goal 10: [Young adolescents] respect and value the diverse ways people look, speak, think, and act within the immediate community and around the world.

Self-Check 3.2

LO 3.3 Socioeconomic Diversity

Twenty-one percent of children in the United States live in homes where the income is below the poverty line. Poverty in early adolescence transcends differences in gender, culture, language, family, and religion and has widespread effects on success in school.

Although **socioeconomic status (SES)** includes occupation and education, the primary determinant of SES is how much money a family makes. To be considered in poverty, a family of four (two adults, two children) makes less than $24,036 a year. The state with the lowest poverty rate is New Hampshire (11%), with Mississippi having the highest rate at 31%. By race, 36% of African Americans live in poverty, 31% of Hispanic Americans live in poverty, and 11% of whites live in poverty. Considering families with no adult having secure year-round employment, North Dakota and Utah have the lowest percentage and Mississippi and West Virginia have the highest at 37%. More students than those living in poverty qualify for free or reduced-price lunch, allowing families who struggle, but are not considered in poverty, to receive benefits for their children (National Center for Children in Poverty, 2017).

In *Disrupting Poverty*, we read that the U.S. child poverty is the highest of all developed nations and that the percentage of children living in poverty continues to rise. Over half of K–12 students qualify for free or reduced-price lunch (Budge & Parrett, 2018). As teachers we often feel helpless in the face of these horrifying facts. While it's true we can't solve the economic disparities that plague our country, we *can* do something to nurture the spirits and build the coping skills of the young adolescents in our classrooms and our schools. Figure 3.1 is a brief overview of five ways to disrupt the devastation of poverty. As you read the five principles, consider that they are all addressed in *This We Believe*.

Perhaps the most devastating result of poverty is homelessness of children and youth, defined by the federal government as those who lack a fixed, regular, and adequate nighttime shelter. They may share overcrowded temporary housing (76%) or live in emergency or transitional shelters or motels (21%), with about 3% having little to no shelter and spending nights in cars or public spaces (National Center for Homeless Education, 2016). Hard to imagine, isn't it? The United States has more homeless women and children than any other industrialized nation (Project HOME, 2017). This is a shameful and disgusting fact. These are the kids in our classrooms.

The socioeconomic gap in the United States is often referred to as the **privilege gap**. Title I funding is the U.S. government's method of assisting schools with more than 40% of their students qualifying for free or reduced-price meals. Our government is correct in the notion that it takes more money to educate a child who lives near or below the poverty line. By some estimates, it takes as much as twice as much money to educate a child from a poor home than a child from a middle-income home.

Individual teachers can make a difference in the lives of students who are poor. Given all we have explored in terms of young adolescent development, even middle level students with unlimited financial resources struggle with the passage from childhood to adolescence. Think about how much more difficult it may be for those young adolescents who live in low-income settings. To add to their problems, many studies show that teachers expect less of students from lower socioeconomic homes than they do of middle class students. We must examine what part we play in the ongoing failure of poor students due, in part, to communicating to them that they lack potential. Young adolescents need us to have high expectations for them. Teachers must believe their students can achieve before they put forth their best effort to teach them. Likewise, students must believe that they can achieve before they are willing to try. In April 2012,

FIGURE 3.1 Five ways to disrupt poverty

1. Develop relationships as the foundational principle
2. Hold high expectations and provide needed support
3. Commit to equity
4. Accept professional accountability for learning
5. Have the courage and will to take action.

Based on: *Disrupting Poverty* by K.M. Budge and W.H. Parrett, 2018. Alexandria, VA: ASCD.

an AMLE research summary written by E.C. Ruiz stated in part, "If teachers demand high expectations from their students and engage them in tasks that interest and involve them, they will promote self-esteem and build students' confidence and academic performance." High expectations matter.

Self-Check 3.3

LO 3.4 Family Diversity

Some of the family structures experienced by young adolescents today are far different from what was considered "normal" during much of the past century. Regardless of the family/home structure, it strongly influences a child's development. Likewise, as young adolescents try to figure out who they are within the family unit, their struggle affects the way family members interact with each other.

Defining Family

With only about one-fourth of school-age children living in traditional, two biological parent homes, we need to examine the structures in which our students live. In 2015, 35% of single-parent families had incomes below the poverty level, compared to 8% of married-couple families. With the divorce rate more than 50%, single-parent homes have increased more than 300% in the past 30 years. In 2015, 35% of K–12 students lived in single-parent homes (unchanged since 2010), with Mississippi at 48% and Utah at 19%, representing the range of state percentages. Two-thirds (66%) of African American children, more than half (52%) of Native American children, 42% of Hispanic children, and 41% of multiracial children lived in single-parent families in 2015. By comparison, 25% of white children and 16% of Asian and Pacific Islander children lived in single-parent households (Annie E. Casey, 2017). In 2014, more than 40% of births in the United States were to unwed mothers including 36% of white babies, 53% of Hispanic babies, and 71% of black babies (Child Trends, 2015). All these statistics and more tell us that young adolescents in our classrooms may live with:

- Two biological parents
- One biological parent
- One biological parent and a stepparent
- One stepparent
- One or two adoptive parents
- Grandparents
- Aunts and uncles
- Adult siblings
- Foster families
- Other students in a group home

It is not uncommon for students to "time share" in two houses because their parents have joint custody following a divorce. These houses may have any number of others living there as well (stepparent, stepsiblings, half-siblings, etc.). Our migrant family population is also significant. These families often move repeatedly according to the season and the available work, so that children are in several different schools during the year. A relatively new family structure for which there are no statistics as yet are same-sex partners who choose to be parents. And we must never forget the children who, by themselves or in a variety of family units, find themselves homeless.

Standard 5

Middle Level Professional Roles

Element c. Working with Family Members and Community Involvement: Middle level teacher candidates understand and value the ways diverse family structures and cultural backgrounds influence and enrich learning. They communicate and collaborate with all family members and community partners, and participate in school and community activities. They engage in practices that build positive, collaborative relationships with families from diverse cultures and backgrounds (e.g., race, ethnicity, culture, age, appearance, ability, sexual orientation, socioeconomic status, and family composition).

Involving Family

One of the 16 keys to educating young adolescents in *This We Believe* states that the effective school "actively involves families in the education of their children" (National Middle School Association, 2010, p. 40). It is well-documented that parents and other adults in the home play significant roles in the academic achievement of middle level students. All family structures carry with them inherent strengths and weaknesses in terms of the amount of support offered to our students. We may be the only stable, consistent factor in a student's life, or we may be one of many supports of fortunate young adolescents. Only by knowing the home situations and understanding the challenges of students whose lives we touch, will we know best how to help them grow.

Getting to know the adults with whom our students live is more difficult in middle level settings when family involvement often plummets. The significant adults in our young adolescents' lives are only half as likely to attend family conferences as the families of elementary students. Overall, family involvement drops as students age, with middle and high school rates significantly lower than primary and elementary rates (Child Trends, 2013). Developmental changes occurring during early adolescence affect not only the children themselves but also everyone else in the household. Parents, guardians, and families are often surprised by the rapid and unexpected changes they see in their young adolescents. Adults in the home are confused and often look for faults on which to blame behavior changes, not recognizing that many of the changes have very little to do with them. As students strive for greater independence, the adults in their homes may interpret the struggle as a signal to disengage. When students enter middle school, they leave what many experience as the comfort zone of the self-contained elementary classroom. School becomes more complex with class changes, course options, and larger numbers of students with which to contend. Families often feel as if they are lost in the maze. Their attitudes may turn to merely hoping to survive the middle level experiences of their children.

Teachers tell us that lack of home support is a major obstacle to raising student achievement. So far, the picture painted of family and home structures of our middle level students has been generally negative. We need to gratefully acknowledge, however, that there may be many adults in the lives of our students who are very supportive. There are whole schools that experience overwhelming support from the majority of parents and guardians, resulting in an environment conducive to increased student achievement. Offering unique settings such as weekend and weeknight volunteer opportunities, child care, and transportation will likely increase family involvement.

There are ways we can invite family involvement; incorporating these strategies requires an attitude that values both students and the adults closest to them.

Some students are fortunate enough to have family support and encouragement, but others rarely see sparks of interest in what they do in or out of school.

Not only must we value them, we must overcome our timidity and determine to take the time necessary to genuinely invite families to participate. There are impediments to family involvement that will be difficult to overcome including socioeconomic barriers, cultural and language barriers, and educational background barriers (Powell, 2019). Be persistent. Here are some ways we can increase the likelihood of family involvement:

- Begin the year with a questionnaire asking for student and family information that may help you meet the young adolescent's needs.

- Back-to-school night can be an ideal time to introduce yourself and talk about ways families can be involved in your classroom and school. Families can meet and share questions and concerns.

- Integrate families into the curriculum by inviting them to share their cultural traditions, interests, and skills with students.

- Establish effective and varied communication strategies that suit family circumstances.

- Design family education events such as Family Math Night and Science Extravaganza that involve the kids as teachers. For families with cultural and language differences who may need to know ways they can support their students and how to navigate life in the United States, have a special event with translators and community resources available (Eisenbach, Clark, & Gooden, 2016).

Self-Check 3.4

LO 3.5 Academic Diversity

Young adolescents experience intellectual development at varying rates and to varying degrees, as discussed in Chapter 2. This variance, along with other developmental changes taking place within the context of a student's world, contributes to academic success, or the lack of it. We should not expect all students to learn the same knowledge and skills in the same way at the same rate.

Learning Differences

Until recently a section on academic or learning differences would have included multiple intelligences theory and learning styles, concepts held in high esteem by many for a long time. The value of them has now been disparaged by new philosophies and research. But let's not forget the point both made: learning occurs in many ways. Some students learn best when content and skills are presented visually; others learn best from hearing about the knowledge and skills. Some students prefer having **manipulatives**, or objects designed so that learners can perceive a concept through developmentally appropriate hands-on experiences; others learn best by moving.

The great majority of students can learn in a variety of ways, even though they may prefer certain types of strategies. Preferences can be enhanced and weaker modes of learning can be strengthened. In our classrooms, we must provide an environment that is conducive to all learners. Figure 3.2 helps us understand characteristics we may observe in students who learn best through hearing, seeing, moving, and touching.

It's important to discover as much as we can about how we, as teachers, learn. Because it is natural to teach in the same ways we learn, knowing our own learning preferences helps us recognize when we are teaching like we learn, rather than teaching in a variety of ways to meet the needs of more of our students. We should first know ourselves as learners, and then discover the ways in which our students learn to increase their understanding and skills.

FIGURE 3.2   Tendencies of students who prefer to learn in particular ways

Students who prefer to learn through sight tend to . . .

> enjoy reading and being read to.
> be able to verbally explain concepts and scenarios.
> like music and hum to themselves.
> enjoy both talking and listening.

Students who prefer to learn through hearing tend to . . .

> have good spelling, note-taking, and organizational skills.
> notice details and prefer neatness.
> learn more if illustrations and charts accompany reading.
> prefer quiet, serene surroundings.

Students who prefer to learn through moving tend to . . .

> be demonstrative, animated, and outgoing.
> enjoy physical movement and manipulatives.
> be willing to try new things.
> be messy in habits and surroundings.

Students who prefer to learn through touch tend to . . .

> prefer manipulatives when being introduced to a topic.
> literally translate events and phenomena.
> tolerate clutter.
> be artistic in nature.

Ability and Effort

Academic success is dependent on both ability and effort, along with other factors that determine how much and when our students learn. In any heterogeneous middle level classroom, we may find **intelligence quotient (IQ)** scores ranging from 70 to 140, or with possibly even a wider range. An IQ of 70 or below generally indicates intellectual disability; an IQ of 140 or above indicates a high level of intellectual giftedness/ability (Woolfolk, 2018). We know now that IQ is not fixed. Studies have shown that IQ can change based on many complex factors in a person's environment. Intelligence (often measured by IQ), motivation and resulting effort, and the quality of instruction all factor into student learning (Slavin, 2018). As variable as measures of intelligence may be, the variability related to motivation and resulting effort may be just as wide. As shown in Figure 3.3, the wide variances in, and interplay between, both IQ and level of effort can lead to failure by very capable students as well as success by those who may be only marginally capable. Most students exhibit moderate levels of both IQ and effort.

When children are young, they see ability and effort as one and the same. If they try hard, they are successful. By middle school, students tend to see the "smart" kids appearing not to try as hard for good grades. Assuming that if you have ability, effort isn't important, their logic may lead them to believe that if you have to try hard, you must not be very "smart." In an attempt to avoid failure, students may appear not to try so they won't feel unable.

FIGURE 3.3   Effects of ability (as measured by IQ) and effort on academic success

High IQ	Low Effort	May or May Not Succeed
High Effort	Low IQ	May or May Not Succeed

Will Succeed   Will Not Succeed

Academic Self-Esteem

If students experience academic success, they will assign more importance to **academic self-esteem**, or the belief that they have the ability to be academically successful. On the other hand, if students do poorly in school, they face a difficult psychological dilemma. In an attempt to preserve some measure of self-esteem, these students will discount academics. They may adopt a "school doesn't matter" attitude. They may display lack of effort, procrastination, putting blame on others, and purposefully turning in poorly done assignments.

Self-Check 3.5

LO 3.6 Students with Exceptionalities

Students with **exceptionalities** are those who have abilities or disabilities that set them apart from other students (Heward, 2017). Students with enhanced abilities are often referred to as **gifted and talented**. Students with disabilities fall into a wide gamut of descriptors. Some exceptionalities are the result of nature, or genes, chromosomes, or birth defects; others may be the result of injury or illness, aspects of nurture. Two factors are especially important when we consider the education of students with exceptionalities:

- **Identification:** Deciding who has what exceptionality and to what degree
- **Intervention:** Determining how best to meet their educational needs

Millions of students are receiving special services in American public schools, accounting for about 12% of all public school students. Delivery of these special services is the source of continual controversy regarding which students to serve, and how and where to serve them. This section is a broad overview rather than a comprehensive look at special services for students with exceptionalities.

Students with Exceptional Abilities

Students who are considered gifted and talented are identified in a variety of ways, from IQ scores of 125 or more, to teacher and parent recommendation, to observation of a particular gift such as music or art. Students designated as gifted and talented may excel in intellectual, creative, artistic, or leadership abilities.

Gifted and talented young adolescents face the same challenges as others their age, but with some twists that may make their lives even more complicated. Their needs and how they experience development may be different. There are distinct characteristics that may accompany giftedness, according to clinical and research literature, including sensitivity, intensity, perceptiveness, and over-excitability (National Association for Gifted Children, n.d.). For many, going from elementary school, where having an "A" paper posted by the teacher meant a good day, to middle school, where achievement may be ridiculed by insecure peers, may be reason to shrink from the spotlight and stop achieving. They need our support—academically, emotionally, and socially.

Services for gifted and talented students vary significantly and include pull-out programs one period a day with other gifted students, grade skipping, learning the curriculum at a faster pace (compacting), and tracking with other gifted and talented students for part or all of the school day. As classroom teachers, we need to be flexible and accepting of novel ideas and approaches to problem solving. We must not be intimidated by students who may have higher IQ scores than our own; we must encourage them to use their gifts and talents in positive ways. The National Association for Gifted Children is an organization of parents, teachers, educators, other professionals, and community leaders who unite to address the unique needs of children and youth with demonstrated gifts and talents, as well as those children who may be able to develop their talent potential with appropriate educational experiences.

Students with Disabilities

Disabilities that impair daily functioning such as orthopedic impediments and vision impairment are generally diagnosed at a very young age. Some disabilities, however, are masked until a later age because students find ways to compensate for their problems. Table 3.2 lists the various categories of students with disabilities receiving services in schools.

HISTORY OF SERVICES   The official history of special services delivery is very recent. Until 1975, a student with disabilities was accorded no federal rights to an education. Children with disabilities were often denied access to public education and placed in separate schools to be educated, often minimally, with other children with disabilities. The 1975 **Education for All Handicapped Children Act** (PL 94–142) mandated, among other things, that all children with handicaps be given the right to a free and appropriate public education in the **least restrictive environment (LRE)** guided by an **Individualized Education Program (IEP)**. The least restrictive environment is the setting that has the fewest restrictions within which a student can function at capacity. This is most commonly the regular classroom.

An Individualized Education Program (IEP) serves students with disabilities. An IEP is developed by educators, the family, and others as appropriate and involves a detailed plan to reach specific goals. IEP formats may vary, but all must be revisited annually and the student's progress evaluated. An important part of an IEP is the designation of where and with whom students with disabilities will spend their school time.

In 1990, PL 94–142 was reauthorized as the **Individuals with Disabilities Education Act (IDEA)**. The disabilities listed in the 1990 law include autism, deafness, deaf-blindness, hearing impairment, mental retardation, multiple disabilities, orthopedic impairments, other health impairments, serious emotional disturbance, specific learning disabilities, speech or language impairments, traumatic brain injuries, and visual impairments. The 1990 legislation reiterated the principles of the 1975 law and added guidelines for transitioning students. Grade-to-grade transitions for regular education

TABLE 3.2   Percentage of students served in disability categories

Disability	Students Served (%)
Learning disabilities	38.6
Speech or language impairments	19.1
Other health impairments	16.9
Intellectual disability	7.3
Emotional disturbance	6.2
Autism	8.4
Multiple disabilities	2.5
Developmental delay	2.4
Hearing impairments	1.2
Orthopedic impairments	0.9
Visual impairments	0.4
Traumatic brain injury	0.4
Deaf-blindness	<0.1

Based on: University of New Hampshire. (2015). Annual disability statistics compendium. Retrieved July 22, 2016, from http://disabilitycompendium.org/statistics/special-education

students are generally uneventful, requiring minimal support. However, for students with developmental disabilities, transitions may be quite traumatic.

In 1997, the law was reauthorized with an emphasis on accountability, requiring districts and states to include students with disabilities in their assessment plans and to provide appropriate alternative assessments when needed. Other highlights included the mandate for schools to support professional development for all staff to better involve them in the IEP process and to raise academic expectations and performances of students with disabilities. The law also called for more involvement of students with disabilities in extracurricular activities.

LEARNING DISABILITIES   A student with a **learning disability** has a significant discrepancy between learning potential and achievement and, most often, displays problems understanding and using language (Turnbull, Turnbull, Wehmeyer, & Shogren, 2016). Students with learning disabilities (LD) are often not diagnosed until late elementary or middle school. Almost half of the students receiving special services are learning disabled. Because LD has so many forms, it is often misdiagnosed or not diagnosed at all. Many students develop coping strategies that mask their learning problems for years and very possibly for life. Students with LD may:

- Have difficulties with word recognition and text comprehension
- Feel overwhelmed by the idea of getting started
- Struggle to organize and use the mechanics of writing
- Have difficulty differentiating numbers or copying shapes
- Have difficulty identifying, using, and monitoring problem-solving strategies (Turnbull et al., 2016)

Most middle level schools include resource teachers with whom students with learning disabilities may spend part of each day. These skilled teachers help students develop personalized ways to be academically successful.

ATTENTION DEFICIT DISORDER   Encountered more and more in the classroom, and only coincidentally assigned to any kind of special education setting, are students with Attention Deficit Disorder (ADD) and Attention Deficit Hyperactivity Disorder (ADHD). Students with **Attention Deficit Disorder** try to pay attention to everything rather than focusing attention on the task at hand. **Attention Deficit Hyperactivity Disorder** adds two dimensions to ADD—hyperactivity and impulsivity. **Hyperactivity** is a level of activity that is not age-appropriate. **Impulsivity** refers to reacting quickly to a situation without taking time to think about results or consequences (Vaughn, Bos, & Schumm, 2014). Most researchers say that ADD and ADHD have biological causes and behavioral symptoms. To be diagnosed with either, symptoms must be excessive and long-term. More than 7% of all children ages 5 to 18 are diagnosed with ADD or ADHD. Many take medication in attempts to manage the condition. In addition to medication, behavioral interventions may be used in the classroom—social skills groups, daily report cards, positive reinforcement, preferred seating, "time out" arrangements, and so on. In some schools, as many as 10% of the students are on medication for ADD and ADHD (Turnbull et al., 2016). Students are not considered disabled because of a diagnosis of ADD or ADHD. They must have some other disabling characteristic to receive special education services.

Many educators and researchers believe ADHD is over-diagnosed or misdiagnosed. They say the causes of disruptive behavior often associated with ADHD may actually be from overcrowded classrooms, lack of self-discipline skills, or teachers who demand inappropriate amounts of attention. Still others bemoan the fact that many students whom they suspect have the disorder go undiagnosed.

AUTISM SPECTRUM   Autism, or **autism spectrum disorder (ASD)**, is receiving increasing attention as the rates of diagnosis appear to be multiplying at a dismaying rate.

According to the National Institutes of Health (2013), ASD is "a complex developmental disorder that affects how a person behaves, interacts with others, communicates, and learns." It is common for children with autism to have medical problems such as allergies, chronic digestive disorders, limited gross and fine motor skills, seizures, sleep problems, and low pain threshold (Autism Society, 2016). Because there is no medical test to diagnose ASD, we rely on observation by parents, educators, psychologists, and doctors. Autism-specific evaluations are becoming more detailed and precise. **Autism Speaks** is a national organization dedicated to promoting solutions for the children and adults diagnosed with ASD. Their website offers a tremendous amount of information.

Autism spectrum disorder is often diagnosed between the ages of 18 and 24 months, using a series of "red flags" to determine the likelihood of the disorder, including no big smiles or other warm, joyful expressions by age 6 months or thereafter; no babbling, pointing, or waving by age 12 months; and no words by age 16 months (Autism Speaks, 2016). Symptoms begin to surface in school if diagnosis isn't made early because they are rooted in social issues involving interactions and communication. Diagnosis of autism spectrum disorder should become the basis for an individualized educational program (IEP) for the child. Note that Asperger syndrome, once a stand-alone diagnosis, is now one of several subtypes of the single diagnosis of autism.

INCLUSION Perhaps the most hotly debated question may be where to serve students with disabilities and the determination of the least restrictive environment. The assignment of students to the regular classroom for some or all of the day is known as **inclusion. Mainstreaming** is a term often used interchangeably with inclusion. Because middle level philosophy espouses heterogeneity in most learning settings, inclusion is a natural fit. Inclusion supports social development and awareness as it gives all students opportunities to interact.

Because writing an IEP involves both special education and regular classroom teachers, placement of students in inclusive settings is a collaborative effort. Although most general education teachers agree that inclusion can be a positive practice, they don't necessarily feel adequately prepared to serve the wide range of needs often accompanying inclusion. In fact, not all parents of children with disabilities believe that inclusion provides the most effective learning environment for their children.

Schools are required by IDEA to have a continuum of alternative placements available that vary in terms of restrictiveness because a particular level of inclusion is not mandated by law. The "where" of the delivery of services is based on the individual student's IEP and must be revisited annually. Placement decisions often pose scheduling difficulties, as well as staffing, planning, and resource dilemmas. No single model of services can be prescribed. To learn more about serving students with exceptionalities, visit the **Council for Exceptional Children (CEC)** website for information and support.

As a young adolescent with Down syndrome, Trista Kutcher finds success in many areas of her life because of tremendous support at home and in school. Trista has just entered high school, where she is thriving. She is an example of a young adolescent whose family, teachers, and peers look for and promote her development. As the first child of her mom and dad, both teachers, she was diagnosed with Down syndrome at birth so *identification* was early. *Intervention* has been part of her entire life. Many children diagnosed with disabilities are not as fortunate. Be aware that support levels vary widely.

Sara Davis Powell

Trista is a cheerleader. She has Down syndrome. Surprised? With support, many young adolescents with disabilities can thrive.

Enhanced eText
Video Example 3.2

Student Trista Kutcher has excellent home support as she navigates public school. She enjoys inclusion in some classes and participates in extracurricular activities.

Why It Matters

We've explored a variety of diversity issues and should consider both the richness these differences represent and the opportunities they provide as we plan all aspects of teaching and learning. Our responsibility is to affirm each individual and help all young adolescents appreciate each other for what they have in common, as well as the diversity that is inevitable. Creating environments that go beyond tolerance to a real celebration of diversity, both in the classroom and in the school, should be a major goal of middle level education.

Group Activities

1. Refer to your class file of local middle schools. Divide them among class members to find the total number of students, the percentage of students who qualify for free and reduced-priced lunch, and a breakdown of racial identification in each school. All schools should have these data and they are likely even available through district and state websites. Add the data to your class file.

2. Together, brainstorm ways that you as middle level teachers might help create an appreciation of diversity among your students.

Individual Activities

1. Why is it important for your students to understand their particular strengths? Is there value in students understanding the areas where they have less strength?

2. Choose a subject area and a topic you can imagine teaching. Think of ways you might approach the topic to address each of the four ways of learning: visual, auditory, tactile (touching), kinesthetic (moving). Write a brief description of each approach and be ready to share your ideas with your class.

Personal Journal

1. Describe your own cultural identity, including the areas of diversity discussed in this chapter and more.

2. Did you experience any kind of prejudice because of ways you may have been different from other kids in middle school? This may be painful to remember, but "reliving" it and writing about it may lead you toward a better understanding of your students.

3. Are there certain areas of diversity that make you more uncomfortable than others? Do you have personal experiences that contribute to your comfort levels with a variety of areas of diversity?

Professional Practice

Cario Middle School has a diverse population, even though the majority of the kids are white and middle- to upper-income. In a growing and mostly prosperous town, Cario has recently seen an influx of students from various parts of Asia, as well as immigrants from Mexico whose families have come to work in service industries. At Cario the socioeconomic gap seems to be increasing, as does the academic gap, and teachers are scrambling to cope with their changing student population. This is referred to as changing demographics.

Traci Peters

Traci Peters teaches 7th grade math and Deirdre McGrew teaches kids who are at risk for academic failure in a program called Cario Academic Recovery and Enrichment (CARE). Both teachers are concerned that Cario is not keeping up with the rapid student population changes, and, therefore, not meeting the needs of the kids who walk through the doors now. Most of the teachers are well aware of the middle level philosophy that recommends that kids from a wide array of achievement backgrounds be placed in classes together whenever possible. They have had staff

Deirdre McGrew

development sessions about how to successfully teach heterogeneous groups. But nothing prepared them for the realities of this new demographic situation.

Remember that for some items, more than one choice may be defensible. The purpose of the items is to stimulate thought and discussion.

1. Ms. Peters looks around her classroom during an algebra class and is struck by how white it appears. There are two students from Japan and the rest are Caucasian. This group looks so very different from the mix of kids she supervised in the gym this morning before school. How might Ms. Peters work with 6th grade teachers to attempt to have a more diverse 7th grade algebra class next year?

   a. Explore the backgrounds of some of the students who show academic promise in 6th grade to see what their achievement levels were in their previous schools, even if outside the United States, with the intent of putting them in an algebra class in 7th grade.

   b. Ask the principal to assign an ethnic balance of students next year to an algebra class without pretesting or teacher recommendation, to see if having high expectations of all of the kids will bring about success in algebra.

   c. Contact parents of non-white students to ask if they believe their student would thrive in an advanced setting.

   d. Work with her team to adjust certain students' schedules so they can give algebra a try.

2. Ms. McGrew is used to working with the kids who had been placed in CARE in the past. She knew that most would be African American from the lower SES areas of the community. What she was not prepared for were the new students in her group from Mexico and Southeast Asian countries who speak little English. Even with only 15 students in her class, when four speak two different languages, she is at a loss to know how to meet their needs. Which course of action is likely to have the most immediate benefit for all the kids in CARE?

   a. Meet with all the parents of her students to ask about their learning preferences.

   b. Ask her principal to explore the idea of an assistant who will work with CARE kids on English language development.

   c. Increase the variety of the instructional strategies to increase student understanding.

   d. Check with the publisher of her materials to see if audio recordings are available so students can listen and follow along in order to increase their reading skills in English.

3. What can Cario teachers do to establish stronger relationships among themselves and their students, even as the school becomes more diverse? How might they build a sense of community among all the adults and students? What steps could they use to validate that all learners are capable of contributing positively in class and to the school in general?

Chapter 4
Societal Context of Middle Level Education

Sara Davis Powell

Developmentally responsive middle level schools help students develop and maintain healthy minds and bodies. . . . An emphasis on health, wellness, and safety permeates the entire school, with faculty members sharing responsibility for maintaining a healthy school environment. The risks associated with tobacco, alcohol, drugs, unhealthy eating habits, and sexual activities are addressed.

THIS WE BELIEVE, P. 38.

 Learning Outcomes

After studying this chapter, you will have knowledge and skills to:

4.1 Compare and contrast the variations in middle level school experiences based on suburban, urban, and rural settings.

4.2 Explore bullying in its many forms, including consideration of the bully, the bullied, and the bystander.

64

4.3 Examine technologies used by young adolescents and their impact on students' lives.

4.4 Comprehend the impact of poverty on teaching and learning.

4.5 Discover ways to meet the needs of English learners.

4.6 Describe how wellness issues affect young adolescents.

Dear Future Middle Level Teacher,

Our students come to us with complicated pasts and, for many, uncertain presents. The societal context of some students' lives includes lots of positive aspects: a supportive family, community opportunities, and higher education possibilities, to name a few. Other students have challenges that must either be confronted and overcome or managed through coping skills. The more we understand about the societal context of our students, the better equipped we will be to celebrate the positive and help correct or compensate for the negative.

Each generation considers itself unique, and every generation faces particular challenges. To say that the current societal context of middle level education is unlike any other is true. The 21st century is well under way, ushered in by the Columbine tragedy of 1999 and followed just two years later by September 11, 2001, a date that defines much of the political and social climate in which we live today. More recently, the 17 deaths in 2018 at a high school in Parkland, Florida, spurred some to political action on behalf of school safety and gun control. Protracted wars, political upheaval, the fast-paced lives of both adults and children, and our rapidly changing American population all contribute to the societal context of education.

There's a saying that "We cannot control the wind, but we can adjust our sails." Middle level teachers become experts at adjusting sails. Many of the "winds" in this chapter are out of our control, but providing a safe, caring environment for at least a few hours a day, five days a week, can make a world of difference to kids caught in the gusts of negative societal context. This is not a "happy" chapter, but one that's necessary. Let's stick together through these less-than-positive topics and think about how we can make a difference for our kids.

SDP

Standard 1
Young Adolescent Development

Element b. Knowledge of the Implications of Diversity on Young Adolescent Development: Middle level teacher candidates demonstrate their understanding of the implications of diversity on the development of young adolescents. They implement curriculum and instruction that is responsive to young adolescents' local, national, and international histories, language/dialects, and individual identities (e.g., race, ethnicity, culture, age, appearance, ability, sexual orientation, socioeconomic status, family composition). They participate successfully in middle level practices that consider and celebrate the diversity of all young adolescents.

LO 4.1 Suburban, Urban, and Rural Settings

Where kids live and go to school shapes their experiences in many ways. The three principal settings of schools are suburban, urban, and rural. **Suburban settings** are generally small to medium-sized towns, or communities on the outskirts of cities. They typically have distinct neighborhoods or subdivisions. **Urban settings** are large cities with downtowns. **Rural settings** are communities with lots of open spaces and limited retail and services.

Suburban schools account for about 40% of all public schools; urban schools make up about 25%of the schools; and rural schools account for about 35%. Let's look first at suburban schools.

Suburban Settings

Most kids who attend suburban schools live in single-family homes or in apartment complexes. There are generally lawns, schools, churches, recreational options, shopping malls, health facilities, and well-lighted streets and sidewalks. About two thirds of the students in suburban schools are white and the vast majority do not live in poverty (Schneider, 2017).

The school experiences of students in suburban settings often include attendance at neighborhood schools with friends on their block. Even with the increasing mobility of our society, many students in suburbs attend most or all of their K–12 years with the same kids. They may move to a different house, but the chances are pretty good that their schools will be stable. Most suburban schools offer afterschool options, some for fun and others for extra help with schoolwork. There is a sense of safety and continuity that perhaps isn't prominent in large cities.

Even in tough financial times, suburban schools provide the necessities for learning. Facilities are maintained. Families and communities pull together and provide those things not considered necessities—band uniforms, afterschool sports, field trips, and so on—the stuff that often hooks young adolescents and keeps them in school.

In education we are fond of saying "Kids are kids are kids." By this we mean that they are alike in so many ways. And that's true. But for many students, life in urban schools presents challenges suburban kids may never face.

Urban Settings

What I write about urban schools are generalizations, just as they are about suburban and rural schools. The difference is that the picture painted of suburban schools tends not to offend. By generalizing about urban settings and schools, I run the risk of offending those who live and learn in them. This is not my intent.

Urban schools are usually older facilities with problems, such as heating or cooling failures, restroom sanitation issues, limited parking, vandalism, and so on. Two thirds of urban students are nonwhite. Urban school students are increasingly likely to live in disadvantaged homes. The majority of black and Hispanic students in urban schools attend schools that are 90% to 100% non-white (Schneider, 2017). As we've discussed, schools with the majority of students living in poverty receive extra government funding called **Title I** funds. Research supports this added funding because it takes more resources to provide education for students in disadvantaged settings. Is it enough? Obviously not; achievement levels among students in urban settings generally fall well below those of students in suburban and rural settings.

The kids who attend urban schools may live in crowded apartment buildings or government project housing. They may have unstable home lives that often accompany poverty. They may find themselves in dangerous situations simply by walking on the streets that lead to their schools.

See How They Grow

DeVante and Kim 8th grade

If you look back at DeVante and Kim as 6th graders, you'll see how much they have grown by 8th grade. While attending Jefferson Middle School, an urban magnet school for technology and communication, DeVante and Kim became good friends. She first approached DeVante as a "bad boy" she needed to "fix." By 7th grade she was viewing him as an intelligent, charismatic buddy. Through Kim, and several other students and teachers, DeVante began to see life as full of possibilities, and that he wasn't destined to join a gang and live in the conditions in which he had grown up. Kim and her family introduced him to the possibilities of college and careers. By 8th grade DeVante and Kim were almost inseparable.

Some urban schools have been converted into **magnet schools**, schools that attract students because of a particular emphasis. With intriguing themes, the promise of specialization, and the draw of expert teachers and perhaps small, specialized classes, some urban magnet schools have successfully recruited kids from suburban and rural areas, creating a healthy diversity among students. Two of our focus students, DeVante and Kim, attend Jefferson Middle School, an urban magnet. Read more about them in See How They Grow.

Rural Settings

In communities where kids live in very small towns, or are perhaps scattered across large areas of land, there may be K–12 schools out of necessity with fewer than 100 students. In Alaska, 20% of schools have three or fewer teachers. In Montana, 70% of the schools are rural. Most rural schools are small, but some are as large as suburban and urban schools. Students in geographically large rural school districts may be bused to very large K–2, 3–4, 5–6, 7–8, and 9–12 schools, some as large as 1,000 students per grade span.

Rural areas tend to be fairly stable, with the possibility of increasingly large populations of migrant farm families who may move with the season. This is a particularly challenging situation for some rural educators. Some of the other challenges of rural schools include the relative isolation of students and the resulting lack of various forms of diversity (cultural, social, etc.). It may also be difficult to hire new teachers, many of whom want more social and graduate education opportunities than many rural areas offer. It may also be harder to provide extracurricular opportunities for kids in widespread locations. Bus transportation may be difficult to arrange and pay for. Small schools often find it challenging to offer a wide range of courses because of lack of teacher expertise and few students having the same interests. Fortunately, today there are e-options that expand curricular choices.

Rural settings have a number of advantages. With relatively stable populations, there may be a real sense of community and continuity. In smaller schools, teachers and students may know each other better, with parents who attended the same schools, sometimes with the same teachers. In many rural settings, the teachers sense that they are really extended family to students. They know parents and grandparents and often watch children grow through elementary, middle, and high school. They cheer them on through college. The school may be the center of community life, with families involved in athletics, spelling bees, school carnivals, and so on. Yes, it sounds idyllic, but it's the reality of many living in rural areas. Remember that again we are dealing in generalities. Not all rural settings mirror Mayberry. (If this reference eludes you, try watching reruns of the *Andy Griffith Show*. Ron Howard wasn't always a famous director!)

Make A Difference

You may spend your entire career in one setting. Or you may have the opportunity to teach in two or three different settings. Even though what you have just read is an overview, you will likely find parts that hold true for each setting. We know they are not alike. Our responsibility as teachers is to make the teaching and learning connection for all students, regardless of where they live. With available technology, the least we can do is show students what the world looks like outside their schools and immediate surroundings.

Advocate for kids, wherever you teach. That advocacy may look different based on circumstances. Be sensitive to needs and be vocal about what you, the school, the district, and the state need to do to make opportunities for learning and growing available to your students.

We now turn our attention to a societal issue that transcends home and school settings. Unfortunately, bullying happens in the suburbs, the inner city, and in rural areas all across our country.

Self-Check 4.1

LO 4.2 Bullying

Let's begin with what bullying is and what it is not. **Bullying** is aggression with intent to harm; it is about exerting power over another person. Bullying is using this power in a relationship where one person (the bully) hurts and humiliates another (the bullied), often to the indifference or amusement of those who watch (the bystanders). Bullying is *not* a rite of passage, nor an expectation of growing up. Bullying does *not* include spontaneous acts that arise in particular circumstances; it is willful and intentional, used as a dangerous weapon. It may be verbal, physical, or social/emotional—a sharp weapon indeed.

Young adolescents know about bullying. They see it in the halls, in the cafeteria, on the playground, and, unfortunately, right under our noses in the classroom. Many experience bullying through the Internet. In fact, some studies tell us almost twice as many middle level kids experience bullying as do their elementary and high school counterparts.

Bullying may be physical aggression in the form of slapping, kicking, bumping, tripping, or shoving. It may relate to possessions and involve vandalism or stealing. Or bullying may be verbal in the form of taunting, name-calling, sexual comments, or threats. Social/emotional bullying may be comprised of leaving someone out on purpose, talking about students behind their backs or online, embarrassing another in public, or spreading rumors. Young adolescents are faced with the possibility of being targets of bullying or being bystanders daily. And obviously some choose to be the bully. No one is immune from involvement. This inevitability doesn't mean that it's OK to just let it happen. Because middle level schools are where social interactions continually occur and self-concepts are formed, dismantled, and reformed, it is the place where students must learn civility and what it means to be humane.

The Harm of Bullying

Bullying has very real consequences. Nationally, more than 20% of students ages 12 to 18 reported being bullied in 2015. Let's consider some consequences found on the government website stopbulling.gov.

Kids who are bullied can experience negative physical, school, and mental health issues. Kids who are bullied are more likely to experience:

- Depression and anxiety, increased feelings of sadness and loneliness, changes in sleep and eating patterns, and loss of interest in activities they used to enjoy. These issues may persist into adulthood.
- Health complaints.
- Decreased academic achievement—GPA and standardized test scores—and school participation. They are more likely to miss, skip, or drop out of school.
- A very small number of bullied children might retaliate through extremely violent measures. In 12 of 15 school shooting cases in the 1990s, the shooters had a history of being bullied.

Kids who bully others can also engage in violent and other risky behaviors into adulthood. Kids who bully are more likely to:

- Abuse alcohol and other drugs in adolescence and as adults.
- Get into fights, vandalize property, and drop out of school.
- Engage in early sexual activity.
- Have criminal convictions and traffic citations as adults.
- Be abusive toward their romantic partners, spouses, or children as adults.

Kids who witness bullying are more likely to:

- Have increased use of tobacco, alcohol, or other drugs.
- Have increased mental health problems, including depression and anxiety.
- Miss or skip school (U.S. Department of Health and Human Services, 2018).

Gender Differences in Bullying

Both boys and girls are bullies and/or victims, and we can make generalizations about each. But when it comes to verbal bullying, both sexes do it. Verbal bullying usually involves name-calling. It may be done quietly in a whisper or yelled on the field. It is a quick way for a bully to powerfully use words to hurt a victim. Racial slurs, sexual innuendo, cruel jokes aimed at hurting feelings, and taunts such as "retard," "fag," and "geek" will continue if not dealt with by adults and could lead to even more severe forms of bullying.

Boys tend to use physical bullying more than girls. It's more visible than other forms. Choking, punching, pinching, tearing clothes, breaking or stealing possessions—these forms of bullying are used by boys who are older or bigger or who have more social capital than their victims. Girls who engage in physical bullying are most often the larger girls who tend to be louder and depend on fear to hold onto others as companions.

Relational bullying, most often practiced by girls, involves humiliation through ignoring, excluding, or shunning. What horrible words! I feel bad just writing them. Imagine experiencing these things. Maybe you have.

Socially aggressive behavior involved in relational bullying may be just as harmful, or more so, than physical bullying. Certainly, the hurt lasts longer. Facial expressions alone can be a devastatingly effective tool of bullying. Girls are often very sensitive to a particular look that tells them in no uncertain terms that they are not welcome at a table in the cafeteria. Emotional games girls play that result in hurt feelings and make themselves appear powerful leave lasting scars on the girls who fall victim.

Relational bullying is a kind of psychological warfare and, therefore, is often hard to detect. Victims are often hesitant to tell anyone, much less accuse a classmate. Ratting on a peer is often forbidden in the social order of early adolescence.

Sara Davis Powell

Even if not intended, girls often perceive relational aggression when they think other students are talking about them.

Lesbian, Gay, Bisexual, Transgender Bullying

Lesbian, gay, bisexual, transgender, and youth questioning their sexual preference or gender identity (LGBTQ) have a 91% greater chance of being victims of bullying than their heterosexual peers (Marx & Kettrey, 2016). A large-scale study indicates that while society appears to be more open and accepting of LGBTQ individuals, the rate of victimization has not decreased since statistics specifically addressing sexual minority people started being collected in the 1990s. This same study revealed that bias-related forms of victimization have particularly pronounced, long-term effects on physical and behavioral health and achievement of children and youth (McKay, Misra, & Lindquist, 2017). If young adolescents who are LGBTQ are not accepted in their own homes and then are bullied in school, they often have nowhere to turn. When kids don't mirror what may be accepted in society as normal, they become more prone to being bullied, often suffering isolation, verbal and physical abuse, and humiliation. We need to explore our own biases as teachers and be sensitive to issues affecting LGBTQ young adolescents.

The Bully

The act of bullying generates more attention than the bully, but perhaps it shouldn't. Young adolescents fill all three roles: bully, bullied, and bystander. Until we understand why and how a child becomes a bully, we will not be completely effective in deterring bullying. A large study reveals that there's a relationship between being considered "cool" and being a bully. About 2,000 students in Los Angeles schools were asked to name the cool kids as well as those who are physically aggressive or rumor spreaders. The same 7th and 8th graders were repeatedly named in both categories, leading researchers to conclude that some students who are socially prominent likely maintain their popularity by being socially aggressive in bullying ways (Juvonen, Wang, & Espinoza, 2012). Of course, the cool kids aren't the only ones who bully, and certainly not all cool kids are bullies. But it's helpful when research can increase our understanding of bullying.

Bullies may have been, or are, victims of bullying themselves. Bullies are seeking power they may not feel they have in other parts of their lives. They exert power by harming others, by intimidating and being dominant. Yes, we need to try to prevent them from exerting this power, but we also need to dig deeply for the cause of their actions, not just the symptoms, or they will never be whole and productive.

Sara Davis Powell

Some student behaviors and mannerisms make them more likely to be targets of bullying. We don't want to harm a student's self-concept by telling him to stop acting in ways that may seem very natural to him, but we also don't want the target status to continue. Teacher-student relationships that include respect and trust help us talk with students in ways that can help, not harm, their sense of self.

The Bullied

Everyone has a right to be treated with dignity, no matter how he or she fits in, or doesn't fit in, with others. The **bullied**, kids who are targets of bullies, may be passive, physically weak/unattractive, have low self-concepts, be socially unskilled, cognitively or academically gifted, lesbian, gay, or maybe just new to the area. Targets come in all shapes and sizes, all races and ethnicities. Young adolescents often are convinced that there's nothing that can be done about bullying. We need to show them that they're wrong.

The Bystander

We are all **bystanders**. We have seen bullying in progress and done nothing—if not as adults, then certainly as kids. It's understandable that 12-year-olds would perhaps watch and then turn away out of fear of being called names and ostracized themselves, or out of a sense of helplessness. But for adults, it's unforgivable.

We must teach students that being a bystander and doing nothing is not acceptable. They must never join in and should immediately try to find an adult. Remember that it takes a lot of nerve for a young adolescent to ask the bullied peer to join him and together find an adult.

Make A Difference

While making a difference in terms of perpetrator and victim in a bullying scenario may seem like a natural fit for teachers, in reality too many teachers either ignore bullying, as part of kids growing and learning to make their way in life, or are not tuned in to what's happening around them. It may be easy to spot overt bullying and send a student to the principal or a counselor. But just stopping the behavior isn't enough. We have to get at the cause in order to eradicate it. That's the tough part. When bullying occurs, it creates ready-made teachable moments not to be missed by effective middle level teachers. Helping our students understand that we all deserve to be respected despite how we differ is part of being developmentally responsive. Figure 4.1 lists some ways we can make a difference with regard to bullying.

Some communities are taking bullying very seriously. Districts are establishing antibullying policies with uniform consequences. States are passing legislation requiring school personnel to report all suspicions of bullying to the school administration. In the legislation, characteristics that motivate harassment are often listed. A compilation of these characteristics include race, color, religion, ancestry, national origin, gender, socioeconomic status, academic status, gender identity, physical appearance, sexual orientation, and mental/physical/developmental/sensory disability. Concern about bullying goes well beyond the schoolhouse door. In fact, it's quite difficult to isolate anything inside the school, given the proliferation of technology.

FIGURE 4.1 Ways to make a difference with regard to bullying

- Create a climate where "telling" is not only OK, but expected and appreciated. Reporting bullying should be viewed as a classroom community responsibility where an open atmosphere consistently says that all are welcome and valued.
- Be totally present in mind, body, and spirit. This means our personal problems wait for us in the car for the trip home and do not interfere with giving students our full attention.
- Practice "withitness." This is a term coined decades ago that means we act as though we have eyes in the back of our heads. We see all, hear all, and protect all.
- Use discussion groups, advisory periods, literature focusing on tolerance and civility, and other means of continuing conversations about why bullying is wrong.
- Know what bullying looks like. Learn to recognize both the bully and the bullied. Act on what you see; act on what you hear.
- Never underestimate the fears of a student. Take reports seriously and don't stop interventions until the bully is put out of the bullying business and the bullied is able to function comfortably in the school setting.
- Step in when there is an unhealthy imbalance of power. The better we know our students, the easier it will be to spot these situations.
- Consistently intervene, protect, and teach civility.
- Stay calm and model respectful behavior when you intervene.
- Don't question those involved in front of other kids and don't force bystanders to say publicly what they saw.

LO 4.3 Technology and Young Adolescents

Not only do the ways young adolescents relate to technology have implications for how we teach and how they learn, but we are in classrooms with kids who take to technological innovations in natural ways and consider social media just part of everyday life. Technology is definitely an attraction, often a distraction, and may become an obsession. Young adolescents don't know a world without smartphones, iPads, blogs, instant messaging, Twitter, social networking sites, and whatever is new on a given day that allows kids to be in touch with friends, family, and the whole world through the Internet.

It's shocking to realize that on any given day, teenagers average about nine hours of entertainment media use, excluding time spent at school or for homework. Preteens average about six hours a day. Media of all sorts are an enormous presence in young adolescents' lives, claiming a huge share of their time and attention. Sadly, students from low-income homes and those who are black and Hispanic spend far more time with media, especially television, than white children and children from higher- and middle-income homes. Watching TV and listening to music are the most popular media regardless of age, gender, race, ethnicity, and socioeconomic status (Common Sense, 2015).

> *TWB* **Goal 4.** [Young adolescents] use digital tools to explore, communicate, and collaborate with the world and learn from the rich and varied resources available.

Sara Davis Powell

Most young adolescents sense the need to connect electronically with friends.

Social Media

Have you sat outside a middle school lately when the final bell rings? Here's what you'll see: ear buds immediately dangle from almost every bobbing head, thumbs go into full blown aerobic texting mode, small groups pose in silly and sometimes provocative ways as smartphones or tablets snap photos, and so on. The word **ubiquitous** means "everywhere at the same time, constantly encountered, widespread." Could there be a better word to describe **social media** among young adolescents?

Some argue that the ubiquitous nature of social media is bad for kids, that the constant communication through texting and instant messaging is damaging our ability to communicate verbally, to express our thoughts and opinions in reasoned, nonabbreviated ways, that spelling skills and correctness are things of the past, that civilization is damned. Well, that last one may be extreme. As a backlash, we hear reports of wealthy, technologically sophisticated parents insisting on schools for their children that incorporate nothing more tech-savvy than a whiteboard and colored markers. The children and young adolescents in the California Waldorf School of the Peninsula in Silicon Valley read actual paperback books, they use their fingers as math manipulatives, they learn to knit. The parents apparently see the possible downside of their children becoming engrossed in the very tools they themselves use to conduct business. They say there's plenty of time for technology use when the kids are older.

Cyberbullying

Teachers should learn to recognize, prevent, and help kids know how to respond when **cyberbullying** occurs. Sometimes it's easy to see cyberbullying for what it is: sudden mean messages. Other instances of cyberbullying take time to have an effect: posting of other kids' personal information, videos circulated that were meant for a few friends, and so on.

RECOGNIZE CYBERBULLYING   When a young adolescent is the target of cyberbullying, there are signs we should learn to recognize. When young adolescents decide to *be* the cyberbully, identical signs may be observed. They may:

- Be overly protective or secretive about online activities.
- Turn off the screen when someone comes near.
- Become withdrawn or show signs of depression.
- Be anxious or overly stressed.
- Stop using the computer and other technology.
- Suddenly avoid or change friends.
- Lose interest in activities or school.

PREVENT CYBERBULLYING   There are specific things we can do to help prevent cyberbullying, including:

- Implementing and enforcing a school antibullying code of conduct.
- Having students sign an antibullying and anticyberbullying pledge (to not participate and to speak up if someone is being bullied).
- Creating a safe place for students to voice concerns or problems.
- Talking with students about cyberbullying: what it is, the impact it has, and its consequences.
- Making it clear that cyberbullying will not be tolerated.
- Working with students to help raise cyberbullying awareness within the school through student-led clubs, assemblies, or posters (National Crime Prevention Council, 2017).

In addition, teachers should tell students to *never*:

- Post or share personal information, or that of a friend, online (including full name, address, telephone number, school name, parents' names, credit card, or Social Security number).
- Share Internet passwords with anyone, except your parents.
- Meet face to face with someone previously known only online (Powell, 2019).

HELP KIDS KNOW HOW TO RESPOND   If students suspect, or are certain, cyberbullying is occurring, teachers may advise them to:

- Tell an adult they trust about what's going on.
- Not delete any of the emails, texts, or messages. They can serve as evidence.
- Keep a record of incidents.
- Never forward any mean messages that spread rumors.
- Never plot revenge because it won't solve anything.
- Report the incident to the administrator of the website (National Crime Prevention Center, 2017).

FIGURE 4.2 Technology safeguards

- Never give identifying personal information such as home address, Social Security number, telephone number, and so on.
- Never send pictures that are in any way incriminating or suggestive.
- Never give out online passwords to anyone other than parents.
- Never "meet" anyone online.
- Never pass along anything hurtful about anyone.
- Never download software without parental permission.

SEXTING   One of the most frightening and potentially harmful types of cyberbullying is known as **sexting**. Yes, it's texting about sex. Many kids think sending, or passing along to others, nude or suggestive photos and texts is fun and/or semi-innocent flirting. However, it's much more, with social and legal consequences they never imagined. For the sender who thinks only a select person or group will see the photo or read the message, the surprise is that with a single click it can all be on the Internet where millions may view what was assumed would remain private. For the receiver who decides to broadcast the images of a minor child, pornography charges are possible, with his or her inclusion on police public pedophile lists. Parents and school personnel are justified in their concern that unthinking actions of kids may haunt them for the rest of their lives.

Cybercitizenship

We should teach students how to be good citizens in the cyberworld, hence the newly coined word **cybercitizenship**. In 2012, the federal government passed the Children's Online Privacy Protection Act (COPPA), a bill designed to make more transparent the operations of websites that cater to children. Legislating safety must be accompanied by both vigilance and common sense.

Make A Difference

It is important for middle level teachers to know what's going on around them concerning technology. For one thing, most technological advances have tremendous potential as teaching tools. But even if that's not the intent, we need to be aware of what our kids have access to. We need to see it all both as positive new means of communication and as potentially harmful innovations when used improperly. Figure 4.2 lists safeguards we can teach kids. Each safeguard should be accompanied by serious discussions about the harm that may come to young adolescents if they don't follow the guidelines. As middle level teachers, we must remember that the decision-making capabilities of our students are not fully developed. What we consider common sense may not even cross their still developing minds.

Some students have very serious concerns on their developing minds, like surviving from day to day and justifiably worrying about their futures. Let's next consider students who may need us the most—those living in low socioeconomic status (SES) homes and neighborhoods.

Self-Check 4. 3

LO 4.4 Poverty and Schooling

We defined and explored poverty in Chapter 3. Now we'll consider the effects of low socioeconomic status (SES) on teaching and learning. Many young adolescents who grow up in low SES circumstances are living in very loving homes with parents who sacrifice every day to provide shelter, food, and other life necessities. Their lives may be difficult, but they are supported by family and other adults. Then there are other kids in situations that are difficult not only financially but also in terms of support. Still others live in neighborhoods where gunfire is common and safety is elusive.

Making the Teaching and Learning Connection

 Hello, courageous future middle school teachers!

My name is Charles and I teach in the Dayton school district, one of the lowest SES areas in Ohio. Let me quickly add that I wouldn't want to teach in any other setting! Our focus is on preparing kids to be the first in their families to attend college. I am totally convinced my students can thrive when they are actively engaged in what they're learning.

Yes, most of my students are poor. They didn't choose to be poor. They didn't choose to live in neighborhoods that many people would never walk through in the day, much less after the sun goes down. They rely on us to teach them the knowledge and skills that will prepare them for today, for high school, for college, and for life. Pretty challenging, don't you think? The classmates I graduated with from University of Dayton often have trouble understanding why I teach, much less why I teach "those kids." But let me tell you, there's no greater challenge, nor more fulfilling satisfaction, than knowing these young men and women are motivated to learn in direct response to my faith in them.

I admit that my personality in the classroom comes naturally to me, but may not come naturally to you. I suppose my sense of humor and self-confidence have a lot to do with both my enjoyment and effectiveness in the classroom. But I have friends who don't sing songs, lead chants, or dance to illustrate vocabulary, and their students learn from them. Use your personality but don't be phony. Be who you are. Kids can see right through us.

My parting words of advice: Don't let poverty or any other obvious attribute of your kids daunt your enthusiasm for teaching. If you believe they can learn and achieve, they will believe it, too. Learning will happen and you can all celebrate. Go for it, my friends!

Charlie

Only 62% of children in persistently low-income homes, or those who spend more than half of their young lives in poverty, complete high school compared with 90% of children who never experience poverty (Radcliffe & Kalish, 2017). There are many reasons for this, with one actually dealing with brain development. **Toxic stress**, a possible result of living in poverty, can lead to impaired memory, making it harder to learn, solve problems, follow rules, pay attention, and control impulses (Boghani, 2017).

The more we know about our students' life circumstances, the better able we are to meet their needs. When a student acts out, we need to consider that the actions could be from the effects of poverty. We should be respectful, caring, and empathetic as we provide a solid foundation upon which learning can be built. A problem cited over and over in the literature is the lack of qualified teachers in schools with high percentages of kids in poverty. Yes, they have special challenges and, no, it's not easy. But think about the progress that's possible. One of our focus teachers, Jesse White, has chosen to focus his efforts on kids who live in low SES settings. He has options each year to teach in suburban schools and makes the choice to stay in an urban setting with kids who need him most. Read what he has to say about his decision in Teachers Speak.

Enhanced etext
Video Example 4. 1
One of the most enthusiastic teachers I have ever observed teaches in a Title I school in Dayton, Ohio. Watch as he teaches and then tells us about his love of the profession and of young adolescents.

Teachers Speak

Jesse White

My university teacher preparation program was for K–8 certification. When it came time to student teach, I asked for 4th or 5th grade. I was placed in an upscale elementary school where all but two of my 4th graders were Caucasian. Dream assignment, right? Well, that's what I thought. I was the envy of other student teachers. But I discovered early on that my heart wasn't in it. The kids were great, and my cooperating teacher was supportive. But something was missing. When I walked through the front door of Lincoln Middle School, I knew what it was. It took a while for me to put it in words, and sometimes it's still difficult to express my "calling" to other people, even to teachers. The kids at Lincoln both won my heart, and broke it at the same time. You see, they all live in public housing projects, qualify for free breakfast and lunch, are almost all black or Hispanic, and many have already failed a grade or two by the time they get to our 8th grade team. There are a few academic stars, but not many. And it seems like when one student begins to do well, he or she will often slip back very quickly because standing out isn't cool.

I try to celebrate progress, no matter how small, in ways that are special and not embarrassing to the kids. It's a fine line. There are days when there's absolutely nothing to celebrate . . . days when there's a cloud over our team of kids. Parent arrested, cousin shot, or frightening rumblings among gangs, and kids know something's up. Unfortunately, some of my kids are already junior gang members; some have no choice but to join. Then there are other days when what we're discussing or experiencing in social studies strikes a positive chord or catches their interest. One of my goals is to relate what's in the curriculum standards to something the kids can understand.

This is my sixth year in the classroom. It's time for me to begin a master's program, and I'm sure I will soon. Some of my teacher friends are in administrator-prep programs, but I don't see myself leaving the classroom. It may sound hokey, but I love my students. When I see a lightbulb come on in their heads as they get a concept, or when they just can't help but grin when I return a paper on which I've written a compliment, or they walk down the hall saying, "What's up, Mr. White?" I know I am where I need to be, and where I want to be.

Make a Difference

We can make a difference in the lives of students who struggle because of low socioeconomic status. Here are some suggestions:

- Know students well, acknowledge their challenges, and do what's necessary to understand how poverty affects them.
- Look for student strengths and find ways to build on them.
- Reject deficit theories that concentrate on what kids in poverty lack.
- Reach out to families and involve them in ways that suit their availability.
- Fight to ensure school meal programs are accessible.
- Teach a curriculum that includes people from all arenas of life.
- Increase reading instruction and reading activities to build basic skills.
- Teach the whole student, not just what relates to the curriculum.
- Build relationships with students.
- Monitor progress and celebrate even small successes.

Many young adolescents living in poverty have an additional challenge. English is not their first language.

Self-Check 4. 4

LO 4.5 English Learners

We began our discussion of English learners in Chapter 3. The following list illustrates the variability that may exist among EL students in your classroom and school:

- How long they have lived in the United States
- English proficiency of parents and other family members
- Educational attainment of parents and family members
- Ethnic/racial minority status
- Economic and social resources
- Permanency of lifestyle
- Literacy level in native language
- Academic success in native country.

> *TWB* Goal 10. [Young adolescents] respect and value the diverse ways people look, speak, think, and act within the immediate community and around the world.

Some EL students come to us from families whose parents are professionals with good jobs and have a record of academic success, but others arrive in our classrooms for short periods of time from families who struggle to support their children through intermittent work they must follow in order to survive. Some are legally in the United States, whereas others must continually look over their shoulders to watch for a U.S. immigration official who may send them back to their native country. These students are young adolescents who deserve our very best efforts in providing teaching and learning environments that help them succeed, not only in efforts to speak and comprehend English but to learn all of the content in our standards—a tall order.

Programs Designed for EL Students

Currently schools address the needs of English learners in one or more of three ways. The selection of a plan by a community depends on political and demographic profiles in the local population, as well as on what the district or state embraces philosophically.

Standard 5

Middle Level Professional Roles

Element c. Working with Family Members and Community Involvement: Middle level teacher candidates understand and value the ways diverse family structures and cultural backgrounds influence and enrich learning. They communicate and collaborate with all family members and community partners and participate in school and community activities. They engage in practices that build positive, collaborative relationships with families from diverse cultures and backgrounds (e.g., race, ethnicity, culture, age, appearance, ability, sexual orientation, socioeconomic status, family composition).

Enhanced eText
Video Example 4. 2
Teacher Angelica Reynosa in Fresno, California, exemplifies the skills required to effectively incorporate bilingual instruction.

- In **English as a second language (ESL)** programs, students receive individualized assistance once or twice a week for about an hour each session. With ESL, little or no emphasis is placed on preserving native language or culture, and ESL teachers do not need to speak another language. ESL programs are less expensive than bilingual programs for school districts to implement if they have limited numbers of students to serve.

- **Bilingual education** involves the delivery of instruction in two languages, with attempts to preserve and build on native language skills. A major barrier to bilingual instruction is the lack of teachers who are not only fluent in two languages but also qualified to teach math, science, social studies, and language arts, and, of course, basic reading and writing.

- **Structured English immersion (SEI)** is an approach to serving ELs that includes a significant amount of the school day spent in explicit instruction of the English language. Although other content areas are touched on, the primary focus is on teaching students to become proficient in reading, writing, and conversing in English. Students and teachers in SEI settings speak, read, and write in English. Teachers treat English as a foreign language and apply instructional methods of teachers of foreign languages. Students transition out of SEI programs on a specified timetable with the skills necessary to be successful in English-only classes.

As a "regular" classroom teacher, you will undoubtedly face the challenge of teaching young adolescents who are English learners. These students add a rich diversity to our classrooms. Take advantage of whatever assistance is offered.

Make a Difference

The literature about language diversity contains many suggestions concerning English learners in the classroom. Some are doable for teachers with little or no formal training in instructing ELs, and others may require more expertise and professional development than is readily available. Here are some things that may be within your reach in your middle level classroom:

- Know your students and their English proficiency levels. (Remember that no learning can be student-centered until we know our students.)
- Do what you can to activate the prior knowledge of EL students.
- Use as many relevant graphics and visuals relating to your curriculum as possible.
- View a variety of languages as an asset. Demonstrate and verbalize this both in attitude and action.
- Make real objects part of your instruction to illustrate concepts.
- Use clear scoring rubrics that enable you to be culturally sensitive in feedback.
- Monitor learning problems as best you can, given language barriers.
- Try peer-assisted learning if you have bilingual students in your classes.
- Encourage family involvement in your classroom and school.
- Utilize translating services for home communication.

Sara Davis Powell

Bilingual teacher Carmen Esparza teaches 90 minutes a day in each of three classes, one with 6th graders, one with 7th graders, and one with 8th graders. She teaches language arts and social studies, about half in English and half in Spanish. Students concentrate on becoming fluent in English, while strengthening their skills in Spanish as well.

- Make all languages visible through welcome signs, directions for routines, and so on.
- Validate other cultures in your classroom with artifacts, posters, anecdotes, inclusion of cultural customs, and persons of diversity in the curriculum.

Our efforts to meet the needs of English learners will no doubt change as more research and teacher experiences are incorporated into the body of knowledge. You will likely have ELs in your classroom, whether in the small towns of Maine or in the metropolises of California. Be innovative, be sensitive, and be respectful.

Now we focus on issues that cross cultural, language, and socioeconomic lines—wellness issues.

Self-Check 4. 5

LO 4.6 Wellness Issues

Although there are many wellness issues, we will focus on just a few, including substance abuse, sexuality-related concerns, childhood obesity, and a seemingly simple one to correct, lack of sleep. Day-to-day choices matter. Following each of the four topics—substance abuse, sexuality-related concerns, childhood obesity, sleeplessness—there's a Make a Difference section.

> *TWB* Goal 9. [Young adolescents] recognize, articulate, and make responsible, ethical decisions concerning his or her own health and wellness needs.

Substance Abuse

We need to have a realistic picture of what the situation is before talking about what we can do to help our students. A discussion of substance abuse benefits from the inclusion of data, so let's begin. You may need to read the numbers and percentages a couple of times to understand their impact. Take the time to let it sink in.

In 2016, approximately 2 million adolescents ages 12 to 17 used illicit drugs, which represents 8% of adolescents. We begin with statistics about the lesser-used drugs published by the Substance Abuse and Mental Health Services Administration (SAMHSA, 2016). When you read percentages like 1, or less than 1, don't dismiss the devastation. One percent of adolescents ages 12 to 17 amounts to 250,000 kids. Even one young adolescent is one too many. But 250,000? Devastating, indeed.

An estimated 389,000 young adolescents and adolescents misused prescription psychotherapeutic drugs (pain relievers, tranquilizers, stimulants, and sedatives) at least once in a given month. This is about 1 in 60 adolescents (1.6%) who misused psychotherapeutic drugs in 2016. That same year, 28,000, or 0.1% of adolescents, used cocaine. In the same group, less than 0.1% used heroin. An estimated 114,000 12- to 17-year-olds used hallucinogens, or 0.5% of adolescents.

Inhalants include a variety of substances, such as nitrous oxide, amyl nitrite, cleaning fluids, gasoline, spray paint, computer keyboard cleaner, felt-tip pens, and glue. Middle schoolers abuse potentially fatal chemicals more than any other age group. Inhalants are easy to obtain and use anywhere, even in school. One state reports 3,800 inhalant-related ER visits each year. Referring to death due to inhalants as Sudden Sniffing Death Syndrome, it's so sad that about 20% of those who die do so from one experimental use (The Recovery Village, 2017).

We have all heard news reports about opioid use, abuse, and substance use disorder. More than 64,000 American deaths were blamed on this relatively new phenomenon in 2017.

In 2016, approximately 11.8 million people ages 12 or older misused opioids. This number represents 4.4% of the population of the entire United States. About 891,000 adolescents (almost 4%) ages 12 to 17 misused opioids in 2016. In fact, deaths by overdose of all the substances listed so far have risen dramatically since 2010 (National Institute on Drug Abuse, 2017). Here's a list and the percentages of middle school students who have tried a variety of drugs (The Recovery Village, 2017).

- Marijuana (11.7%)
- Inhalants (5.3%)
- Synthetic marijuana (3.3%)
- Cough medicine (2%)
- Tranquilizers (1.7%)
- Adderall (1.3%) as a "study drug"
- Hallucinogens (1.3%)
- OxyContin (1%)
- Vicodin (1%)
- Cocaine (1%)
- Ecstasy or MDMA (0.9%)
- Ritalin (0.9%).

In addition to what we consider illicit drugs, young adolescents also abuse over-the-counter substances like cough syrup and pills that have to be consumed in large amounts to get what may be considered a high. There's no age limit, so kids can easily purchase the substances. Using them generally results in a miserable sickness that is often bad enough for the abuser to learn a valuable lesson. Some result in emergency room visits that reveal to parents that there's a problem. Anabolic steroids are abused by some middle level students who want to "bulk up." Most don't see using steroids as problematic (The Recovery Village, 2017).

Now let's look at use by adolescents of the more easily attained and commonly used substances—tobacco, alcohol, and marijuana. Table 4.1 provides basic information.

In 2016, 855,000 adolescents (3.4%) ages 12 to 17 smoked cigarettes in a given month. This percentage is a decline, and we want to keep the downward trend going. Tobacco use remains the leading preventable killer of Americans (SAMHSA, 2016).

Boys are more likely to try drinking alcohol before girls, with the average age of 11, around the end of elementary school. Among 12- to 20-year-olds, all underage and drinking illegally, about 7.3 million, or 19%, report alcohol use—12% were binge drinkers, and 3% were heavy drinkers. The relatively good news is that underage drinking in 2016 was lower than the percentages in 2002 through 2015 (SAMHSA, 2016).

TABLE 4.1 Percent of 12- to 17-year-olds reporting use of substances within a specific month in 2016 compared to 2002, 2008, 2012

Substance	2002	2008	2012	2016
Tobacco	13	9	7	3
Alcohol	29	27	24	19
Alcohol use disorder*	6	5	3	2
Marijuana	8	7	7	7
Marijuana use disorder**	4	3	3	2

*Alcohol use disorder was defined as meeting DSM-IV criteria for either dependence or abuse for alcohol.
**#x002A;Marijuana use disorder occurs when someone experiences clinically significant impairment caused by the recurrent use of marijuana, including health problems, persistent or increasing use, and failure to meet major responsibilities at work, school, or home.

Late in 2016, and again 2017 and 2018, more states voted to legalize recreational marijuana. For all of 2016 when our statistics were collected, marijuana (pot or weed) was legal for recreational use in Alaska, Colorado, Oregon, Washington, and the District of Columbia. It's actually surprising, then, that in 2016 only an estimated 24 million Americans ages 12 and older were current users of marijuana, a number that corresponds to 9% of the U.S. population. Even so, this percentage was higher than the percentages from 2002 to 2015. This increase in marijuana use reflects use by adults ages 26 or older and, to a lesser extent, the increase in marijuana use among young adults ages 18 to 25. In 2016, 6.5%, or approximately 1.6 million adolescents ages 12 to 17, used marijuana in a given month (SAMHSA, 2016).

Marijuana remains the most popular drug among middle school students, as it is with high school students. This isn't surprising since many of those high school students report starting to use marijuana before they were 13. Besides smoking it, young adolescents buy and sell edibles like cookies and brownies laced with marijuana. Sadly, about 40% of 8th graders say marijuana is easy to get, and the same percentage thinks regular use of the drug has no adverse side effects on their health or on their futures.

After reading these statistics, you are no doubt thinking about the harm of substance abuse for young adolescents. A brief list is in Figure 4.3. As teachers, we need to be aware of signs that students are experimenting in dangerous ways. Some of the behavioral signs of substance abuse correspond with what's considered normal behaviors of young adolescents; indeed, in small measure or infrequency, what you read in the list probably doesn't signal substance abuse, just expected stages many young adolescents experience. When we are observant and know our kids, we should be able to spot the behaviors in severity or in combination that may signal real problems. The list is long in Figure 4.4. Take the time to read and think through a scenario that might alert you to issues. Our kids' lives depend on it.

Make a Difference

Amid all the planning for instruction and creating a positive environment and the seemingly endless tasks of teaching middle level students, we must also do what we can to steer kids away from substances that will harm them. Here are some things to consider:

- Know the warning signs of substance abuse.
- Model good judgment in the use of legal substances and abstinence of illegal substances.
- Develop strong, trusting relationships with students so they will confide in you and respect your opinions.
- Make information available not only about the harm of substances but also about community resources kids can contact for support and help.

FIGURE 4.3 Possible ramifications of substance abuse

- Casual drug abuse can turn into full-fledged addiction
- Impaired thinking, decreased memory, and learning disability
- Lower graduation rates
- Trouble getting into college
- Struggles to find employment and become financially independent
- A life of crime
- Potentially fatal overdose
- Lack of judgment leading to a variety of risky behaviors.

FIGURE 4.4 Some of the behavioral signs of substance abuse

- Personality shifts with no apparent cause
- Changes in hobbies or activities
- Loss of interest in family activities
- Shifts in social circles, such as spending less time with old friends and more time with new friends, particularly if the new friends are known drug users
- Neglect of personal hygiene habits
- Loss of motivation, self-esteem, or energy
- Sudden drop in grades or work performance
- Being late for or skipping work or school
- Repeated dishonesty or deceit
- Suspicious or secretive behavior
- Excessive desire for privacy at strange times
- Forgetfulness and difficulty paying attention
- Unexplained temper tantrums or oversensitivity
- Unexplained giddiness, bounciness, or silliness
- Unexplained nervousness, moodiness, or irritability
- Unexplained scrapes, scratches, or injuries
- Paranoia
- Unexplained need for money
- Financial irresponsibility
- Stealing money or prescription pills
- Repeated dishonesty or deceit
- Tremors or shakiness in the hands or feet
- Slowed or swaying walk
- Loss of physical coordination
- Runny nose or cough
- Red or watery eyes
- Pupils that are larger or smaller than normal
- Flushing or paleness
- Uncharacteristic sluggishness, laziness, hyperactivity, or talkativeness
- Strange odors on breath or clothes.

Source: The Recovery Village, 2017.

Sexuality-Related Issues

It's hard to imagine that Jenny, as we see her in her 7th grade school photo, would know about sexual intercourse, much less actually experience it. But she did. She's 12 and pregnant. Jenny lives with her grandparents and plans to keep her baby. She tells me the father of her baby, age 16, will be involved in her life and the life of the precious child she will soon have. The vast majority of teen mothers are unmarried, a fact that puts them and their babies at high risk of living in poverty.

Teen pregnancy rates have declined steadily since the 1960s. That fact doesn't matter now to Jenny. Too many young adolescents are engaging in sexual activity, and many are suffering physical, as well as psychological, consequences. Sexual experimentation can result in sexually transmitted diseases (STDs) and transmission of the HIV virus that can lead to AIDS. Although their bodies may accommodate sexual activities, young adolescents aren't ready for the emotional and social dilemmas that accompany early sexual activity.

Sara Davis Powell

Sara Davis Powell

In her school picture, Jenny is a pretty, emerging young adolescent. Months after this picture was taken, what sets her apart among her 12- and 13-year-old friends is that she'll soon be a mom.

Make a Difference

This is a sensitive area of development that some schools address in well-conceived health education programs, while other schools fail to address the issues in any kind of organized, effective way. Young adolescents need information delivered in understandable, matter-of-fact ways. As with any form of self-destruction, students' ability to use refusal skills increases with their own sense of self-worth and self-confidence. Teachers can be instrumental in helping kids become better decision makers, armed with knowledge of what's wise and healthy.

Childhood Obesity

More than one third of the children and adolescents in America are overweight or obese (Kids Health, 2017). That's triple the number since 1970. It's an epidemic with no legal remedy. Food is legal, and abundant for most children; exercise isn't mandated. Obese children are well above the normal weight for their age and height. The causes of this obesity epidemic are numerous and well documented. According to the Centers for Disease Control and Prevention (CDC), they include:

- Genetics
- Metabolism
- Eating and physical activity barriers
- Environmental factors
- Social and individual psychology (CDC, 2017).

They continue by stating, "Over time, consuming more energy from foods and beverages than the body uses for healthy functioning, growth, and physical activity, leads to extra weight gain. Energy imbalance is a key factor behind the high rates of obesity seen in the United States and globally" (CDC, 2017). Allow me to add these causes:

Sara Davis Powell

Childhood obesity may set today's youth apart from all others in the history of our country. Because of health problems related to obesity, this generation of kids may live shorter, less healthy lives on average than their parents.

- increases in media use leading to young "couch potatoes"
- fast food restaurants
- decrease in family dinner time, with reliance on "junk food"
- failure of some schools to follow mandates for physical activity required daily minutes
- adult obesity. It seems that with each passing year the parents of my students have gotten fatter and fatter. I understand that I'm not being politically correct to say this, but it's true. When I meet some parents I think, "This poor child doesn't stand a chance of being a healthy weight." Home role models of healthy living are becoming harder and harder to find.

For the first time in generations, today's adolescents may live, on average, shorter and less healthy life spans than their parents. And it's not drugs, alcohol, tobacco, or early sexual activity that will prove to be the culprit. It's unhealthy food, accompanied by a sedentary lifestyle. Serious health problems once thought to strike only adults are becoming commonplace among overweight adolescents, including:

- High blood pressure and high cholesterol, risk factors for cardiovascular disease
- Increased risk of impaired glucose tolerance, insulin resistance, and type 2 diabetes
- Breathing problems, such as asthma
- Joint problems and musculoskeletal discomfort
- Fatty liver disease, gallstones, and gastroesophageal reflux (i.e., heartburn)
- Psychological problems such as anxiety and depression
- Low self-esteem and lower self-reported quality of life
- Social problems such as bullying and stigma. (CDC, 2017)

Make a Difference

The Child Nutrition Reauthorization Act of 2004 mandated that school districts develop wellness policies that address what students eat in school, the kinds and amounts of physical activity they experience, and the provisions for health education. Most schools have removed machines that offer sugary drinks and unhealthy snacks. However, some cafeteria food contributes to both lack of nutrition and obesity. When choices routinely include pizza, hamburgers, and fries, kids will likely gravitate to them. When students may or may not participate in exercise, many will opt out.

We can be role models for our students. We can make wise choices in terms of nutrition and be physically active. We can be vocal advocates for young adolescents' health. To not do so contributes to this growing, serious problem of childhood obesity.

Sleep Issues

We hear it all the time, and often pay little attention. Sleep matters. Sleep has much to do with overall health. Sleep is essential to concentration and productivity. Research labeled "bell time studies" abound, telling us that the decades-old battle over when to start school is almost always won by arguments about when adults go to work, necessitating start times, bus route transportation issues, and just plain "this is the way we've always done it." Poor excuses for requiring early start times for adolescents whose circadian rhythms, or how our bodies naturally dictate things like waking and sleeping, are different for both young children and many adults.

Sleep is food for the brain (National Sleep Foundation, 2018). Important body functions and brain activity occur when we sleep. Aside from moodiness and poor school performance, sleepiness accounts for more than 100,000 car crashes each year. Staggering, isn't it? The foundation says that a body and brain hungry for sleep will get it, and often when we don't expect it and without our consent. When a student falls asleep in your class or eyelids flutter during an American Revolution discussion or the factoring of binomials, it's sleep deprivation—a health issue.

Sara Davis Powell

Schools can help young adolescents live healthier lives by providing snack choices that promote better nutrition.

Today, sleep deprivation is one of the most common and easily fixable public health issues in the United States. The American Academy of Pediatrics recommends that middle and high schools never start before 8:30 a.m. Any earlier is unhealthy, unsafe, and counterproductive. Most teenagers can't fall asleep before 11 p.m. Needing 8 to 9 hours of sleep, catching a 6 a.m. bus for a 7 a.m. start time, simply doesn't work. According to James Maas, a sleep expert at Cornell University, "Almost all teenagers, as they reach puberty, become walking zombies because they are getting far too little sleep" (Snider, 2014).

"Children and adolescents who don't get enough sleep are at increased risk for obesity, diabetes, injuries, poor mental health, and attention and behavior problems, which can affect them academically," according to the CDC. A major CDC study reveals that 58% of middle school students and 73% of high school students don't get a healthy amount of sleep on weeknights (Reinberg, 2018). That's a majority of U.S. kids. All the health and behavior issues in this chapter could result merely from young adolescents' lack of sleep. I wish it were that simple, but, of course, it isn't. However, it is something we need to understand about our kids and, when the opportunity presents itself, take a stand and fight for change. School districts will almost always fight the idea of later start times, but it's a winnable battle if we rally enough stakeholders for the cause.

Make a Difference

As educators we can't ignore health issues, so let's educate our students about the benefits of adequate sleep and how they may increase their sleep amounts. What can we do besides talk to our kids and fight a steep uphill battle concerning delayed start times? Not much, unfortunately, without the help of families.

- This will also be a battle, but because strong light before bedtime is detrimental to falling asleep, that light from phones and iPads kids stare at late at night may be keeping them awake longer. If they won't turn them off at 9 p.m., then perhaps turning the brightness down may help. Or how about the radical idea of no media in the bedroom?

- Parents can be encouraged to set a good example by turning in earlier and insisting on all lights out by 10 p.m. Media curfews may be something parents haven't realized can actually be very important to adolescent health. Tell them!

- When we wake, studies show that letting in light immediately wakes our brains. Tell families this.

- Going to bed worried prevents the most restful sleep. Relaxation techniques may help such as an opportunity each evening to talk about how the day went or simply a warm bath or shower.

- A high-carb snack may help, such as pretzels, cereal, fruit, cookies, toast with jelly, and more. These snacks can bring on sleepiness. No caffeine after 8 p.m. is also a good rule. One cup of hot herbal tea works, but may require a bit of coaxing (Asp, 2016).

Self-Check 4. 6

Why It Matters

For many young adolescents, growing up is not easy. This isn't a new phenomenon, but as a future middle level teacher you should be aware of the societal context in which your students live. There are some issues we are helpless to affect, but with others, we can make a difference. Be that difference for your students. They're depending on you.

Sometimes as teachers we feel like so much of what happens in the lives of our students is out of our control. And it's true. As part of a school, we have about seven hours a day, 180 days a year, to have a positive impact. That's a big chunk of time, but time alone won't change developmental aspects of their lives, their homes, neighborhoods, socioeconomic status, health-related choices, and so on. What we can control is ourselves—our attitudes, our levels of effort, our careful consideration when making decisions, our passion for the teaching profession and its inherent responsibilities and opportunities. This chapter began with an analogy we should consider again as we close.

"We cannot control the wind, but we can adjust our sails." Teachers recognize that the social issues that negatively affect our students are complex and multidimensional. They don't begin with us, and most won't be completely resolved through us. Our responsibility is to do what we can, for whom we can, as often as we can.

Group Activities

1. As a group, think about the negative societal context issues the young adolescents in your area may be most likely to encounter. Other issues to consider include violence, theft, neglectful parents, and child abuse. Decide on several and, in small groups, do Web searches for more information about them. Share what you discover.

2. Brainstorm ways teachers might positively affect the decision-making skills of students on issues such as substance abuse, sexuality-related issues, and obesity.

3. Have a discussion about where and when you have experienced or witnessed bullying. What harm occurred because of the incidences?

Individual Activities

1. Why is it important for teachers and schools to be involved in student wellness issues? Why do you think some educators hesitate to do so? What role do you think parents and the community should play in setting limits for school involvement in sensitive issues?

2. Think about the subject(s) you want to teach. At what point in your curriculum do you think you might address one of the societal issues discussed in this chapter?

3. Have you encountered English learners either as a middle school student or as an adult? If so, what do you remember about the experience(s)?

Personal Journal

1. Think about the societal context in which you grew up. What influenced you most?

2. What societal elements have the most influence on you today? Are there influences that you have now that are also applicable to young adolescents?

3. Have you ever been bullied? If so, what were the circumstances? Have you ever been a bully? If so, what were the circumstances? Have you ever been a bystander of bullying? If so, what were the circumstances?

Professional Practice

(It will be helpful to reread the descriptions of Keith Richardson in Chapter 1 and Andy in Chapter 2.)

Keith Richardson

Because Keith is only in his second year of teaching, after an 18-year career in business, he is still looking at students through new eyes. A number of things bother him. One problem he sees not only in his classroom, but also in his community, is obesity. In fact, there are times when he goes to Walmart or to a restaurant and has a hard time spotting people around him who are not overweight. He and his wife have talked about this growing problem for years. They are both fit, as are their children. Now that Keith is a teacher, he is continually reminded of the problem when he looks at the 6th graders on his team and the rest of the young adolescents at Hamilton Middle School.

Kids at Hamilton take P.E. one semester each year. That's not enough to meet the state guidelines, but no one appears concerned. There are still unhealthy snack machines in the hallway and frequent lunch choices include fries, hot dogs, hamburgers, and pizza. Because Keith is a relatively new teacher, he hesitates to speak up for fear of offending his grossly overweight principal, as well as one of his team teachers.

Andy sixth grade

One of Keith's students who is well on his way to being obese is Andy. Recall from Chapter 3 that Andy is an only child whose mom died a couple of years ago. Andy's dad is overweight. Besides being overweight, Andy shows signs of being a bully, although he doesn't display overt bullying behaviors that get him into trouble, at least not yet. Keith is observing subtle signs of bullying like the looks he gives a couple of the smaller boys on the team. The looks are "evil," with squinting eyes and a frown. The other boys look away, and walk away. As he becomes more watchful, he notices that the two other boys often end up without their supplies and lunch money. He suspects this may have something to do with Andy. He wonders if Andy's expanding size has anything to do with what appears to be bullying behavior.

Remember that for some items, more than one choice may be defensible. The purpose of the items is to stimulate thought and discussion.

1. Keith wants to start an initiative that might have an impact on the activity level of the kids at Hamilton. He wants to develop a walking trail on the school property that consists of five fenced-in acres. Here's the problem he wants to address with his initiative. When kids finish lunch, they are allowed to either go outside or stay in the cafeteria. Those who stay inside just sit and talk. Those who go outside generally do the same. The few kids who are active are those who are normal weight. Keith wants to propose that all kids go outside, weather permitting, when they finish lunch and walk the trail until it's time to go back to class. Which of the following obstacles will be the most critical for Keith to overcome?

   a. His principal may not see the need for the project.
   b. It will take time and energy, along with volunteers, to make the trail a reality.

(Continued)

c. The teachers at Hamilton will have to be "on board" and support the initiative for it to work.

d. There may be be some expenses involved in the project.

2. If Keith's initiative is put in place, the students at Hamilton can simply be told that this is how they will spend their lunch breaks. However, for the walking trail to succeed in not only increasing activity for 15 minutes a day but also affecting how students view fitness, which of the following actions will likely have the most impact?

a. Teachers enthusiastically walk the trail and show obvious enjoyment of the experience.

b. The kids are encouraged to both run and walk to see who can make the most laps.

c. Each student is given a pedometer so data can be kept and math problems developed around this authentic experience.

d. The walk includes a weekly scavenger hunt for items on the trail.

3. While Keith is working on his plan, he is trying to figure out how to approach the fact that Hamilton P.E. classes don't provide either enough minutes or the activity levels that are addressed in state guidelines. What should he do?

a. Make a suggestion at a faculty meeting that the issue be addressed by the principal.

b. Talk with the P.E. teacher to become smarter about the history of P.E. at Hamilton to better understand why classes are not full-year and why many days are spent indoors in a classroom rather than outside or in the gym.

c. Call the district office and speak with the director of Health and Physical Education.

d. Continue working on the walking trail and wait until he has accomplished this initiative before tackling another.

4. Although Keith may never know for sure whether Andy's weight contributes to what he is now certain is bullying, he knows something needs to happen. What are three things Keith might do to address this issue?

Chapter 5
Structures of Middle Level Education

Sara Davis Powell

The ways schools organize teachers and group and schedule students have a significant impact on the learning environment. . . . The team is the foundation for a strong learning community characterized by a sense of family.

THIS WE BELIEVE, P. 31.

 Learning Outcomes

After studying this chapter, you will have knowledge and skills to:

5.1 Articulate *structures of people* in middle level settings, including student groupings, teaming, and advisory programs.

5.2 Describe *structures of time* appropriate for young adolescents, including traditional schedules and block schedules.

5.3 Focus on ways to enhance *structures of place* in middle level settings, specifically in the classroom.

Dear Future Middle Level Teacher,

When I was hired for my first teaching assignment, 6th grade math, I was very anxious about the logistics of the position: When are my classes? Where is my classroom? What classes will I teach? Will I work with other teachers? These are the classic *when, where, what,* and *who* questions that set the stage for the work to be done. No doubt you will be anxious to know the same things when you begin your career. Once these questions are answered, we're free to make plans for teaching and learning.

Structure gives shape and support to middle level education. Developmentally responsive structures provide both framework and opportunity for the middle level educator to build on best practices with as few impediments as possible. As you read, there's a big *if* to keep in mind. The structures will only be effective *if* teachers make the most of the opportunities. Without intentional, concerted effort, the structures fall flat. For instance, organizing teachers and students into interdisciplinary teams is an organizational change and not a guarantee that the potential benefits of teaming will be realized.

In this chapter we explore structures of people, time, and place that are believed to be appropriate for young adolescents. These are elements to look for when determining a school's degree of adherence to middle level philosophy as articulated in *Turning Points* (Carnegie Council on Adolescent Development, 1989) and *This We Believe* (National Middle School Association, 2010). I hope you have the good fortune to be part of a school that aligns with middle level philosophy.

SDP

LO 5.1 Structures of People

As dynamic, living organizations, middle schools revolve around relationships that set the tone and determine the climate. Our challenge as teachers is to create structures of people that best promote learning and growth. In this section, we examine homogeneous and heterogeneous grouping, interdisciplinary teaming, looping, school-within-a-school, and advisory programs.

Grouping Students

Perhaps the most controversial of all philosophical dilemmas concerning structuring adolescents within middle level settings is the homogeneous versus heterogeneous grouping debate. **Homogeneous ability grouping**, or **tracking** as it is commonly called, has been the norm in most levels of schooling for many years. It seems to make sense to test students and put them into classes based on their abilities and achievement levels so curriculum and instruction can be tailored to meet their specific needs. It appears reasonable to expect teachers to teach at their best when presented with groups of students who fall within narrow bands of intelligence and aptitude. What "makes sense" and "appears reasonable" dictates what often prevails in practice, in direct opposition to middle level philosophy. Keep in mind that a *homogeneous middle level classroom* is really an oxymoron. There are not 2, much less 20, middle level students who respond in the same way and at the same time to any given scenario.

Tracking indicates static grouping where kids are placed in a particular class, or group within a class, without opportunities to move up or down based on learning progress or the lack of it. *Turning Points 2000* clearly calls for **heterogeneous ability grouping** of students, meaning that students in any given class represent the spectrum of ability levels in the school student population (Jackson & Davis, 2000). Still, homogeneous ability grouping is prevalent in schools that otherwise follow the tenets of middle grades education. The arguments for and against **ability grouping** have been the same for decades. It seems clear that ongoing research is needed on the topic of homogeneous versus heterogeneous ability grouping.

THE CASE FOR TRACKING   The literature available on the topic of tracking indicates that the case for it is based on the following propositions: tracking helps schools meet the varying needs of students; tracking provides low-achieving students with the attention and slower pace they require; high-achieving students are provided with challenges when tracked; tracking is necessary for individualizing instruction; and tracking will prevent low-achievers from hindering the progress of high-achievers.

It's easier to plan for instruction for a homogeneous class. Materials and teaching methods can be chosen specifically for the ability level of the students. High-achieving groups can sometimes "teach themselves." They often seem to thrive regardless of the curriculum and instruction. At the other end of the spectrum, teaching a class of low-achievers has been, and often still is, a matter of drill and practice in a worksheet-rich environment if the teacher is not committed to a type of instruction that is more interesting and challenging to students, and more difficult to plan. Perhaps it's not the grouping but the quality of instruction that makes a difference.

THE CASE AGAINST TRACKING   The literature available on tracking indicates that the case against it relies on the following propositions: tracking is detrimental to young adolescent peer relationships; it is harmful to the self-esteem of low-achievers; it perpetuates class and racial inequities; the grouping process is often biased; it reinforces inaccurate assumptions about intelligence; and the least experienced teachers are typically assigned to low-achieving classes. Donna San Antonio states that in her 30-year-long experience of studying the world of young adolescents, "No area of my study surprised me more than the connections among ability grouping, social class, and the development of social perceptions. Students in accelerated classes were more than three times more likely to be from wealthier communities than from poorer ones" (2006, p. 10). Her findings extend to the reality that most gifted classes consist primarily of white and Asian students from middle income or above homes (Grissom and Redding, 2016).

Middle level philosophy in *Turning Points 2000* tells us that diversity of all kinds is important in classrooms—achievement levels, interests, learning preferences, and more—with instruction varied to address differences (Jackson & Davis, 2000). The reality of what actually occurs in our schools often does not follow this philosophy. A major benefit of the team structure is that it supports heterogeneous grouping of students while allowing for grouping and regrouping as determined by individual student needs and the curriculum.

There is perhaps, a viable compromise that exists in many middle level settings. Some middle level schools restrict grouping to subjects that are overtly hierarchical in nature. A common configuration of courses involves tracking in math and language arts, with heterogeneous grouping in science, social studies, and noncore classes. For those adamantly opposed to any kind of tracking, it may be difficult to accept this compromise. Tracking is deeply embedded in our schools and is unlikely to be eliminated. Chances are you will encounter some form of tracking in your school and may have no choice as to whether or not to practice it.

FLEXIBLE ABILITY GROUPING   Let's establish the difference between tracking and **flexible ability grouping**. Whereas tracking, or ability grouping, calls for static groups, flexible ability grouping calls for grouping and regrouping that meets individual learning needs. Flexible ability grouping is a no-cost way to boost student

Sara Davis Powell

With flexible ability grouping students move in and out of groups, depending on individual progress.

achievement. However, even though there's evidence that using time in flexible ways benefits learners, some have called flexible ability grouping the evil twin of tracking (Olszewski-Kubilius, 2013). Implemented effectively, flexible ability grouping does not have the stigma, nor cause the potential harm, of inflexible tracking.

Flexible ability grouping requires ongoing and varied assessment practices, record keeping, and vigilance on the part of teachers. To avoid permanently labeling students, teachers must carefully reassign groups based on assessment results. Flexible ability grouping allows us to provide instruction that matches student readiness. When used appropriately, flexible grouping helps us implement instruction at the right time for varying student levels of mastery. Teachers must be able and willing to detect when and where students should be grouped to maximize students' abilities and learning.

Teaming

"No single educational idea has come to characterize the middle school concept as certainly as has interdisciplinary **teaming**" (Lounsbury, 1991, p. 58). Creating teams of teachers and students is vital to the development of a middle level **community of learners**. This partnership of shared time, space, instructional and curricular emphases, and philosophy can make a large school feel smaller and reduce anonymity for young adolescents and adults alike. Within a team, a small group of teachers takes primary responsibility for facilitating academic and social growth of a specific group of students. I am convinced that the adage "An individual can make a difference: a team can make a miracle" is true.

As with any organizational structure, teaming is as powerful as the people involved choose to make it. The structure provides the opportunity, but teacher determination and creativity are necessary for successful implementation.

TEAM ORGANIZATION Teams in middle schools are most often **interdisciplinary teams**, with each teacher responsible for one or more subject areas. They represent at least the subjects considered core: language arts, social studies, science, and math.

Standard 3
Middle Level Philosophy and School Organization

Element b. Middle Level Organization and Best Practices: Middle level teacher candidates utilize their knowledge of the effective components of middle level programs and schools to foster equitable educational practices and to enhance learning for all students (e.g., race, ethnicity, culture, age, appearance, ability, sexual orientation, socioeconomic status, family composition). They demonstrate their ability to apply this knowledge and to function successfully within a variety of school organizational settings (e.g., grades K–8, 6–8, 7–12). Middle level teacher candidates perform successfully in middle level programs and practices such as interdisciplinary teaming, advisory programs, flexible block schedules, and common teacher planning time.

Positive results are achieved from a wide variety of team sizes. Teams commonly consist of as few as 2 teachers and 40 students to as many as 4 core teachers plus related arts, special education, and resource teachers and more than 125 students. Because "one size fits all" does not make sense when it comes to team configurations, many decisions are required about the composition of teacher expertise, space, time, student demographics, and other relevant variables. The goal is to create an effective organizational scheme that produces a learning environment that meets the needs of middle level students. Smaller teams of two or three teachers are often created for 5th and 6th grade to more closely resemble self-contained classrooms, whereas larger teams are dominant in 7th and 8th grade. Regardless of the size of the team, teachers planning together is vital to ensure success.

COMMON PLANNING TIME To function effectively, team teachers need adequate time to meet and plan. **Common planning time** is defined as "a regularly scheduled time for teachers with the same students to meet and plan" (Caskey, Anfara, Mertens, & Flowers, 2013). The definition is in *Common Planning Time in Middle Level Schools,* a chronicle of research studies conducted by middle level teacher educators from around the country as part of the National Middle Grades Project on Common Planning Time. This project was a study involving 500 surveys in 23 schools in seven states to determine teachers' perceptions and uses of common planning time. In 2012, as the project was underway, researchers strongly agreed that common planning time has the potential to affect student learning through, among other things, serving as a valuable tool for increasing teacher knowledge and skills (Caskey & Carpenter, 2012). With common planning time, teachers learn from each other through meaningful peer interaction as they coordinate assignments, assessments, and activities.

Teachers report that this time together allows them to use their collective knowledge to be on the same page in terms of recognizing student needs, planning for curriculum and instruction, and, in general, providing stability for young adolescents. The frequency and length of common planning time have a major impact on the effective functioning of teachers on a team. Team planning time typically occurs during students' related arts classes when all the core teachers are available to meet. So much can be accomplished by teachers working together. As team members, we should respect team planning by being on time and focused. Having an agenda for topics to be discussed and decisions to be made over the course of a week helps us stay on task. Team planning time should be separate from, and in addition to, individual planning time. A school and administration that value effective team functioning will arrange the schedule to accommodate both. Having to choose between using a planning period for individual planning or team planning is no choice at all. Both are vital to instructional effectiveness with young adolescents. Figure 5.1 gives you an idea of the variety of decisions and projects that teams of teachers confront. This list is by no means exhaustive. So many issues, so little time!

Mertens, Hurd, and Tilford (2013) found that the two endeavors ranked as most frequent in their research were discussing student learning issues and discussing student behavior issues. While these problems are daily attention-getters, and for very legitimate reasons, the researchers propose that if teachers were better trained in how to effectively use common planning time, perhaps concepts that require large measures of collaboration and interdisciplinary approaches, such as developing curriculum and integrating concepts, might garner a larger percentage of team time. An efficient and focused team can do so much with 4 or 5 days of 30 to 45 minutes common planning time each!

In the project, common planning time was considered essential by the interdisciplinary teams. The researchers found that there were three necessary components of effective use of common planning time: a common vision and mission, clearly defined

---

FIGURE 5.1 Possible agenda items for team planning

- Upcoming thematic unit
- Student progress reports
- Scheduling of parent conference(s)
- Student disciplinary issues
- Overlapping curricular topics
- Special education referrals
- Field trip to museum
- Problem with graffiti in boys' bathroom
- Encouraging parent participation
- Rotating responsibility for student teacher
- Participation in writing competitions
- New rules during construction on field
- Use of computer lab time
- Discussing article given to team by principal
- Jointly grading unit projects
- Discussion of individual students as need arises
- Preparing for long-term substitute for teacher requiring maternity leave
- Book fair approaching
- Bulletin board display rotation
- Choosing liaison to a district committee.

---

goals, and effective building-level leadership, namely a supportive principal. They tell us that common planning time can be "the vehicle by which [the principal] enhances communication, demonstrates support, encourages professionalism, and empowers teachers to collaborate, make decisions, and share in the leadership of the school" (Faulkner & Cook, 2013, p. 85). Everyone wins, particularly the kids, when these conditions pervade a school's culture.

TEAM LEADERSHIP AND MEMBERSHIP Every team needs a designated facilitator, usually called the *team leader*. This task is sometimes rotated among members for varying lengths of time. Being a team leader takes more time than being a team member. Agendas must be made, extra meetings are often required with schoolwide leadership teams, communication among team members and school administrators generally falls to the team leader, and the day-to-day functioning of the team relies in great measure on the team leader's efficiency.

Being a good team member is a task to be taken seriously. Traits that are common among those who are valued team members include the following:

- Participatory, carrying through with all team decisions
- Collaborative, even when things aren't going their way
- Pleasant, even when circumstances make it difficult
- Responsible, completing tasks and showing up on time
- Energetic, finding ways to do what's needed when it's needed
- Honest and trustworthy, avoiding talking behind teammates' backs
- Open-minded, willing to learn and try new strategies
- Caring, always putting student needs first.

The choice of teachers and students who will comprise a team should not be random. Teams need to bring together teachers who have varying subject-area expertise, different backgrounds to add diversity, and personalities that combine to give the team collective power. Best friends do not necessarily make the best teammates.

The composition of students on a team is as important as the mix of teachers. A team should be a microcosm of the whole school, reflecting heterogeneity in terms of ethnicity, socioeconomic background, gender, special education status, and academic achievement. We should be careful not to weight a team heavily with either high-achievers or low-achievers (Jackson & Davis, 2000).

The quality of teaming is enhanced by staff development, both before implementing teaming and on a regular basis after teams are established to promote increased effectiveness. Learning how to set goals, provide consistent support, communicate openly, and collaborate willingly requires concerted effort and training.

A recommendation that enhances the well-made choice of team members, staff development to help members grow, and efficient use of team planning time is the stabilization of team continuity for at least 3 years. Newly formed teams function differently than teams that have been together for a number of years. If norms have been established that foster effectiveness, then keeping teams together makes sense (Jackson & Davis, 2000). Teams can take specific actions to help members grow together and enhance one another, some of which are listed in Figure 5.2. Most important, student welfare must guide all decisions and actions. Effective teams put students first.

BENEFITS OF TEAMING   As you can imagine after reading the preceding discussion, effective teaming has far-reaching benefits. The benefits of teaming are listed on the next page in Figure 5.3 and are referred to throughout the rest of this text.

Curriculum integration is a major benefit of teaming because it helps students understand who and why and how of the curriculum. It's not about making forced connections, but rather looking for and being conscious of natural links. Teams of teachers can coordinate assignments, focus on larger skills and concepts, and progress logically through subject matter. In Chapter 6, we explore ways to plan for curriculum integration.

INVOLVING OTHER SCHOOL PROFESSIONALS   Most middle school teams are limited to core curriculum teachers. Our students spend the majority of their school time with this group of two to five teachers. However, involving other school professionals makes the teaching/learning connection more viable.

Courses taught outside the core are sometimes called related arts, **exploratory** curriculum, **wheel courses** (referring to the fact that they are rotated), or **encore courses** (Get it? Encore, as opposed to *core*?). Perhaps the most generic term is **related arts**, so we'll stick with that. Related arts courses are vital to middle level philosophy. They provide skills training, use talents, and motivate students to pursue real-life activities. As an unintended benefit, related arts teachers and their courses are the main reason teams are able to benefit from common planning time. While appreciating related arts teachers for the valuable learning resources they provide to our students, we also realize that without them core teams could not function effectively. Often, related arts teachers

---

FIGURE 5.2 Ways for teams to increase effectiveness

- Establish a team name and motto
- Build ownership and enthusiasm
- Spend time together in productive ways as they show care and concern for one another and for students
- Come to consensus on a philosophy, and then publicize and teach according to that philosophy
- Take advantage of opportunities to alter their schedule within flexible blocks of time
- Group and regroup students for instruction
- Work together to accomplish all the items on their ever-growing, ever-changing agenda
- Meet with students and confer with parents as a unit
- Plan curriculum together and make connections among concepts and topics using varied instructional strategies.

FIGURE 5.3 Benefits of teaming for teachers and students

Benefits for Teachers

Teachers get to know students well.
Procedures and routines are consistent.
Decisions are made collaboratively.
Collegiality and professionalism are enhanced.
Synergy is created by combining strengths.
Intellectual stimulation is the result of collaboration.
Instructional strategies may be shared.
Curriculum integration is easier to implement.
Assessment is enhanced by joint evaluation.
Classroom management is more consistent.

Benefits for Students

Teachers get to know students well.
Learning environment is more personalized.
Sense of belonging is created.
Connections among curricular areas are more obvious.
Support from teachers is comprehensive.
More opportunities for grouping and regrouping exist.

---

have insights about student motivation, behavior, and talent that core teachers do not. Finding ways to involve related arts teachers in team planning benefits everyone. Perhaps a substitute could be arranged for the related arts teachers periodically to allow them to participate in team planning time.

The **principal** plays a pivotal role in the success of teaming. When first implemented, teaming requires fundamental changes in any school's organization. To make the logistics work, principals have to rethink staffing, time allocations, scheduling, and use of facilities. To begin and then continue the structure of teaming requires the principal to understand and support the concept and benefits of interdisciplinary teams. Providing ways for related arts teachers to meet with teams of core teachers is an example of principal support.

The structure of special education in middle school is increasingly inclusive. This means that students who qualify for special services, or students with **exceptionalities**, are part of both core and related arts courses. If the schedule can be arranged, everyone involved benefits from having *special educators* in the classroom alongside core and related arts teachers, all working in concert with students with special needs and other students in need of assistance. Some schools have even arranged schedules that support co-planning and co-teaching. As teams of students reflect the school population, they share equally the students who have physical and learning differences. Many schools designate special education teachers to be part of specific teams and serve the students of those teams. In smaller schools, the special educators may serve the entire population of students with special needs.

Guidance counselors can have a tremendous influence in middle level settings. Counselors who are compassionate, committed, and specially trained to work with young adolescents have the potential to make significant differences in the life of a school. Teams of teachers should communicate regularly with guidance counselors about the students they serve.

CREATING TEAM IDENTITY   The teachers' vision for their team leads the team to a unique persona, an identity that is recognizable. An element of "this is who we are" does much to unify and motivate both teachers and students.

A team name is essential. Don't announce to students in August that they should be proud to be members of team 7B. Screams excitement, doesn't it? How about "Welcome to the Stargazers! Stargazers dream big and aspire to reach the stars," as the lights go out and stars are projected around the room? Now that's an attention-getter! Some teams of teachers choose a name and a theme and stick with it year after year. They accumulate "stuff" that speaks to their theme. It grows with time. Other teams allow students to choose a name and theme each year. They let the students experience the democratic process and take ownership of team identity. There are pros and cons with each method. No matter how it's chosen, the team's name and theme should be proudly displayed in each team classroom and used in fun ways all year.

Choosing team colors and a team chant helps students feel that they belong. If fabric painting is part of art, then banners and T-shirts can be made. The music teacher may help students write a chant or song. Most 6th graders will participate willingly, but many 7th graders will consider it all pretty silly, although they may secretly take a good deal of pride in their team identity. Eighth graders will often take a renewed interest in team identity and relish being the "big guys" of the middle school. Students of each grade level will generally reflect the enthusiasm of the team teachers. Team identity will be as meaningful as teachers choose to make it. Read that again. We are responsible for team identity and enthusiasm!

The majority of middle schools are organized in teams by grade level, but there are other possible organizational structures. In some schools, more than one structure is operating and variations of basic organizational schemes may be found. It would be impossible to describe all the possibilities, so as we briefly discuss two of these structures, keep the basics of teaming in mind. Sadie Fox, our focus teacher at Valley View Middle School, describes her dedication to her students and tells us about teaming in Teachers Speak.

Creative Grouping Alternatives

The possibility of creating alternative structures is very real. Let's explore two possibilities.

LOOPING   The rationale for this grouping alternative is this: If teams of students and teachers have many benefits, why not extend those relationships, and consequently

Teachers Speak

Sadie Fox

For me, teaching is all about the kids. Yes, I love science and teaching it to my students, but I decided to teach so I could make a difference in the lives of kids.

I chose middle school for a number of reasons. One reason is that I enjoy their sense of humor—bizarre and unpredictable! I also am drawn to the concept of teaming. When I was in college, I was president of our chapter of the Collegiate Middle Level Association and attended two Association for Middle Level Education conferences. There I participated in sessions on teaming and found the concept to be the best thing going!

I think the enthusiasm of the younger teachers at Valley View convinced other teachers to make the most of the concept. When I started teaching here, teams were in place, but if you walked down the halls you couldn't tell one team from another. Several of us got together and decided the 8th grade teachers and students would change that. We decided to develop team identities and come up with names, colors, chants, logos, and anything else the kids could think of. We had several team meetings and brainstormed with the

kids. Our team decided they wanted to be the Valley View Vampires. I wasn't crazy about it but decided to let them run with it. They chose red, of course, for blood and resurrected the old "Monster Mash" song as the theme. I went to the dollar store that evening and surprised them with plastic vampire teeth. Well, we all put them on and posed for a team photo. I had the photo enlarged to poster size and we hung it in our team hall. The kids wanted to get a vampire movie and read books about vampires. We agreed to study the legend of Dracula, but the only movie we could show in school about vampires was *Scooby-Doo and the Legend of the Vampire*. This wasn't exactly what they had in mind, but we used it as a behavior incentive for the end of the term, and the kids had a great time at the event, complete with red soda and popcorn.

Can we do splashy team events all the time? No, of course not. But has a team identity with lots of student input brought us closer together, involved reluctant kids, and motivated participation in not only activities but also learning? You bet! Teaming is at the heart of middle school. It makes sense, and makes teaching more effective and enjoyable.

the benefits, over longer periods of time? A continuous year-to-year instructional plan involving the same team of students and teachers has been called teacher rotation, student-teacher progression, and, most recently, **looping**. "Looping . . . promotes real communication, mediation, resolution, and deeper understanding of other perspectives that foster a sense of community and teach our students lessons about maintaining the relationships in their lives" (Fenter, 2009, p. 29).

Although research is sparse concerning achievement benefits, anecdotal accounts tell us that looping is a very positive experience. Some have reported that this gift of time is experienced in the second and third years when moving ahead instructionally is not hampered by the necessity of getting acquainted, becoming familiar with achievement status, and working out procedures. A common medical analogy is that finding a new dentist or doctor for a child every year makes no sense. If it's important for physicians to know their patients as they develop, how can we not see that it's equally important for teachers to know their students as they grow? This is a powerful argument.

SCHOOL-WITHIN-A-SCHOOL This second alternative method of grouping also takes advantage of long-term relationships. In large middle schools, separate community systems may be established composed of a 6th-grade team, a 7th-grade team, and an 8th-grade team (or teams). **School-within-a-school** is also known as a house plan.

In this grouping, each **house** is a microcosm of the total school population. If facilities permit, each house has its own distinct area of the building(s), where at least the core classes are held. Ideally each house has its own administrative area, along with related arts classrooms. If this isn't possible, houses stay together for core classes and then join others on individual grade levels for related arts and intramural activities.

Schools-within-a-school have been around for years. The organization requires fewer alterations and less teacher effort than looping. Teachers remain with a team of students for one grade level, but because they are part of a "house," their contact with their teams of students remains throughout the students' 6th-, 7th-, and 8th-grade school years. The benefits are derived from grade to grade by teams continuing to work together closely as a unit. They can plan for ongoing themes as they build a curriculum for a specific group of students. Sixth graders know who their teachers will be in subsequent years. They also know that the students on their team will remain constant. So, the benefits of a small learning community can be realized.

Regardless of the organizational structure of a middle school, or any school that serves young adolescents, advisory programs are developmentally appropriate.

Advisory Programs

A special time regularly set aside for small groups of students to meet with specific adults is known as advisory period, or just **advisory**. Some schools call it advisor/advisee, home-based guidance, or teacher-based guidance. Typically, advisory groups meet for 20 to 30 minutes, at least three days a week. *This We Believe* (National Middle School Association, 2010) tells us that when advisors and advisees meet regularly,

Standard 1

Young Adolescent Development

Element d. Implications of Young Adolescent Development for Middle Level Programs and Practices: Middle level teacher candidates apply their knowledge of young adolescent development when making decisions about their respective roles in creating and maintaining developmentally responsive learning environments. They demonstrate their ability to participate successfully in effective middle level school organizational practices such as interdisciplinary team organization and advisory programs.

they help students internalize respect, compassion, and positive values, as well as collaborative skills.

Turning Points directs middle schools to provide opportunities such as advisory periods for each student to have a close relationship with an adult within the school. Advisory accommodates close relationships as teachers better understand student needs and can use available resources to meet these needs (Carnegie Council on Adolescent Development, 1989).

ORGANIZING ADVISORY   Schools vary in their approaches to advisory. Some are quite structured, with all advisory periods following basically the same plan—possibly a prescribed program using purchased materials to guide discussions and activities. Other schools leave advisory up to individual teams that decide how to best use the time. Some advisories are organized by day. For instance, Monday may be used for administrative "housekeeping" activities, Tuesday for planned discussion, Wednesday for intramurals, Thursday for silent reading, and Friday for test preparation and homework completion. This kind of arrangement closely resembles the traditional homeroom and doesn't meet the developmental and affective needs of the middle level student in optimal ways. It does, however, afford the advisor a daily forum within which developmentally appropriate topics may be addressed if desired. Another approach might be for the team to decide on weekly or monthly themes that guide discussions and activities. Possible themes include self-awareness, respect, dangers of substance abuse, healthy lifestyles, and celebrating differences.

The primary purpose of advisory is to meet the developmental and affective needs of students (Pearsall, 2017). Whatever schedule may be in place and regardless of the "plan," advisors should respond to crisis situations by giving advisees opportunities to ask questions, express fear or frustration, and, in general, draw comfort and guidance from the advisory setting. Incidents of school violence, such as the 2018 school shooting in Parkland, Florida, local happenings, or whatever is of concern to our students is appropriate advisory content.

BENEFITS OF ADVISORY   Here's a list of some of the benefits of establishing and maintaining viable advisory periods in middle level settings:

- Because all young adolescents want to be heard, advisory periods provide opportunities for peers and a trusted adult to listen.

- All kids have occasional struggles as they make their way through early adolescence. Advisory periods provide a forum for discussions of their struggles and a safe place to explore options and solutions.

- Advisory groups serve to fortify identity. They bring together kids who normally may not have a lot of contact and who don't naturally gravitate to each other in social settings. This diverse group of kids has a unique identity as they spend time together.

- In stressful times, whether personal, school-based, regionally generated, or as a result of national or international crisis, young adolescents gather in advisory and can vent their fears and anxiety under the watchful guidance of a trusted adult.

- Advisory period provides time for administrative functions much like traditional homerooms when needed.

- Healthy and flourishing advisory programs often lead to better attendance and higher academic achievement for students (Pearsall, 2017).

TWB **Goal 11.** [Young adolescents] develop the interpersonal and social skills needed to learn, work, and play with others harmoniously and confidently.

Sara Davis Powell

Advisory is an excellent way to help young adolescents learn valuable life lessons.

ROADBLOCKS TO ADVISORY Although advisory by definition and in practice is a major tenet of middle level philosophy, its widespread implementation remains elusive. Most middle schools have a nonacademic and nonrelated arts period during the day that serves as an administrative time, like a homeroom, but may be labeled "advisory." Close examination is required to determine if the period is being used for purposes similar to those described in this section. As with so many concepts, having a designated period of time provides opportunity. What is done with the time makes the difference. Many teachers view advisory as another class preparation and are often unwilling to commit the time necessary to make it valuable for students. Comprehensive professional development is vital to the successful implementation of advisory that realizes the many possible benefits.

Please consider carefully how advisory can make a difference in the lives of young adolescents. You may find yourself in a school where advisory exists in name only. If you have the designated period, use it to benefit your students. The effort will be worth it. And remember that advisory is an *attitude* more than a program, one that leads us to commit to know our students well, to advocate for them when possible, and to wear our advisor hats all day, every day.

Self-Check 5.1

LO 5.2 Structures of Time

Time is the one thing we are guaranteed to have with our students, typically 180 days or so. That's a constant. How we choose to use these days is a critically important variable. As with other variables in life, there isn't just one right way. Fortunately, there are many options and variations. As educators, we have an awesome responsibility for organizing the time our students spend with us so optimal benefit is achieved. Although some configurations appear to be more developmentally conducive than others, ultimately schools have to choose a schedule that facilitates their priorities. In this section we delve into how days can be scheduled to enhance student growth during their middle level experience.

This We Believe calls for flexible grouping, scheduling, and staffing, with teams designing and operating much of what occurs each day (National Middle School

Standard 5
Middle Level Professional Roles

Element b. Advocacy for Young Adolescents and Developmentally Responsive Schooling Practices: Middle level teacher candidates serve as advocates for all young adolescents and for developmentally responsive schooling practices. They are informed advocates for effective middle level educational practices and policies, and use their professional leadership responsibilities to create equitable opportunities for all young adolescents in order to maximize their students' learning.

Association, 2010). Ideally, teams have the power to arrange blocks of instructional time in ways that best meet the needs of the students, as well as the curricular and instructional plan. *Turning Points 2000* echoes this point by recommending that team teachers lengthen and shorten classes, as well as determine the frequency and order of classes, to reflect instructional and student needs (Jackson & Davis, 2000).

Sounds great, doesn't it? With flexible scheduling we can have team autonomy to use time in ways that respond to the needs of students. Reality? Rarely.

Traditional Schedule

Although opportunity exists for flexibility and creativity in scheduling, the majority of middle level class periods remain 45 to 55 minutes long. Many schools schedule six or seven fixed periods a day, every day, all year long. I'll be the first to say that a well-planned instructional period of 50 minutes is far preferable to a 90-minute period, half wasted. However, limiting instructional time in each subject to an arbitrary 50 minutes is traditional, but perhaps not as effective as alternatives. If we view time as a resource rather than an element of schooling to be managed, we see that perceived obstacles to using time in more constructive ways are worth overcoming.

Dissatisfaction with both the limits of shorter classes and the inflexibility of traditional schedules has led increasing numbers of schools to reconfigure the way students and staff spend their days. No schedule is perfect, nor should any schedule be considered permanent. There are advantages and disadvantages to each that grow or recede in importance based on numerous variables. It's not necessary—and indeed prohibitive or downright impossible—to wait until all the anticipated kinks are ironed out of any given plan. Schedules need to stay fixed for given periods of time, but they should be evolving and moldable from semester to semester, year to year.

Block Schedule

The word *block* is used in many ways when discussing schedules. A block of time is a chunk of time—a longer period than the traditional 50-minute period. A **block schedule** is any schedule that allows for more time in class. It is important to understand that whatever the configuration of a block schedule, there are three major distinctions to be considered:

- Some forms of block scheduling increase the time spent in a given class period, but because the class may not meet every day the total minutes allotted to the class over the course of the year don't change.

- Some forms of block scheduling increase not only the time in a particular class but also the total minutes for the year because the number of times the class meets is not altered.

- Flexible block scheduling provides time that is divided by teachers as appropriate for the day's academic plan. Let's look at a variety of block scheduling models.

4 × 4 SEMESTER BLOCK MODEL   The 4 × 4 is used in many high schools, and some middle schools are adapting the basics of the plan. In this model, four courses are completed during each semester. Figure 5.4 illustrates a variation for middle schools. In this sample, the student would have 90 minutes of math and 90 minutes of language arts every day of the year, but 90 minutes of science *or* social studies every day for only a semester. This plan would work well for a three-teacher team—one math, one language arts, and one who can teach both science and social studies.

ALTERNATING DAY MODEL   This model is also popular in high schools where it's often referred to as the A/B schedule. In middle school this model allows for three related arts periods or a course repeated daily. Figure 5.5 illustrates the basics of this

FIGURE 5.4 4 × 4 semester block model: sample of a schedule for one student on a team

	Semester I	Semester II
8:00–9:30	Math	Math
9:30–11:00	Language Arts	Language Arts
11:00–12:00	Lunch and Advisory	Lunch and Advisory
12:00–1:30	Science	Social Studies
1:30–3:00	Related Arts	Related Arts

model using eight periods on a two-week cycle. Like the 4 × 4, a benefit of this model is that students change classes only four times a day and thus spend more minutes in each period.

A variation of the previous model is the alternating day model, which follows a weekly cycle as illustrated in Figure 5.6, allowing for each class to meet three times a week rather than some two times and some three.

DAILY PLUS ALTERNATING DAY MODEL Some schools declare curricular emphasis in certain subjects such as science and math. Others have a "back to basics" approach that invests more time in math and language arts. The daily plus alternating day model in Figure 5.7 shows how a schedule can create time frames to accommodate some classes having twice as much time as others. This model still provides the benefit of longer class periods for all subjects.

FLEXIBLE BLOCK MODEL The schedules presented so far provide longer class periods and, for some courses, considerably more total time overall. What the schedules don't provide for is flexibility. The model that best approximates the vision for scheduling in *This We Believe* (National Middle School Association, 2010) and *Turning Points* (Carnegie Council on Adolescent Development, 1989) is the **flexible block schedule**. This model provides large blocks of time allotted to teams to be used for instruction. With the flexible block, time is available for large group experiences, uninterrupted video viewing, co-teaching, grouping/regrouping, guest speakers, joint projects—the list can go on and on.

FIGURE 5.5 Alternating day model (2-week cycle)

Time	Monday	Tuesday	Wednesday	Thursday	Friday
8:00–9:25	1	5	1	5	1
9:25–10:50	2	6	2	6	2
10:50–12:10	Lunch/Advisory/Recess				
12:10–1:35	3	7	3	7	3
1:35–3:00	4	8	4	8	4

Time	Monday	Tuesday	Wednesday	Thursday	Friday
8:00–9:25	5	1	5	1	5
9:25–10:50	6	2	6	2	6
10:50–12:10	Lunch/Advisory/Recess				
12:10–1:35	7	3	7	3	7
1:35–3:00	8	4	8	4	8

Time	Sixth Grade	Seventh Grade	Eighth Grade
10:50–11:15	Advisory	Recess	Lunch
11:15–11:40	Lunch	Advisory	Recess
11:40–12:10	Recess	Lunch	Advisory

FIGURE 5.6 Alternating day model (weekly cycle)

Time	Monday	Tuesday	Wednesday	Thursday	Friday
8:00–8:45	1	1	5	1	5
8:45–9:30	2				
9:30–10:15	3	2	6	2	6
10:15–11:00	4				
11:00–12:00			Lunch/Advisory/Recess		
12:00–12:45	5	3	7	3	7
12:45–1:30	6				
1:30–2:15	7	4	8	4	8
2:15–3:00	8				

A sample flexible block schedule is shown in Figure 5.8. Grade levels and, therefore, interdisciplinary teams, have two large blocks to use as they deem appropriate. Examining the figure reveals how easily a team could take its 250 minutes and divide them into five neat 50-minute periods: math, language arts, science, social studies, and reading. Or it might divide them into four periods of 60-plus minutes with one split around lunch or related arts. Either choice is OK to do as a base schedule. However, neither is OK to do every day for 180 days.

To make optimal use of the flexible block, teams of teachers should spend time devising about five different ways the schedule might be altered and brainstorm reasons for making the alterations. For instance, the science teacher plans to have students conduct a lab experiment that requires more than 50 minutes. The schedule is altered so that one science class meets for 150 minutes each day. The other teachers divide the remaining students (in the case of a four-person team, that would be 75% of the students) and rotate them through their subjects. Perhaps the team wants to see a special exhibit at the local museum. They would have 150 minutes for the trip without interrupting related arts schedules.

When teams have the autonomy to use their time, it is possible to rotate classes from day to day. We discussed the changeability of middle level students, how they may behave very differently from one day to the next. In fact, a student may approach school at 9:00 a.m. very differently than at 1:30 p.m. Teachers who rotate student schedules on a regular basis report that students respond differently to their teaching depending on the time of day. Not surprisingly, they find that their teaching styles and attitudes also vary—some are "morning people" and others function more enthusiastically as the day goes on. Thus, there are benefits in rotating classes of students to spread out the advantages, and to share the low moments equitably. On Monday, you may see groups A, B, C, and D in that order (ABCD). On Tuesday, you would see them in BCDA order and then on Wednesday in CDAB. Given uninterrupted team time, rotation is possible without altering schedules outside the team.

FIGURE 5.7 Daily plus alternating day model

Time	Monday	Tuesday	Wednesday	Thursday	Friday
8:00–9:25	1	1	1	1	1
9:25–10:50	2	2	2	2	2
10:50–12:10			Lunch/Advisory/Recess		
12:10–1:35	3	5	3	5	3
1:35–3:00	4	6	4	6	4

FIGURE 5.8 Flexible block model

Time	Sixth Grade	Seventh Grade	Eighth Grade
7:35–8:00	Homeroom/Advisory	Homeroom/Advisory	Homeroom/Advisory
8:00–8:25	Related Arts/ Exploratory	Instructional Block	Instructional Block
8:25–8:50			
8:50–9:15			
9:15–9:40			
9:40–10:05	Instructional Block		
10:05–10:30			
10:30–10:55		Related Arts/ Exploratory	Lunch
10:55–11:20			Recess
11:20–11:45	Lunch		Instructional Block
11:45–12:10			
12:10–12:35	Instructional Block	Lunch	
12:35–1:00		Recess	
1:00–1:25		Instructional Block	Related Arts/ Exploratory
1:25–1:50			

UTILIZING LONGER BLOCKS OF TIME Two elements are absolutely necessary to make longer blocks of time the effective instructional tools they can be. One element is continuing professional development. A 90-minute lesson is not two 45-minute lessons back to back. Teachers need strategies appropriate for longer class periods. More hands-on learning is possible with time for projects and opportunities for active student participation.

The second necessary element is planning. With adequate professional development, teachers are equipped to open their instructional toolboxes and apply varying strategies to longer blocks of time. To do so in effective ways, both individual and common team planning time are vital.

Both traditional and alternative scheduling can provide opportunities for curricular and instructional improvement. Maximizing the potential of any structure requires commitment, energy, and continually developing expertise.

Self-Check 5.2

LO 5.3 Structures of Place

An important feature in the life of a middle school team is shared space. The core classes should be as close together as possible—either next door to one another, or at least on the same hallway. Proximity means fewer minutes lost in changing classes, fewer discipline problems in the hallways, and more opportunities for informal teacher-to-teacher contact. Having an identifiable part of the building to call our own is a vital aspect of teaming. This is generally a built-in feature if a facility is constructed to accommodate middle level philosophy. Ideally, there is a pod of classrooms including a science lab and a teacher workroom. With flexible scheduling, teams of students need to be free to move from classroom to classroom without disturbing other teams.

You will have choices of where you teach young adolescents. Most attend public middle schools with grades 5 or 6 through 8 and some are in K–8 or 7–12 settings. Others attend private schools with various grade configurations. Still others choose magnet schools and charter schools, two public options.

Magnet Schools

A **magnet school** is a public school that offers a special emphasis or focus in addition to the core curriculum. This focus may involve specialized curriculum, instruction, or both. Magnet schools may bring together academically gifted students, students with an expressed interest in a specific curricular area, or perhaps students with distinct career aspirations. Because students in a magnet school share aptitude and/or interests, they tend to be more homogeneous. In some cases, magnet schools represent overt tracking. During the 1970s, districts devised magnet plans to draw students from the suburbs into urban areas to create racially mixed populations. Magnet schools are viewed by some as forces for integration.

Sara Davis Powell

Magnet schools are considered by many to be vehicles for improving scholastic standards, providing a broad range of curricular choices, and allowing students to concentrate on distinct interests and talents. Some magnet schools require proof of academic achievement and aptitude through high scores on standardized tests. Once admitted, students must maintain high achievement levels to remain in the school. Some magnet schools require auditions in areas such as music, theater, and dance. Their programs then provide talented students in these areas with opportunities to enhance their skills and to use them in performance. Some middle schools declare a curricular focus such as math and science. They increase their resources and teacher expertise and invite students with interest in, and aptitude for, the chosen focus to apply. Still other magnet schools declare a focus on, for instance, military or career preparation. Interested students are asked to apply, and attendance is determined by lottery.

Magnet schools are more likely to have greater monetary and staff resources. They cost more to operate. So although magnet schools are part of public education, they are inherently unequal to nonmagnet schools in what they can offer students. They often compete with private and charter schools to draw students and parents who are looking for alternatives.

TWB **Goal 8.** [Young adolescents] develop his or her strengths, particular skills, talents, or interests and have an emerging understanding of his or her potential contributions to society and to personal fulfillment.

Charter Schools

A **charter school** is a public school that is freed in specific ways from the typical regulations required of other public schools. Charter schools receive public funding and may use much of the money as they wish to promote student learning. In a middle level school, for instance, if the administration and faculty perceive low reading ability among the students, they can make the decision to use their funding for teams of five teachers: math, language arts, science, social studies, and reading. They will likely need to sacrifice in some other area, but funds may be shifted to staff according to where the needs appear to be. Most charters, however, have networks of private supporters who help with funding for programs they deem valuable.

Charter schools may be started by anyone for a variety of reasons. Some may have the goal of raising achievement for a particular student population; some may want to promote a specific subject area or set of skills. A "charter," or plan, is

Sara Davis Powell

Teachers and students enjoy learning together at STRIVE Prep.

devised and submitted to the state for approval. This is a lengthy and complicated process. If approved, a charter school is considered part of the district in which it is geographically located. Some states limit the number of charters approved. For every charter school, funding is diverted from "regular" public schools because in most states the **expenditure per student** from local, state, and federal sources is allocated to the charter school the student attends. This makes charter schools controversial, along with the perception that the level of accountability may not be high enough, even though students in charter schools take all state-mandated standardized tests and the schools are accountable for the quality of teaching and learning through test results.

Because funding for charter schools depends on how many students attend them, they must recruit students and convince parents that they will provide a better education. Charter schools usually start from scratch and build a facility (this requires private funding) or lease an existing building. While charter schools are considered part of the district in which they are physically located, the district is not obligated to pay for facilities, student transportation, or food services. In charter schools, administrators and teachers usually make most of the decisions. This is often referred to as **site-based management**. In 2015, almost 7,000 charter schools educated about 6% of all public school students. This means more than 3,000,000 attended charter schools, double the number in 2010. In fact, charter student enrollment more than quadrupled between 2000 and 2015 (National Alliance for Public Charter Schools, 2016). Some charter schools operate independently and others are part of a larger system. One of the best known charter systems is the **Knowledge Is Power Program (KIPP)**, a national network of 209 free, open-enrollment charter schools serving more than 87,000 K–12 students. About 88% of KIPP students are eligible for free or reduced-price meals and about 95% are African American or Hispanic. KIPP's success includes a high school graduation rate of 93%, with 80% of KIPP graduates attending college (Knowledge Is Power Program, 2018). This is quite a success story!

STRIVE Preparatory Schools is a network of schools serving the Denver, Colorado, metropolitan area. The student population of STRIVE is similar to that of KIPP schools. STRIVE was established primarily to meet the needs of at-risk children and adolescents in the Denver area. The STRIVE record of achievement is remarkable, with new schools established each year since the founding of the system in 2006. The middle schools have achieved top academic honors for the state of Colorado, even though most STRIVE students live in low-income homes where English is not the first language (STRIVE Preparatory Schools, 2018).

If you choose to teach in a charter school, make sure you have a clear picture of the responsibilities you will have. Remember that charter schools don't have to follow what are considered the norms of other public schools. For example, the teachers in the STRIVE system begin school responsibilities in July rather than August and are expected to answer student phone calls until 9:00 p.m. Monday through Friday. For their extra efforts they are paid more than teachers in the Denver Public Schools. In my visits there, I have discovered a level of dedication and innovation that is refreshing, and a love of the teaching profession that is inspirational.

Just as students succeed at high levels in some public schools, and in others they do not, some charter schools are effective and others are not. The state is responsible for renewing charters and, therefore, bears responsibility for the students who choose the schools. Close supervision of the charters and heavily monitored accountability are needed.

The Inviting Classroom

We may have little control over the existence or location of shared team space, but we have a great deal of control over our individual classrooms and the environments we create. There's not a lot we can do about the amount of money the school district has, or chooses to spend, for physical amenities, and the size of the classroom is rarely a matter of choice.

How can we make our classrooms pleasant and efficient? To answer this question requires thought and planning. Sometimes the only variable within our sphere of influence is our own creativity. We want our rooms to serve as an initial and continuing invitation to students. The environment should say to students "Welcome. This is a place where you belong and are safe." The amount of effort we put into the classroom environment is noticed by our students, whether or not they express it.

First impressions are crucial. Having your classroom ready to go on the first day of school with a big WELCOME banner to greet your students will set the tone. Try standing by the doorway and shaking each student's hand as he or she enters and saying a personal "Welcome! I'm _____." Most 10- to 15-year-olds are not used to being greeted in such an adult way. It will make a lasting impression! Most of them will look away and giggle and give you what my daddy used to call a "dead-fish" handshake. After a week or so, you can talk about the greeting. Ask students how it felt to be welcomed with a handshake. Talk to them about exuding self-confidence, a firm handshake, and eye contact. Repeat the greeting every few weeks.

Students need to feel safe and secure and comfortable. For some, these three factors don't exist outside the classroom. Their home and/or neighborhood environments may be less than desirable. You may bear the responsibility of providing one of the only inviting atmospheres they are currently experiencing. What a burden—and what an opportunity!

If you have the luxury of being hired in early summer for a position that begins in late August, you will have plenty of time to prepare your classroom. Some of you may be hired after school has already started because the enrollment allows the principal to add a position, or perhaps an emergency has led to the need to replace a teacher. Preparation sometimes requires nights and weekends—whatever it takes to create a desirable environment.

PLANNING THE BASIC SETUP   The kind of environment we create may depend on the subject(s) we teach and on our personal preferences. There are two imperatives for basic room arrangement. When setting up desks or student tables, we must provide for teacher *access* to all students. We also must provide ways for students to *transition* from individual to small group to whole-class instruction.

You need room to walk in order to have access to students and quickly reach each one in your classroom. **Proximity** to students has both instructional and management advantages. Having a walking loop is an important way to accomplish proximity.

The configuration of desks in rows was typical in the recent past, and this configuration persists in many classrooms. If lecture is the most frequently used form of instruction, then rows will work. Rows are easy to keep orderly. However, desks in rows often confine the teacher to the front of the room in the traditional power position. For standardized testing days or days dedicated to strictly individualized work, desks in rows may be advantageous. But on typical days in a middle level classroom filled with active involvement, there are other configurations that allow for greater teacher access to all students, as well as student-with-student interactions. Whether you have 45- or 90-minute classes, your students will make **transitions** while following your lesson plans. If you are fortunate enough to have a large classroom that allows for easy movement, there are many room configurations that will work. If you are cramped for space by either a small classroom or a large number of students, your options may be limited.

Enhanced Text

Video Example 5.1

Deirdre McGrew's room tour at Cario Middle School shows distinct areas, each with a purpose.

Arranging desks or tables in small groups is the most usable and flexible configuration. If space permits the seating arrangement to be changed for transitions to individual and whole-class work, that's terrific. If not, students can work individually or as a whole class from small group configurations. When tables or desks are in small group configurations, make sure students understand your expectations for individual work. They may simply pull their desks apart or may turn them so they are not directly facing one another. For transition to whole-class instruction, be sure all students can see and hear what's going on.

FURNITURE, EQUIPMENT, AND MATERIALS   Once you have a basic setup of desks or tables, it's time to plan the rest of the room. Your desk is an important feature of the classroom for you, but not for the students. It is an organizational tool for you where you may want to lay out materials you plan to use and keep information to which you need to refer. But the teacher's desk is not the focal point of a classroom. I suggest you choose a corner for a file cabinet, your desk, and a chair. It is your space and students need to respect that. But don't sit behind a desk and allow it to be a barrier between you and your students.

Learning centers are locations in your classroom where topics can be explored by individuals or small groups. They have been popular in elementary schools for decades. Speaking about learning centers in the secondary classroom, "Learning centers diversify student experience, encourage student voice, leverage available resources, and give teachers built-in opportunities for formative assessment and critical one-on-one conversations" (Malefyt, 2016). Learning centers in a middle level classroom need not be complicated to develop or maintain. A table or shelves with interesting objects and information can enhance any classroom's learning potential.

A classroom library is appropriate regardless of the subject(s) you teach. Having interesting books, both fiction and nonfiction, on shelves for students to peruse and check out encourages reading.

The amount of available technology in your classroom depends on lots of variables including school funding and leadership philosophy. Provide easy access and guidelines for student use of devices.. Frequency of use will depend on the subject you teach, the software available, and your encouragement. As you plan for instruction, there will inevitably be materials involved. Maybe you'll use graph paper, newspapers, markers, maps, calculators, tablets, and so forth. Having materials organized and readily accessible will save valuable instructional time. Plastic crates and boxes that stack neatly work well. Teaching students good organizational habits will pay off now and in their futures. They need to know how to access and how to put away instructional materials. There's a knack to making all this organization work. The key is habit. Instill efficiency and respect for materials in your students from day one. These routines will pay off for each of the other 179!

WALL SPACE   Classroom wall space can be a dynamic teaching tool. Many teachers merely purchase an assortment of posters, put them on the walls and bulletin boards, and then leave them all year. This is boring, and the posters rapidly become wasted instructional space once students have lost interest. You may have a few favorites that seem appropriate for the entire year, but choose carefully. Class, team, and school expectations may be left up and some inspirational posters are acceptable to use as permanent displays, but changing bulletin board displays is a creative and efficient way of bringing new information into the classroom. Bulletin board displays need to correspond to what's being taught and learned. Make them interesting and interactive. Have groups of students design and make displays. Use student art or class work and display projects. There should be a designated area where assignments and necessary books/materials are posted. This should be in a consistent location. Each afternoon before leaving for the day, get into the habit of posting information for the following day. You do not necessarily need to write out the exact assignment, but have the space ready so you only have to fill in the details when it's appropriate.

Making the Teaching and Learning Connection

Hello, future middle school teachers! As someone who prepared to teach elementary students, every day I'm delighted my path led me to young adolescents. There's never a dull moment! We laugh and cry and learn together.

My family and friends sometimes refer to me as an organization geek. While they may say it in a joking way, I respond with pride that I never have to hurry or worry when I go to school. I plan ahead, gather materials, grade assignments, and know where everything is. I never go home until everything is ready for the next day. I'm convinced that this is a major reason I enjoy my job. When others are scrambling for position in the copier line at 7:45 a.m., I'm calmly sipping my coffee and smiling. When another math teacher rushes into my room saying she can't find her set of protractors and class starts in 35 seconds, I hand her my set and ask for her car keys to hold until the protractors are returned. When a parent stops by for an impromptu conference, I simply pull his up-to-date file from my drawer. So, you see, I'll take the ribbing in exchange for peace of mind!

Please don't assume that I'm rigid or cold with my kids. My obsessive organization just gives me more time to relax and be personal with them. One thing they love is my "Mrs. Peters board." Just as I want to know my students as whole people, I want them to know me as a happy, well-rounded person. Even though they may have looked at the board multiple times, they will inevitably laugh again at my 7th grade school photo or my less-than-perfect 7th grade report card.

I've always found that students appreciate structure. They like the fact that they know what to expect in my classroom from the standpoint of routines. It saves time, too. They know where to put things, where to gather what they need, and where to find what they missed when they are absent. They also know that I am all smiles when our lessons run smoothly. I rarely have any discipline concerns, while some of my teammates occasionally do. Sure, there are lots of reasons for kids misbehaving, but I like to think my organization helps with classroom management, too.

Teaching middle level students is not always rosy, but I wouldn't trade it for any other position. You're in for a career that will challenge you and provide lots of joy at the same time. Stay organized!

Sincerely,

Traci

Home Away from Home

Think about it—at least 7 of every 24 hours of every school day are spent mostly within the walls of our classrooms. Let your classroom reflect you, your care for students, and your enthusiasm for learning. Chances are you will experiment with configurations and move things around as the year goes by. You will learn what works best for your students in terms of your access and their transitioning. Learning centers will change and bulletin boards will develop in direct proportion to your creativity and the time you spend to make it happen.

Enhanced Text

Video Example 5.2

Traci Peters maintains her own personal bulletin board that encourages her students to get to know her.

You may want to add personal touches like plants to your classroom (let students rotate the responsibility for their care), couches, comfortable chairs, lamps, and so on. These items are a matter of space and availability and your own style. If time for individual reading is part of your day, seating options are enjoyed by students. Again, if they are in the habit of moving about the room in respectful ways, they will not abuse the privilege of sitting on a rug or in an overstuffed chair occasionally to enjoy silent reading.

Remember that students spend time with you in your classroom. Their curiosity and subsequent motivation depend in large measure on your keeping an organized and comfortable environment as part of your instructional planning. Use your classroom as a haven of security, a motivator of interest, and a workshop for organizational habits.

Self-Check 5.3

Why It Matters

How we choose to structure people, time, and place in middle level settings affects school climate and academic success. Some of the effects have been verified through research, and others are reported anecdotally. Although many structures fall within an acceptable range, some more closely follow the tenets of *Turning Points* and *This We Believe*.

Creating small learning communities is a hallmark attribute of middle level philosophy. The middle level teacher-student team is most widely accepted as the optimum people structure. As we've seen in this chapter, there are many possible team configurations, some incorporating tracking, and some that group entirely heterogeneously. Some are quite small, and some are large. Some teams of teachers and students stay together for one year; others practice looping for two or more years.

Time, as a tremendous resource, is ours to use every school day. As educators, we are obligated to make the most of the 180 or so days we spend with our students. Longer blocks of time in classes provide opportunities for complete cycles of introductory experiences, inquiry, understanding, practice, reflection, and assessment. Putting blocks of time together for optimal learning and then incorporating flexibility both serve vital functions in the middle level.

Manipulating our physical environments may be an ongoing process of working toward efficiency and comfort. Choices of desk/table arrangements, use of wall space, movement and storage areas, and the atmosphere we create are all ours to make. The total effect of place relies on our efforts.

The structures described in this chapter align with middle level philosophy, but there are schools all across America that are successfully educating young adolescents through responsive dispositions without many of the structures we have discussed. Understanding and appreciating the development of young adolescents and framing curriculum, instruction, and assessment around their needs and unique qualities will produce an environment that fosters healthy physical, intellectual, emotional, social, and moral growth. It is possible for a school for middle level students to be subject-area based, with six classes a day, and without clustering of classrooms, and still meet the needs of the students. It's possible, but certainly more difficult than if structures are in place that accommodate young adolescent development. Keep in mind that structures aligning with middle level philosophy provide opportunities. They don't guarantee success. It's up to us to take full advantage of the opportunities provided by developmentally responsive structures of people, time, and place.

Group Activities

1. In groups of two or three, arrange to visit with teachers from a school in your file. Your instructor will give you guidelines for arranging the visit. Your group will want to spend about 30 minutes with the teachers you visit to find out about their structures of people, time, and place. Using this chapter as a reference, work with your class to formulate questions/prompts that will lead to an understanding of the degree to which the teachers and students team, if and how tracking or flexible ability grouping is used, the format of advisory, the schedule, and the physical layout of the building as it is used by teams and/or grade levels. The results of the school visits will be added to your school file.

2. Divide your class into two groups. One group will be assigned looping and one will be assigned the school-within-a-school configuration. Each group will formulate its best reasoning in support of its structure. The groups will present their reasoning to the class as "panels of experts." If possible, invite other students (education majors and others) to listen to the panels and then allow the audience, even if it's only your classmates, to critique the panel discussions.

Individual Activities

1. Knowing what we do about the development of middle level students, write a description of what you would consider to be the most appropriate use of a week of daily 30-minute advisory periods.

2. Draw an overview diagram of a classroom arrangement you might want for the subject area you plan to teach. Be prepared to explain (and possibly defend) your arrangement choices.

3. How do you feel about the "to track or not to track" debate? Specifically, what kind of grouping (and regrouping) do you feel might be most appropriate for your chosen subject area(s)?

4. Explain in your own words the statement, "An individual can make a difference: a team can make a miracle."

Personal Journal

1. Think back to your days in middle school. Was tracking used at your school? Was it formally orchestrated so that it was obvious to everyone, or was it more covertly arranged and just understood by students? Were you in a particular track in certain subjects? How did you feel personally, and how do you think you were perceived?

2. Do you remember classrooms that seemed to "invite" students? If so, what qualities did the classroom have? Was it a function of the physical amenities or of the teacher's personality? Was it a combination? If you don't remember any of your classrooms as obvious "invitations," what elements might have created this kind of atmosphere?

3. Do you think you have the personal skills to function as a cooperative and effective member of a teaching team? If so, what personal qualities give you this ability? If not, and if you want to be part of teaming, what personal qualities do you want to cultivate to enable you to participate productively on a team?

Professional Practice

(It would be helpful to reread the descriptions of Sarah Gardner in Chapter 1 and Darma in Chapter 2.)

Sarah Gardner
Sarah Gardner is student teaching with two teachers who each have more than 20 years in the classroom. They are comfortable with young adolescents and the subjects they teach. The only thing Sarah finds to question is their use of time set aside for advisory. Ms. Morris and Ms. Cunningham each have a group of about 25 kids for the 30-minute period. So far, she hasn't seen the daily 30-minute period utilized the way she has read about in the *Middle School Journal*. It's a homeroom where lunch money is collected, announcements are made, and homework is finished. On Fridays, they go outside or to the gym for games. It's not a bad use of time, just not what it could be.

(Continued)

Darma • sixth grade

Kids like Darma thrive during the daily session. His homework already done, he uses the time to trade comic books or play chess or cards. His advisory group is the same as his first period class—all AIG (academically and intellectually gifted) students meet with Ms. Morris. The other 25 kids meet with Ms. Cunningham.

Remember that for some items, more than one choice may be defensible. The purpose of the items is to stimulate thought and discussion.

1. Sarah is disappointed in the use of advisory time. What is the most likely cause of her disappointment?

   a. She wants the time to be structured around academic assistance.

   b. She thinks the time would be better spent for an additional related arts class.

   c. She would rather divide the 30 minutes among the core courses so there would be more time in them.

   d. She would like to address non-academic topics that will help kids grow.

2. Which of the following would not be appropriate for Sarah's team teachers to do to change the way they have always approached advisory period?

   a. Call the district office and ask if anyone knows of a middle school that uses advisory in ways they don't at Lake Park Middle School.

   b. Ask kids to come up with topics and then write reports and present topics to the whole advisory group.

   c. Look into programs that address the affective side of young adolescent development and consider

   following a daily plan based on themes of the program.

   d. Make a plan for each day of the week such as current events on Monday, character traits on Tuesday, intramurals on Wednesday, and so on.

3. Darma enjoys the 30-minute period each day. Given what we know about him, which of the following would likely not be Darma's reaction to changes in format?

   a. Darma would go along with changes.

   b. Darma would ask to change teams if Sarah got her way and mixed the two groups.

   c. Darma would still complete his homework early and take a wait-and-see attitude toward changes.

   d. Darma would actively work with his friends on whatever projects were planned.

4. Knowing Sarah as we do, what one thing would she want most to change about advisory that links to her interests in graduate school?

   a. She would like to mix the AIG and "regular" kids in advisory period.

   b. She would like to design a research study on student perceptions of advisory.

   c. She would like to visit each team's advisory periods to observe differences.

   d. She would like to plan focused reading and discussion.

5. Advisory is one of the most underutilized facets of middle level philosophy. One reason for this cited in research studies is that teachers view advisory as another course preparation. What ideas do you have for taking advisory from the realm of drudgery or ambivalence to a pleasure for teachers and students?

Chapter 6
Middle Level Curriculum

Sara Davis Powell

Curriculum is the primary vehicle for achieving the goals and objectives of a school. In developmentally responsive middle grades schools, curriculum encompasses every planned aspect of the educational program. It includes not only the basic classes designed to advance skills and knowledge but also school-wide services and programs such as guidance, clubs and interest groups, music and drama productions, student government, service activities, and sports.

THIS WE BELIEVE, P. 17.

Learning Outcomes

After studying this chapter, you will have knowledge and skills to:

6.1 Summarize major aspects of curriculum in middle level settings, including Common Core State Standards, the impact of national subject-area organizations, and how standards are addressed in the classroom.

6.2   Categorize ways to connect the curriculum, including complementary, multidisciplinary, interdisciplinary, and integrative approaches.

6.3   Explain why and how all teachers are teachers of reading and writing.

Dear Future Middle Level Teacher,

What we teach in middle level settings matters. Being a content expert provides the background we need to make subjects not only accurate but also interesting. You may teach one subject all day, or possibly two. Unlike elementary teachers who must keep up with all the core subjects, you will specialize. Chances are one subject is your primary interest, but you'll be required to make another subject a second focus. These subjects are what we refer to as part of the **formal curriculum**, mandated by district and state, and guided by standards.

Now let's think briefly about another kind of curriculum we teach, whether we realize it or not . . . the **informal curriculum**. We teach who we are, and who we are speaks volumes to young adolescents. John Lounsbury, outstanding leader of middle level education, first coined the phrase **wayside teaching** in 1991, meaning "the teaching that is done between classes, when walking in the halls, after school, and in dozens of one-on-one encounters, however brief" (1991, p. 29). Wayside teaching is all about relationships with students, colleagues, families, the curriculum, instruction, assessment, and every other aspect of our profession. Understanding this informal curriculum helps us make all our relationships more positive. It's up to us to recognize that "harnessing the *power of our presence* has tremendous implications" (Powell, 2010, p. 15).

What you will read in this chapter is an overview. It will, however, give you a glimpse of just how complex and challenging the issue of curriculum, and in particular, middle level curriculum, can be.

SDP

LO 6.1 Curriculum in the Middle Grades

Middle level education's guiding document tells us that "curriculum embraces every planned aspect of a school's educational program" (National Middle School Association, 2010, p. 19). **Curriculum** consists of specific classes, core and otherwise, as well as guidance, advisory, activities of all kinds, and provided services. Whatever is intentionally designed to support and accomplish the mission of the school is curriculum, along with what's accomplished through wayside teaching, the elements of teaching and learning that may not be planned but are the result of our care and concern for kids.

This We Believe about Curriculum

A developmentally responsive middle level school will embrace a curriculum that is *relevant, challenging, integrative,* and *exploratory,* finely tuned to the characteristics and needs of young adolescents. The quotes in the following descriptions of these four elements are found in *This We Believe.*

Standard 2
Middle Level Curriculum

Middle level teacher candidates understand and use the central concepts, standards, research, and structures of content to plan and implement curriculum that develops all young adolescents' competence in subject matter. They use their knowledge and available resources to design, implement, and evaluate challenging, developmentally responsive curriculum that results in meaningful learning outcomes. Middle level teacher candidates demonstrate their ability to assist all young adolescents in understanding the interdisciplinary nature of knowledge. They design and teach curriculum that is responsive to all young adolescents' local, national, and international histories, language/dialects, and individual identities (e.g., race, ethnicity, culture, age, appearance, ability, sexual orientation, socioeconomic status, and family composition).

RELEVANT   "Curriculum is relevant when it allows students to pursue answers to questions they have about themselves, content, and the world" (p. 20). A relevant curriculum results in student understanding of the connected, "holistic nature of all knowledge" (p. 20). A relevant curriculum is "rich in all personal meaning" (p. 21). By creating new interests, a relevant curriculum stretches "students to higher levels of learning" (p. 21).

CHALLENGING   To be challenging, a curriculum must address three issues. Let's look at them separately.

A challenging curriculum must include "substantive issues and skills" (p. 18). Substantive issues are those that are worthwhile in the eyes of both adults and students. They are issues that are important enough to study in depth. This in-depth study uses basic principles along with alternative points of view involving skills that are contextually based. A challenging curriculum addresses both why and how things happen.

Given the diversity exhibited by middle level students, implementing a curriculum that is appropriate for their varying levels of understanding is a daunting task. Finding ways to meet our students where they are, build on prior knowledge and experiences, and continue to challenge them should become our daily ritual requiring multiple levels of curriculum.

The third component requires that the curriculum enable students to take responsibility for their learning. Exercising decision making must be a component of a developmentally responsive curriculum that is challenging.

INTEGRATIVE   "Curriculum is integrative when it helps students make sense of their lives and the world around them" (p. 21). To be integrative, *This We Believe* tells us curriculum must be coherent, must connect school to students' daily lives, and must encourage students to grasp the totality of their experiences. Applications, connections, construction of knowledge—making sense of content and experiences is what integrative curriculum is all about.

EXPLORATORY   *This We Believe* tells us that "the general approach for the entire curriculum at this level should be exploratory" (p. 20). Exploratory, then, does not refer to a set of courses, but rather an attitude and an approach. Discovery and choice are embedded in the disposition that encourages exploration.

This We Believe states that "[e]xploration, in fact, is the aspect of a successful middle school's curriculum that most directly and fully reflects the nature and needs of the majority of young adolescents" (p. 20).

Keep in mind that in middle level we view curriculum as more than just what is taught/learned in the classroom. Don't lose sight of the broader view of curriculum as everything that is planned for students in our schools. But for the sake of the discussion that follows, we deal with that part of the curriculum that is planned by classroom teachers for students.

Curriculum Standards

Perhaps the most profound influence on what is taught/learned in schools is wielded by standards developed by national and subject-area organizations, and individual states. Very simply, **standards** define what students should know and be able to do.

It's rare to pick up an education journal dated 1998 or later and not find numerous references to standards. Although standards aren't (and shouldn't be) stagnant, the concept of standards will endure. Standards documents are not effective if we fail to make them living documents, subject to our best thinking over time. In 1989, the National Council of Teachers of Mathematics introduced us to standards for teaching and learning math in prekindergarten through grade 12. In the 1990s, national organizations for language arts, science, and social studies followed suit. Other classes taught at the middle level have also formulated standards. These subject-area organizations have used groups of experts to determine essential knowledge and skills in the disciplines that students should master. Familiarity with these standards is essential for middle grades teachers as we specialize in one or two subject areas.

COMMON CORE STATE STANDARDS INITIATIVE Many educators believe that schools should teach basically the same things at approximately the same time. A growing body of research indicating state-to-state differences in standards and testing led to the development of the common core standards for English language arts and math. The common standards were initiated by two organizations that are made up of representatives from all of the states: the **National Governors Association (NGA)** and the **Council of Chief State School Officers (CCSSO)**. Together they developed the **Common Core State Standards Initiative**.

The NGA and CCSSO tell us that the Common Core State Standards are clear, understandable, and consistent and include rigorous content and application of knowledge through higher-order skills. They contend that the standards are evidence-based and research-based.

Adoption of the Common Core State Standards in K–12 English language arts and math is voluntary for states (Common Core State Standards Initiative, 2018). The NGA and CCSSO do not plan to develop standards in any other subject areas. Developing and implementing standards that are common across the United States is a complicated undertaking. Read some frequently asked questions (FAQ) in Figure 6.1. The Common Core State Standards will likely be part of what you teach in middle level English language arts and math classrooms.

You can imagine the controversy that swirls around common standards for all states. Even though they are voluntary, most states have adopted them. Table 6.1 presents a variety of views of both advocates and critics.

State Standards and Subject-Area Organizations

All 50 states now have standards documents that are followed by school districts. Most state standards for math and ELA align with the Common Core State Standards. Standards for other subject areas are similar to the standards of the national subject-area organizations and contain assessment criteria aligned with these standards. You will no doubt be handed copies of the standards for your teaching area(s) and grade level(s) and urged by your administrators, mentors, and teammates to make the standards the guide and dominant "playbook" in your classroom. Your state standards will be the

FIGURE 6.1 FAQ: Common Core State Standards

What are the Common Core State Standards?

The Common Core State Standards are standards written for K–12 English language arts and math to provide consistency of learning expectations across states. Before these standards, each individual state developed its own standards and standardized exams, resulting in widely varying topic emphases and levels of rigor in American public schools.

Who is leading the Common Core State Standards movement?

The Common Core State Standards are the result of collaboration between the Council of Chief State School Officers (CCSSO) and the National Governors Association Center for Best Practices (NGA). The CCSSO and NGA are state-based organizations that brought together teachers, school administrators, subject area experts, and education organizations from across the country to develop a common core of state standards for K–12 English language arts and math.

Why are the Common Core State Standards believed to be a valuable reform in K–12 education?

The developers of the common standards tell us they want every child to receive an education that provides tools necessary to succeed in college and beyond, no matter where they live. Because standards varied widely from state to state, consistency can only be accomplished through a set of common rigorous standards that provide clear expectations for how students, parents, administrators, education policy makers, and the community can work together toward providing the tools for success.

The Common Core State Standards make it easier for states to work together on ways to meet the standards and share helpful information and resources.

Common standards prompt textbook and digital media producers to concentrate on one set of standards and improve the resources available to all teachers and students.

The standards provide a measuring stick for student learning that is consistent from state to state. This is important for policy makers and education leaders who watch for progress on a national level.

Now that the English language arts and math standards are written, will they ever change?

Yes. The standards for K–12 English language arts and math are considered dynamic documents, meaning that they will be revised based on feedback as teachers use them and discover ways to improve them.

Will the common core state standards prevent teachers from making decisions about how to teach?

No. The standards provide expectations for the knowledge and skills needed for student success. Teachers, principals, and others will decide how to help students meet the standards. Teachers will write lessons that address both the standards and student needs in their own classrooms.

Did teachers help create the common core state standards?

Yes. Teachers participated in the development of the standards through multiple organizations including the National Education Association (NEA), American Federation of Teachers (AFT), National Council of Teachers of Mathematics (NCTM), and National Council of Teachers of English (NCTE). The CCSSO and NGA continually ask for comments and feedback.

Will more standards mean more tests?

No. The CCSS allow states to develop and share appropriate assessments. A test based on individual state standards is replaced by a test based on the common standards.

Will common standards be developed for other subjects?

No, that's not part of the plan. English language arts and math were chosen because they are considered the basic subjects necessary for learning all subjects. Other subject areas are very important to education, but NGA and CCSSO will not develop standards in other subjects. States will continue to develop and revise rigorous and effective standards for other subjects with the help of organizations such as the National Coalition for Core Arts Standards; National Art Education Association; National Research Council; the National Science Teachers Association; the American Association for the Advancement of Science; the National Council for the Social Studies; the American Alliance for Health, Physical Education, Recreation and Dance; and the American Council on the Teaching of Foreign Languages.

Are the Common Core State Standards an attempt by the federal government to control public education?

The creation of the CCSS is a state-led endeavor, not a result of federal government efforts. However, the federal Department of Education agrees in principle with a common set of standards and uses financial incentives to encourage states to adopt the Common Core State Standards.

Based on: National Governors Association Center for Best Practices, Council of Chief State School Officers. (2010). *Common Core State Standards*. Retrieved January 1, 2013, from www.corestandards.org/

basis of your curriculum. Standards are typically organized by disciplines, but this in no way prevents the blending of subjects. Both discipline-based curriculum and curriculum based on connections among disciplines are not only possible but desirable.

CORE SUBJECT-AREA STANDARDS   Each core subject area has its own national organization. These organizations are made up of teachers, administrators, subject experts, and others with keen interest in the discipline represented. The organizations

TABLE 6.1 Advocates and critics of common core standards

Advocates believe that common core standards	Critics believe that common core standards
provide clear and consistent goals for learning, regardless of where in the United States students may live.	take away states' rights to determine what is taught and learned.
prepare U.S. children for success in college and work.	are premature and that state standards have not had sufficient time to succeed.
unite teachers and students across the United States as a cooperative effort.	do not allow for local educational values and use of local resources.
provide common ground around which strategies and programs may be shared.	detract from individualism of states and teachers.
build on strengths and lessons of current state standards.	are unwieldy and will not be enforceable.
level the academic playing field for all students.	will bring all states' standards down to the lowest common denominator.

Based on: Your Introduction to Education: Explorations in Teaching (4e) by S. D. Powell, 2019, Upper Saddle River, NJ: Pearson.

have governance structures, position statements, multiple conferences, publications, resource guides, websites, and more. They also formulate standards. Middle level teachers derive numerous benefits from membership in these organizations. I urge you to go online and explore the organizations that represent the subject(s) you want to teach.

English Language Arts

Major Organization: **National Council of Teachers of English (NCTE)**

Website: www.ncte.org

Journals for middle grades: *Language Arts* (for elementary and middle level), *Voices from the Middle* (middle level)

Standards

The Common Core State Standards now dominate what is taught and learned in English language arts classes, as well as emphasis on literacy in other subject areas. The official name of the standards for grades 6–12 is *Common Core State Standards for English Language Arts & Literacy in History/Social Studies, Science, and Technical Subjects*. The overarching purpose of the standards is to help ensure that all students are college and career ready in literacy. The National Governors Association and the Council of Chief State School Officers do not intend for the emphasis on literacy in other subject areas to replace 6–12 standards in history/social studies, science, and technical subjects, but rather to supplement them.

According to the CCSS document, extensive research establishes the need for college and career-ready students to be proficient in independently reading complex informational text. For this reason, the emphasis on nonfiction has increased dramatically. In middle level the emphasis is half on literary texts and half on informational texts.

Standard 2
Middle Level Curriculum

Element b. Middle Level Student Standards: Middle level teacher candidates use their knowledge of local, state, national, and common core standards to frame their teaching. They draw on their knowledge of these standards to design, implement, and evaluate developmentally responsive, meaningful, and challenging curriculum for all young adolescents.

Mathematics

Major Organization: **National Council of Teachers of Mathematics (NCTM)**

Website: www.nctm.org

Journal for middle grades: *Mathematics Teaching in the Middle School*

Special feature: Illumination website with interactive multimedia investigations

Standards

As with English language arts, the Common Core State Standards now dominate what is taught and learned in mathematics. Comparing the major aspects of the CCSS standards and the long-standing NCTM standards in the document *Principles and Standards for School Mathematics*, published in 2000, we see that they are very much alike. In addition to the major content areas in the standards, NCTM acknowledges five process-oriented standards: problem solving, reasoning and proof, communication, connections, and representation.

You may be among the many students who have struggled, and continue to struggle, with math. On the first day of my Introduction to Education classes we always do an activity to help us get to know each other. Part of the activity involves revealing our favorite subject and our *least* favorite subject. Math is most likely to not be the favorite and is almost always the least favorite subject. As a math teacher, this is disappointing to me and I spend a good deal of time tutoring and encouraging. If you plan to teach middle level math, please find ways to actively engage your students and take the "mystery" out of the logic and patterns, and emphasize the beauty of mathematics!

Science

Major Organization: **National Science Teachers Association (NSTA)**

Website: www.nsta.org

Journal for middle grades: *Science Scope*

Special feature: NSTA works collaboratively with other organizations to sponsor science competitions to actively involve young adolescents and their teachers.

Standards

The **Next Generation Science Standards** were developed by a partnership that includes NSTA, the National Research Council, and the American Association for the Advancement of Science and are being adopted by many states. The standards outline what students need to know and be able to do to be scientifically literate, grade level by grade level, and promote excellence and equity for all students in science and state that science should be an active process for students. In other words, science is something students do, not just read about, with inquiry central to science learning. The four major categories of standards are life science, earth and space, physical science, and engineering and technology.

Social Studies

Major Organization: **National Council for the Social Studies (NCSS)**

Website: www.socialstudies.org

Journal for middle grades: *Middle Level Learning*

Standards

NCSS proposed the *National Curriculum Standards for Social Studies: A Framework for Teaching, Learning, and Assessment* in 2010. Like the original 1994 standards, the revised standards encompass 10 strands: culture; time, continuity,

Enhanced eText
Video Example 6.1
Kadean Maddix explains how he became a math teacher and his viewpoint about how to make math accessible to all students.

and change; people, places, and environments; individual development and identity; individuals, groups, and institutions; power, authority, and governance; production, distribution, and consumption; science, technology, and society; global connections; and civic ideals and practices. In addition, the standards focus on questions for inquiry, what learners should know and be able to do, and how learning will be demonstrated.

The integrative nature of social studies is a big factor in middle grades education. Most of the themes used in interdisciplinary instruction and integrative approaches are derived from social studies. No longer a subject in which memorizing dates and names is paramount, social studies in the middle grades can and should be an exciting and worthwhile learning adventure. NCSS tells us that the primary purpose of social studies is to help students make informed decisions with the public good in mind as they actively support a democratic society with a culturally diverse population.

RELATED ARTS   English language arts, math, science, and social studies are considered core subjects. A variety of other courses are typically offered in middle school that we refer to as related arts. These courses are vital to developmentally responsive middle level education.

Related arts courses may include art, physical education, health, vocal music, instrumental music, technology, home/consumer arts, industrial arts, foreign language, and others. Although middle level teachers and schools openly acknowledge the value of related arts to student development and learning, there often appears to be a rift, real or perceived, between core and related arts teachers. We should be careful not to classify courses as academic and non-academic because this kind of terminology can be inflammatory. Scheduling necessarily restricts many related arts teachers from fully participating in team meetings and functions and makes participation in interdisciplinary teaching and units difficult. What follows are very brief overviews of some of the related arts areas.

Arts Education   This broad category includes related arts courses typically available in middle school. Major arts-related organizations joined to create standards that apply to what the Consortium of National Arts Educators Association considers the four categories of arts disciplines: visual arts, music, theater, and dance.

Most middle schools offer visual arts classes, often allowing students to discover and demonstrate talent that hasn't yet become evident in other areas. Students with artistic talent should be encouraged to use and expand their talent in other courses. Many middle level settings offer theater and dance classes that provide students who wish to participate opportunities to explore their interests and talents.

The National Association for Music Education developed goals for vocal and instrumental music courses available in most middle schools. These classes are usually attended by choice, rather than as required courses. In elementary school, students are often exposed to vocal music on a regular basis and consequently choose chorus as an option in middle school. On the other hand, students who take private music lessons often form the backbone of instrumental music in middle school. Music programs in some middle schools serve primarily to give students awareness of the art form, whereas in others musical groups present entertainment on occasion and participate in competitions.

> *TWB* Goal 7. [Young adolescents] explore music, art, and careers, and recognize their importance to personal growth and learning.

Health and Physical Education   Most middle schools require students to be part of physical education classes each year. Health education is approached in a variety of ways, varying by state and by district. Elements of health education are sometimes incorporated in science, but most frequently health education is part of physical education. Some middle schools even contract with outside organizations to provide health education.

The Centers for Disease Control developed *National Health Education Standards—Achieving Excellence* in 2004 and revised the document in 2012 to promote health education and to challenge schools to continue efforts toward excellence in health education (CDC, 2016). The topics include health promotion, disease prevention, healthy behaviors, influence of media on young adolescent health, goal setting, and decision making.

Experts in the field of health education have identified 10 content areas as necessary for a comprehensive school health education and recommend a developmentally appropriate program based on community needs, with at least 50 hours per year of instruction in health-related areas. The 10 content areas are community health, consumer health, environmental health, personal health and fitness, family life education, nutrition and healthy eating, disease prevention and control, safety and injury prevention, prevention of substance use and abuse, and growth and development.

The content areas addressing personal health, fitness, nutrition, and healthy eating are vital in today's middle level schools. Childhood obesity is at an all-time high and steadily increasing, with life-threatening consequences.

> *TWB* Goal 9. [Young adolescents] recognize, articulate, and make responsible, ethical decisions concerning his or her own health and wellness needs.

Technology Education   The broader phrase associated with technology is "information literacy." We all know that there is absolutely too much information in any discipline for any of us to "know it all." Not only is there a wealth of information, the information is constantly changing. Our greatest impact is in helping students know how to search for what they need and how to judge reliability.

> Our libraries are now media centers. Regardless of the subject, we are all responsible for introducing students to resource generators and requiring that they use them. Many middle schools offer specific courses that are basically technology centered. Courses in keyboarding are prevalent, as are courses that relate to software programs and how to use them. The **International Society for Technology in Education (ISTE)** guides us regarding technology skills appropriate in middle level education.

> *TWB* Goal 4. [Young adolescents] use digital tools to explore, communicate, and collaborate with the world and learn from the rich and varied resources available.

Industrial, Home Arts, and Consumer Education   When I was in middle school (junior high), courses in this general category were simply called "shop" and "home economics." With advancements in technology and added sophistication, we have changed both names and content. Middle schools now offer courses with titles like "Family and Consumer Science," "Trade and Industrial Arts," and "Technology and Design." The classes are coed, with girls and boys learning similar information and skills. By virtue of their content, the classes are interactive and hands-on in nature, ideal attributes of courses for young adolescents.

Foreign Language   Typically there are two levels of foreign language instruction in middle school. Foreign language classes with curriculum equivalent to what students encounter in courses for which they receive high school credit are usually offered to 8th graders who show promise and interest in languages.

Many middle schools have language classes that expose students to the culture of one or more countries, with minimal exposure to the associated language. Courses of this nature are often short in duration, possibly six weeks, allowing a student to become familiar with a number of cultures and languages. For instance, a 7th grader may have six weeks of Spanish culture and six weeks of French culture interspersed with other brief related arts courses.

The American Council on the Teaching of Foreign Languages (ACTFL) developed a vision statement that includes the philosophy that all Americans should be proficient in at least one language and culture in addition to English.

> *TWB* Goal 6. [Young adolescents] understand and use the major concepts, skills, and tools of inquiry in the areas of health and physical education, language arts, world languages, mathematics, natural and physical sciences, and the social sciences.

Standards in the Classroom

Standards should be viewed as empowering. They give us structure and consistency without dictating instruction. They are not restrictive and don't necessarily dictate sequence. In most cases, we are free to take a set of standards for our subject(s) and grade(s) and move them around to match our classroom and team goals. They can be introduced in one unit, emphasized in another, practiced in another, and assessed and reinforced as often as desired. Within the structure of curriculum standards, we can create learning experiences that are developmentally responsive for middle level students. This should be a collaborative effort among teammates, administrators, central office personnel, curriculum leaders, and so on.

A reality check must be included at this point: Standards are often overwhelming. They may provide not only the skeletal structure of a body of knowledge but also many details of a discipline. Rather than fit and efficient, we often seem to have an obese body of prescribed knowledge that simply won't fit in a 180-day school year. Our best judgment tells us that something must be trimmed in order to spend ample time on more

See How They Grow

Maria • 7th grade

Maria grew increasingly restless being cooped up in the apartment she shares with her mother each afternoon and most weekends. When she was younger, TV and toys occupied her time. Now that she's in 7th grade, she frequently leaves the apartment and stays away for longer periods of time. She goes down the block to a corner grocery store and sits outside with neighborhood kids, not a bad thing in and of itself, but the potential for harm is present. On several occasions she has accepted rides with high school teens and knows her mother would not approve. She has tried beer and now will have one any time it's available. She has smoked cigarettes but doesn't particularly care for them. She has been offered marijuana but so far has turned it down. Many in the older crowd she now seeks dropped out of school and speak mostly Spanish.

Maria's mother knows she sneaks out occasionally, and they argue about it. Mom would like to have another job so she could be home more when Maria isn't in school, but she has had no luck finding other work. Maria's teacher, Ms. Esparza, is also concerned about her.

We recognize that the purpose of middle level education involves both academic and affective domains. Middle level education receives criticism both in philosophy and practice if less than optimal progress of middle level students on standardized assessments is announced. In our efforts to strengthen this level of schooling, our focus must continually rest on what we teach and how we teach it—in both the four core subjects and the related arts. Strong programs require teachers who are competent and confident in the disciplines, those who understand how and when to help students make connections both to, and among, the concepts we teach.

foundational aspects. Perhaps the best way to put our curriculum standards on a diet is thoughtful and ongoing discussions with colleagues about what to emphasize and what to minimize.

LO 6.2 Connecting Curriculum

Sara Davis Powell

Young adolescents eagerly learn together when the curriculum is interesting.

Most of us who teach young adolescents realize the benefits of connecting curricular areas to whatever extent is feasible and appropriate. The terms *connecting* and *integrating/integration* are often used interchangeably in defining the process of looking for bridges or commonalities among historically distinct subject-area curriculum strands. In the interest of clarity, when we discuss the various approaches to connecting curriculum, I'll refer to the four most widespread methods described briefly in Figure 6.2.

Regardless of definitions, procedures, and components, helping our students see and study connections within, between, and among subject areas can bring concepts to life, increase understanding, and make content more relevant. As teachers, it is our responsibility to determine approaches to curriculum that work best for our students.

What you're about to read represents both a compilation of what others have said about curricular connections and how I have come to understand and practice the broad concept.

Complementary Content and Skills

Connecting the curriculum through **complementary content and skills** is the easiest and least intrusive method, involving only support and acknowledgment of other content areas through shared components or concepts. Before we can support each other's curricular plans, we have to be aware of them. The first step is do what's called **curriculum mapping**, an effective way for teachers to plan a year of instruction. The primary elements to consider include:

- Process and skills
- Essential concepts and topics
- Assessment products and performances.

Individual teachers on a team arrange these elements on a calendar in sequences so the elements build on one another. A team of teachers then shares their calendars. Carefully, they view the curriculum of their fellow teachers. They look for gaps and repetitions in individual calendars and complementary fits among subject areas. When complementary content and skills are spotted, teachers negotiate timing so that a cohesive plan emerges that makes sense for student learning. Using a large calendar, with teachers writing planned elements and units on sticky notes, works well. Plans can be moved around to accommodate complementary content and skills. Ideally this is done before the school year begins.

FIGURE 6.2 Connecting the curriculum

Simple			Comprehensive
• May alter timing	• Alters timing	• Alters timing	• Alters timing
• Uses content mapping	• Uses content mapping	• Uses content mapping	• Uses content mapping
• Subjects separate	• Subjects separate	• Subject boundaries blurred	• Subjects interwoven
• Teacher driven	• Teacher driven	• Teacher driven	• Student and teacher driven
	• Content-based	• Concept-based	• Themes derived by student-teacher interaction and are based on student concerns and societal issues

Sara Davis Powell

A well-planned and connected curriculum will open a world of possibilities for young adolescents.

Through curriculum mapping, it's possible for teams of middle level teachers to recognize content topics and skills emphases that naturally fit together. For example, the science teacher may plan to use pendulum swings the second week in October as part of a six-week study of physics. This would be an ideal time for the students to study circles, radii, and arcs in math. The language arts teacher may plan to study the elements of short stories, including Edgar Allan Poe's "The Pit and the Pendulum." The three teachers don't change their lesson plans. They alter the timing of topics. Pendulums do not constitute a theme, merely a focal point around which multiple content areas and skills fit.

The complementary content and skills approach requires little extra effort on the part of teachers. A curriculum map makes tweaking timing a relatively simple thing to do. The multidisciplinary approach also uses curriculum mapping, but in a more complex way.

Multidisciplinary Approach

With **multidisciplinary instruction**, teachers share their curriculum maps with the intent of choosing a theme around which complementary content and skills may revolve, a theme that unifies topics and concepts in two or more subject areas. Teams will typically determine a theme and then decide what each subject area can contribute and when and for how long the theme will guide and unite their disciplines. Themes in social studies work well because they are generally broad.

TWB **Goal 1.** [Young adolescents] become actively aware of the larger world, asking significant and relevant questions about the world and wrestling with big ideas and questions for which there may not be one right answer.

Along with curriculum mapping, a process called **webbing** is valuable. Take a look at the thematic web used in multidisciplinary instruction illustrated in Figure 6.3. The theme is in the middle and the subject areas form the web. In multidisciplinary instruction, the subject areas remain distinct, and, through the theme, students see connections. They see that content learning in one area applies to another area.

Multidisciplinary, or thematic, teaching will serve its purpose of enriching the curriculum through connections only if those connections are genuine, not artificial. Just as connections should be meaningful, so should the choice of themes. The theme becomes even more important when we move to the interdisciplinary unit approach.

Standard 2
Middle Level Curriculum

Element c. Interdisciplinary Nature of Knowledge: Middle level teacher candidates demonstrate the interdisciplinary nature of knowledge by helping all young adolescents make connections among subject areas. They facilitate relationships among content, ideas, interests, and experiences by developing and implementing relevant, challenging, integrative, and exploratory curriculum. They provide learning opportunities that enhance information literacy (e.g., critical thinking, problem solving, evaluation of information gained) in their specialty fields (e.g., mathematics, social studies, health).

FIGURE 6.3 A multidisciplinary approach web

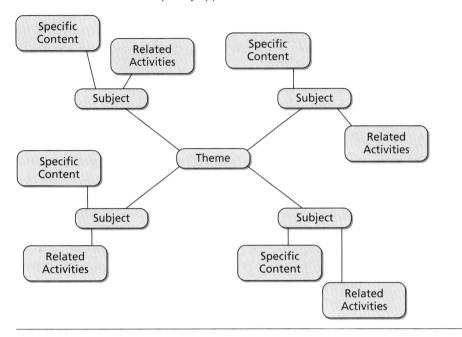

Interdisciplinary Unit Approach

An interdisciplinary approach involves a theme, with teachers altering both timing and content. An **interdisciplinary unit** usually lasts two to three weeks, with almost all content revolving around a theme that's more conceptual in nature rather than content-based. For example, multidisciplinary teaching may revolve around "seasons," whereas an interdisciplinary approach might have "change" as the theme. A theme of seasons is more limited with fewer avenues to explore than a theme of change.

When teachers work together to explore a concept such as "change" by connecting multiple subjects, subject-area boundaries are often blurred. Teachers often go outside the subject(s) they teach to promote understanding of the conceptual theme. Figure 6.4 lists some themes that are more concept-based as opposed to content-based.

FIGURE 6.4 Conceptual themes

- Activism
- Beginnings
- Celebrating differences
- Change
- Conflict resolution
- Conservation
- Freedom
- Heroes
- Independence
- Innovations
- Interdependency
- Journeys
- Justice
- Prejudice
- Self-awareness
- Societal Dilemmas
- Symbolism
- Wellness

Integrative Curriculum

Although *This We Believe* calls for middle level curriculum to be integrative, or connected to students' lives, the Association for Middle Level Education does not ask that the entire scope of middle level curriculum be integrative in the sense that James Beane defines it.

> Curriculum integration is a curriculum design that promotes personal and social integration through the organization of curriculum around significant problems and issues, collaboratively identified by educators and young people, without regard for subject area lines (Association for Middle Level Education, n.d.).

Of all the terms used to describe connecting the curriculum, "integrative" is the most complex to implement. An **integrative curriculum** is intended to be the whole, planned curriculum of the middle school, distinguished by the themes chosen for study that result from the intersection of *problem-based student concerns* and *large social issues*. Students and teachers determine themes jointly and plan the direction of study together. A broad range of skills are necessary in integrative curriculum, including those in Figure 6.5. While the less complex forms of connecting the curriculum require some of the skills, the list provides admirable goals for all of us.

An integrative curriculum includes both core and related arts subject areas, blended in the study of meaningful themes. It should be conducive to heterogeneous ability grouping and accommodate individual differences. Teachers are facilitators who are also learners right along with students.

The benefits of all curricular designs rest with well-prepared, committed teachers. With strong subject foundations and connections among disciplines established to any degree considered appropriate, curriculum in middle grades will foster learning and motivate interest and achievement.

FIGURE 6.5 Skills for integrative curriculum

1. Reflective thinking, both critical and creative, about the meanings and consequences of ideas and behaviors
2. Identifying and judging the morality in problem situations and ethical dilemmas
3. Problem solving, including problem identification and analysis
4. Identifying and clarifying personal beliefs and standards upon which decisions and behaviors are based
5. Describing and evaluating personal aspirations, interests, self-conception and self-esteem
6. Acting in problem situations both individually and collectively; social action skills
7. Searching for meaning in such areas as cultural diversity and poverty

LO 6.3 We Are All Teachers of Reading

We often hear that children learn to read by 3rd grade and read to learn from then on. If only that were true. Two misconceptions exist. One is the expectation that students who enter middle level classes are proficient readers, particularly readers for literary experiences, including short stories and simple novels. The second is that students who have mastered reading for literary experiences will naturally read for information and for learning how to do something without direct instruction and guided practice. The solution to the first misconception may be best accomplished through reading specialists. In the absence of funding (or the fact that reading instruction is not a priority), it is up to all of us to teach the basics of decoding and comprehension. Many of us are not prepared to do this. Professional development is essential to accomplish the task.

The second misconception implies that all types of reading are the same. We must address this misconception if our students are to be successful. They must be able to read with comprehension, regardless of the subject area. Reading a math book requires rereading. Once through is rarely sufficient. Students may need to read a paragraph, consider examples, and then reread. Reading a science text often involves calling up prior knowledge to provide context. Social studies material is often laden with names of people and places that are difficult to decipher. We must help students understand how to get beyond pronunciation to substance, to envision an event and get the big picture of a sequence. When we use opportunities provided in the content we teach to reinforce reading skills, then reading has purpose and relevancy. We could tweak the reading adage to say, "We read in middle level to learn content and, as we learn content, our reading skills improve." After all, is there a content area that doesn't rely heavily on reading proficiency?

Strategies for Encouraging Reading

Regardless of the subject(s) you teach, there are steps you can take to increase both the reading skills and enjoyment of your students:

1. Know your students' reading habits. Do they read only because it's assigned? Do they read novels? Magazines? Comic books (graphic novels)? Newspapers? Internet websites? Text messages? When is reading meaningful to them?

2. Provide a variety of reading opportunities—individual, small group, whole group, for pleasure, to learn specific information, to learn how to do something, and so on.

3. Explicitly teach students how to read for a variety of purposes and in appropriate ways. We have to teach them to read poetry, a math book, information in journals or online for a report, a piece of historical fiction, the newspaper, and so on.

4. Establish a classroom library, no matter what subject(s) you teach. As a math teacher, I have favorite authors—such as Greg Tang and Jon Scieszka—who write wonderfully entertaining books that teach math skills. But I don't stop with books that deal with math. I buy books at book fairs, library sales, garage sales, 75% off tables at large bookstores, and flea markets . . . anywhere young adolescent-appropriate books can be found. Don't forget to include magazines, such as *Time for Kids*, *National Geographic*, *Wildlife*, *Sports Illustrated for Kids*, and so on.

5. Consistently incorporate Sustained Silent Reading (SSR) or Drop Everything And Read (DEAR) into the school day. A well-stocked classroom library will provide plenty of choices so students may self-select what they read.

TWB **Goal 3.** [Young adolescents] read deeply to independently gather, assess, and interpret information from a variety of sources and read avidly for enjoyment and lifelong learning.

Standard 2
Middle Level Curriculum

Element a. Subject Matter Content Knowledge: Middle level teacher candidates demonstrate a depth and breadth of subject matter content knowledge in the subjects they teach (e.g., English language arts, mathematics, reading, social studies, health, physical education, and family and consumer science). They incorporate information literacy skills and state-of-the-art technologies into teaching their subjects.

Enhanced eText Video
Example 6.2

Derek Boucher discusses his
classroom library and suggests
ways to encourage students to read.

Making the Teaching and Learning Connection

Dear new teacher,

I began my career as an American History teacher more than 10 years ago. I enjoyed it, but it wasn't long before a glaring problem hit me in the face. The problems my students faced in American History, they also had in other subjects. I talked with my teammates and others and we all concluded the issue was READING. The students' inadequate reading abilities were keeping them from comprehending content and learning the skills of every subject area.

I went back to college and earned a master's degree in reading instruction. I learned how to teach students to decode and then comprehend what they were assigned to read. This has become my passion! I was always an avid reader and knew the value of reading, but before this awakening of sorts I guess I assumed reading came naturally to everyone while in elementary school.

Just having an adequate classroom library isn't enough. If kids have low reading ability and the lack of self-confidence that goes with it, they will only pick up a book when it's required. And when they only read out of necessity, they will never do so for pleasure. If they don't read for pleasure, their reading skills won't improve. It's a vicious cycle of underachievement.

Bottom line is that you have to be a reading teacher, regardless of your subject area expertise. You may not feel qualified; you may not get a master's degree in reading instruction. But you understand your content area and how reading in your area is unique. Teach your students how to read like a mathematician, like a scientist, like a historian, like a novelist or poet or artist or video game designer. You will be changing the lives of your students, one bit of text by one bit of text.

Sincerely,
Derek Boucher

Strategy to Help with Memory

Students often tell us they read a particular piece of text but can't remember anything about it. They're generally not exaggerating. So, what do we do?

The answer may lie in *connections*. It has long been acknowledged that we learn new material most easily when we link the information to something we already know. This connection forms a brain hook to catch the new information. "Optimal brain engagement, understanding, and storage occur when new information is identified as being related to an existing memory pattern" (Willis, 2018). In addition to connections, we learn new material best when we are prompted to make predictions, given what we've already read.

Willis (2018) developed an easy-to-implement strategy that prompts students to pause in their reading and think about what they know so far. She calls it "talking back to the text," an ideal approach for young adolescents! She simply uses sticky notes with prompts on them. The students put the notes at preplanned places in what they're reading to remind them to think about:

- Here's what I think I'm learning . . .
- I already know that . . .
- From here I predict that . . .
- This is like . . .
- This graph tells me . . .

What a simple strategy to try! Besides helping students comprehend and remember, it can serve as a perfect assessment to tell us if students are learning what we want them to learn. This is formative assessment, a vital teaching and learning strategy that we discuss in Chapter 8. When the students write brief responses to the prompts, we can have them put the sticky notes on one page of paper and submit them. These sticky notes have the power to lead to what Willis calls "optimal brain engagement."

Writing

A discussion of reading would not be complete without addressing writing. Reading is, of course, a prerequisite for writing. But more than a prerequisite, the two are inextricably linked. Good readers have most of the skills necessary for good writing, but instruction is necessary for students to successfully engage in the different genres and purposes of writing. Both reading and writing are necessary to succeed in our increasingly literacy-based society. Whether for pleasure, for information, or for knowing how to do something, reading and writing are essential skills. As middle level teachers, we are all teachers of reading and writing. In Teachers Speak, focus teacher Keith Richardson relates his views on teaching all students to read and write.

Why It Matters

Curriculum is more than textbooks, district guides, lists of facts, and even more than standards. Curriculum involves all the aspects of students' interactions with teachers, with each other, with specific discipline-based knowledge, with connections among concepts, and with their worlds and beyond. Young adolescents are with us for only a few brief years. During that time they grow and change and become. Our daunting responsibility is to frame a curriculum that will bring out all their potential and catapult them forward with knowledge, skills, awareness, a sense of responsibility—all those positive and healthy attributes called for in *This We Believe*. You may hear the phrase "curriculum wars" referring to what some seem to perceive as conflicting viewpoints of curriculum—academic and affective. There is absolutely no need for conflict here. Developmental responsiveness does not adversely affect high academic expectations and vice versa. They work in concert and complement one another.

Teachers with strong content knowledge coupled with an understanding of young adolescent development are prepared for discipline-based and connected curriculum designs. Balanced curriculum includes core and related arts subjects, service-learning, support of affective growth—a holistic approach to middle level. In all these areas, our curriculum is to be relevant, challenging, integrative, and exploratory.

Teachers Speak

Keith Richardson

I can't express strongly enough the benefits of a robust reading and writing program. My classroom library is a vital part of teaching language arts, as is daily reading for pleasure. I see my responsibilities as a middle school teacher to include the following:

1. Teach kids to read with fluency and comprehension.

2. Teach kids to write with proper mechanics, to address particular audiences, and to express their thoughts clearly and concisely.

3. Encourage a love of, and appreciation for, language expression in all its many genres.

I have these responsibilities posted near my desk. Each day I challenge myself to engage students in their own learning to bring them closer and closer to these three goals. It's work I love.

Group Activities

1. In groups, acquire your state standards for each of the core disciplines for grades 5, 6, 7, and 8. Add these standards to your class files. You will use them in future activities.

2. Add to your school files by finding out what related arts courses are offered at each of the middle level schools. Are any of them required? Are any offered only at certain grade levels? Do any require auditions or other qualifications?

3. In groups of three to five, choose a theme from Figure 6.4. Draw a web similar to Figure 6.3. Write your chosen theme in the middle and fill in the core four subjects plus at least two related arts areas. Now spend 15 minutes brainstorming concepts that could be explored in the core and related arts areas to support the theme. You should have no problem filling a page. Conceptual themes invite so many interesting topics. Be prepared as a group to share with other groups an overview of the results of your brainstorming.

Individual Activities

1. Consider the subject area(s) you want to teach. Was anything discussed in this chapter pertaining to that subject new information to you? If so, what?

2. Choose a subject-area organization website to visit. Prepare a brief report of what's included to share with classmates.

3. Think of one related arts course that particularly stands out in your memory. Write at least five attributes of this course to share with your class.

Personal Journal

1. What was your favorite subject in middle school? In retrospect, was it your favorite because of the subject/curriculum or did other factors weigh more heavily (teacher, instructional approach, time of day, cute boy/girl sitting in front of you, etc.)?

2. Why have you chosen the particular subject area(s) you want to teach? What influences led to your decision?

Professional Practice

(It will be helpful to reread the profile of Carmen Esparza in Chapter 1 and the description of Maria in Chapter 2.)

Carmen Esparza
Ms. Esparza's career as a bilingual teacher is ever-evolving. The rapidly increasing interest in teaching English language learners provides new articles on the topic in many journals. She diligently seeks them out, reads what educators have to say, and adjusts her strategies. But at the end of the day, it all boils down to one goal—English fluency. Ms. Esparza understands and appreciates the need to keep other cultures alive in her class and to validate home languages. But it doesn't change the fact that her students must learn to communicate in English, read it with accuracy and comprehension, and express themselves in written standard English.

Maria 7th grade

Ms. Esparza is particularly concerned about Maria, now a 7th grader. She has had her in class for almost two years and has watched her change from a shy, compliant 6th grader to a withdrawn, almost defiant 7th grader. Her English skills showed improvement in 6th grade, but her lack of effort is showing in 7th grade.

Remember that for some items, more than one choice may be defensible. The purpose of the items is to stimulate thought and discussion.

1. Bilingual education has critics. Some people don't see its value. Among them are teachers. What can Ms. Esparza do to influence the perceptions of those who disparage what she does?

   a. Be as informed as possible about studies addressing bilingual education and, when opportunities arise, reasonably express what she learns to others.

   b. Make the bilingual program more visible in the building through projects and posters.

   c. Ask her principal to talk with teachers about the need for support.

   d. Keep to herself and let teachers watch the progress.

2. Which of the following should Ms. Esparza not do as she tries to positively influence Maria?

   a. Ask a professionally successful Latina woman to meet with Maria and other girls to talk about issues she faced and what contributes to her success.

   b. Remind Maria daily of the value of speaking and writing fluently in English.

   c. Continue to speak in both Spanish and English in whole-group sessions but change to mostly English when speaking with Maria.

   d. Involve Maria in afterschool activities.

3. As a nonbilingual teacher, how could you support Ms. Esparza's efforts to legitimize and promote bilingual education at Martin Luther King Middle School?

Chapter 7
Middle Level Instruction

Courtesy of Warren Cobb

The distinctive development characteristics of young adolescents provide the foundation for selecting learning and teaching strategies. . . . Teaching approaches should capitalize on the skills, abilities, and prior knowledge of young adolescents; use multiple intelligences; involve students' individual learning styles; and recognize the need for regular physical movement.

THIS WE BELIEVE, P. 22.

 ## Learning Outcomes

After studying this chapter, you will have knowledge and skills to:

7.1   Comprehend the impact of brain research on instructional decision making.

7.2   Implement student-focused instruction.

7.3   Explore a variety of instructional strategies.

Dear Future Middle Level Teacher,

Instruction is the obvious part of teaching; it's what we see when we walk into a classroom. It's communication among teachers and students, with learning as the optimal result. Instruction involves interactions, and it can be so much fun!

There are principles to guide and support how teachers teach and students learn. One principle is that we have to thoroughly understand the curriculum ourselves before we design ways to facilitate student understanding and skill development. The variability of student aptitude and achievement makes knowing our content vital. There are times when doing this may mean studying for hours before teaching a concept or content. If that's what it takes, then that's what we do.

Another principle is that the more we understand about how learning takes place, the more effective we will be as teachers. The field of neuroscience has much to teach us, even as we are likely just in the beginning stages of this huge field of inquiry.

Another principle is that we have to be constant observers of students, picking up on indications that learning is happening, or not. In Chapter 8, we learn ways of assessing learning to guide instruction. We must be flexible and willing to change course right in the middle of a lesson plan or strategy that's not working.

An undisputable principle is that the more extensive our repertoire of instructional strategies, the more effective we will be as teachers. In this chapter, we discuss big ideas of instruction and then explore 15 strategies that work well to promote young adolescent learning. So, let's get started on a creative journey.

SDP

LO 7.1 Brain Function and Learning

An analogy from the 1980s is partially credited for educators' fascination with how brain functioning applies to teaching and learning. It goes like this: "Designing educational experiences without an understanding of the brain is like designing a glove without an understanding of the human hand" (Tokuhama-Espinosa, 2012). Research on how our brains work is a dynamic area of science, often referred to as **Mind, Brain, and Education (MBE)**. This emerging field of research connects diverse disciplines to discover more about how we learn.

The last three decades have seen rapid progress in our understanding of how the brain functions during learning, part of a larger field of study labeled as **neuroscience**. Many articles and books have been written about how best to teach students given what some refer to as brain research. As the frenzy to apply neuroscience to teaching and learning has decreased, we are becoming aware that not all research and learning theories about brain functioning have been credible. Some parts of the theories that we relied on in the past are being labeled neuromyths: right-brain and left-brain theories, learning style theories, the concept that we only use 10% of our brains, and more (Tokuhama-Espinosa, 2012). However, study continues, and that's a good thing.

There are some theories that appear at this point in time to be well-established that can help teachers improve student learning. Given that the field of brain research is ever-evolving, we have to base our strategies on what we believe at the time to be confirmed by science.

Brains Are Unique

Human brains are unique; not all are created equal. This isn't at all new to anyone and the fact has given rise to concepts such as multiple intelligence theory and learning styles. Even though elements of the theories have been debunked, their message is unmistakable: our brains are unique.

IMPLICATIONS

- Having high expectations for all students does not mean having the *same* expectations for each student. It's well-established that not all brains can approach specific challenges successfully.

- When measuring intelligence, the IQ test doesn't tell the whole story. However, when it comes to academic aptitude and achievement, a person's IQ certainly plays a big part in what, how much, and when students learn, as well as how they go about it.

- Differentiation of instruction is a valid and necessary goal for teachers. Differentiating basically means we find ways to teach that address the varying learning needs of unique brains.

Brains Can Change

"The brain is the only organ of our body that changes each day as a result of our experiences" (Burns, 2015). This is the good news for teachers! What we do and how we do it matters, not just in students learning bits of information, but in stretching their brain capacity. This is referred to as **plasticity**. It explains how we make connections between what we know and new concepts, content, and skills.

IMPLICATIONS

- Once students understand a concept, practice solidifies it. This is why we include guided and independent practice in our lesson plans (more on this in Chapter 9).

- When new knowledge or skills are presented, they are learned more readily if they are connected to previous learning or personal interests.

- Our old conception of intelligence as a fixed commodity now gives way to the belief that intelligence can grow, although how much is still a mystery.

- Exercising the brain helps strengthen it, just as exercising the body makes us stronger. For instance, playing chess for several hours makes us better players, and increases reasoning capabilities, as we think through the board and strategize.

Brains Jump to Conclusions

People judge one another's faces, and even tones of voice, almost immediately and unconsciously (Stigler & Hiebert, 2009). This fact doesn't apply directly to choice of instructional strategies, but it certainly applies to how we as teachers impact students.

IMPLICATIONS

- First impressions matter! The first time we meet our students they are sizing us up. Is she smiling? Does she seem happy to be in the classroom? Is she excited about the new year and her subject area?

- Every day should be a fresh start. Kids know if we are holding grudges or carrying resentment for their behavior or something they may have said in haste. They see it in our faces and hear it in our tone of voice.

- Teaching students to understand that first impressions matter is giving them tools for life.

- Videotaping a class has never been easier. Perhaps we aren't aware of our expressions or our tone of voice. Watching ourselves teach is rarely a pleasant experience, but it reveals so much that we can learn from.

Brains Respond to New Stimuli

We quickly recognize when things are different. We notice unexpected movements, sounds, smells, anything that's sensory. We know, often instantly, if patterns are changed. But because this brain function is unique to individuals, it's difficult to know how individuals will respond to change.

IMPLICATIONS

- There's comfort in sameness, so be careful to keep some elements of your classroom unchanging. For instance, routines should be established so everyone knows how to function within your classroom community.
- Keep in mind that kids like to know they can count on us to be consistent. It's important to have a demeanor that is life-giving and positive!
- Even though we can't know exactly how individual students will react, we do know that change is recognized and we can use this to our advantage as an attention-getter.
- Engaging students in learning is often the result of change. The brain likes novelty and kids will often become excited about something new or different in our instruction.

Eric Jensen is perhaps the best-known advocate of using brain research to improve teaching and learning. He tells us that enriched learning has two critical ingredients—the learning must be *challenging* and *interactive feedback* must be present (Jensen, 2016). Challenge may come through problem solving and critical thinking opportunities, relevant projects, and complex activities. Be aware that too much challenge may lead students to give up, while too little challenge will lead to boredom. Determining the right amount of challenge calls for us to know our students well, and then to individualize levels of challenge to maximize enrichment. Interactive feedback is the second ingredient of enrichment. Feedback should be specific and immediate. As we proceed through this chapter, keep challenge and feedback in mind. These two elements should be infused in every facet of our classroom instruction.

No doubt the field of Mind, Brain, and Education research will continue to thrive. As it does, my hope is that this overview will pique your interest and that your heightened awareness of how brain function can influence teaching and learning will grow.

Standard 4
Middle Level Instruction and Assessment

Middle level teacher candidates understand, use, and reflect on the major concepts, principles, theories, and research related to data-informed instruction and assessment. They employ a variety of developmentally appropriate instructional strategies, information literacy skills, and technologies to meet the learning needs of all young adolescents (e.g., race, ethnicity, culture, age, appearance, ability, sexual orientation, socioeconomic status, and family composition).

Self-Check 7.1

LO 7.2 Student-Focused Instruction

Student-focused instruction calls for us to create opportunities that empower students to be self-directed learners. Student-focused instruction requires us to be facilitators of learning, not merely dispensers of information and skill trainers. Filling our instructional toolboxes with strategies, some of which are discussed later in this chapter, enables us to tailor what happens in the classroom to meet the needs of our students. A balanced classroom will include student-directed activities as well as more traditional strategies such as lecture, note-taking, worksheets, and whole-class instruction. Regardless of the strategy, we must keep our focus on students. The characteristics of student-focused instruction include:

- Active student engagement
- Variety of strategies
- Student choice
- Student inquiry
- Student responsibility
- Challenge and feedback
- Ongoing assessment of learning.

Differentiation of Instruction

Differentiation of instruction calls for us to meet our students where they are, to accept them as learners with differing strengths and weaknesses, and to do all we can to help each and every student grow as much as possible. Since the mid-1990s the words "differentiating instruction" have caused us to examine classroom practices in a new light. The concept of differentiated instruction is linked to Carol Ann Tomlinson (1999) and her book, *The Differentiated Classroom*. In this book and many subsequent books and articles, Tomlinson makes a commonsense case for the importance of differentiating instruction, describes the philosophy and ways to begin, and provides classroom scenarios (many in middle level) that give us vivid pictures of what a classroom looks like when the instruction is differentiated to meet the needs of students.

Tomlinson tells us that we can differentiate content, process, and product. *Content* is what students should know and be able to do. *Process* includes ways students make sense of and use the content. A *product* allows students to demonstrate what they know and can do. We can use student affect, readiness, interests, and learning profile to guide our differentiation practices. Student *affect* includes how he or she responds emotionally to the content and process. Student *readiness* is how close students are to grasping content. Student *interest* is obvious and student *learning profile* includes a number of variables including learning preferences, cultural influences, and gender. Keep in mind that differentiating one aspect of instruction will affect the other aspects.

Whole-class instruction is entirely appropriate in many instances. Tomlinson tells teachers they may adapt one or more of the curricular elements (content, process, and product) based on one or more of the student characteristics (affect, readiness, interest, and learning profile) at any point in a lesson or unit. She emphasizes that there is no one right way or time to differentiate. She cautions us to move slowly as we develop ways to differentiate and to start small as we build our repertoire of strategies.

To begin to differentiate according to affect, readiness, interests, and learning profile requires us to know our students well. At the heart of middle level education is the premise that doing schooling right requires us to have knowledge of, and closeness to, our students. Characteristics of a differentiated classroom include:

- Student differences are considered.
- Diagnostic assessment is used to determine student needs (more on this in Chapter 8).

Enhanced etext
Video Example 7.1

In *Providing Students Options for Learning,* we hear several educators discussing differentiation of instruction.

- Student grouping strategies are varied.
- Student choice is exercised.

Critical Thinking Skills

"**Critical thinking** involves observing, comparing and contrasting, interpreting, analysing, seeing issues from a variety of perspectives, weighing variables, and then making decisions and solving problems based on these thinking skills" (Powell, 2019). Using **thinking skills** is a cognitive act that may simply involve awareness of surroundings or may be as complex as making judgments that lead to actions. **Bloom's taxonomy** (1956) presents the classic six levels of thinking: knowledge, comprehension, application, analysis, synthesis, and evaluation. In 2001, Anderson and Krathwohl provided an update to Bloom's taxonomy using the terminology in Table 7.1 and changed the order of highest level of thinking to "creating" rather than "evaluation" (Anderson and Krathwohl, 2001).

Each level may be accessed through the use of active verbs and questions. I strongly urge you to explore the levels fully, to read books and articles about them, and to internalize them. Regardless of the content area, we can provide thinking opportunities at all six levels. Teach them to your students. Then occasionally ask: "Which level of Bloom's taxonomy are we using here?" The flower in Figure 7.1 is a fun way to keep the levels visible in your classroom.

Teaching students thinking skills can be accomplished through focused instruction outside a specific content area. Modeling is vital. We can model, for instance, the difference between reading and recalling the steps required to successfully learn to juggle two balls and actually doing it. We can read the steps out loud, close the book and recite them (*knowledge* or *remembering*), paraphrase the steps (*understand* or *comprehend*), and then hold two balls and ineptly toss them into the air, bungling the process. We then explain to our students that remembering and understanding are quite different from applying. We would then ask students to *analyze* what went wrong when we attempted to *apply* what we knew and then to *create* or *synthesize* a plan for learning to actually juggle. Finally, we would ask the students to predict the success of our attempts, or perhaps the value of learning to juggle (*evaluation*).

Although it is possible to teach critical thinking skills in isolation, teaching critical thinking skills within the context of the curriculum should be ongoing. To extend a skill presented in isolation, such as categorization (*analysis*), a math teacher might give a small group of students a bucket of attribute blocks and ask them to develop categories in which the blocks might be divided and lists of blocks that fit each. A language arts teacher might ask students to read an essay, write a summary (*understand* or *comprehend*), organize the main points (*apply* and *analyze*), compose an essay on the same topic (*create* or *synthesize*), and then examine both essays critically to defend the value of each (*evaluate*). A science teacher might ask students to name the parts of an insect (*remember*), ask students to illustrate the parts (*understand* or *comprehend*), dissect an insect into basic parts (*apply* and *analyze*), and build a clay model of an anatomically accurate insect they imagine (*create* or *synthesize*).

> *TWB* **Goal 2.** [Young adolescents will] be able to think rationally and critically and express thought clearly.

Inquiry-Based Learning

Inquiry-based learning is just what it sounds like—learning from questions and investigations. The process of inquiry is open-ended, beginning with a topic or scenario and involving a brief exploration or in-depth research. There are many levels of inquiry. A quick check on Google or a telephone call or an informal

Enhanced eText
Video Example 7.2
Fifth grade teacher Dee Lanier shares how he and his teammates approach differentiation of instruction.

FIGURE 7.1 We're bloomin'
Edited by L. W. Anderson, and D. R. Krathwohl,
Source: Adapted from Anderson, L. W., & Krathwohl, D. R. (Ed.). (2001). A taxonomy for learning, teaching, and assessing. New York: Longman., Pearson Education

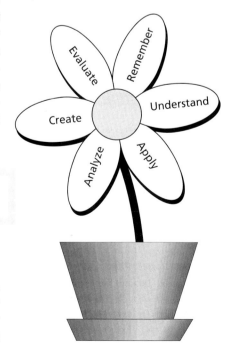

TABLE 7.1 Bloom's taxonomy

Categories	Key Verbs		Question Stems
Remember (Knowledge)	recognize	retrieve	When did _____?
	identify	list	Who was _____?
	recall	define	Where is _____?
	memorize	duplicate	Why did _____?
			Can you list four _____?
Understand (Comprehension)	interpret	classify	How would you compare _____ to _____?
	summarize	compare	What is the main idea of _____?
	infer	explain	What is meant by _____?
	illustrate		
Apply	implement	dramatize	How would you use _____ to _____?
	use	illustrate	What approach would you use to _____?
	operate	solve	Can you _____ by _____?
Analyze	organize	categorize	What evidence can you find to conclude that _____?
	integrate	differentiate	What does _____ have to do with _____?
	focus	examine	
		test	
Evaluate	check	monitor	What is your opinion of _____?
	critique	defend	How valuable is _____ for _____?
	judge	support	Why would you recommend _____?
Create (Synthesis)	generate	construct	How would you change _____ to form _____?
	plan	produce	Can you propose a different way to _____?
	design	develop	How would you design _____ to _____?

Edited by L. W. Anderson, and D. R. Krathwohl, *Source:* Adapted from Anderson, L. W., & Krathwohl, D. R. (Ed.). (2001). A taxonomy for learning, teaching, and assessing. New York: Longman., Pearson Education

Enhanced eText
Video Example 7.3

Eighth grade teacher Dave Uelmen discusses a project that revolves around inquiry learning.

interview constitutes inquiry, or inquiry-based learning may involve a well-planned project with multiple levels. It is not passive, not characterized by middle level students in straight rows taking notes as the teacher lectures. Inquiry-based learning is good for young adolescents because it cultivates students' responsibility for their own learning.

> *TWB* **Goal 6.** [Young adolescents] understand and use the major concepts, skills, and tools of inquiry in the areas of health and physical education, language arts, world languages, mathematics, natural and physical sciences, and the social sciences.

One manifestation of inquiry-based learning is **constructivism**. A teacher facilitating students as they use critical or higher-order thinking skills to construct their own learning is constructivism. Constructivism is good for young adolescents because most prefer active learning, they are generally very social creatures, and they have the capacity to be quite creative. Constructivism takes emphasis off teaching and places it squarely on learning and the learner. Constructivist strategies are time consuming and most appropriate for complex learning, such as analyzing events, proving theories, and scientific experimentation. Although using them in every lesson is appealing, there simply isn't enough time in a school day, or school year.

Enhanced eText
Video Example 7.4

Focus teacher Traci Peters's lesson demonstrates a structure that includes students working in groups.

Cooperative Learning

There's cooperative learning, and then there's **cooperative learning**. The two words can be a catchall for any instance of students working together, or they can represent an instructional strategy with defined guidelines and requirements. Let's examine both viewpoints.

On any given day in any middle school, you will probably hear teachers referring to cooperative learning or cooperative groups or simply group work. Although proponents of stricter definitions may wince, I believe that any time young adolescents work together they experience both cooperation and learning. This has to be good for them.

More formalized cooperative learning involves the creation of scenarios that require students to do the following:

- Depend on each other for success.
- Interact in a variety of ways, using positive interpersonal skills.
- Be responsible for both individual tasks and group tasks.
- Consider how their group is functioning and making progress toward the end product(s).

When these elements are planned as part of a lesson or project, students will experience a host of benefits. The presence of these elements, according to many researchers and teachers, sets "true" cooperative learning apart from more loosely constructed group work.

Both heterogeneous ability grouping and homogeneous ability grouping may be utilized to group students for cooperative learning experiences. Sometimes teachers designate groups and purposefully put particular students together. At other times students are grouped using random strategies or are allowed to choose their own groups.

The length of time groups remain intact will vary. Changing the size and composition of your groups depends on the activity or task. If you assign a group project, the groups of students will remain constant for the duration of the assignment. Some teachers have great success with forming heterogeneous cooperative groups that stay together for nine weeks, or longer. The philosophy behind this is that students in stable groups, with appropriate guidance, develop trusting and nurturing relationships along with social skills and commitment.

The participants in cooperative groups are often assigned specific roles to help the groups function effectively and efficiently. The roles may include a facilitator to keep things moving, a recorder to take notes, a timer to keep members on schedule, a gatherer of materials, an encourager to ensure everyone provides input, and an artist to illustrate for the group.

There are multiple benefits of cooperative learning, including development of racial and gender tolerance, promotion of friendships, increased understanding of children with disabilities, and greater abilities to problem solve. With benefits like these, the practice of cooperative learning is a must in middle level education. The steps in Figure 7.2 will help you begin and maintain cooperative learning in your classroom.

Sara Davis Powell

Any time students work together cooperatively they are learning important skills.

> *TWB* **Goal 11.** [Young adolescents] develop the interpersonal and social skills needed to learn, work, and play with others harmoniously and confidently.

Technology in the Classroom

We make our choices among the many instructional technology tools according to lesson objectives, availability, our expertise in using the tools, and the appropriateness of the tool to the particular situation. Our challenge is to mesh curriculum, our students and their needs, and instructional tools to foster effective learning opportunities. The use of calculators, videos, audiotapes, and other tools considered "lower tech" in the 21st century is common. Most classrooms have higher-tech options including Smart technology, instructional software, tablets, e-books, digital games, and more. **Educational technology** is any technology-based device or program that enhances teaching and learning.

Technology use in the classroom can be motivating. Young adolescents take for granted that technology is part of everyday life. To walk into a classroom and find no technology can be disconcerting. Access to information provided by the World Wide Web has the potential to enhance how we approach research in all content areas and helps put research responsibility in the hands of students. The interactive nature of websites allows for simulations in which students manipulate variables and receive immediate feedback. The possibilities are tremendous. A relatively recent innovation using technology is the concept of the **flipped classroom**. Basically, flipping a classroom entails using technology to digitally deliver a mini-lecture or provide content that's accessible on electronic devices. Students watch the video after school, freeing classroom time for engaging in discussion and activities that may have been formerly reserved for homework (Cohen & Brugar, 2013). In a flipped classroom, students spend more time working together at the higher levels of Bloom's taxonomy. Jonathan Bergmann, one of the pioneers of the flipped classroom, provides some positive results of flipping your classroom on his website, including:

- In a flipped classroom, students have more opportunities to direct their own learning.
- Students may access material presented electronically any time.
- Teachers have more time to work with students individually during class periods.

Creating the take-home lesson component is possible through tech tools such as **Jing**, a program that allows you to capture your brief lesson and make it available to your students through screencasts, or specifically designed videos.

FIGURE 7.2 Getting started and maintaining cooperative learning

1. Read about and experience cooperative learning in university classes and staff development opportunities.
2. Determine to implement cooperative learning in your own classroom.
3. Give several simple tasks to students in random groups that will show them the benefits of working together. Make sure success is built into the tasks.
4. Define a task for cooperative groups in your classroom.
5. Make decisions about grouping students, roles for the task, materials needed, time guidelines, and desired results of cooperative work.
6. Plan for positive interdependence, face-to-face interactions, individual accountability, interpersonal skills, and group processing.
7. Talk with your students about the process of cooperative learning. Include your expectations, guidelines for interactions, and how work will be assessed.
8. Assign roles to students in groups.
9. Observe closely as groups work together. Take notes on what you see.
10. Involve students in debriefing the cooperative learning experience.
11. Plan your next venture into cooperative learning!

Teachers Speak

Jermaine Joyner
Using technology is so much a part of who I am and what I do. I teach kids about it all day long. I have my own website and blog. My smartphone is my means of voice communication, text messaging, surfing the Internet, reading books, etc. It's my alarm clock and my camera. I often joke that I'm married to it and don't need a traditional wife. But then I fully understand that

I'm exaggerating. If I forget, my girlfriend gladly reminds me. My point is that I depend on technology and enjoy it as well. I view technology as a vital teaching tool, and I have a hard time understanding teachers who don't take advantage of at least a few of the tools available. Fortunately, I have a principal who calms me down when I get agitated and frustrated by some colleagues' lack of interest and motivation to incorporate tools I know would benefit student learning. Calm or not, I'm on a mission to bring the wonderful digital world into every teacher's repertoire of strategies.

The **International Society for Technology in Education (ISTE)** gives us detailed descriptions of the knowledge and skills related to technology use appropriate for young adolescents. You'll notice that the AMLE Teacher Preparation Standards repeatedly include technology. As with any teaching and learning tool, technology should enhance what we do in our classrooms or not be used.

> *TWB* Goal 4. [Young adolescents] use digital tools to explore, communicate, and collaborate with the world and learn from the rich and varied resources available.

Now that we have established a foundation for instructional practices, let's examine some instructional strategies that are appropriate for young adolescents in middle level settings.

Self-Check 7.2

LO 7.3 Instructional Strategies

Our instructional toolboxes should be overflowing with strategies to effectively address the learning needs and preferences of all students. To be developmentally responsive requires it.

Standard 4

Middle Level Instruction and Assessment

Element b. Middle Level Instructional Strategies: Middle level teacher candidates employ a wide variety of effective teaching, learning, and assessment strategies. They use instructional strategies and technologies in ways that encourage exploration, creativity, and information literacy skills (e.g., critical thinking, problem solving, evaluation of information gained) so that young adolescents are actively engaged in their learning. They use instruction that is responsive to young adolescents' local, national, and international histories, language/dialects, and individual identities (e.g., race, ethnicity, culture, age, appearance, ability, sexual orientation, socioeconomic status, and family composition).

The Importance of Choice

Choice accommodates differentiation, one of the most daunting challenges for teachers. This is the overarching benefit of choice. Our discussion of differentiating instruction included a Video Example 7.1 depicting a teacher giving students three choices of assignments, all relating to the problem of erosion of the Georgia coastline. This sort of choice allows students to choose based on affect, readiness, interest or learning profile. Think about your future heterogeneous classroom and how well-designed choices will make it possible for students, whether designated as gifted or those with varying disabilities, to "fully participate in appropriately challenging and personally interesting work because they had meaningful choices about what to study, what goals to challenge themselves with, and what projects to create to share their learning" (Anderson, 2016, p. 10). Differentiation accomplished!

Choice is motivational. In Chapter 10, we discuss two forms of motivation. One is extrinsic, or motivation that depends on the actions of another. The other is intrinsic, or motivation that comes from within. Choice has the potential to be intrinsically motivating. Giving students choices when appropriate leads them to sense some ownership over their learning (Chandler, 2017). And ownership is intrinsically motivating.

Choice should be purposeful. We can't give students choices about every aspect of their learning. We have standards to meet that must guide much of the content and dictate some of our instructional choices. There are skills that must be learned and often there's little time for choice. Anderson (2016) reminds us that choice is a means to an end, and rarely the end in and of itself. He also suggests three guidelines to consider as we develop meaningful choices for our students.

- Keep the number of choices small, two to five, for assignments. We don't want to overwhelm the students.
- Consider the students and make sure there's one that suits what he terms outliers.
- Be realistic. Consider time, resources, and amount of preparation you will have to do.

It's vital to teach students how to make good choices. The first step is to thoroughly explain the logistics of each choice. Students should understand the level of effort that will be required and have time to think through their decisions, often with our guidance. After all, when we create the choices we will do so with our students in mind. This is another benefit of knowing our students well. Having a full toolbox of instructional strategies allows us to carefully choose the ones that are appropriate for our students, as well as for the content, skill, and standard to be addressed. This toolbox also allows us to give students choices. One of many excellent resources for expanding our instructional repertoire is *Teachers Network*, a website loaded with free lesson plans, resources, professional development opportunities, grant writing information, and videos that help us hone our skills.

Sara Davis Powell

Sara Davis Powell

The unique characteristics of young adolescents make it important to provide variety and choices in lessons and assignments. Their spontaneous personalities add so much joy to our lives!

Standard 4

Middle Level Instruction and Assessment

Element a. Content Pedagogy: Middle level teacher candidates use their knowledge of instruction and assessment strategies that are especially effective in the subjects they teach.

Let's look briefly at nine categories of instruction before exploring a variety of strategies.

Nine Categories of Instruction

Marzano, Pickering, and Pollock (2012) tell us there are nine categories of instruction shown in Figure 7.3 that correlate positively and most often with student learning. Some of the categories are stand-alone strategies, but others may encompass multiple individual strategies. The categories are all shown to be highly effective through a meta-analysis of strategies and, although they are listed in descending order of effectiveness, each comes highly recommended as a tool for classroom instruction. Don't just glance at this list. Study it and think about why these strategies may be so effective. Take particular note of the hierarchal nature of the list. As we examine individual recommended strategies in the next section, refer to Figure 7.3 to see how each strategy might fit into one or more of the nine categories.

Recommended Strategies

Brief descriptions of instructional strategies that fit in one, or more than one, of the nine categories of instruction and are vehicles for implementing the big ideas of instruction are discussed next. Keep in mind that not all strategies are appropriate for all subject areas or groups of young adolescents.

LECTURE   Overuse and misuse of the lecture format, along with some of our own memories of fighting to stay awake through the Prussian Wars or the contributions of automation to the Industrial Revolution, have left many of us with a bad taste. However, with certain guidelines, the **lecture**, or mini-lecture, is a valuable teaching strategy to introduce a lesson, describe a problem, and/or provide information in concise ways.

FIGURE 7.3   Categories of instructional strategies that affect student achievement

Identifying similarities and differences—involves identification of important characteristics and then comparing, classifying, creating metaphors and analogies

Summarizing and note-taking—powerful study skills for identifying and understanding the most important aspects of what students are learning

Reinforcing effort and providing recognition—techniques that address students' attitudes, beliefs, and motivation concerning the connection of effort and success

Homework and practice—provide opportunities for students to refine and extend knowledge

Non-linguistic representations—graphic representations and physical models that elaborate on knowledge

Cooperative learning—flexible and powerful tool for grouping students to promote collaboration

Setting objectives and providing feedback—process of establishing a direction for learning and then providing an explanation of what students are doing that is correct and what they are doing that is incorrect

Generating and testing hypotheses—process of understanding a principle, making a conjecture, and applying the knowledge to see if it holds true

Cues, questions, and advance organizers—techniques that activate prior knowledge and/or set the stage for, and bridge the way to, new knowledge

---

Based on: R. J. Marzano, D. J. Pickering, and J. E. Pollock (2012). *Classroom Instruction That Works* (2nd ed.). Alexandria, VA: ASCDLearn. Teach. Lead.

A **mini-lecture** is simply a brief lecture. Keeping the mini-lecture to 10 minutes or so will allow it to be used effectively and as often as appropriate.

When planning a mini-lecture, identify the main points. Develop an **advance organizer**, an attention-grabbing opener that sets the stage for the content to come. Then decide on examples to include that will illustrate the main points. Finally, develop a summary of the content that refers to the advance organizer and main points.

DEMONSTRATION   A **demonstration** is a way of showing students something that would be difficult to convey through words alone. Whether showing steps in solving a math problem, describing the symbols for editing and their applications, or conducting a science experiment, demonstrations can be very effective instructional tools applicable in every subject area. When coupled with a mini-lecture, a demonstration complements auditory learning with visual stimulation.

TEACHER THINK-ALOUD   Modeling thinking processes through **think-alouds** shows our students how they might go about solving problems, approaching tasks, or processing new information. Think-alouds can make invisible mental processes visible.

Here's an example of a think-aloud: Margo purchased a CD on sale that had an original price of $15. All the CDs on the rack were 20% off. The sales tax was 8%. How much change did Margo receive from a $20 bill?

A think-aloud example:

> Ummmm . . . Let's see what I know. The CD is on sale so she's not going to pay $15. Does she pay 20%? No, that's the discount. So I have to find 20% of $15. That's $3. I should subtract it because the CD is on sale. Okay, that's $12. Now I need to add the tax. I have to multiply again (write .08 × 12 on board and multiply). I subtracted the $3 but now I have to add the $.96 (write on board 12.00 + .96). That means she paid $12.96 for the CD. She used a $20 bill so I have to subtract $12.96 from $20 (do this on board). So she got $7.04 back in change.

Think-alouds can demonstrate to students how to bring personal background and prior knowledge into reading. Try reading an article or passage in a short story and then stop to verbalize an experience you had that relates to the text. In this way you are showing your students how to internalize what they read.

Aside from academics, try using the think-aloud strategy when you hear students arguing or you become aware of a friendship rift or when students have decisions to make. Think aloud about how you might deal with the situation. For young adolescents this is so much more effective than "preaching" or talking "at them."

QUESTIONING   Effective questioning takes thought and planning. We can prompt our students to think on all six levels of Bloom's taxonomy on any topic in any subject by asking relevant questions and asking them to create their own questions.

Questions may be convergent and tend to have one best answer. **Convergent questions** lead to exercising Bloom's remembering and understanding/comprehending levels. **Divergent questions** are those that are open-ended and often have many possible responses. When we are looking for application in thinking, our questions should allow for a number of correct responses. Analysis is often personal and based on prior knowledge, so answers will vary. Creating can be engaging because we are asking our students to come up with something new based on what they know. The responses to questions aimed at evaluative thinking can take many directions. Figure 7.4 includes very practical guidelines for using questioning as a thoughtfully planned instructional strategy.

One of the best ways we can help our students learn a concept deeply is to guide them in framing good questions. After a reading assignment or an activity, rather than requiring students to write a summary or an outline, have them write questions. Without guidance you will likely get a lot of "When did . . . ?" "Who was . . . ?" "What happened when . . . ?"—all *remembering*, with maybe a smattering of *understanding*.

FIGURE 7.4 Questioning techniques

1. Plan key questions that are clear and specific to provide lesson structure and direction. Ask spontaneous questions based on student responses.

2. Adapt questions to student ability level. This enhances understanding and reduces anxiety. Phrase questions in natural, simple language.

3. Ask questions at a variety of levels. Keep Bloom's taxonomy in mind.

4. Respond to students in ways that encourage them to clarify initial answers and support their points of view and opinions.

5. Give students time to think before requiring an answer. Wait-time after asking a question should be five seconds or more to both increase the frequency of student responses and encourage higher-level thinking.

6. Encourage a wide range of student participation. Call on non-volunteers, being careful to consider difficulty levels of questions.

7. Encourage student questioning. Prompt students to phrase questions that stimulate higher cognitive levels of thought.

Making the Teaching and Learning Connection

Pearson Education, Inc

Dear future teachers,

I discovered after being a 5th grade teacher for several years that I am happiest teaching science. I've found the perfect position as the science teacher for all the 4th and 5th graders at my large intermediate school.

Middle level science is such an exciting field! I spend my days with kids who learn using the most hands-on methods I can find or create. As the school's science specialist, I am able to impact not only what and how students learn, but also how they perceive science. I remember my own science experiences in middle and high school, most of which consisted of reading about a concept, taking notes as the teacher lectured or demonstrated, and then having tests on Fridays over material I learned for a week and then forgot.

Once I started teaching and using the 5E lesson plan—engage, explore, explain, elaborate, evaluate – I realized what I had missed in my own science education. With the exception of a few high school lab sessions, I never engaged. Now in my classes, the kids engage almost every day. I make sure they don't just follow a set of steps to reach a conclusion. They build their own conclusions, what some call constructivism, and learn through inquiry. They wonder and discover by asking their own questions. When they need a little boost, I step in with questions. It's an effective way to teach and so much fun, as a side benefit not just for the kids, but for me, too.

If you will be teaching science, or really any other subject, use the concepts of the 5E plan, engage kids when you can, ask lots of questions and encourage them to do the same, and enjoy the adventure!

Macy Ingle

Enhanced eText
Video Example 7.5

A middle level science teacher demonstrates the use of student engagement and inquiry learning in her classroom.

Standard 1

Young Adolescent Development

Element c. Implications of Young Adolescent Development for Middle Level Curriculum and Instruction. Middle level teacher candidates use their knowledge of young adolescent development when planning and implementing middle level curriculum and when selecting and using instructional strategies.

To make the strategy effective, use question prompts like the ones in Table 7.1 Bloom's taxonomy. As a homework assignment you might ask students to read a particular text and develop three questions using these prompts. The next day, form groups and have students exchange and answer each other's questions.

CLASS DISCUSSIONS Class discussions occur every day in almost every class in every middle school. It is the nature of most young adolescents to like to talk and voice opinions. Most want to be heard and have great things to contribute. Focus the discussion to keep it on track and ensure that everyone participates. Keep in mind that a discussion is a conversation, not just a question and answer session. Ideally student voices are heard more frequently than the teacher's.

BRAINSTORMING The goal of brainstorming is to produce as many responses as possible. All contributions are allowed without judgment (of course, within guidelines of good taste). We want students to think in divergent ways as they contribute. The results of brainstorming can be recorded in many ways using the chalk/whiteboard, chart paper, or SMARTBoard.

Brainstorming is also the first stage of a very popular and useful instructional tool, the **K-W-L chart**. Figure 7.5 shows a K-W-L chart and an example of how it might be used. The K stands for what we KNOW. Brainstorming fills that column. From the brainstorming will come questions, perhaps about things listed in the K column. The W stands for what we WANT to know, so the W column will be filled with questions. The L stands for what we LEARNED. The K-W-L chart should be displayed for the duration of the study of a topic so entries can continually be added to the columns.

Another important use of brainstorming is to begin the writing process. To write an essay, students can brainstorm all the things they might possibly want to include. They group them, and the groups become logical paragraphs. The paragraphs are then sequenced, and an introduction is written followed by the body paragraphs and then a conclusion.

When a class decision is needed, perhaps choosing a field trip location or a topic to be studied in more depth, brainstorming is a valuable tool to encourage everyone

FIGURE 7.5 K-W-L chart

Constitution of the United States		
K What We Know	**W** What We Want to Know	**L** What We Learned
• Written in 1700s • Tells how to run our country • Displayed in Washington • Fancy penmanship • Signed by a bunch of men • Has amendments	• Who actually wrote it? • Can it be changed? • What do we do about things that aren't covered in the Constitution? • What are some things that we hear about that are "unconstitutional"?	This column is for students to record answers to their questions and other things of interest learned in their study. Have a way of adding lots of paper for a long list.

to participate. Once students have experienced the process, it can be student-led rather than teacher-led. Brainstorming is an effective way to create ownership of decisions.

NOTE-TAKING   Taking notes is part of our everyday lives. We make lists for groceries and things to do, notes to help us follow directions to a location, instructions for how to order something we see on television, and so on. Of course, this isn't the same thing as taking notes on a lecture or a reading assignment, but the reasons for note-taking are similar. Note-taking, whether practical or academic, helps us remember and saves us time.

Note-taking can be thought of as "listening with your pencil" (Ernst, 1996, p. 71). Note-taking requires both listening skills and **critical thinking** skills as we decide what is important to remember, organize information to write, and determine if it's enough or if further clarification is needed. This is a lot to ask of a 10- to 14-year-old. We must model the process.

We can give students a framework for notes and have them fill in details either as they listen to a lecture, participate in a discussion, read text, or watch a video. For these guided notes, you may want to simply write statements with key words and phrases omitted. Allow time for students to read through the guided notes before the lecture, discussion, or video so they will be reading or listening for specific information. This strategy focuses attention and also provides a study guide.

In an inclusive classroom you will likely have students for whom note-taking will be difficult because of some condition that impairs their ability to be successful with the skill. Try providing carbon paper for several students who are willing to share their note-taking abilities with students who need assistance.

DRILL AND PRACTICE   Clarifying and consolidating material already learned and then repeating the information or skill is what the drill and practice strategy is all about. The process helps with long-term retention and aids in developing speed and accuracy (Burden & Byrd, 2016).

When you use drill and practice, always make sure the material is familiar enough so students won't have to stop to look something up or ask questions. Students should be able to work independently and always have a way of knowing quickly how well they did. Using computer software to practice skills and recall information is both efficient and effective. Use drill and practice in moderation, but don't fail to employ it when there are obvious benefits.

GRAPHIC ORGANIZERS   As powerful instructional tools, **graphic organizers** help us think critically as we visualize knowledge and comprehend relationships in organized ways. They enhance teaching and learning in any subject area to sequence events, prioritize actions, categorize information, compare and contrast ideas and objects, show part/whole relationships, illustrate connectivity, show cause and effect—you name it, and a graphic organizer can enhance it.

Following a brainstorming session, students can take all the random, scattered information and make sense of it using a graphic organizer. A simple web design illustrated in Figure 7.6 works well for this purpose, with supporting ideas radiating from a central topic or theme, like spokes on a wheel. Talking students through the creation of such a web is the best way for them to understand the process.

After reading a story or novel, an effective way to review the events is to use a sequencing organizer like the one shown in Figure 7.7. You can do this as a whole class a few times, then assign the task to small groups of students who can post their graphic organizers for others to view.

You'll find that many students will start to really catch on to the significance of concepts such as *recognizing similarities and differences* when they

FIGURE 7.6 Simple web

FIGURE 7.7 Sequencing organizer

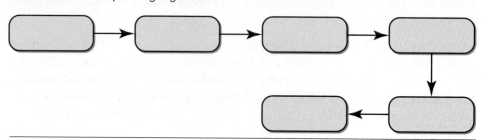

understand the use of Venn diagrams. Do you remember from the beginning of this section that this is the top ranked category of instructional strategies in terms of student learning? Figure 7.8 shows a simple Venn diagram, one of the most useful graphic organizers.

ENHANCING VOCABULARY The more words students *own*, the higher their comprehension levels will be and the easier learning and conceptualizing will become. Creating a word-rich environment will immerse our students in vocabulary. When a new word surfaces in class readings, videos, or discussions, have a student write the word on an index card along with a definition that is appropriate for the context. Then have the student put the card in a classroom pocket chart with a pocket for each letter in the alphabet. In this way we create our own classroom dictionaries that are full of relevant words. Encourage students to use the words in the pocket chart in their writing. As the words increase, occasionally pull out all the cards in one letter pocket and review the words with students. Ask them to recall the context of the creation of each card. The words can also be used in games and exercises.

Graphic organizers can be very effective in vocabulary study. Knowing that visual stimulation promotes learning, graphically portraying words makes sense. Figure 7.9 shows two visually pleasing ways for students to study new words.

FIGURE 7.8 Venn diagram

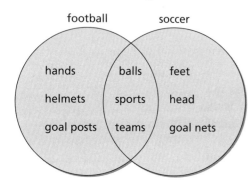

FIGURE 7.9 Vocabulary approaches

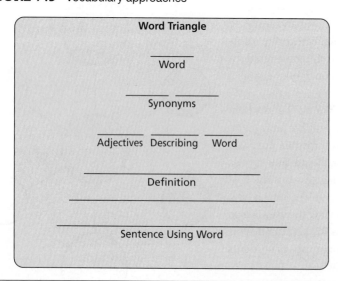
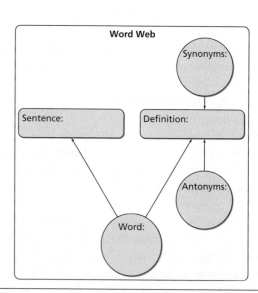

SHARING VOCABULARY   Every subject has a unique vocabulary. There are lots of ways to bring these unique vocabularies alive for our students. We no longer need to perpetuate the drudgery of writing an assigned word, indicating part of speech, then writing a dictionary definition along with a sentence that may or may not illustrate meaning, followed by the task of reading this structure over and over to memorize it. Far more interesting and productive strategies are available to us.

One of the richest benefits of the team structure in middle level settings is the possibility of sharing the vocabulary used in all our subjects all day long. Team vocabulary sharing can be accomplished in a very simple way. Here are the steps:

1. Devise a rotation system that designates one team teacher to be in charge of vocabulary each week.

2. On Thursday, pass a clipboard with a page similar to Figure 7.10 on it among team teachers (or use email).

3. Each team teacher writes a brief description of the next week's content/plans and five or six key vocabulary words. Include related arts teachers who teach students on your team.

4. By Friday the designated teacher should have the clipboard. This teacher makes a wall chart of the words for each team classroom and perhaps the gym, cafeteria, art room, and so on. Colored paper from the big rolls available in most schools works well. A wide marker will make the words easily visible. Use the same colored paper and marker for all classrooms for any given week.

5. Teachers post vocabulary lists in the same places in each classroom every week.

The lists are visual reminders of the words that will be key to understanding the concepts and skills emphasized during the week. All teachers should attempt to use every word on the list within the context of their classes. Although *photosynthesis* rarely comes up in language arts, the word can still be examined because of its compound nature. The art teacher may use the word *symmetry* to describe a painting rather than just mentioning the balance of elements, while the math teacher works with the concept of symmetry. As you use a word, walk over to the list and point to it. Our students are then hearing the word in different contexts and seeing the word on the list. Great reinforcement! Sharing vocabulary lets our students know we talk and plan together. Students learn vocabulary in deeper, more contextualized ways. All this is accomplished through a painless process that takes very little time.

ROLE-PLAY   When students act out or dramatize a situation or idea in a class setting we call it role-play. To be useful as an instructional strategy, **role-play** requires structure that includes a clear purpose and role descriptions. Expectations and incentives

---

FIGURE 7.10 Shared vocabulary

Team _____

Week of _____

Subject: Key vocabulary

Overview of plan:

Subject: Key vocabulary

Overview of plan:

Subject: Key vocabulary

Overview of plan:

Subject: Key vocabulary

Overview of plan:

are needed both for those actively participating, as well those students not actively filling the roles but who need to pay attention. It is vital to debrief a role-play session to make sure students get the point(s). Once the students are accustomed to role-playing, we can be more spontaneous about initiating it.

Role-play helps students gain empathy for others, test solutions to dilemmas, and more deeply understand an event or situation. Other benefits include increased verbal and nonverbal learning, encouragement of divergent thinking, enhanced mental stimulation, and expansion of communication skills.

PROJECT-BASED LEARNING   One of the most student-centered strategies we can use in our classroom is **project-based learning** (PBL). I have watched with great joy as young adolescents suddenly "come alive" in the midst of a project experience that is full of choices. Students who seldom show any semblance of interest in schoolwork often blossom when given the opportunity to choose a topic, a strategy, and/or a work product. Project-based learning allows students to show initiative, take responsibility, be physically involved, make decisions, and create.

Implementing PBL can be much "messier" than other strategies. We must set expectations, ask questions that help students define their projects, assist them in sequencing tasks and organizing procedures (graphic organizers are ideal), remind them of problem-solving strategies for the big and small dilemmas that are inevitable, provide encouragement to stay on task, and celebrate with them as their work culminates into a product. In other words, we facilitate the acquisition and practice of life skills. Worthy effort! There are a number of excellent books about PBL, including those by Thom Markham, to explore.

THINK-PAIR-SHARE   As a versatile and useful tool, **think-pair-share (TPS)** can be employed almost any time, in almost any setting, and for any purpose. TPS encourages the students who rarely join class discussions to participate in pairs where there is less chance of intimidation. Here are the simple steps:

1. Ask a thought-provoking question or give a prompt.
2. Instruct students to think for 30 seconds or so.
3. Have students turn to a neighbor and briefly discuss their thoughts.
4. Ask for volunteers to share with the class what they have discussed.

I often have students write brief notes about their thinking before talking with a partner to lend some accountability to the process. You might want to establish a think-pair-share journal in which students date their thoughts and add their partner's opinions/answers to their own.

A variation of think-pair-share, sometimes called pyramid think-pair-share, involves having pairs of students share with other pairs. In this way, a student goes from individual opinions/answers, to hearing from another student and building on ideas or possibly being persuaded to change an opinion, and then on to benefiting from two additional students' thought processes. This could be followed by whole-group sharing.

JIGSAW   There is great power in students teaching students, and the **jigsaw** model of cooperative learning is an excellent technique that requires them to do so. Here are the basic steps involved in using the jigsaw model:

1. Choose a reading that can be logically divided into sections.
2. Divide your students into groups the same size as the number of sections in the reading. For instance, if a chapter has four sections, your students should form "base" groups of four students each.

FIGURE 7.11 Jigsaw

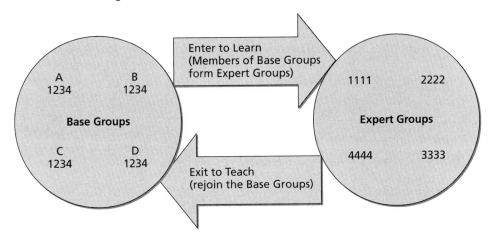

3. Within each group, have students number off one to four. Ask all the ones to get together, all the twos, all the threes, and all the fours. These groups become "expert" groups.

4. Assign each expert group a section of the reading to discuss. Their task is to formulate a plan to teach the material to members of their individual base groups. Encourage groups to develop graphics, written summaries, or other unique ways to make the material meaningful.

5. Reconvene base groups to teach each other the material they have mastered in their expert groups.

Figure 7.11 graphically shows how the model works. Students like the idea of being experts and teachers. Naturally, your watchful facilitation will play a critical role in the success of this valuable instructional strategy.

Self-Check 7.3

Why It Matters

To be effective, instructional practices must pass numerous tests—developmentally responsive, research-based, content or skill appropriate, time efficient, standards supporting, and so on. It takes time to build a repertoire of strategies and experience to make decisions about the what, how, and when of approaches.

Consistently using only one or two strategies is not developmentally responsive. We should choose our instructional strategies based on student needs, the concepts to be taught/learned, and the classroom situation at hand.

Group Activities

1. In small groups (three or four), agree on a broad topic that would be taught in middle school. Brainstorm aspects of the topic *content*, *process* of learning, and *product* that might be differentiated. Then think of ways to determine student *affect*, *readiness*, *interests*, and *learning profiles* concerning the topic. Organize your best collective thoughts for the six italicized areas and be prepared to share with your whole class.

2. In pairs, make an appointment to talk with a middle school teacher. Ask about how he approaches heterogeneous ability grouped classes. How often and in what ways does he differentiate instruction? Add your findings to your school files.

3. So far in this class you've had numerous cooperative learning experiences. As a class, discuss the experiences that seemed more successful than others. Can you determine the factors that may have affected the relative success of the experiences?

4. There are 15 instructional strategies in this chapter. In pairs, choose one strategy and write three questions about it using the question stems provided in this chapter. Use the questions to teach another pair more about your chosen strategy.

5. Think-pair-share time. Individually think of how using procedures to share vocabulary within your team is developmentally responsive. Write your thoughts on a note card. Now pair with someone in your class and share what you have written. As a pair, connect with another pair, and share responses. As a whole class, debrief the process.

6. In conjunction with your instructor, decide on sections of Chapter 8 that appear conducive to using the Jigsaw model. Determine base and expert groups. Use this model to teach each other about various aspects of assessment.

Individual Activities

1. Choose a topic within a subject you plan to teach. Write a narrative explaining how you might address each of the categories in Bloom's taxonomy.

2. Think of a process or skill that would be included in a subject you plan to teach that lends itself to a teacher think-aloud. Plan what you would say to help students understand the process or skill and be prepared to think-aloud for your classmates.

3. During one of your university classes, pay attention to the dynamics of a typical class discussion. Pay close attention to process, as well as keeping up with the content. Take notes on what you observe. Write a critique of the experience and include ways the professor might have improved the discussion time.

4. By this point in your life you have no doubt developed note-taking techniques that you find effective for your learning style. Write a brief description of your technique to share with the class.

Personal Journal

1. Do you recall cooperative learning experiences in your middle level school years? Write about your participation in, and reactions to, the experiences.

2. Did you ever have that "lost" feeling in a middle level class? What subject and what topic? Now that you know more about differentiation, explain what your teacher might have done to better meet your needs.

3. How comfortable are you with classroom technology? Explain.

4. What motivated you as a student? Can you remember teachers, projects, or other circumstances that prompted you to achieve? Explain.

5. Were you an eager participant in class discussion? Why or why not?

6. Can you recall any time as a student when having a choice in your academic work made a task more meaningful for you? When would choices have made an experience more productive?

7. What instructional strategies dominated your young adolescent experience? High school? University?

Professional Practice

(It would be helpful to reread the description of Mr. White in Chapter 1, as well as the description of Zach in Chapter 2.)

Jesse White
Recently Jesse attended an in-service workshop designed to create awareness of how teacher-focused and student-focused methods of instruction differ. He has attended other workshops during his six years of teaching in which he has learned about cooperative learning and the importance of differentiating instruction.

Mr. White decided to plan and implement a cooperative learning project that would take about four weeks to complete. Because the project requires significant monitoring and he wants to "work out the bugs" before implementing it with all 107 students he teaches, he decides to pilot the project in his first-period class. He forms heterogeneous groups of five students each. He gives them an overview of the project and reminds them of the basics of their recent class study of media influences and the importance of an informed citizenry. Students are given the individual task of watching television news and reading newspapers for a week with the purpose of choosing one local, one national, or one international issue on which they would like their group project to be based. The groups will decide on an issue and together write a statement justifying their decision. They must be ready to defend their choices using notes that Mr. White will collect. The main product is a poster. One side will include newspaper articles, summaries of television news reports, and personal commentaries that explain the issue. The other side will be used to follow up on other related events and/or solutions as they unfold over a period of two weeks.

Zach • 8th grade
Remember that for some items, more than one choice may be defensible. The purpose of the items is to stimulate thought and discussion.

1. Zach is an 8th grader. and is now on Ritalin for his diagnosed ADHD. While he appears to be better able to concentrate, he still lacks the motivation to work up to his potential. Mr. White recognizes this. Zach has warmed up to Mr. White, and this is a good first step. Every once in a while, Zach shines in social studies. How might this project be most positive for Zach's usual lack of motivation?

a. Zach will have an opportunity to use his creative streak to successfully design a good poster, something that he will likely enjoy.
b. In the role of facilitator, Zach could prove to other kids that he can be a leader.
c. From what Mr. White has heard from his teammates, Zach's interest level is more acute early in the day, so being a student in first period is a real plus.
d. Zach may develop an interest in a current events topic.

2. Zach rarely participates in class. He is quiet most of the time. Mr. White knows Zach's interest in academics will continue to decline if he isn't somehow "hooked" on learning. Which one of the following would be the least beneficial aspect of this project for Zach?

a. He may find an issue that sparks his interest.
b. He may feel a sense of belonging as a result of being part of a small learning group.
c. He will be expected to do some individual work.
d. Because there is an element of choice involved, he may find the project inviting.

3. As part of the information presented to Mr. White on student-focused instruction, he learned that using primary sources of data is desirable. Which one of these responses illustrates this concept?

a. As an authority in the class, Mr. White should give an overview of local, national, and international issues.
b. The posters will result from the work of the students in each group.
c. Students can ask the adults in their homes for opinions about the issues.
d. The project requires students to get information directly from newspaper articles.

4. What aspects of teaming could Mr. White use to enhance this project? What characteristics of effective teams might help facilitate a project like the one described?

Chapter 8
Assessment of Middle Level Learners

Ian Allenden/123RF

Continuous, authentic, and appropriate assessment measures provide evidence about each student's learning progress. Such information helps students, teachers, and family members select immediate learning goals and plan further education. . . . Means of assessing student progress should serve a learning function, helping students clarify understandings and providing information on which to base judgments.

THIS WE BELIEVE, PP. 24–25

Learning Outcomes

After studying this chapter, you will have knowledge and skills to:

8.1 Articulate major tenets of classroom assessment.

8.2 Explore evaluation and grading strategies.

8.3 Describe standardized assessment and related issues.

Dear Future Middle Level Teacher,

"Remember students, we have a big test tomorrow!" strikes terror, or at least dread, in the hearts of most of us. As a teacher, I've attempted to encourage, or even excite, my students by saying over and over that tests give us opportunities to show what we know and can do. Sounds good, doesn't it? Feel inspired? Honestly? Probably not. What I tell students is true, but it's still a test. Anxiety rises . . . that sick feeling in the pit of the stomach. Can we change this negative approach by young adolescents? The only way to lessen the dread of **assessment**, or the gathering of evidence about student learning, is to build both comprehension and self-confidence.

Young adolescents can show what they know and are able to do in a wide variety of ways, from traditional paper-and-pencil tests to projects and performances. They may illustrate, report, build, demonstrate, and so on. How we assess in our classrooms can be more palatable with creativity and effort on our part. But standardized testing, or tests given to large groups, aren't quite so kind. Multiple-choice items, bubble sheets, and the ever-grueling "Write 3 grammatically correct and organized paragraphs based on the following topic" abound.

Curriculum, instruction, and assessment are intertwined and interdependent. Curriculum is meaningless without appropriate instruction. The only way to move forward with the curriculum is to assess what students know and are able to do, and then adjust instruction. It's vital that teachers understand both how to create classroom assessments and how to interpret and use the results; it's imperative that teachers know how to help students be more comfortable with standardized assessments.

So let's dive into the topic of assessment and explore why it's an essential component of effective teaching and learning.

SDP

LO 8.1 Classroom Assessment

The most important purpose of classroom assessment is the information it provides as we make instructional decisions. Plainly stated, if the kids don't "get it," we find another way to provide learning opportunities. If they do "get it," we are free to move on, move up the Bloom's taxonomy hierarchy, and offer enrichment. In addition to using assessment to improve instruction, assessment allows us to monitor student progress, with a view toward promoting student growth. Another purpose is to evaluate student achievement (i.e., grading) in order to recognize accomplishment (or the lack of it). A fourth purpose involves the collection of data to substantiate program decisions (National Council of Teachers of Mathematics, 1995). Deciding to modify, discontinue, or adopt new programs should be based on assessment results, generally gathered over time or from larger samples than one classroom.

Our responsibility is to assess purposefully, in a variety of ways, and with an eye toward using the results to promote increased learning.

Categories of Assessment

There are three broad categories of classroom assessment, each having distinct functions. **Diagnostic assessment** is what we commonly think of as pretesting, serving the function of revealing what students already know about a topic or unit to come. **Formative assessment** helps monitor student progress and, in doing so, provides valuable information to help with lesson planning. **Summative assessment** comes at the end of a unit of study and is used to measure the amount and quality of learning or of a product.

DIAGNOSTIC ASSESSMENT   How can we plan curriculum and instruction if we don't have information about what our students know and don't know, what they can and can't do? Content area standards give us broad expectations by subject, topic, and grade level. Classroom time is too precious to use on content and skills that students have already mastered. Conversely, jumping right into standards and realizing days later that students lack the prior knowledge necessary to relate meaningfully to new content, or lack the skills necessary to progress to new skill levels, also wastes valuable instruction time. The solution is diagnostic assessment. This form of assessment is an important teaching and learning tool that is often neglected.

Diagnostic assessment may indicate deficiency or mastery of whole groups of students, or it may help us in planning for differentiation if we discover wide variations in prior knowledge or achievement levels among students. Diagnostic assessment informs us about our students and increases our ability to develop a classroom perspective more closely matched to reality. This information is powerful when it comes to effectively planning for teaching and learning.

FORMATIVE ASSESSMENT   The purpose of formative assessment is to monitor learning during instruction and take advantage of multiple opportunities to give feedback. Formative assessment methods vary according to content, skills, and instructional strategies and may be as informal as teacher observation. In fact, we can't help but observe. How we record our observations and use what we see and hear separates useful formative assessment from wasted opportunities. The results of formative assessment should guide our instructional decisions and help us find out where our students are on the path toward mastery. Formative assessment also provides opportunities to give meaningful feedback. We should rarely record grades from formative assessment to keep them as risk-free as possible. We want students to try new skills and express learning in many ways without a grade attached.

Formative assessment may be accomplished in many ways, depending on continually varying classroom circumstances. Here are some formative assessment methods you may want to try:

- **Questioning:** anytime, anywhere in the learning process.
- **Student self-reporting:** thumbs-up or thumbs-down when you ask about comprehension.
- **Exit cards:** This simple assessment requires paper and pencil and can take many forms. Students use the last few minutes of class to respond to prompts such as: "Three things I learned today . . . "; "I'm still confused about . . . "; "The main use of today's skill is . . . "
- **Graphic organizers:** create an organizer that allows you to see what students have learned; could be as simple as a Venn diagram.

The feedback provided as a result of formative assessment helps students know where they are in relation to learning goals, as well as what they need to do to continue to improve. Feedback should be as timely as possible to allow us to take advantage of

Standard 4
Middle Level Instruction And Assessment

Element c. Middle Level Assessment and Data-informed Instruction: Middle level teacher candidates develop and administer assessments and use them as formative and summative tools to create meaningful learning experiences by assessing prior learning, implementing effective lessons, reflecting on young adolescent learning, and adjusting instruction based on the knowledge gained.

FIGURE 8.1 Diagnostic, formative, and summative assessment

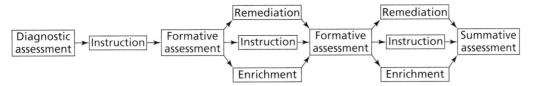

"teachable moments." It may be as simple as saying "You're on the right track" or, even better, detailed feedback that specifically addresses areas of progress, or lack of, during teaching and learning. Giving specific corrective feedback not only guides future efforts, but also tells our students loudly and clearly that what they do and learn is important to us, and therefore *they* are important to us. What we know about young adolescent development tells us that providing feedback promotes positive cognitive and emotional development.

SUMMATIVE ASSESSMENT   Summative assessment typically occurs at the end of a unit of study and is designed to make judgments about the quality of a process or product. It's more formal than diagnostic or formative assessment and is a major factor in determining student **grades**. Summative assessment should allow students to demonstrate what they can do with what they know. To be effective, summative assessment should not be limited to paper-and-pencil exams.

Figure 8.1 shows the interactions among instruction, diagnostic assessment, formative assessment, and summative assessment. Because formative assessment occurs all along the journey toward mastery, it guides our instruction, providing multiple opportunities to alter what we do and how we do it. Take a few minutes to follow the paths that exist between and among these four important aspects of teaching and classroom assessment.

Forms of Classroom Assessment

Classroom assessment can take multiple forms. Any time we gather information about student achievement and behavior, we are assessing. Robert Marzano has contributed to what we know about assessment for decades. In 2016, Marzano published *The Marzano Compendium of Instructional Strategies* on his website. Here is a brief explanation of each of the forms of assessment in Figure 8.2.

COMMON ASSESSMENTS   While not an actual form of assessment because it can take almost any form, common assessments are composed of formative and summative assessments that teachers who are responsible for the same content design to assess and provide feedback to their students. The teachers typically implement the assessments and then compare student results. This sort of assessment would be ideal in middle level settings with two or more teams in a grade level. For instance, the two or more ELA teachers could create common assessments and then use them with the specific students on each team. This leads to grade level consistency and perhaps better assessments because they result from teacher collaboration.

SELECTED-RESPONSE   In earlier works Marzano referred to selected-response as *forced choice*. This means the student must simply recognize the correct response as in multiple

FIGURE 8.2 Marzano forms of assessment

Common assessments
Selected-response
Short constructed-response items
Student demonstration
Student interviews
Observations of students
Student-generated assessments
Response patterns

Based on: Marzano, R.J. (2016). *The Marzano Compendium of Instructional Strategies.*
file:///C:/Users/1/Downloads/FormalAssessmentsofIndividualStudents-1.pdf

choice, true-false, and matching. Remember that while selected-response assessments may be labeled as *objective*, they actually are only objective in that they can be scored consistently since there's only one correct answer. But someone writes the items and provides the choices for the answers. Because of this, selected-response items are not really objective.

SHORT CONSTRUCTED-RESPONSE ITEMS Constructed-response items require students to think of correct answers instead of just recognizing them. These are questions that have one-word or one or more sentence answers that may have some leeway in the words used, but there remains a basic right answer. Most teachers give this sort of assessment often. Fill-in-the-blank and short essay are forms of short constructed-response items.

STUDENT DEMONSTRATION When skills or processes are assessed, student demonstration is the ideal assessment. It may be as simple as asking a student to think aloud or write about a strategy or mental process used, or as complex as the creation of an actual demonstration requiring materials and time to create. Student demonstration accommodates any area that requires a physical skill like science and the arts.

STUDENT INTERVIEWS These one-on-one conversations are excellent assessment tools, but also very time-consuming. In a perfect instructional world, teachers would have time to interview each student regularly. In most middle level settings, however, a team may consist of more than 100 students. For a teacher to have even a 5-minute conversation with each student would require more than 8 hours straight through with no breaks. Even scattered across a 9-week period, that would mean 10 interviews a week. Given most schedules of 50- to 100-minute classes periods, by the time a teacher would get to the tenth student, the content would have changed. Don't let this discourage you from interviewing particular students for whom this may be the best way to assess their understanding and abilities.

OBSERVATION OF STUDENTS We've already established that observation is inevitable for teachers. Marzano refers to observation as unobtrusive assessment, meaning that it's ongoing and doesn't disrupt the flow of learning. It's important to record our observations in some way. This may be accomplished with a chart on a clip board or notes in a folder. You may think you won't forget that Martin thought the Constitution was written before 1776, but by the end of the day this observation will likely have faded or have been overridden by other observations.

Teacher observation may be the only way to assess nonachievement factors such as attitude, effort, behavior, time on task, and so on. Having definite aspects to observe and then creating a system for recording those observations are vital to lend consistency and a measure of objectivity (though admittedly small) when using teacher observation as assessment. Think about this—it's impossible *not* to observe in our classrooms. It will happen continually. The danger in using teacher observation in overt ways as a form of assessment is that the "squeaky wheel gets the grease." By this I mean that certain young adolescents may draw more attention than others, either positively or negatively. If we don't occasionally make teacher observation very purposeful, we are likely to miss key growth-enhancing or remediation opportunities.

STUDENT-GENERATED ASSESSMENTS This form of assessment requires a large measure of coaching to help students generate effective assessments of their own accomplishments. This works best when students have a common assignment or project allowing them to talk together about how they want to view the quality of what they know or can do. Simply saying "Tell me how you think you did," or "Did you do a good job?" will not elicit thoughtful responses from most middle level students. They need specific aspects to assess, an array of understood descriptors from which to choose, and a reporting process that ensures them respect and confidentiality.

Teacher think-alouds can be valuable for teaching students to self-assess. Through teacher self-assessment we can demonstrate to students how to think about progress, accomplishment, quality factors, and indicators of understanding.

Teachers who use student self-assessment extensively report that students tend to assess their own work quite realistically, with honesty and candor. Their remarks and criticisms are often more severe than those of the teachers. Having students self-assess following corrective measures builds independence and proactive behavior.

A question to consider is whether student self-assessment, if recorded in some viable way, should have some bearing on a teacher's assessment or if it should be its own category added to many forms of assessment used within a unit of study. The answer to this question depends on circumstances such as how the self-assessments are gathered, how much guidance students have in doing the self-assessment, and the stated purpose of the self-assessment.

RESPONSE PATTERNS   This form of assessment involves teachers assessing what students know by classifying what is correct, what's incorrect, or what's partially correct as opposed to adding up points and coming up with a score for the assessment. Teachers then analyse patterns of learning. This allows for more specific feedback to each student. Again, this can be very time-consuming in a middle level setting. I suggest using what I'll call an **item analysis**, a way of looking in a more general way at patterns of what an entire class knows, doesn't know, or partially knows. For instance, if a selected-response assessment is administered, the teacher tallies how many students answer each item incorrectly. In this way, a picture emerges of patterns of knowledge. In a class of 24, if two students miss an item, the teacher finds a way to address the item with the two students to help them understand the content. If, however, eight students miss the same item, it would be logical to reteach the content to the entire class in a different way. The students who missed the item will hopefully understand it, and the ones who may have guessed may understand the content better because it's presented in a different way. Those who answered correctly out of understanding may see the content in a new light. Everyone wins.

In Teachers Speak, Deirdre McGrew tells us that assessment is a snapshot rather than a holistic view of student capabilities.

Teachers Speak

Deirdre McGrew
I've never been very comfortable with the whole idea of testing. As a student, I always felt I knew more than any particular test might indicate. But tests are considered necessary in education, and, in my opinion, they are necessary evils. That being said, let me tell you what I've learned about assessment that makes it palatable to me.

An assessment is a snapshot of what a student knows and can do at a given time under particular circumstances. One snapshot is not an album. It takes lots of snapshots to get a real view of learning. The kids in our CARE program would still be in 5th grade if their capabilities were measured only by a once-a-year standardized test score. They know more than the state tests show. I take notes on what I observe them doing and what they tell me in interviews. I watch them work in small groups and listen as they teach each other. They complete lots of their work on the classroom computers, and the software tracks progress. When I view assessment as a collection of these measurements plus more, it makes sense to me. I'm exploring portfolio assessment for my students' collections. That may be a great way for them to follow their own progress.

ESSAY QUESTIONS   Essay questions require students to write responses in narrative form, to answer questions in complete sentences and in an organized fashion. In that respect, essay questions can assess knowledge (remembering), comprehension (understanding), application, analysis, synthesis (creating), and evaluation, as well as communication skills. Essays are, of course, more difficult to score and involve greater levels of subjectivity.

Marzano only addresses essay as a form of assessment in the section of his work about student-generated assessment. He lists the essay item as one of the choices students may want to use to show mastery of content. Regardless, we need to acknowledge that essay is a legitimate and useful form of assessment.

Enhanced eText
Video Example 8.1

Grant Wiggins and others discuss and demonstrate a variety of classroom assessments that prompt students to show what they know and can do.

Standard 4
Middle Level Instruction And Assessment

Element a. Content Pedagogy: Middle level teacher candidates use their knowledge of instruction and assessment strategies that are especially effective in the subjects they teach.

Performance Assessment

Alternative and *authentic* are words often used interchangeably with *performance* assessment. **Alternative assessment** generally refers to any assessment that is not primarily a selected-response, essay, or short written response. **Authentic assessment** tends to be real-life in nature. **Performance assessment** usually refers to tasks that require students to apply knowledge. *Performance* tends to be an umbrella term in that it includes both real-life and contrived aspects of assessment. The Venn diagram in Figure 8.3 illustrates that both authentic and performance assessments are alternative in nature, that authentic assessment is performance-based, and that performance assessment is broader than authentic assessment.

Performance assessment methods are generally considered to be those outside the realm of traditional assessment. In *Turning Points 2000*, Jackson and Davis tell us that authentic performance tasks help students figure out complex issues, show what they know, make connections between what they are learning and the real world, and apply what they know to new situations. Read about focus student Gabe's experience with performance assessment in See How They Grow.

FIGURE 8.3 Alternative, performance, authentic assessment

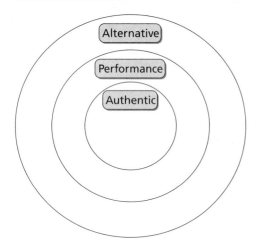

See How They Grow

Gabe • 8th grade

Gabe is enjoying 8th grade much more than 6th or 7th, in part because his family no longer leaves the area for three months each year. Dad got a job working construction, with a backup job in landscaping. The family now lives in a small house near Valley View Middle School. Gabe can walk to school.

Another reason for Gabe's renewed interest in school is his fascination with robotics. In Ms. Fox's science class he learned the basics, and she encouraged him to stay after school with the kids who are in the robotics club. He was hesitant because they already knew so much more than he but soon discovered that his long-time love of transformers was good preparation for being part of the club. For several years he searched the Goodwill store for transformers while his mom bought the family clothes. Occasionally she would buy one for him. Ms. Fox is very enthusiastic and asked if he would bring his collection to a club meeting. She brought the DVDs of both the transformer movies and loaned them to him.

No, this isn't what we think of as a traditional way to hook a student on school, but genuine attention from a teacher, coupled with a captivating topic, is probably the best way to keep reluctant learners coming back. Ms. Fox can use Gabe's knowledge as expressed through club activities as a performance-based indicator.

Portfolio Assessment

A **portfolio** is a collection of student work that may be selected to showcase best quality, show progress over time, or both. Portfolios are flexible vehicles for organizing and viewing all kinds of assessment tools, from traditional paper-and-pencil tests to performances that include teacher feedback and student self-assessment. A comprehensive portfolio should emphasize both process and product and should serve as a short evolutionary record of progress toward learning goals.

As collections of work, portfolios allow individual differences to be seen as assets. If students are given opportunities to make choices within guidelines as to what to include, they stand a good chance of being able to express their own strengths. For instance, they may have the opportunity to include artwork, video productions, photographs of sporting events, items from nature, Internet searches and results, annotated lists of books they've read, timelines, graphic organizers, poems . . . the list is endless. If a portfolio is to show what a student knows and can do in a discipline or multiple disciplines, then student choice leads to student self-expression. As with project learning, lightbulbs go on in some young adolescents' heads when they see learning as a whole rather than as isolated assignments, and when they make decisions to shape a product they can proudly display.

> *TWB* **Goal 2.** [Young adolescents will] be able to think rationally and critically and express thought clearly.

Many books and articles have been written about portfolios, detailing their development and benefits. Teams that use portfolios can share advice and the lessons learned in implementing them. Whole middle schools that use portfolios reap the benefits of having students view them as a "way of life" and excellent evidence of the depth and breadth of their learning and maturing progress.

> **Self-Check 8. 1**

LO 8.2 Evaluating and Grading

We examined broad categories of classroom assessment and discovered there are many ways to diagnose prior knowledge and skills, to monitor progress along the way through formative assessment, and to determine if goals are reached through summative assessment. We looked at single assessment as well as collections of performances in portfolio format.

Now let's address the issue of distinguishing degrees of understanding and clarifying the criteria for judging performance. Here are some necessary terms and definitions.

- **Evaluation:** the process of judging levels of quality of student work, performance, and understanding
- **Score:** the number given to student work to indicate evaluation
- **Weight:** the value given to specific student work relative to other assignments
- **Grade:** the number or letter representing scores of evaluations received over time and reported to students and adults.

For decades, some educators have questioned the wisdom of assigning grades to students. Some argue that grades are meaningless, do not represent understanding and the application potential of knowledge, are harmful to student self-esteem, impede progress if either too low or too high—the list goes on and each flaw has a degree of

FIGURE 8.4 Generic rubric

Criteria	4	3	2	1	0
Choice of topic	Interesting and current	Interesting, but not current	Generic and uninteresting	Not at all relevant	Not enough information for judgment
Depth of research	Evident and compelling	Evident, but not compelling	Some research	Little evidence	Not enough information for judgment
Organization of ideas	Clear, easy to follow	Can be followed	Little organization evident	Ideas cannot be followed	Not enough information for judgment
Quality of information	Correct and detailed	Correct but without detail	Incomplete, some incorrect	Mostly incorrect or missing	Not enough information for judgment
Use of conventions	Correct usage of grammar and punctuation	Some errors but not distracting	Errors that interfere with content	Too many errors to be coherent	Not enough information for judgment

validity. But for Americans, grading is ingrained in our schools. Recently researchers have taken up the challenge of looking at grades in new ways. With the advent of standards and acceptance of differentiating instruction, we may see meaningful change in grading practices in the future.

Rubrics

To assess in ways that speak to "how good is good enough," we turn to rubrics, both as valuable instructional tools and as means of assessment. A **rubric** is a scoring guide that provides the criteria for assessing the quality of a piece of work and includes a gradation for each criterion, generally from excellent to poor, with quality often indicated by numbers. You have probably experienced rubrics as scoring tools and have discovered their benefits in education courses. Figure 8.4 shows a generic rubric that could be adapted for specific topics in most any subject area. Figure 8.5 provides sample descriptors when numbers are used to judge work quality.

Some schools use rubrics frequently. Chances are that these schools had a few rubric zealots who attended a workshop or a session at a conference where rubrics were explained and the development process was clarified. Once teachers experience their benefits, they are willing to take the time to develop rubrics to assess the performance of their students. And they are willing to share their success with other teachers.

When you share a rubric with your students, it becomes an excellent instructional tool. If detailed enough, a rubric lets students know the expectations for an assignment. Rubrics paint a clear picture; they're much more explicit than simple directions. If you have examples of products, share them with students and discuss what each criterion looks like. Be sure to save products so you'll have some to show the next time you make similar assignments. Rubrics serve as valuable communication tools between teacher and student, teacher and parent, and student and parent. The clear expectations and level of feedback communicate thoughtful, purposeful assignments with rubrics providing feedback and the basis of conversations about teaching and learning. Figure 8.6 summarizes some of the benefits of using rubrics.

FIGURE 8.5 Number scale for rubrics

4—Students understand the important information accurately and with detail.
3—Students understand the important information, but the details are fuzzy or nonexistent.
2—Students have a basic understanding of the information mixed with some misconceptions and gaps.
1—Students have so many misconceptions that the basic information is not understood.
0—Students provide insufficient indicators on which to judge their understanding.

FIGURE 8.6 Reasons to use instructional rubrics

Instructional rubrics . . .

- provide clear expectations for assignments.
- make teachers' expectations very clear and consistent.
- help teachers differentiate among performance levels.
- provide clear guidelines for how students can improve.
- help families understand expectations and assessment of assignments.

Purposes of Grades

Grades provide information. A grade assigned to a student serves multiple purposes depending on who views it.

- **As viewed by students.** An obvious purpose of grades is to inform students about their achievement. With ongoing formative assessment, summative grades should not surprise students. What they do is lend seriousness to the whole assessment process. The surprise is often perceived by the adults who receive grade reports without adequate communication about sources of grades and student progress.

    Low letter grades without accompanying details and descriptions of deficits have never been shown to be motivators. The threat of even lower grades if study habits aren't changed will probably prove to have negative effects. However, descriptive narratives, even if they contain negative comments, can be motivational

Making the Teaching and Learning Connection

Hello, future teachers!

It is my pleasure to teach in an environment where students solve real-world challenges and begin to understand themselves as learners and contributors. I have the privilege of teaching at the Charlotte Lab School, an innovative charter school serving students in kindergarten through 8th grade. The waiting list continues to grow, and for good reason. I believe the model we use can be achieved in many other schools that have a vision of students learning by doing.

We continually assess. We talk to our students; we watch their growth and their struggles. Not only do we assess academic progress, but also the skills our kids need to be successful personally and in their future professional lives. We watch for problem solving thinking skills and coach the students to help them improve all along Bloom's taxonomy levels. We look for collaboration skills, again coaching the kids on how to talk with one another and contribute.

Rubrics play a big role in our assessment methods. Most teachers acknowledge how important rubrics are in assessing students. We take it a major step beyond by making sure our students understand the scales they develop with us and view rubrics as self-evaluation tools.

My wish for you is that you find an environment that encourages both teachers and students to participate in a productive teaching and learning community. Spending my days with developing young adolescents is the best profession in the world!

Dee

Enhanced eText
Video Example 8.2
Teacher Dee Lanier tells us about his methods on ongoing assessment.

if approached as opportunities for improvement (Burden & Byrd, 2016). Receiving a high grade, especially if it shows progress, can be motivating with or without an explanation. As with so many aspects of middle level education, perspective and teacher attitude determine in large measure the receptiveness and dispositions of students toward grades.

- **As viewed by parents.** Grades are expected features of school. Attempts at the middle level to convey progress, or lack of it, with narratives alone (replacing letter grades) have generally been met with disapproval and been considered unacceptable by families. Grades are traditional, and even though parents may realize they are subjective measures, they usually still want to know if Johnny's work is of A, B, C, D, or F quality. Praise and punishment may both be doled out based on the grades received by students.

- **As viewed by teachers.** If grades and the process of grading do not guide instructional planning, then we are missing a major function of assessment and evaluation. We have already discussed the value of diagnostic assessment in decision making. The same premise applies to grades. We look at the academic achievement of our students, or lack of it. We determine content depth, remediation, instructional strategies, sequencing, pacing, and so on. At the same time, individual student grades give us guidance for grouping, regrouping, and differentiating instruction.

  When considering placement in what are considered advanced courses in middle schools, such as Algebra I and foreign language, grades provide a guidance function. They also provide information used in determining summer school or afterschool options often used for remediation.

- **As viewed by administrators.** Administrators at school and district levels use grades as indicators of academic success of groups of students—classes, grade levels, and whole schools. Individual student grades influence promotion and retention and help determine placement of students in homogeneous or heterogeneous groups.

Your school and your team will have established grading procedures in terms of scales and reporting. Be sure you understand these procedures and what leeway you may have in determining student grades. Some schools will require a minimum number of grades per quarter or semester. Many principals will ask to see your record-keeping system, and parents expect clearly defined criteria. As a team, you will want the message that grades send to students and adults to have a measure of consistency and absolute fairness.

Establishing Scoring Criteria

Regardless of the assignment or assessment, scoring needs to be based on preestablished criteria. For select-response assessments, students need to know how many points each item is worth and then how those points translate to scores and figure into overall grades. For projects, students need rubrics that provide number scores when points are assigned to each descriptor of quality.

Clear and precise scoring criteria set targets for our students. With assignments that receive scores, and assessments that are evaluated, knowing what is expected in terms of standards to be met and the credit to be given adds clarity and definitive goals.

Having defined criteria helps us deal with the basic question of what grades mean. What, after all, is an A? How about a C? There are general notions, but consistency from state to state, school to school, and even classroom to classroom does not exist. As we look at the different percentages commonly associated with letter grades in Table 8.1, keep in mind that even with percentages established for a district, the assignments and assessments that are evaluated and scored to come up with the percentages are subjective, and very often up to you.

TABLE 8.1 Varying grade scales

A	B	C	D	F
90–100%	80–89%	70–79%	60–69%	<60%
93–100%	85–92%	78–84%	70–77%	<70%
95–100%	85–94%	75–84%	65–74%	<65%
95–100%	88–94%	81–87%	75–80%	<75%

WHAT TO INCLUDE Even though academic achievement is the implied focus of grades, we know that other factors are often included. In some schools and on some teams, it is understood that dispositions such as effort, participation, attitude, and other behaviors receive weight in a grade. However, great caution needs to be applied when including dispositions in academic scores to develop letter grades. Unless a non-academic outcome or behavior process is part of a stated learning goal, it should not be part of a content area grade. Nonacademic attributes are difficult to define and even more difficult to measure.

Along with reporting academic grades, it is entirely appropriate to give feedback on dispositions and behavior. A commonly used rating scale for non-academic outcomes includes descriptors such as superior, excellent, above average, average, satisfactory, and so on. An alternative to these scales, which sometimes lack specificity, are checklists of specific behaviors such as uses time wisely, organizes work well, works effectively with others, or completes assignments on time.

WEIGHTING GRADES Some assignments and assessments are more valuable than others because they demonstrate learning more accurately and require more knowledge and skills to complete. For this reason, we don't want a homework assignment to be scored on a 0- to 100-point scale and a major writing project to also be scored 0 to 100. We need to do what's referred to as **weighting grades**. You will want to designate the compiled or mean-averaged scores of major assignments and assessments as a larger percentage of the overall grade. You might reserve 0 to 100 points for the bigger assignments and assessments and relegate fewer points (0 to 5) for daily work. This is what weighting is all about.

When using a rubric, you could have five criteria with a 0 to 4 scale for each. This would give a score range of 0 to 20. If the rubric is applied to a major assessment, you would multiply the achieved score by a factor that would show its relative importance. For instance, if the assignment needs to be worth 100 points, simply multiply a score on this particular rubric by 5.

AN ALTERNATIVE TO MEAN AVERAGE When an idea required more than passive consideration, my mother would say, "Put your thinking cap on." Here's a concept so simple, yet so radical, that it may require your thinking cap. For me it resulted in a response of "Wow! What a revelation!"

My experience leads me to believe that the overwhelming majority of teachers use the mean average to compute grades. Recall that the mean is the sum of scores divided by the number of scores. The mean is a measure of central tendency, and so is the median. The median is the middle value when the scores are placed in numerical order.

When using the mean, all scores or possible scores are added, even the zeros. The mean emphasizes quantity over quality and values assignment completion as much as mastery of content and skills. (O'Connor, 2009). Few students, and unfortunately not all teachers, realize what one or two zeros will do to a mean average. If a student has four scores, three of which are 100% and one of which is zero, the mean average is 75%. According to Table 8.1 that means a C or a D. Do either of these letters accurately indicate the student's likely level of achievement? The median (100, 100, 100, 0) of 100 is not accurate either, especially if the zero resulted from a lack of understanding or skill. But chances are a zero indicates a behavior (nonacademic) outcome and perhaps should not even be included in calculating a content-area letter grade. Perhaps the student had a disturbing event at home or some social dilemma that totally threw her off when the low assessment occurred. This is something that should be perceived or known by teachers.

Using the median as a measure of central tendency rather than the mean takes into consideration that we all stumble occasionally and have days when we are not at our best. If this philosophy applies at any age, it should definitely apply in early adolescence. We expect variability. Being developmentally responsive calls for us to validate achievement and growth over time while diminishing the effects of social and emotional changes and traumas.

Take time to examine Table 8.2 illustrating issues with the mean from *How to Grade for Learning* (O'Connor, 2009). Note that the mean for each of the four students is 72%. Now look at the medians. Consider the 10 scores for each student. Which students appear to have a solid grasp of the knowledge and skills? Should they all receive low Cs and Ds? Their point totals are the same, but their degrees of understanding are certainly different.

REPORTING GRADES   Progress reports and report cards are standard fare in most schools. They should be considered the bare minimum in terms of efforts to communicate progress, or lack of it, to students and parents/guardians. The traditional system calls for grade reporting every four to five weeks. Ideally your team will have a system to communicate with families more frequently in cases where outstanding progress is being made or a sudden or chronic lack of progress is noted.

Report cards vary in the amount and types of information included. This is often outside your control. You and your team will want to supplement communication in ways that keep parents/guardians informed and invite their participation.

Grading for Success

Here are some general guidelines for assigning grades:

1. Grade students for what they know and are able to do, without comparing them to other students.

2. Grade individual achievement more frequently than group achievement.

TABLE 8.2   Issues with the mean or median used alone

Assessments of the semester, from beginning to end	Enriquez	Marguarite	Lindsey	Marcus
Assessment 1	0	10	30	40
Assessment 2	20	72	40	50
Assessment 3	0	72	30	62
Assessment 4	100	82	20	62
Assessment 5	100	72	100	90
Assessment 6	100	72	100	90
Assessment 7	100	72	100	63
Assessment 8	100	94	100	63
Assessment 9	100	84	100	100
Assessment 10	100	80	100	100
Total	720	720	720	720
Mean	72%	72%	72%	72%
Median	100%	72%	100%	90%

Based on: O'Connor, K. (2009). *How to grade for learning.* Arlington Heights, IL: Skylight Professional Development.

3. Include a wide variety of assessment methods.

4. Weight grades to reflect mastery of content and skills more than progress toward mastery.

5. Arrive at a final grade by considering outlier grades such as zeros and their effect when using mean averaging (Powell, 2019, p. 126).

Self-Check 8. 2

LO 8.3 Standardized Assessment

Standardized tests are a fact of life in public education. The demand for accountability in our schools has never been greater. We hear it from families, legislators, and citizen groups. Standards of learning established by the Common Core State Standards, subject-area organizations, and state departments of education provide goals. How to measure progress toward those goals is a dilemma. Calls for accountability lead to standardized testing, but the process itself and the results are often controversial.

Validity and reliability are two concepts important for all assessment but are of particular importance for **standardized assessment**. **Validity** refers to the degree to which an assessment measures what it is supposed to measure. For classroom assessment, validity is within our control. For standardized testing based on imposed standards, validity can be verified through comparisons of standards and test items. However, most teachers do not have access to state items, so establishing validity is usually a state issue. **Reliability** refers to the consistency with which an assessment measures what it is meant to measure. Reliability can be complicated to establish, requiring field testing of sample populations.

Comparing Standardized and Classroom Assessment

As classroom teachers we can follow the adage of "Teach what you test and test what you teach." If classroom assessment is interwoven with curriculum and instruction, and standards are incorporated, then the package of learning and testing can be neatly and cohesively bundled. Classroom assessment in its many forms derives content and skills to be tested from the learning opportunities of the classroom.

Most standardized tests derive content and skills from many sources including Common Core State Standards and national subject-area organizations. They are written to match grade level expectations but often contain items and complete sections that are unfamiliar to our students. We can use published preparation materials, but in doing so we may find that we actually end up presenting isolated facts out of context.

With classroom assessments, we are free to determine the value of items in the overall scheme of our planned assessment and measure student success against our learning goals. We then assign a score to the assessment and a weight to indicate its importance relative to other assessments. Assessing student success in meeting stated learning goals and expectations is referred to as **criterion-referenced assessment**. Student scores reflect what they know and the degree to which they know it. With **norm-referenced assessments**, students are rated relative to other students within a like population. Norm-referenced tests are expressed in percentiles. On a classroom assessment (criterion-referenced), an "85%" means that 85% of the knowledge and skills assessed were correct. On a standardized assessment, usually norm-referenced, a student in the 85th percentile means that 85 of every 100 students tested lower and 15 of 100 students tested higher. This simply compares student performance and provides little information about the level of achievement or mastery of learning goals. If most of the students did very poorly on the assessment, then a norm score of 85th percentile would represent questionable success. If most of the students did exceptionally well on the assessment, then a norm score of 85th percentile would represent outstanding success. Based on student success relative to learning goals, standardized test results typically place students in one of four groups labeled "below basic," "basic," "proficient," and "advanced." This information is reported in ways that facilitate individuals being compared with other students within the same class, school, district, or state. In the same way, schools and districts are compared with others within a state. The only way to compare states to states in the same way is if all states administer the same assessment, perhaps an assessment based on the Common Core State Standards. Coming close to comparing states is the National Assessment of Educational Progress, discussed later.

Benefits of Standardized Assessment

Standardized assessment is not going away in the foreseeable future. The capacity, debatable as it is, to provide comparisons and gauge annual progress makes standardized assessment a fixture in public education. I have often referred to it as a "rite of spring" since most standardized assessments are administered March through May. Given their undeniable presence, our best stance is to be proactive. To be both proactive and positive, we must consider the possible benefits of standardized assessment. Figure 8.7 lists a sampling of benefits.

Preparing for Standardized Assessment

There is a prevailing fear that preparing for standardized assessments will lead to almost exclusive drill and practice, or, as some call it, drill and kill, instruction. Obviously, that would be very inappropriate, particularly for middle level students. Most researchers who study test preparation practices and their results tell us that we should avoid the temptation to drill isolated information, not just because we know it's not developmentally responsive, but because it doesn't work. Classrooms that concentrate on the "big ideas," active student engagement, and a comprehensive curriculum are likely to see their students excel on standardized assessment. Here are some practices to consider:

1. **Be positive concerning the necessity of standardized tests.** If we convey (even if we don't say out loud) the message, "We've got to put up with those stupid standardized tests in April," our students will sense our negativity, and their preparation, and subsequently their scores, will suffer. If we approach standardized tests with an attitude of, "This is a great opportunity to show what we know and can do!" I guarantee you happier, more productive students along with the real possibility of higher scores.

2. **Focus on student reading ability,** regardless of the subject area tested. Remember that we are all teachers of reading. Help students improve their reading skills within the context of your subject area and continually assist them with vocabulary acquisition.

FIGURE 8.7 Benefits of standardized tests

Standardized tests . . .

- provide data on how well students, and consequently teachers, schools, districts, and states, are performing.
- if directly tied to standards, promote a common instructional focus.
- show patterns of strengths and weaknesses to guide decision making.
- when results indicate mastery and/or improvement, build public trust.
- provide a mode of comparison, although approximate, for schools, districts, and states.
- may prompt us to ask probing and important questions concerning instructional practice as we analyze results.

3. **Know your state curriculum standards intimately,** including the ones written for previous and subsequent grade levels, and incorporate them into your lesson plans.

4. **Obtain and use previous standardized test results for your students.** Look for strengths, weaknesses, and both individual and team trends. Use these results diagnostically for instructional planning.

5. **Provide an abundance of authentic opportunities** that call not only for knowledge and comprehension, but also application, analysis, synthesis, and evaluation.

6. **Emphasize problem solving** in all content areas. Math does not have a monopoly when it comes to problem-solving opportunities. After all, history is just one problem after another, with attempted resolutions along the way.

7. **Teach the skills of editing** and then give lots of opportunity for practice. Help students recognize errors and areas for improvement in their own and others' writing.

8. **Provide frequent opportunities for students to interpret and create representations** like tables, graphs, and maps. As with problem solving, this is not the exclusive purview of math. Some estimates tell us that 25% of the standardized test items in social studies and science involve charts, tables, graphs, and maps.

9. **Use a variety of assessment methods** to help develop student flexibility. We know it is beneficial to assess the same content and skills in many ways.

10. **Locate and use appropriate test preparation and test-specific materials** from publishers and as provided by state departments of education. Using material that is written in the same format as the test to be administered is advisable. After all, we don't want the test to measure format familiarity more than content knowledge and skills.

Preparation for standardized testing should not be thought of as separate from daily instruction. Using a variety of instructional practices to present a broad and comprehensive curriculum is the best possible preparation.

National and International Standardized Tests

The **National Assessment of Educational Progress (NAEP)**, is known as the nation's report card. It is currently the only standardized test systematically administered to a sampling of students across the country to compare states. The NAEP is given to fourth-, eighth-, and twelfth-grade students in math, reading, writing, science, history, civics, economics, geography, foreign language, and a variety of the arts. Results of NAEP are not reported by individual student, school, or district, but only by race, grade level, and state.

Two standardized tests are administered in about 50 countries through the **International Association for the Evaluation of Educational Achievement,** an independent cooperative of national research institutions and governmental research agencies. One of the tests, **Trends in International Math and Science Study (TIMSS)**, compares students in math and science worldwide through randomized assessment every four years. The **Progress in International Reading Literacy Study (PIRLS)** compares students worldwide in two specific types of reading: literary and informational. In both TIMSS and PIRLS, the United States ranks consistently in the top 10 countries.

Self-Check 8. 3

Why It Matters

Curriculum, instruction, and assessment are interwoven. We have looked at each separately and examined components and issues. What we teach, how we teach it, and then how we gather evidence of learning must be developmentally appropriate and responsive, as well as interdependent. Diagnostic assessment informs our decisions concerning curriculum and instruction; formative assessment tells us if we need to move toward enrichment or remediation; and summative assessment provides information for grading and signals the timing for moving on to new curriculum.

Assessment can be accomplished through a rich variety of means, whether diagnostic, formative, or summative. Assessment allows us to evaluate student achievement and recognize accomplishment; make informed decisions and improve instruction; monitor student progress and promote growth; and evaluate and modify programs.

Classroom assessment establishes hallmarks of understanding. To distinguish degrees of understanding and skill development, we use classroom assessment. Rubrics allow us to set criteria and measures of quality in advance of assignments, use narratives and descriptions to give feedback, and be specific and open in what otherwise can be a very subjective and vague process.

Performance assessment involves any task in which students are required to demonstrate understanding and skills. Paper-and-pencil tests that require more than recitation of facts, complex tasks requiring extensive planning, and every level in between may be considered performance assessment.

Standardized assessment is a stable feature of public education. It's not going away. Standardized assessment has limitations, but it also has benefits. Taking a proactive stance involves including strong instructional practices that strengthen learning and lead to improved standardized test scores.

Accountability is essential for all of us involved in teaching and learning. Assessment allows our students to show what they know and what they are able to do. The results of assessment serve as accountability measures. Schools and districts are responsible for providing support for teaching and learning. Assessment results hold them accountable to us and to our students. The important roles of classroom and standardized assessment cannot be overstated.

Group Activities

1. In pairs, interview a middle school teacher to discuss assessment. Ask the teacher about diagnostic, formative, and summative assessment in the classroom. Write a summary of this information to be shared with the class. Include summaries in your school file.

2. In subject-area groups, choose a standard and develop an overview of a performance that would assess a hallmark of understanding. Be prepared to share your overview and assessment with the class.

3. In subject-area groups, write lists of items that might be included in a student portfolio for a particular topic of study.

4. Respond to these and other questions and prompts appropriate for your area/state.

- Does your state mandate a state-written test? If so, in what subject areas and at what grade levels?
- Does your state mandate a nationally produced standardized test? If so, find information on the administration of the test (timing, grade levels, frequency, use of results, etc.).
- What information is available concerning your state's standardized assessment (grade levels, developers, website for preparation, uses of results, etc.)?
- Locate state and district test results. Put in a form to share with the class.
- Locate state test results for the middle schools in your school file. Put in a form to share with the class.

Add information gathered to your class files.

Individual Activities

1. What type of assessment can you remember from your middle school years? High school? College? Which type did you find easiest? Most difficult? Most meaningful?

2. Write a paragraph that compares and contrasts alternative, performance, and authentic assessment.

3. Do you think a missing homework assignment should receive a grade of zero? Why or why not? What might you do to lessen the impact of an "off day" or "off week" for a student?

4. Discuss the pros and cons of using the median rather than the mean to determine grades. What about a combination of the two?

5. How are the concepts of performance assessment especially appropriate for young adolescents?

6. Write a letter you might send home to parents to explain the value of rubrics. Assume they are unfamiliar with the concept and you plan to use a rubric to assess a student project.

Personal Journal

1. How do you typically react to assessment? Do your grades generally mirror your self-assessment of knowledge/skill level?

2. Do you remember taking standardized tests? SAT or ACT? Praxis? Write about your anxiety levels for these tests.

Professional Practice

(It would be helpful to reread the descriptions of Joey Huber in Chapter 1 and Emily in Chapter 2.)

Joey Huber

Joey is in his last week of full-time student teaching. He can't believe it's almost over. Things have gotten a little tense at Madison because it's almost time for the state standardized tests. The principal at Madison is making a very big deal out of it, sending letters home asking parents to go over fact sheets and practice materials with kids. He's also planning a big test pep rally. The teachers have told Joey that at least an hour a day must be spent doing practice tests and then going over the material with the kids, who, by the way, are less than enthusiastic about the whole thing. They're used to the testing, but that doesn't make them like it any more. They know that if they don't score in the basic category or above, they could be held back in 6th grade. Joey volunteered to conduct daily help sessions after school now that middle school baseball season has ended.

Remember that for some items, more than one choice may be defensible. The purpose of the items is to stimulate thought and discussion.

1. All of the following would be good things to do to prepare for the help sessions *except*:

   a. find items in the same format as the tests and explain to the kids how to approach them.

   b. make charts that show how the 6th grade students performed on the tests last year to give this year's kids something to aim for.

   c. develop exercises that require students to take apart problem-solving scenarios to figure out steps to a solution.

   d. find sample reading passages and accompanying questions for kids to use as practice.

Emily • 7th grade

2. Emily and her friends are particularly anxious about the tests. They get nervous every year, but the thought of not going to 8th grade is terrifying to them. Which of the following would be the most appropriate for Joey to say to them?

   a. Don't worry about it. You'll do fine.

   b. We have a week to go, and I'll work with you to study for the tests.

(Continued)

   c. You've learned so much this year. Remember this as we review.

   d. These tests don't matter that much anyway.

3. Which order of assessments and instruction is correct?

   a. Diagnostic, instruction, formative, instruction, summative

   b. Diagnostic, formative, instruction, diagnostic, instruction, summative

   c. Formative, instruction, diagnostic, instruction, summative

   d. Formative, diagnostic, instruction, summative

4. Why is the assessment rubric considered an important innovation? What are the major benefits of rubrics for both teachers and students?

Chapter 9
Planning for Teaching and Learning

Sara Davis Powell

Adapting curriculum to challenge and provide continuous progress for each and every student requires significant planning, flexibility, and collaboration among all teachers, counselors, school social workers, parents, and the students themselves.

THIS WE BELIEVE, P. 19.

 ## Learning Outcomes

After studying this chapter, you will have knowledge and skills to:

9.1 Summarize the importance of planning, including emphasis on life skills.

9.2 Articulate essential components of effective planning for teaching and learning.

9.3 Explain the steps involved in interdisciplinary planning.

> ### Dear Future Middle Level Teacher,
>
> In this chapter, we put it all together—curriculum, instruction, and assessment, tempered by what we know about student developmental characteristics and differences. Planning the days, the weeks, the semesters, and the year is the task that will determine the level of success we, and our students, achieve in making the teaching and learning connection.
>
> We don't have to plan alone. In fact, we shouldn't! First, there are guidelines for planning provided by states and districts, along with national subject-area organizations. These guidelines aren't optional. They provide the required framework for planning instruction. Second, we are fortunate that planning with colleagues in middle level settings is the norm. We plan with teachers who teach the same subjects to make sure students have the same high-quality learning opportunities, regardless of who teaches them math or English language arts, science or social studies. We plan with teammates to show young adolescents connections among, and relevance of, what they are learning. In middle school, we don't close our doors and become islands unto ourselves. We communicate, share, and collaborate because it's good for the kids. And kids are not left out of the planning process. We know them well—what interests them, what motivates them. We ask them to help plan activities and projects. We give them choices. Involving students in planning helps ensure their engagement and teaches them cooperative and organizational skills.
>
> Overwhelmed? Possibly—well, probably. But take heart. Like any other active endeavor that requires hard work and energy, planning for teaching and learning builds cognitive muscles that may seem overworked or incapable in the beginning but become stronger and more suited for the challenge as we gain momentum in the process. This isn't to say that it's ever easy, but with experience we become more comfortable with the planning process.
>
> *SDP*

LO 9.1 The Importance of Planning

To understand how important planning is, simply consider some of the elements involved: content; sequence; strategies; who does what, when, where, and in what order; resources and materials; standards; learner needs; technology; homework; classroom climate; student assessment, and so on. The elements of planning involved on a daily, weekly, semester, and yearly basis must all be organized and coordinated. Decisions must be made that involve student needs and interests, curricular requirements, and lesson delivery. Effective, comprehensive planning requires thoughtful and wise decision making. We take the time to plan because teaching is more than a job. It's an adventure to create experiences and connections for kids.

Planning for teaching and learning serves many purposes. Burden and Byrd (2016) tell us that among other things, planning can help us do the following:

- Give a sense of direction and, through this, a feeling of confidence and security. Planning can help you stay on course and reduce your anxiety about instruction.

- Organize, sequence, and increase familiarity with course content.

- Prepare to interact with students during instruction. This may include preparing a list of important questions or guidelines for a cooperative group activity.

- Incorporate techniques in each lesson to motivate students to learn.

- Take into account individual differences and the diversity of students when selecting objectives, content, strategies, materials, and products.

Standard 4

Middle Level Instruction and Assessment

Element b. Middle Level Instructional Strategies: Middle level teacher candidates employ a wide variety of effective teaching, learning, and assessment strategies. They use instructional strategies and technologies in ways that encourage exploration, creativity, and information literacy skills (e.g., critical thinking, problem solving, evaluation of information gained) so that young adolescents are actively engaged in their learning. They use instruction that is responsive to young adolescents' local, national, and international histories, language, dialects, and individual identities (e.g., race, ethnicity, culture, age, appearance, ability, sexual orientation, socioeconomic status, family composition).

- Arrange for appropriate requirements and evaluation of student performance.
- Become reflective decision makers about curriculum and instruction.

And you thought a plan was whatever you could squeeze into a 2-by-2-inch box on a page with many other boxes to remind you which pages to cover in a textbook! In this chapter, we take an in-depth look at this extremely important function of a classroom teacher.

Incorporating Organizational Skills

We have the responsibility to teach organizational skills required for success. Organizational skills involve forming habits. Our students are going to form habits with or without our guidance. Helping them be "creatures of habit" in positive ways that promote learning and success is one of our greatest services to young adolescents. Planning for organizational skill acquisition involving productive habits enhances students' chances of success in current and future academic situations and will also serve them later in life.

The acquisition of organizational skills is not an innate or inevitable process. The late Robert Sylwester (2007), an expert on brain-based learning, was fond of using the word *hover* to express how we should approach the teaching of specific life skills to young adolescents. Because the frontal lobe of the brain dealing with problem solving, critical thinking, and organizational skills develops between ages 10 and 14, this is the ideal time to *hover* over and around them. The implication here is that we need to plan to include consistent practice and monitoring when it comes to teaching organizational skills.

Incorporating Study Skills

We have already discussed the necessity of directly teaching students how to read the material in specific subject areas—that reading a math text requires different skills and approaches than reading a short story. Here are some more lessons that often require us to *hover*:

- Looking up vocabulary in a glossary and thinking about words in context
- Reading captions under pictures
- Understanding information in tables and graphs
- Knowing how to use a map legend
- Recognizing the importance of key names and timelines
- Taking time to dissect a formula and its applications
- Reading a story carefully to determine main ideas, characters, plot, setting, and voice.

Summarizing and note-taking are vitally important instructional strategies that correlate with student learning. As with reading in content areas, they must be explicitly taught and monitored. Outlining is a related skill that will prove invaluable.

The skills needed to study for a test often elude many middle level students. Some think simply sitting in class should be enough, even when they are unsuccessful over and over again. Others don't have a clue or rely on last-minute cramming with possible short-term, but little long-term, success. If we teach what we test, and test what we teach, then assessment in the form of quizzes and exams should not be a mystery. We need to help our students learn how to show what they know and can do.

Even with our emphasis on the big concepts and in-depth understanding, we ask our students to memorize numerous things in order to problem solve, accurately complete a timeline, perform an experiment, and so on. Most of us have tricks that work for our learning preferences. Share them with your students. Try new ones yourself and then think aloud about them for your students as you model how they work. Figure 9.1 provides a brief list of memorization techniques.

Incorporating Time Management

As adults we know how important time management is, not only to our productivity but also to our comfort and enjoyment of both work and leisure. Middle level students are moving from the dependency of childhood toward independence when their own personal decision making concerning time will affect what they accomplish, or fail to accomplish.

In the classroom, with effective planning on our part, students work within a structure on various tasks. However, simply having the structure does not guarantee that young adolescents will use their classroom time productively. They may go from sitting alone at a desk with a book open during silent reading time, to sitting in a circle during group discussion time, and back to a desk for journal writing, and still accomplish *absolutely nothing*. To an outside observer they appear to have cooperated with the teacher and followed directions. Well, physically *yes*, but cognitively *no*. Our emphasis must be on using class time wisely to engage students mentally. Interesting lessons requiring individual and group accountability will help engage and elicit participation from

---

FIGURE 9.1 Techniques for memorization

1. Visualize the information. Create a picture in your mind that portrays what you want to remember.

2. Divide the information you want to memorize into small chunks. In dividing the information, do so as logically as possible. The act of categorizing will make retention even easier.

3. Recite out loud the information you need to remember. Listen to your own voice. When trying to recall, it is easier when you can remember what your voice sounded like as you recited.

4. Make flash cards. No, they're not just for math facts. You can use them for words/definitions, events/people and dates, sequencing, random bits of information, etc.

5. Create acronyms for lists or groups. Did you know that radar stands for "radio detection and ranging"? It's an acronym that is so accepted that it has become a word in itself. To create an acronym, simply arrange the first letters of each item you want to memorize into a real or made-up word.

6. Write what you want to memorize in varying ink colors. The color will help you visualize the information you want to recall.

the reticent, sometimes mentally lazy, occasionally daydreaming kids who inevitably inhabit our middle level classrooms.

When given work/study time in school and homework to do at home, our students need to understand that assignments take time and that the amount of time varies from student to student. If, for instance, we ask Noah to show the solution steps and find the answers to three math items, read the social studies text section on reconstruction, fill in a lab sheet with science experiment data from class, and write a paragraph summarizing the setting of *The Cay*—all this while preparing for a band presentation at Tuesday's PTA meeting—we need to provide time management guidelines that realistically portray his Monday afternoon and evening. He needs to understand approximately how much time he will have to devote to academics and how much time he will have for other activities such as sports, video games, dinner, home chores, and, perhaps most important to him, hanging out.

Many middle schools require students to use assignment pads. Some even provide these valuable organizational tools and insist that they be maintained in consistent ways. I agree with this practice. My calendar (adult electronic assignment pad) is invaluable. It is my ultimate time management tool. Of course having an assignment pad doesn't guarantee accomplishment, but when adequately filled in, and then consistently checked upon arrival home by a family member, a student stands a greater chance of managing time and completing work. Assignment pads also serve as reminders of what materials need to be taken both to class and home.

Time is certainly saved when students have the correct tools in class and at home. Providing a team-coordinated list of required school supplies is essential. For instance, if your teacher team prefers mechanical pencils and black ink, then specifically state that these are necessary. If three classes require pocket and brad folders, then they should be on the list. Binders for subject areas and spiral notebooks for journaling; calculators, protractors, and rulers for math; colored pencils for social studies—whatever is needed must be listed explicitly. If your students all have laptops or tablets, they must be charged and ready when needed.

Some teachers provide an extra service for students by having a dry-erase board outside their classroom doors to list what is required for the day. For instance, vocabulary notebook, poetry anthology, and highlighters may be needed Wednesday, but not literature books, with the opposite being true for Friday. Staples such as paper, pencils, and assignment pads are a given.

Depending on your particular situation, you may want to keep extra supplies in a drawer to be loaned to students who infrequently arrive without what they need. For students who perpetually forget or intentionally fail to have needed supplies, team action may be required to emphasize the importance of having necessary items.

Courtesy of Rhonda VanPelt

Many young adolescents have lots of activities that occupy their out-of-school hours, making time management a valuable skill. Focus student teacher Joey Huber (far right) adds baseball coaching to his clinical experience.

Self-Check 9.1

LO 9.2 Planning for Teaching and Learning

Planning for teaching and learning is a monumental task of teachers. All our knowledge and skills concerning curriculum, instruction, and assessment have to be interwoven with what we know about our students to create lessons that are content-specific, engaging, and that result in student learning. Before we begin to examine the components of planning lessons, let's look at where the daily plans fit into the overall scheme of a school year.

Long-Range Planning

Too often when we think of planning we concentrate primarily on daily lesson plans. There are other levels that are significant to student learning and warrant careful consideration as they provide the context for daily planning. Figure 9.2 illustrates levels of planning and some of the factors that guide decision making at each level.

Long-range planning serves as a framework for unit planning. Unit planning, or "chunking" content into large, logical segments, provides a framework for both weekly and daily planning. By beginning with long-range planning, we are planning from whole to part. Long-range plans are comprehensive guides for facilitating learning involving student profiles, content and sequencing, classroom management philosophy, instructional strategies, and overall organizational factors. Writing a long-range plan requires that we think ahead and consider the big picture.

Your district or school may require that you write a long-range plan for the school year, providing detailed guidelines for the plan and checking to make sure certain

---

FIGURE 9.2 Levels of planning

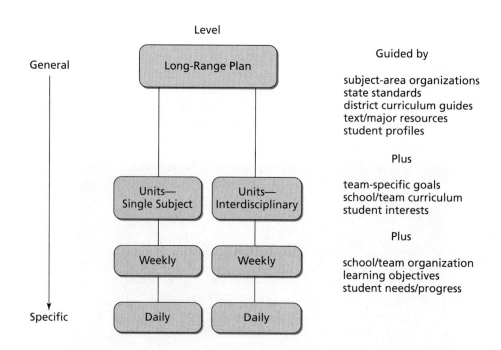

elements are included. Even if you are not required to write a long-range plan, I strongly urge you to do so. Here are some key components to include:

- **Student information:** Develop a student profile by reading permanent files, looking at test scores, talking with teachers who have taught them, driving through the neighborhoods where your students live, considering socioeconomic factors (e.g., free and reduced lunch status), and gauging student interests through some sort of survey in the first few days of school.

- **Content information:** Identify the body of knowledge and skills that compose your course content (standards).

- **Sequence:** Determine a general sequence of the content you will teach. Develop a timeline.

- **Materials:** List the instructional resources you will need to organize or order.

- **Assessment:** Determine major forms of assessment for evaluating student progress.

- **Units of study:** Determine large "chunks" of content that may be considered units of study.

- **Records:** Select or design a system of record keeping for student progress and achievement.

- **Management:** Develop expectations, consequences, and procedures for classroom management, as well as non-instructional routines. We explore this area in Chapter 10.

- **Communication:** Determine ways to communicate with students, colleagues, parents, and the community.

Writing a long-range plan that includes all of these components may seem like a daunting task, particularly if you don't have a mentor or teammates to emulate. Even if you do not produce a formal document to be reviewed, the process of thinking through the key components and making notes concerning your plans will provide a structure for life in your classroom.

Developing and adjusting a long-range plan is part of being a reflective practitioner. Just as navigators rely on maps and charts to determine the track they want to follow from starting point to destination, teachers rely on plans and their decision-making abilities to effectively and efficiently orchestrate learning. Long-range plans should be thought of as working documents that are flexible enough to be altered to accommodate varied rates of learning and to respond to unforeseen events.

Students like Janie who have favorite authors and/or strong interests appreciate opportunities to be part of planning for learning. Keep this in mind as we explore various levels of instructional planning. Read about how Janie is changing in See How They Grow.

See How They Grow

Janie 6th grade
Of all our focus students, I'd say Janie changed the most between 6th and 7th grade. You have to look closely to know the girl in each picture is actually the same young adolescent. As you recall from her introduction in Chapter 2, Janie became concerned about her weight right before entering Cario Middle School. Concern for physical development aligned with social development and a metamorphosis of sorts took place.

(Continued)

Janie 7th grade

Janie's parents weren't thrilled with the transformation. When the first purple streak appeared in her hair, along with the black fingernails, they were horrified. Mom said she should have known when Janie's taste in literature went from Judy Blume to Jodi Picoult. Mom and Dad called a parent-teacher conference to try to find out why their daughter had turned "goth." When Traci Peters and her teammates sat down with Janie's parents, they listened to their concerns and then began to reassure them. Had Janie gotten in trouble in any setting? No. Had Janie's grades fallen in 7th grade? No. Had she become withdrawn or rebellious? No. Of course the teachers noticed the change, but so far it was in outward appearance only. Teachers and parents agreed to stay in close touch and communicate any signs of problems immediately.

Backward Design

Now that we have a better view of the place of lesson planning in the bigger picture of teaching and learning, let's look at the philosophy and practice of **backward design** as it brings curriculum, instruction, and assessment together. The link among the three has traditionally focused on the order in which the words were just stated—we decide what to teach, we develop ways to teach it, and then we determine whether learning occurs. Backward design changes this order. The concept was first presented in an important book titled *Understanding by Design* written by Grant Wiggins and Jay McTighe in 1998. Since that time the framework has been repeatedly both validated and updated.

Backward design calls for us to first consider our desired results. Next, we determine what evidence would assure us the results are accomplished. Once these two decisions are made, we plan the experiences and instruction that will achieve the results and provide evidence of success (Wiggins & McTighe, 2012).

Stage One of backward design involves identifying desired results. There is more content within the national, state, and district standards than can reasonably be addressed, so we have to make choices about what to include in any depth. To help us make our decisions about priorities, we are encouraged to view content on three levels:

- Concepts and skills considered *enduring*—those big ideas that students retain even when they have forgotten facts and details
- *Essential* knowledge and skills—those we want students to remember from lessons and units
- Knowledge and skills that are worth being *familiar* with—the ones that may be peripheral to what is studied and are merely introduced in the current lesson or unit.

A major teaching responsibility involves knowing our subjects deeply and broadly enough to distinguish where along the continuum from enduring understanding to familiarity specific knowledge and skills belong. Experience, reflection, and collaboration among colleagues are important for fulfilling this responsibility.

Standard 2
Middle Level Curriculum

Element a. Subject Matter Content Knowledge: Middle level teacher candidates demonstrate a depth and breadth of subject matter content knowledge in the subjects they teach (e.g., English/language arts, mathematics, reading, social studies, health, physical education, and family and consumer science). They incorporate information literacy skills and state-of-the-art technologies into teaching their subjects.

Stage Two of backward design calls for us to determine what evidence will tell us that students have achieved the desired results. A wide range of assessment methods, including informal checks for understanding, observation, quizzes/tests, and performance tasks/projects serve as evidence.

Stage Three of backward design involves planning learning experiences and instruction to give students opportunities to achieve desired results and to demonstrate those results with appropriate evidence.

Naming the practice described in the three stages as "backward design" causes many teachers to reconsider their instructional planning practices, while others say it is common sense and they practiced the concept long before it had a name. Backward design supports the standards movement, which provides clear expectations for what the learning should be.

Goals and Objectives

To effectively plan instruction, we have to know where we're going in terms of standards and what the desired outcomes look like. In keeping with backward design, the first step is to know what results we want. In writing goals and objectives, we are practicing backward design as we state the desired learning. Backward design asks us to strengthen our goals and objectives by envisioning the final product or performance as we design paths to get our students where we want them to go.

GOALS   **Goals** are general statements of intent. They are broad and do not specify steps toward reaching them. An educational goal may be written at the national, state, district, or school level to provide a direction for learning. Goal-setting is an essential aspect of teaching that guides our instructional planning.

In writing goals, three broad concepts are considered: needs of the learner, the subject matter, and needs of society (Estes & Mintz, 2016). With what we know about young adolescents, including all three of these components makes sense. Here are some examples of classroom goals:

- Students will understand how math is used in everyday life.
- Students will grasp the importance of conservation with regard to natural resources.
- Students will appreciate the musical contributions of major composers.
- Students will understand the influence of William Faulkner on the image of the South.

OBJECTIVES   A **learning objective** states the learning that is intended to take place as a result of instruction and the results of objectives are measurable. I like this definition for three reasons. First, the term *learning objectives* encompasses other terms you may hear such as performance objectives, cognitive objectives, affective objectives, content objectives, and other modifications of the basic word *objectives*. We realize that regardless of what we want our students to know or do, or the source from which the knowing and doing emanate, the result we're going for is *learning*. Second, I like the definition because of the emphasis on objectives as *measurable*. Although goals may state ideals, objectives use action verbs to define specific learning and provide ways to determine whether the learning occurs. Third, I like the definition because it states that the objective is accomplished as the result of instruction. For an objective to be meaningful, it must guide instruction and be the reason for doing what we do in the classroom. Each chapter in this book begins with a list of learning outcomes that serve as the learning objectives for the chapters.

TWB **Goal 8.** [Young adolescents] develop his or her strengths, particular skills, talents, or interests and have an emerging understanding of his or her potential contributions to society and to personal fulfillment.

Using action verbs to describe the learning we want to occur makes it possible to design assessments to verify the learning (step 2 of backward design) and select instructional strategies to bring about the learning (step 3 of backward design). Most learning objectives begin with the statement "Students will." Keeping a chart of action verbs associated with Bloom's taxonomy on your desk as you write objectives is a good way to check for inclusion of each of the six categories of learning while varying verb usage. Here are some examples of objectives and the category of Bloom's taxonomy they address:

- Students will recall the order of the major wars involving the United States. (remember/knowledge)
- Students will match the authors to the titles of the books listed on the Great American Authors chart. (remember/knowledge)
- Students will classify each polyhedron as a pyramid or a prism. (understand/comprehension)
- Students will summarize a paragraph, preserving the main idea. (understand/comprehension)
- Students will construct an equilateral triangle given their knowledge of angles and a compass. (application)
- Students will interview a community member on the topic of increasing voter participation given the recent study of communication techniques and the political process. (application)
- Students will compare and contrast the Dust Bowl era to the current drought situation. (analysis)
- Students will verify the relative accuracy of information from a variety of graphs. (analysis)
- Students will design an electrical circuit. (creation/synthesis)
- Students will compose a short story with all the prescribed elements. (creation/synthesis)
- Students will support one candidate for governor using recent newspaper reports. (evaluation)
- Students will defend their positions on gun control. (evaluation).

Learning objectives are included in the Common Core State Standards, state standards, textbooks, and other instructional materials. If they express what you want your students to know and be able to do, then use them—if not verbatim, then as starting points. You will probably not have to write objectives from scratch, but you will be the decision maker regarding both the depth of content and the order in which the desired learning will take place.

Writing your learning objectives in a particular place on the board each day gives students a sense of organization and purpose. Refer to the objective at the beginning of a class period and then draw student attention to it again toward the end of the class and ask for opinions on whether or not the objective was reached. If so, ask how we know. If not, ask what needs to happen to bring about the learning. Young adolescents are capable of this kind of critical thought. Let's give them opportunities to practice.

Daily Lesson Planning

The quality of day-to-day classroom experiences depends in large measure on the quality of teacher-designed lesson plans. There is no one right way to plan a lesson. The variability of our students and our subject areas determine appropriate approaches.

Very few teachers can "wing it" successfully, at least not for long. Certainly experience helps, but the process of writing a lesson plan in an organized way is beneficial to 30-year veterans as well as first-year teachers. The veteran's plan may be more concise with just reminder words, whereas the novice may want to actually script the lesson. The mere act of putting in writing what we envision for our time with students will lead to more ideas, changes that will enhance, material or resource reminders, and structuring that will alert us to gaps. You have probably seen lesson plan books in resource stores or in classrooms during field experiences. Could all the information needed to successfully teach a lesson possibly fit in a 2-by-2-inch square? For experienced teachers, perhaps, but for beginners, absolutely not! What plan books, either paper or electronic, do is provide overviews, usually a week at a time. They help organize and sequence days and structure whole weeks. Many administrators require teachers to submit copies of a week's worth of plans on Friday or Monday. This accountability check is necessary, unfortunately, as an impetus for some teachers to structure their content and delivery practices. Teachers who thoughtfully plan with or without periodic accountability checks shouldn't mind administrative oversight. The weekly plan book is a great way to map out five days at a time within a single subject or interdisciplinary unit. For instance, if you know from unit planning that you will spend four weeks on Egypt and Egyptian history in 6th grade social studies, dividing the unit into four major chunks, one a week, will help organize and give direction to your unit.

Keeping a three-ring binder of daily plans, or keeping them in an online file, is a positive habit you will value more and more with time. When you have thorough, written plans, it's simple to transfer the main points to a weekly planner. The binder provides a complete picture of classroom activities that will aid in future planning.

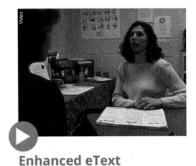

Enhanced eText
Video Example 9.1
Traci Peters discusses how she plans for instruction.

GRADUAL RELEASE Before looking at components of a lesson plan, I want you to think about a concept that benefits every level and type of planning. We want our students to become independent learners and doers. The **gradual release model** reminds us to support learning and then step back as learners take responsibility for themselves. The gradual release teaching and learning framework shifts responsibility for learning to the learner through a series of steps that rely on us knowing both our students and our content very well. To optimize learning, teachers orchestrate a lesson to go from "I do it" to "We do it." This involves modeling first and then working through guided practice with our students. The next step is for students to work together in the "We do it together" phase. These three steps lead to "You do it alone," a sign of independent learning and doing. A shortened version goes like this: "I do, we do, you do."

COMPONENTS OF LESSONS Regardless of the lesson planning format you choose, there are basic components to consider when structuring a class period. However, not every component will be present in every class period. Your basic plan will often extend into a second or even third day. These components of a lesson have been described by many authors and delineated in school and school district guidelines. Here are some components common to most lesson plan guideline documents:

1. **Lesson launch.** This is a distinct beginning of the lesson that helps learners focus on what's ahead. Focus can be established in many ways. You might want to try:
   - Reading a current events article
   - Telling a relevant brief story or joke
   - Placing an object in the room to garner attention
   - Projecting a picture on the ceiling
   - Demonstrating something interesting
   - Asking a provocative question.

The beginning of a lesson makes the difference between our students anticipating what's ahead or simply following along when and where they are led.

2. **Objective clarification.** Thoughtful planning will include a clear view of the lesson's objective(s), often established through state or Common Core content standards. Just as rubrics let students know expectations for products, objectives tell students what they are expected to learn and be able to do as a result of the instruction. A clear objective communicated to students, along with an attention-getting launch, will "kick start" a lesson.

3. **Academic language.** For many teachers and teacher education programs, **edTPA** is an acronym that is quite familiar. For those of you who will not participate in this performance-based assessment, edTPA stands for educational Teacher Performance Assessment. It is a subject-specific portfolio including lesson plans, videos of parts of lessons, a collection of student artifacts, and very lengthy commentary on each separate component of planning, instruction, and assessment. The whole portfolio is assessed using rubrics. As part of the planning segment, edTPA calls for teachers to list **academic language**, the vocabulary used for academic purposes and the language of a particular discipline. For instance, in a lesson centered on the various kinds of triangles, academic language may consist of compare, contrast, angles, sides, acute, obtuse, equilateral, and scalene. Whether or not you are required to complete edTPA, thinking about academic language and how you plan to teach it, is an important focus.

4. **Presentation of new knowledge and skills.** This step is wide open in terms of instructional strategies. All of the strategies discussed in Chapter 8 may be used in this step of lesson planning. The decisions we make about the appropriateness of strategies based on the content, and student interests and needs, must be made during the planning process, as well as decisions about individual and/or group work.

5. **Guided practice with feedback.** This is formative assessment. Practice can take many forms, depending on the content, skills, and classroom circumstances. If what has been taught and learned can be practiced in a traditional paper-and-pencil way, then it is entirely appropriate. If, however, practice involves a more authentic approach, then students may attempt to replicate a demonstration, perform a skill, respond to questioning, and so forth. Guided practice typically occurs during class and is brief enough to allow time for feedback. Teachers may choose to post answers or results and ask students to determine their own success. Students working in pairs or small groups may check each other's work as feedback. Teachers may "spot check" or simply ask students if there are problems or questions. Whatever the method, it's important to gauge student understanding of reasonable chunks of content and skills before moving on to independent practice or new knowledge and skills.

Further student inquiry or reteaching may be necessary. The results of the guided practice will tell us. This part of planning cannot be bypassed. As you give feedback or receive information about student understanding, you will need to make decisions about continuing whatever strategies you used in step four or changing gears to other instructional strategies. Flexibility is a must throughout the planning process, and nowhere more than in the guided practice with feedback phase. Experience helps, but we are all occasionally surprised by the levels of understanding, as well as the pace of understanding, whether rapid or halting.

6. **Assignment of independent practice.** Guided practice generally takes place in class, while independent practice may take place in class or as homework. A discussion of homework comes later. Holding students accountable for completing independent practice is important and worthy of careful consideration. Not everything students do requires a grade, but students need to have their work acknowledged, and, when not complete, they need a consequence. Finding a balance where

independent practice is valuable to student learning and also valued by them as a means to greater understanding and proficiency is one of our planning challenges.

7. **Closure.** A lesson should not end because the bell rings. Flexibility dictates that we not insist on completing all we have planned in a class period just because we wrote it as a class period "package." Closure may come about as planned in the form of summarizing the lesson, asking students to do a brief reflection exercise, or discussing how the lesson relates to what's ahead. Then again, you may glance at the clock and discover you have four minutes left and your lesson is still in the guided practice with feedback phase. Regardless of the phase, you need to focus the students' attention on a closure that helps them see what has been accomplished during the class period and a brief comment about what's to come.

FORMATS FOR LESSON PLANNING The basic components of a lesson can be formatted in many ways. Figure 9.3 shows a commonly used planning form that includes aspects of standards and student variability. Forms such as this one work well because they remind us to include important components. I often need much more space than a single sheet of paper provides. Some lessons need to be "scripted" to a greater extent than others. For instance, if my lesson involves the examination of characters in a short story, I know that appropriate questions to direct student thinking need to be planned and organized. I would want to write the questions I plan to use to elicit thoughtful responses. On the lesson form I may write "Lead class discussion of characters by asking questions." Then I would attach a sheet of the questions.

Young adolescents are wonderfully creative and imaginative. If part of the planned lesson brings out these traits and learning is taking place that perhaps wasn't part of what you anticipated, allow yourself enough flexibility to go with the momentum. On the other hand, if a concept or skill you assumed to be either already mastered or easily grasped turns out to be surprisingly difficult or time consuming, be ready to slow down, change strategies, reteach, or simply allow time for processing. Effective teachers are sensitive to both the level and pace of student understanding and are willing and able to direct classroom activities to accommodate needs.

ENGLISH LEARNERS In Chapter 4, we explored ways to meet the learning needs of English learners. We briefly discussed bilingual education, English as a second language (ESL), and structured English immersion (SEI) as three major categories to help ELs be successful in school. Now let's look specifically at a way of approaching lesson planning that not only makes sense for English learners, but also makes lots of sense for all our students. The model is referred to as **SIOP: Sheltered Instruction Observation Protocol** and was developed by the Center for Applied Linguistics.

SIOP is just plain good teaching, plus the purposeful teaching of vocabulary all students need to know. The emphasis is on language. There are eight components in a SIOP lesson plan as listed in Figure 9.4. With SIOP teachers develop both a content objective and a language objective. Recall the discussion of edTPA. Can you see the similarities? It makes perfect sense to emphasize language for all our students in all our subject areas. Let's look more closely at each of the eight components.

Lesson preparation begins with content objectives and language objectives. Once this is done we need to identify supplementary materials and plan meaningful activities. Next we plan to *build background* by making explicit links to student backgrounds and prior learning as we emphasize key vocabulary.

At every point in the lesson we need to make sure what we do and say is *comprehensible input*. This requires that we make sure our speech is appropriate for student proficiency levels as we explain exactly what we want our students to do. This is where our instructional toolboxes come in handy. Variety in techniques matters. Using action verbs and shorter sentences will help comprehension. Students must have plenty of

---

FIGURE 9.3 Sample lesson plan format

Teacher _____ Class _____ Date _____

Standards to be addressed:

Lesson objective(s):

Academic language:

Launch or opening:

Procedures:

Whole group—

Small group—

Individual—

Plan for differentiation—

Guided practice:

Feedback:

Independent practice:

Assessment:

Closure:

Materials and resources:

---

opportunities to experience the *strategies* we choose. Providing appropriate supports for students is known as scaffolding. A variety of planned questions can help students move to higher-order thinking.

The next component is *interaction*, a very middle-level-appropriate part of SIOP. Students need lots of opportunities to talk with each other and with the teacher as they process information and skills. **Wait-time** is important to give all students opportunities to formulate and clarify responses.

Hands-on *practice and application* will help students internalize knowledge and skills and learn for the long haul, rather than just short-term. For *lesson delivery*, SIOP emphasizes supporting the content and the language objectives clearly and consistently. Students should be actively engaged in the lesson at least 90% of the time, with the lesson paced for student ability levels.

FIGURE 9.4 SIOP components

Lesson preparation
Building background
Comprehensive input
Strategies
Interaction
Practice and application
Lesson delivery
Review and assessment

Enhanced eText
Video Example 9.2

An experienced teacher tells us
how she plans a SIOP lesson with
emphasis on language acquisition.

It's important to *review and assess* concepts, skills, and vocabulary, providing regular feedback. Formative assessments should be varied and take place throughout the lesson.

VARYING CLASS LENGTHS   Class lengths vary in middle schools. Some may be as brief as 45 minutes and others as long as 100 minutes, as we examined in Chapter 5. Teams that use flexible blocks may occasionally have classes that are two to three hours long. The strategies we explored in Chapter 7 may be more or less appropriate depending on the length of the class period. The value of knowing about, and having experienced, a wide variety of strategies is that we can pick and choose what will be best, given the circumstances of the day.

As you plan for a class, keep in mind that there are few activities or assignments that will engage young adolescents for more than 20 minutes or so at a time. A lab experiment, an active group project, or an invigorating class discussion may be exceptions, but planning for variety is the best policy. A brief class period may require only two distinct changes of pace, whereas a longer block of time may require five or six different activities/strategies to motivate and engage students. **Education World** is a large site loaded with practical information and strategies to assist teachers with lesson planning (and a wide array of templates to make life easier!). There's a section titled "Tips for New Teachers," as well as information on the use of technology in classroom instruction.

Planning for a longer block of time is not as simple as putting two short plans together back to back. The need to check for understanding will be different, the pacing of activities will vary, assessments may change in both nature and scope, and independent practice will certainly be different from the simple combination of two separate assignments. Longer blocks of time with our students have many benefits, and the thorough nature of the planning process that is needed to effectively use the gift of more time is worth the effort.

HOMEWORK   For every ardent supporter of homework, you will find a naysayer. The homework controversy is not new and will likely never be resolved to everyone's satisfaction. Every 15 years or so, there's an outcry alternately for more or less homework. The call for increased homework coincided with the launch of *Sputnik* in the 1950s, and in the late 1960s homework was viewed as undue pressure on students. Following the publication of *A Nation at Risk* in 1983, homework gained favor. In the late 1990s, concern grew over stressed-out students and overworked parents. Now, well into the 21st century, the debate continues.

The prevailing opinion for elementary students is that assigning homework has little, if any, effect on achievement. The best assignment may be to read with an adult each day. For high school students, the benefits of being assigned and completing homework are substantial. For middle school students, the benefits are more evident than for elementary students, but no more than half as effective as for high school students. The National Education Association and the national Parent-Teacher Association recommend the 10-minute rule: 10 minutes of homework total per grade level. So, 6th graders would benefit from an hour of homework, 7th graders from 70 minutes, and 8th graders from 80 minutes total (Terada, 2018). As counter-intuitive as it may seem, a 2015 study showed that middle school students assigned more than 90 to 100 minutes of daily homework actually began to decline in their math and science scores (Fernandez-Alonso, Suarez-Alvarez, & Muniz, 2015). The study also concluded that excessive homework can drain young adolescents of motivation and focus.

There are many variables when it comes to why students complete, or do not complete, homework. Home circumstances play a role. Some students have quiet study areas and adults who check assignment pads and encourage students to do their homework. Then there are the rest of the students. Although many believe that education is the "great equalizer," homework definitely is not. We can provide equal working conditions in our classrooms, but the home is basically outside our realm of control. When parents or families no longer understand the assignments, homework becomes an exercise possibly fraught with inequities.

Homework—to assign or not, how much, what kind, what percentage of the grade it will be worth—should be a matter of team concern. One of the beauties of middle grades teaming is the possibility of coordinating the whole school experience for our students. The answers to the questions about homework should be guided by the needs and characteristics of our students.

If homework is assigned, then students should be held accountable for completing it and given some sort of credit. To assign it and never require that it be completed is unfair to students and to the process. If it's important enough for students to use their out-of-school time to complete, then it's important enough to warrant checking, at least for completion or attempted completion. I view homework (and tests, papers, any assignment) as so important that I feel a strong obligation to provide as rapid feedback to students as possible. At the college level, I aim for returning student work with comments by the next class period and view the "midnight oil" it sometimes requires as well worth it. My students are demonstratively appreciative of the extra effort. Middle school students need immediate (or close to it) feedback to enhance their knowledge and skill building. Homework can be used to build responsibility in our students as it reinforces learning. We can model responsibility with our respect and acknowledgment of their efforts.

Not every student will turn in homework on time. As in every other area, there is a great deal of variability. One way to attempt to instill personal responsibility in students is to not only require work, even if late, to be completed, but also require documentation as to why the work was not completed on time. A form similar to Figure 9.5 may work for your classroom, and perhaps for your whole team.

When assigning homework, here are some ideas to consider:

- Arrange with your team/school to provide an afterschool setting for students who want to stay to complete assignments. Yes, this may pose transportation issues that entail a study time during the school day.
- Check homework every time it is assigned to provide feedback, but only record grades for homework periodically or not at all.
- Never make assignments due following a holiday or on a Monday.
- Make homework only a small percentage of the total grade, and then, only as a completion component.
- Allow students to take "open homework" quizzes and tests occasionally as an extra motivation to complete assignments.

We need to think about *designing* homework, as well as *assigning* homework. Instead of asking students to answer questions about a section, we might ask them to write questions about what they read using question stems associated with Bloom's taxonomy. Or maybe we could ask students to talk to three others about a current event

FIGURE 9.5 Student responsibility form

Name _____ Class _____

Today's date _____ Date assignment was due _____

Assignment _____

I did not turn in this assignment on time because

(check all that apply)

_____ I was absent on _____ .

_____ I forgot to do it.

_____ I did not understand how to do it.

_____ I had extra home duties including _____ .

_____ I did not take the right materials home.

_____ I did not have the assignment written down.

_____ I did it but left it at home.

_____ I did it but could not find it when it was time to turn it in.

Here is what I plan to do to make sure my assignments are completed and turned in on time.

_____

_____

_____

_____ (signature)

issue and take notes on their responses. When math practice is needed, 10 problems will usually work better than 40.

Practical Advice

Here are some tips to consider when planning lessons:

1. Overplan, rather than underplan, to avoid wasting valuable class time. It's much easier to eliminate planned elements than it is to improvise in meaningful ways.

2. Check for levels of Bloom's taxonomy and differentiation to meet student needs—all the aspects that help ensure effective instruction.

3. Regardless of where you are in your plan, allow time for closure that wraps up the lesson.

4. Never leave school without a written plan for the following day.

5. Gather materials and arrange for resources at least a day ahead. The copier seems to know when we wait until the last minute—it runs out of toner or the line extends out the workroom door!

6. Be flexible. This is possible when we know the content, practice a variety of instructional strategies, and plan thoughtfully. Interruptions happen. They are inevitable. Altering our plans may be necessary for academic reasons as well as any number of other occurrences totally outside our control.

7. Spend time reflecting on lessons. Consider what worked well, what could have been better, and how to alter/adapt plans to be used in the future. Remember, there's always tomorrow. We can fill in gaps and make adjustments in the following day's plans if we take the time to reflect on our lessons.

8. Keep notes about the things you might change or add as resources for future planning.

If you are fortunate enough to have teachers on your team who plan like Traci Peters, you will both see the benefits and learn a great deal. Read about Traci's philosophy of planning in Teachers Speak.

Teachers Speak

Traci Peters

I've lived with the adjective "obsessive" for my whole teaching career. To me it simply makes sense to plan, and then plan some more. When other teachers see my organization scheme and never see me in a panic in the workroom when the copier jams, it's because I know exactly what I want to do in my classes at least a week in advance. My classroom materials are organized. My groups of four desks each have a number that corresponds to the numbers on the classroom sets of calculators, scissors, rulers, protractors, and so on. I teach my students how to retrieve materials and how to properly return them to their storage place. I walk into Cario each morning knowing my room is ready, my day's state objectives are on the whiteboard, the "What did I miss?" classwork and homework board is complete, and everything I need for the lessons is in place.

I've been asked if this kind of planning carries over into my personal life. My answer is "It used to!" You see, I have a 2-year-old son now and school is about the only place in my life that has any semblance of order! My husband and I enjoy life together so much, and our baby boy has just added to that pleasure. We hope to have several more children. As a math teacher, I think about ratio and proportion and wonder, as my personal life gets messier, how can I possibly get any neater at school?

Resources for Teaching

There is an amazing array of resources for classroom teachers. Visit a teacher resource store and online sites to find books, games, videos, manipulatives, and so on for all subject areas and grade levels. In addition to what's available in the public domain, many teaching resources are available through national organizations. National and subject-area organizations publish materials for teachers to use to increase their effectiveness in the classroom.

SELECTION OF RESOURCES   With all the print and electronic resources continually produced, the dilemma of what to use and when to use it requires commonsense decision making. We can't use it all; we wouldn't want to use it all.

Some districts and schools give teachers set amounts of money to spend each year on classroom resources. This is a luxury, and we need to be good stewards of these funds. Principals have resource budgets that enable them to take teacher requests and buy resources as far as their budgeted dollars allow. Most teachers have more resources at their disposal than they will ever use over the course of a school year. Because of this, new teachers should never feel handicapped by lack of "stuff." Don't be afraid to ask. The resources published by companies not affiliated with school or national organizations should be chosen with care, with our choices guided by the curriculum standards

Standard 4

Middle Level Instruction and Assessment

Element d. Young Adolescent Motivation: Middle level teacher candidates demonstrate their ability to motivate all young adolescents and facilitate their learning through a wide variety of developmentally responsive materials and resources (e.g., technology, manipulative materials, information literacy skills, contemporary media). They establish equitable, caring, and productive learning environments for all young adolescents.

State departments of education and school districts provide resources for teaching and learning. There are curriculum guides, benchmarks and standards documents, sample lesson plans on special websites, practice materials for standardized tests, and other resources deemed important by those who have oversight responsibilities.

we teach and grade/developmental appropriateness. There are many things to consider when choosing resources, including the following:

- Relationship of resources to course objectives and curriculum standards
- Educational value in terms of curricular and instructional goals
- Absence of bias concerning gender, race, religion, and so on
- Relative worthiness of the time necessary to implement or use the resource
- Motivational attributes from a student perspective
- Accuracy and timeliness of content.

Just because software or manipulatives are attractive and potentially fun to use does not qualify them as appropriate for our classrooms. If it does not have the potential to increase student learning, then it is wasting precious minutes.

TEXTBOOKS   When we talk about adopting a textbook series at the state, district, or school level, we are talking about more than a solitary book. Publishers have responded to the call for accountability and ever-burgeoning technology by providing amazing tools for teachers. Along with the basic textbook and teachers' edition, you may receive consumable workbooks (each student gets one each year), CD-ROMs full of supplemental materials, booklets for student and parental interactive practice, special software and workbooks designed specifically for standardized test preparation, interactive software, supplemental literature books, packets of maps, boxes of math and science manipulatives, videos, black-line masters to reproduce, and PowerPoint presentations. Can we use all of these resources over the course of a semester or a year? Absolutely not. The choice of a text series will probably not be yours, but how and when you use the book and assorted "goodies" that come with it will probably be within your control.

Let's consider what a textbook (and its ancillary components) is *not*. It is not the curriculum, it is not the shaper of all instruction, it is not necessarily the sequencer of content, and it is not the only source of information in your subject area. However, a well-chosen text that aligns closely with national and state subject-area/grade level standards can form a basis for our instructional planning. Some schools are now adopting etexts if they have infrastructure to support them.

There are things we can do in the beginning of the school year to make students more comfortable with the basic textbook. For instance, we can prepare a text scavenger hunt that requires students to look at the title page, table of contents, illustrations, organization of chapters, purpose of boldface print, index, appendix, glossary, and more. Middle level students respond positively to creative activities of this kind. The time invested will pay dividends all year long.

Self-Check 9.2

LO 9.3 Interdisciplinary Planning

Any time connections are made among concepts, within or among subject areas, our students benefit, whether the connections are labeled complementary, multidisciplinary, interdisciplinary, or integrative, as we discussed in Chapter 6. The term *interdisciplinary* expresses the cooperative nature of well-planned lessons and units that energize teachers and students and create meaningful learning opportunities for all involved. There are numerous approaches for developing interdisciplinary units, and even more numerous possibilities for implementing them. I hope your interest will lead you to seek out, read, and use books and articles on the topic. What you are about to read is only the proverbial tip of the interdisciplinary unit (IDU) iceberg.

Before we explore interdisciplinary units, let's take a look at the steps that lead to single-subject units. These are units that derive most of their content from within one subject area. You will develop these units, and the connections within them, frequently in your chosen subject area(s). The steps amount to good, basic planning that will help with planning interdisciplinary units.

Single-Subject Unit Planning

As you create your long-range plan, you will be sequencing major chunks of content and skills in your subject area. These chunks may be organized into manageable units of study through **single-subject planning**. Your colleagues are valuable resources for single-subject planning. Most of the content and skills included in middle level curriculum will fall neatly into units around themes. A unit can provide context for learning by revolving around, and being based on, a big idea. Let's look at some basic steps that lead to the creation of a single-subject unit. There are no set rules. The premise is simple—connect learning and build on prior knowledge concerning a unifying big idea. Here are some basic steps:

1. **Select a suitable theme.** The theme may be obvious, such as westward settlement, the writings of Mark Twain, photosynthesis, or measurement, or it may be necessary to combine or divide topics as they occur in your long-range plan.

2. **Determine goals and specific objectives for the unit.** These may be spelled out for you in your standards documents or district curriculum guides. As you examine goals and objectives, you will likely see ways to incorporate standards that may not have been readily apparent. For instance, in a unit on measurement there will be many opportunities for students to practice their knowledge and skills regarding working with fractional and decimal numbers. In a unit on photosynthesis there will be opportunities to discuss the earth's relationship to the sun and other concepts of astronomy.

3. **With your goals and objectives in mind, determine assessments that will gauge learning.** Remember to include variety.

4. **Develop diagnostic assessments to determine prior knowledge.** This may be as simple as a K-W-L session on the unit theme or as traditional as a paper-and-pencil diagnostic test.

5. **Involve students in unit planning.** Tell them the overall goals and give them a sense of where you are heading. Allow them to brainstorm projects and activities that relate to the theme. Incorporate as many of their ideas as possible.

6. **Develop an outline of the breadth of the unit and an approximate timeline.** If you use a textbook as a primary source, determine how much of the text will be included. Be conscious of the school calendar so that your timing makes sense and refer to your long-range plans to make sure your plans will allow for the other units you will teach during the year.

7. **Sequence learning objectives and make daily plans.** We learned about daily lesson plans earlier in the chapter.

8. **Gather resources and arrange for special events that will enhance the unit.** If books need to be reserved and videos ordered, see the media specialist. If guest speakers are desired, call them well in advance. If you want to use facilities other than your classroom, make the arrangements.

All of these steps may be taken independently or in collaboration with other teachers who teach the same subject in the same grade level. Make sure your team knows about your unit plans. Discuss curriculum regularly so that each of you is broadly aware of what's being taught and learned by teammates and students. The whole process of sharing long-range plans leads naturally into discussions of units of study.

Making the Teaching and Learning Connection

Dear teachers-to-be,

I confess that I've always been a science geek. It was the one subject that meant we got out of our desks and were allowed to mess around with stuff. I couldn't understand why it wasn't the favorite subject of all my friends. Then in high school I got the physics bug. I took the two physics courses offered and then majored in physics in college. Along the way I got married and had our first child. Not able to afford to go to grad school straight after my bachelor's degree without a full-time job, I found that local schools were actually looking for science teachers. So, that's what I became. To be licensed, I had to get my master's degree in science education. I chose middle school because I think this is the age when we can "hook" kids on learning!

In the video, what may not be evident is how much planning it takes to successfully engage 7th graders in doing meaningful learning in a gym where they might be easily distracted. I always start with standards when I plan. The lesson you see happened after a week of classroom instruction and is based on Next Generation Science Standard MS-PS2-2 that says, "Plan an investigation to provide evidence that the change in an object's motion depends on the sum of the forces on the object and the mass of the object." This unit on force and motion is just for my science classes, but the ELA teacher on our team linked a Common Core standard with my unit and emphasized how to, "Follow precisely a multistep procedure when carrying out experiments, taking measurements, or performing technical tasks." We're always both surprised and delighted when we find these connections among our subject areas. This is one of the beauties of teaching on a middle school team.

Planning is one of the most important things you will do as a teacher. It's not drudgery for me. I actually enjoy the opportunity to be creative and involve my students in engaging ways.

My best to you!

Kurt Hansen

TWB **Goal 6.** [Young adolescents] understand and use the major concepts, skills, and tools of inquiry in the areas of health and physical education, language arts, world languages, mathematics, natural and physical sciences, and the social sciences.

Enhanced eText
Video Example 9.3

Seventh grade students experience the culmination of a well-planned single-subject unit.

Developing an Interdisciplinary Unit

Let's explore the basic steps necessary for the creation of an *interdisciplinary unit*. Each step is important, but the order of accomplishing the steps can vary. Some teams might have units already written or previously implemented that may only need to be tweaked to make them more effective and engaging. An interdisciplinary unit requires interest and communication among the teachers involved, along with ample time together to plan. Remember from Chapter 5 that common planning time matters!

As we discuss the steps to creating an interdisciplinary unit, refer to Figure 9.6, an IDU my team at Prairie Middle School in Colorado implemented with 8th graders. It will help you understand how the steps fit together.

1. **Choose a theme.** The choice of a theme is crucial. By comparing long-range plans, it is possible for teams to choose a theme that accommodates the standards of

FIGURE 9.6 Celebrating differences

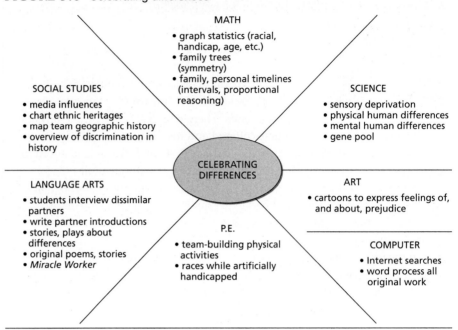

ADDITIONAL CONCEPTS: interaction, cause/effect, perception, interdependence

Big Ideas
1. Differences exist among people.
2. People are often judgmental about differences.
3. Accepting differences and learning from them can make life richer.

Essential Questions
1. How am I the same as, or different from, others?
2. Do I fit in a group? If so, which one(s) and why?
3. Do I do things purposely to conform?
4. What does it feel like to be: excluded, mentally disabled, physically disabled , racially ostracized, economically disadvantaged, youngest/oldest, good/poor athlete, Jewish/Christian/Muslim, etc.?
5. Is the history of discrimination relevant?
6. If we continue on the present course of discrimination, what can we predict for our future?
7. Can we affect the attitudes of others?

each subject area. Typically we think of themes as either content-based or concept-based. A content theme is something tangible or specific, such as airplanes, Native Americans, Middle Ages, or the environment. There is nothing wrong with a content theme as long as related concepts become the focus of lessons and activities. Think about this. A concept related to airplanes is flight. Flight can be a richer theme than airplanes. In an IDU with a theme of airplanes, we can certainly talk about flight. If the IDU theme is flight, however, we can deal with airplanes and much more. An IDU with a theme of Native Americans can deal with culture, heritage, and gentrification. An IDU with a theme of heritage can certainly address Native Americans plus much more. Creating an IDU with a concept theme increases the possibilities of subject-area standards being included in authentic and meaningful ways. Examples of concepts include change, conflict, interdependence, patterns, and power.

2. **Develop essential questions and big ideas.** Essential questions and big ideas are based on standards from each subject area that relate to the theme. They guide students through the unit. They frame the essence of what your class can realistically examine in the amount of time you have to spend. For excellent practical guidance on writing essential questions, refer to *Essential Questions: Opening Doors to Student Understanding* (Wiggins & McTighe, 2013).

The answers to essential questions, which may be many and varied, contribute to the big ideas of the unit. Think of the big ideas of a unit as the principles every student should take away from the unit. These are widely accepted ideas within our shared culture. Figure 9.6 includes additional concepts accompanying the theme of *celebrating differences* along with essential questions, big ideas, and a basic subject web.

TWB **Goal 1.** [Young adolescents] become actively aware of the larger world, asking significant and relevant questions about the world and wrestling with big ideas and questions for which there may not be one right answer.

3. **Web the theme.** Using a simple graphic organizer, the theme/subject web discussed in Chapter 7, team members and related arts teachers should spend considerable time brainstorming ways to use standards, activities, research, readings, and so on, to address the theme. This can be a very invigorating exercise for teachers as we consider our own subject area(s) as well as a wider view of possible connections. As a math teacher, I may have a vague recollection of a song that relates to a particular theme. I hum a line or two and the music teacher recognizes the tune and proceeds to fill in the lyrics that directly relate to the theme. I have experienced brainstorming sessions like this and have found them to be not only productive, but great fun! It's a teacher/team activity that reveals teacher interests and talents that may otherwise lie dormant.

   Now include students in this successful and enjoyable webbing experience. Hold on—they'll surprise you with their ideas and energy. Pick a time frame, perhaps advisory or a common time taken from a block of team time, for each team teacher to conduct a brainstorming session with a group of students. Put the theme in the middle of a web. Tell students that you want their help in planning a study of whatever the theme is and ask them for ideas. Because you have already had the benefit of thinking with others about the theme, you'll be able to prompt the students with suggestions if there is a lull. Remember that inviting and implementing student-generated curriculum infuses developmental responsiveness into our classrooms.

4. **Plan assessments.** In step 2, the essential questions and big ideas are planned, fulfilling the first step of backward design. We know what we want to accomplish in the unit. Once teachers have talked through the parameters of the unit (what, when, how), it's time to create ways of determining *what students know* and *are able to do* as a result of the unit.

   This is not a time for "assessment as usual." Units present wonderful opportunities for combining subject standards in projects and group activities. Students could develop portfolios of their unit work, present a simulation of an event that demonstrates understanding, conduct a research project individually or in groups that incorporates big ideas and new vocabulary, and perform in many other authentic ways.

   You might want to approach the students and ask, "How will I know what you have learned?" They will undoubtedly surprise you with unusual assessment ideas. For instance, when asked this question in connection with a unit based on the theme of flight, one 12-year-old suggested that he make a set of wings for our principal using what he would learn about flight. The principal would then jump off the second-story roof. If he could fly, then learning had taken place. If not, oh well. We all had a good laugh (and, fortunately, so did the principal as the story was told during a faculty meeting). The suggestion broke the ice, and students brainstormed other ideas that actually became part of the unit assessment plan. All of the student suggestions were experiential in nature. No surprise there.

5. **Plan beginning, culminating, and schedule-changing events.** Let the brainstorming session(s) "gel" for a day or so and then plan the major events of the unit. Walking into class on a Monday morning and saying, "For the next few weeks we're going to study flight. Please get out your textbooks and turn to page 146 and begin

reading about Orville and Wilbur Wright" effectively takes a great theme like flight and turns it into instant drudgery. Try this scenario instead:

> Gather your team into a large dark room. Play a recording of bees buzzing, then bird wings flapping, then geese honking, then helicopter blades whirling, and then jets soaring. On a large screen show footage of a rocket launch and then the historic "One small step for man, one giant leap for mankind" sequence. Then turn up the lights and announce that for three weeks we will study flight in many forms and humans' quest to soar. Now *that's* the way to begin a unit!

> It takes planning—from an attention-garnering beginning through schedule-changing events to a meaningful and unforgettable culmination. Guest speakers, field trips, research projects, community involvement, permission forms, bus transportation, parent participation, supply gathering, and more, all take time to arrange. Where imagination takes you, and practical/realistic constraints allow you to go, plan ahead and enjoy the process.

6. **Write daily plans.** This step will make or break the cohesiveness of any unit. A meaningful and well-written unit depends on everyday classroom experiences to draw together the connections related to the theme within and among the subject areas. For instance, the study of aerodynamics, the examination of statistics of passenger airline service, analysis of the significance of President Kennedy's inaugural promise of a man on the moon within a decade, and the study of literature about man's quest to fly all require careful planning and coordination within the unit time frame.

   As teachers begin planning what, when, and how to teach aspects of a unit, they need to talk frequently and share tentative plans. There will be overlaps and obvious connections on which to capitalize. Some topics and activities may be jointly approached because subject-area boundaries are blurred. Combining classes, co-teaching, supporting activities, lengthening/shortening class time—so many educationally sound variations are possible within an interdisciplinary unit.

7. **View the unit as a whole.** Several weeks before implementation, teams need to re-examine the big picture of the unit and focus on support issues. Here are some examples of questions to address:

   - Are all the planned activities meaningful with opportunities for higher-order thinking?
   - Have all arrangements been made? Facilities reserved, permission forms written, phone calls made, materials ordered, transportation confirmed?
   - Have we been realistic in our planning, or overly ambitious?
   - Are the media specialist and others aware of our plans and prepared for the increase in activity resulting from the unit?
   - Has everyone who would be affected by schedule changes been informed?
   - Have responsibilities been equitably delegated?

   As with most anything we undertake in middle grades education, flexibility should rule. We pay attention to our students' needs and follow their lead when possible. When planning a unit, always have mechanisms for monitoring and adjusting. As with any planning and implementation, if something isn't working, change it and move forward.

8. **Enjoy the unit!**

9. **Evaluate the unit.** Allow everyone involved to give feedback. Team teachers and related arts teachers all need to give detailed feedback in a meeting and/or in writing. Debriefing is vital to future success. Figure 9.7 provides sample questions to consider.

   Provide comment or suggestion forms for guest speakers, administrators, personnel at field trip locations, even families. If you call a family member and say, "We'd like your feedback on the unit we just finished" and they reply "What unit?" there's

---

FIGURE 9.7   Unit evaluation for teachers

Unit _____   Team _____   Date _____

 1. Did the plans address the big ideas?
 2. Did the plans address essential questions?
 3. Were all subject-area standards adequately addressed?
 4. Did all students have the opportunity to succeed?
 5. Were all students challenged in some way?
 6. Were higher-order thinking skills promoted?
 7. Were all levels of Bloom's taxonomy addressed?
 8. Was the pace of the unit satisfactory?
 9. Are there other resources that may have enhanced the unit?
10. Were the student assessments appropriate?
11. Was there a balance of independent work and group work?
12. Have we asked the students to evaluate the unit?
13. Have we involved the appropriate people in debriefing the unit?
14. Was there schoolwide or community involvement/interest in the unit?
15. Was the unit successful enough to justify the time and effort it took to plan
    and implement?

---

a good chance that the impact on your students was not what you had hoped. Along with unit-related questions, give family and community participants an opportunity to comment on their interactions with students. In the middle grades, we understand our responsibility to teach the whole child, including attitudes and behaviors.

Asking students to evaluate a unit, or anything else for that matter, requires that our adult egos be intact. Most students will respond to our surveys thoughtfully and with candor, but be aware that there are boyfriend/girlfriend breakups, "I can't say anything positive" attitudes, and "Hey, it will be fun to write nasty stuff" mindsets that may enter the picture. So hold on to your hat when you try a student evaluation similar to Figure 9.8.

10. **Make a detailed log of the unit.** It's very important to keep a comprehensive summary of the planning, implementation, and feedback for each unit. I suggest a three-ring binder to organize plans, lessons, notes, resources, phone numbers, websites, evaluations, pictures—all the artifacts you can gather. Although you may think the unit will remain fresh in your memory, details and reminders will slip your consciousness by the time you want to implement the unit again. A review or critique session and a comprehensive log serve to make the next implementation less work. Why reinvent the wheel each time?

Sara Davis Powell

Traci Peters and her teammates routinely plan together. They look for connections among the content areas and then adjust their individual plans to reflect those connections.

Self-Check 9.3

Why It Matters

In the introduction to this chapter, I stated that with experience we become more comfortable with the planning process. Exactly what will experience do for us in this process? Now

---

FIGURE 9.8 Unit evaluation for students

Name _____ Unit _____ Date _____

1. Three of the most important or interesting things I learned:

_____
_____
_____

2. One question I still have is:

_____
_____

3. The thing(s) I liked best about this unit:

_____
_____
_____

4. The thing(s) I liked least about this unit:

_____
_____
_____

5. If my teachers do this unit again, I would recommend that they:

_____
_____

6. Here are some unit themes I would enjoy:

_____
_____

7. Comments and suggestions:

_____

---

that you have a glimpse at what's involved in long-range, unit, and daily planning, consider some benefits experience will bring:

- Your understanding of the content you teach will deepen and broaden, allowing for more within-discipline and among-disciplines connections to be made naturally as you plan.

- You will have a larger toolbox of instructional strategies to use in your planning.

- You will become more confident in your knowledge of student development, leading to the ability to be more responsive to the needs of young adolescents.

- Your peripheral vision in the classroom will grow wider to allow for more insightful observation of students.

- You will know more about available materials and resources to use in lesson planning.

- Your lesson planning will become more sophisticated as you understand how to use student prior knowledge to build on the potential of your middle level learners.

Most of us find ourselves in charge of a middle grades classroom and 70 to 120 students with only one semester of student teaching under our belts. All the benefits of experience lie out ahead of us as we mature in the teaching profession.

Planning is a series of decisions, each building on other decisions. Thorough, thoughtful, written plans determine to a large extent the learning that happens in your classroom.

Group Activities

1. In pairs, interview a teacher in one of the local schools in your school files. Ask the teachers for information concerning:

   - homework policy
   - long-range planning
   - frequency of interdisciplinary units
   - lesson planning formats
   - If possible, obtain copies of long-range plans, formats for planning, and IDU plans to share with the class.

2. In groups of three or four, brainstorm ways to involve students in the planning process.

3. Form groups composed of different subject-area concentrations. Agree on an interdisciplinary theme and create a web of possible topics or ideas similar to Figure 9.6. Include relevant concepts. Be prepared to explain your web to the whole class.

Individual Activities

1. Briefly describe the memory-enhancing devices that work for you. Be prepared to share with the class.

2. Choose a subject area and find at least three websites that provide subject-specific resources that are user friendly and free.

3. Did you experience an interdisciplinary unit when you were in middle school? If so, briefly describe its impact. If more than one, list the themes you can remember. If not, describe other ways you may have experienced subject connection.

Personal Journal

1. Write about your memories of homework in the middle grades. Did you have a place at home conducive to completing academic work? Were your parents or siblings encouraging and helpful? Were you conscientious about completing independent practice assignments?

2. Do you have the organizational and time management skills to regularly develop thoughtful, written lesson plans? List reasons for an affirmative answer. Think of habits to create or break that may help you develop necessary skills if you feel this is a weak area for you.

Professional Practice

It would be helpful to reread the descriptions of Jesse White in Chapter 1 and Zach in Chapter 2. Also review single-gender education in Chapter 3.

Jesse White

In Chapter 1, we saw that Lincoln Middle School has challenges that it shares with many urban middle schools. The socioeconomic status of most of the students is low or poverty level, and many live in crowded government projects in neighborhoods that have an element of danger. They likely have few role models of academic and professional success. Although this is not an excuse for low levels of achievement and behavior difficulties, the reality is that in many cases this is life in and around urban middle schools. The district administrators have chosen to not grant magnet status to Lincoln as they did to Jefferson Middle School. Instead, they have decided to do something considered pretty radical and controversial. Next year Lincoln Middle School will be two schools in one, and each will be single-gender.

Mr. White observed a suburban school in the district try single-gender math and science classes with reportedly excellent results. The kids, along with some parents, fought it vehemently when the plan was announced. But after two years, praise for the innovation is almost universal. The teachers are happy, the kids are happy, and the parents are happy. Standardized test scores in math and science have improved and behavior office referrals have decreased. Given what we know about gender differences and about planning for instruction, respond to these items.

(Continued)

Remember that for some items, more than one choice may be defensible. The purpose of the items is to stimulate thought and discussion.

1. Some Lincoln teachers object to the change to single-gender. Mr. White is respected among his colleagues. What would be best for him to focus on in discussions with the hesitant teachers?

   a. The district has made a decision and to fight it is futile.
   b. There are books on the learning differences between boys and girls that they can read during summer break.
   c. There is a district school where some objected to the change in the beginning that appears to be very successful and happy with the initiative.
   d. Things can't get a whole lot worse at Lincoln in terms of overall achievement and behavior, so single-gender is worth a shot.

2. To prepare for next year when he will have all boys in his classes, which of the following should Mr. White *not* do?

   a. Read books by authors who write about gender differences.
   b. Arrange to visit with teachers at the school that is successfully implementing single-gender education, at least on a limited scale.
   c. Look for websites that address learning differences and think about strategies to tweak in some way to best suit boys.
   d. Decide that girls and boys do not learn differently so his lesson plans don't need to change.

3. The teams at Lincoln will change as teachers express their preferences for teaching either girls or boys. Which of the following would probably work best in terms of team formation once decisions are made about who will teach boys and who will teach girls?

   a. Allow the faculty to form their own teacher teams.
   b. Ask the faculty to privately submit who they would like to team with, as well as who they absolutely would not want to team with. Then the principal can negotiate team formation.
   c. To be fair, teacher names by subject area could be placed in a bowl. Then math, language arts, science,

and social studies names could be drawn and each group of four becomes a team.

   d. The principal, who knows about teacher styles from a broad perspective and has information only the school "overseer" would have, should put teachers together for this first year of single-gender classes.

Zach 8th grade

4. Zach seems to not care one way or the other about the single-gender decision. Which of the following is probably *not* a benefit for boys in the single-gender school scenario?

   a. The boys in a single-gender class may feel more at liberty to talk about things the way they would when Mom isn't around, allowing for more freedom of expression, that is, gross topics that seem to fascinate boys in puberty.
   b. When only boys are in a middle school classroom, there may be less "posturing" to impress the girls and more attention given to learning.
   c. Because boys tend to learn through kinesthetic activity more than girls, teachers can actually build in more active learning opportunities.
   d. Assignments can be geared more toward typical boy interests, with other choices, of course, because not all boys prefer trucks and frog guts.

5. From what you have read throughout this text, possibly experienced, and think at this point, compare and contrast coeducational and single-gender school settings with regard to academic learning, behavior, and socialization. Do this by completing a chart similar to this one.

Criteria	Coeducational Setting	Single-Gender Setting
Academic learning		
Behavior		
Socialization		

Chapter 10
Maintaining a Positive, Productive Learning Environment

Courtesy of Barbara Hairfield

A successful school for young adolescents is an inviting, supportive, and safe place—a joyful community that promotes in-depth learning and enhances students' physical and emotional well-being. In such a school, human relationships are paramount. . . . The safe and supportive environment encourages students to take intellectual risks, to be bold with their expectations, and to explore new challenges.

THIS WE BELIEVE, PP. 33–34.

⌄ Learning Outcomes

After studying this chapter, you will have knowledge and skills to:

10.1 Describe ways to create a positive and productive learning environment.

10.2 Focus on physical, emotional, and academic safety for young adolescents.

10.3 Explore ways to prevent negative classroom behavior issues.

10.4 Differentiate among ways to intervene when classroom prevention isn't enough.

Dear Future Middle Level Teacher,

We often hear that there are few absolutes in life, and I suppose that's true. But there is one certainty when it comes to teaching that is irrefutable—without effectively managing the classroom environment, learning will be adversely affected, and you will not enjoy your job. Years of experience teaching in the classroom, observing new and veteran teachers, and serving as both a cooperating teacher in the field and as a college supervisor of student teachers have repeatedly confirmed this absolute for me.

People who wince at the thought of teaching middle school don't do so because we study ancient civilizations in 6th grade or learn about the Pythagorean theorem in 7th grade or read *The Outsiders* in 8th grade. They wince at the thought of being the only adult in a room full of young adolescents. Memories of themselves and classmates, perhaps visions of their own 10- to 15-year-olds, and the general portrayal of middle level kids as disturbed links between sweet childhood and maturing adolescence all contribute to the maligning of this wonderful age group. Sure, some of it is justified. There's no denying the element of challenge in middle level classrooms, but there's also no denying that teaching middle level kids is an extraordinary adventure. Young adolescents want parameters. They want their teachers to manage the environment so they can safely learn, grow, and interact.

Being with young adolescents is fun! There's never a dull moment because we are continually required to listen, observe, guide, model, jointly explore, and be *absolutely present* with delightful, curious, and emerging learners who need us. Cool, don't you think?

SDP

LO 10.1 Creating a Positive and Productive Learning Environment

Creating a positive climate, ensuring that curriculum and instruction are engaging, and maintaining a structure conducive to learning all contribute to a productive learning environment. Everything we do and everything that occurs in the classroom enhances or detracts from both student learning and our personal satisfaction with the profession of teaching. Keep in mind that nowhere is developmental appropriateness more critical than when we consider the learning environment.

Sense of Community

A positive and productive learning environment is characterized by a sense of community in which each person (student and teacher) feels connected to both the group and the subject matter. In middle school the whole notion of teaming, with its lengthy list of benefits, is based on the values of belonging and membership. In a school where each teacher plans for and implements strategies that lead to classrooms as caring communities, the teams, the grade levels, and the entire school become productive learning environments.

An environment in which belonging and membership are the norm is especially important for at-risk students whose backgrounds of failure in school, indifference at home, or little support outside the school all threaten their success. Just as belonging in a learning community affects academic success, academic success brings a sense of belonging. Conversely, students who fail academically seldom feel accepted in a learning environment and often seek membership in antisocial settings. Caring about students—all students—leads us to do what Alfie Kohn calls teaching unconditionally. Practicing **unconditional teaching** means we accept students for who they are, not for what they do. Teaching unconditionally is an attitude that lets students know that they matter to us, even when they mess up, don't achieve, or misbehave. An attitude of unconditional teaching tells students that each day is new and what happened in the past is not going to negatively affect what happens in the future. It's especially important to not take young adolescents' words or behaviors personally. They often lash out at the people who mean the most to them. If they know we care about them unconditionally, they may use us to vent, knowing we will still love them. While the labeling of the concept is over a decade old, what Kohn (2005) describes as unconditional teaching is still pertinent to reaching and teaching young adolescents.

- Show students we are glad to see them
- Show students we trust and respect them
- Display an appealing informality
- Spend time with students even when we don't have to
- Ask about students' lives outside school and remember their answers
- Find something appealing about each student.

This is a great list for creating a sense of community where everyone belongs.

Cultural Considerations

The role of culture in determining strategies for managing the classroom environment cannot be overstated. Be sure to review what we discussed about cultural differences

Standard 5
Middle Level Professional Roles

Element b. Advocacy for Young Adolescents and Developmentally Responsive Schooling Practices: Middle level teacher candidates serve as advocates for all young adolescents and for developmentally responsive schooling practices. They are informed advocates for effective middle level educational practices and policies, and use their professional leadership responsibilities to create equitable opportunities for all young adolescents in order to maximize their students' learning.

Sara Davis Powell

Feeling comfortable with a group of friends is important to healthy social development.

in Chapter 3. In the United States, we often stress individualistic values of the dominant European American culture. An individualistic approach to teaching and learning emphasizes the individual and the quest to become independent through growth and development. However, much of the world is based on a collectivistic culture with emphasis on individual development while staying very close to family and others, whose well-being is foremost.

An example of an individualistic classroom practice is almost exclusively asking students to work alone on assignments and projects. A collectivistic approach encourages sharing notes and ideas and solving problems as a group effort. A management expectation of "Raise your hand when you wish to speak," although likely included in many middle level classroom rule sets, is individualistic and will be difficult for students whose cultures are collectivistic in nature.

Teachers' acceptance and understanding of cultural differences can affect the teaching and learning process. A classroom or school that promotes **cultural responsiveness** includes in the curriculum contributions from a variety of cultures; encourages students to express their individual cultures in the school; looks for and then works to close achievement gaps among racial, ethnic, and cultural groups; and makes sure no student is excluded from participation in school activities based on race, ethnicity, or any other aspect of culture (Powell, 2019).

The implications of managing the learning environment with consideration for the cultures of students are important, and pretty daunting. I encourage you to read books such as Laura Pinto's *From Discipline to Culturally Responsive Engagement*. Pinto states, "cultural responsiveness is an approach to education that crosses disciplines and cultures to engage learners by incorporating their ways of being, knowing, and doing. . . . The ultimate goal of cultural responsiveness is to help students succeed" (Pinto, 2013, p. 13). We must keep in mind that students

- Come to us from both social and cultural contexts that influence their learning.
- Benefit from structured classroom organization and management that use what students already know and can do.
- Are profoundly impacted by home and family.
- Can take more responsibility for their own learning as they mature.

It's also vital to be aware of how our own racial and cultural heritages impact the classroom learning environment. We need to honestly identify any existing biases we have toward students from different ethnic, racial, class, and religious backgrounds. Self-examination helps build both understanding and empathy, as well as avoiding mistakes that may negatively affect our students.

Connecting with Students

When there's a pronounced sense of community and we are culturally responsive, connecting with students will come naturally. However, we can't take it for granted. It's a conscious and continual decision to develop relationships with and among young adolescents. Recalling our discussion of wayside teaching in Chapter 6, we know that wayside teachers, or those who purposefully develop strong relationships with students, "positively influence each and every student through seemingly small actions, bolstered by awareness of needs, purposeful observations of students and situations, and a determination to go beyond what's written in our lesson plans. By doing so, we connect with students and support their learning" (Powell, 2010, p. 21). Here are some suggestions for making the most of wayside teaching:

- Before school starts, write a personal postcard welcoming the students who will enter your class. Yes, it's time consuming and the cards and postage will cost (ask your principal to finance it), but the short- and long-term benefits are invaluable. I did this as a middle school teacher and continue the practice at the university level. I consider it a "must." (Parents love it too!)

- Greet your students at the door the first day, and every day.

- Learn student names very quickly, using whatever mnemonic device (memory aid) works for you. Use names often in and out of the classroom. Even if you see 120 students on a team, you should know every name by the end of the second week of classes. It can be done.

- Use "getting to know you" surveys. Kids, like all of us, enjoy talking and writing about themselves. Give them an opportunity to do so, and then use the information throughout the year to connect more personally with them. A simple survey is shown in Figure 10.1.

- Let students know that you understand their need to connect with each other. Experience shows us that if we don't provide socializing opportunities for young adolescents, they will use our instructional time to socialize in ways that have little to do with the content of the lesson. A policy of no talking in the halls or the cafeteria

---

FIGURE 10.1 Who am I?

Name _____

1. I was born in _____.
2. I have lived here for _____ (years, months, weeks).
3. There are _____ people living in my house.
4. My pets are _____, a _____; _____, a _____; and _____, a _____.
5. My favorite subject is _____.
6. My least favorite subject is _____.
7. The best thing I did this summer was _____.
8. After school I most like to _____.
9. On weekends I like to _____.
10. My favorite music group is _____.
11. My favorite movie is _____.
12. The best book I ever read is _____.
13. My favorite food is _____.
14. If I could travel anywhere, I'd most like to go to _____ because _____.
15. The people who know me best would use these three words to describe me:
    _____ , _____ , _____ .

is deadly. Not only is it unenforceable, it's developmentally wrong. Five minutes of free talking time helps ensure attention during the rest of the class period.

Self-Discipline

Helping young adolescents develop **self-discipline** is one of our highest callings. They are in the midst of the transition from dependence to independence. Most have been accustomed to being told what to do, how to do it, and when to do it in elementary school. In middle school it should be to a lesser degree. We want our students to develop self-discipline as members of a community that exists in a positive and productive learning environment. Self-discipline requires a degree of both self-confidence and self-respect as students monitor their own behavior and make adjustments to actions and attitudes when needed.

Teaching students how to monitor their own behavior is an important task. We need to remind them to be aware of their actions and attitudes and to adjust them when needed. Self-monitoring is the ultimate form of **classroom management**. Burden and Byrd (2016) suggest that we teach self-monitoring as a means of achieving self-discipline by prompting students to ask themselves questions when they are tempted to violate a rule or feel like they are about to lose self-control. The questions might include, "Is this worth the trouble it will cause me?" and "Is this what I want to happen?"

As with other traits we want our students to acquire, teaching through modeling self-discipline techniques is very meaningful. Let students see you in a tense situation and how you show self-discipline. Then do a teacher think-aloud about how you felt and how you maintained self-control.

Self-Check 10.1

LO 10.2 Ensuring Physical, Emotional, and Academic Safety

A positive and productive learning environment includes physical, emotional, and academic safety. In recent years we have become increasingly aware of the need for physical safety. From the shocking events at Columbine High School in Littleton, Colorado, in 1999, to Douglas High School in Parkland, Florida, in 2018, to the daily reality of occasional violence in our schools, our heightened focus on physical safety is justified. As important as physical safety is, it is imperative for educators to recognize the need for emotional and academic safety as well. We must minimize, and when possible eliminate, threatening events that may be physical, emotional, or academic in nature.

Physical Safety

Physical safety requires the elimination of threatening and real scenarios including fear of:

- Pushing and shoving in the hallway and on school grounds
- Theft of personal items
- Verbal threats of violence
- Becoming part of a fight
- Weapons being used in school.

The roots of the violence may be family-oriented and related to child abuse, domestic abuse, alcohol or drug abuse, viewing violence in the media and video games, availability of weapons, and other family or social problems happening outside of school. For this reason, school safety should be addressed from many perspectives. When kids are with us, we need to do everything possible to keep them safe. School administrators need to assess the grounds, dark/hidden places, windows, lighting, door closures, and safety hazards. This assessment should lead to security precautions and changes. Most school districts dictate safety procedures for the unexpected, either nature-driven, such as a tornado, or human-driven, such as an active shooter. We need to be aware of threatening situations and how to respond if the following occur:

- An unauthorized or unrecognized person enters the building, possibly with a weapon
- A bomb threat is made
- A natural disaster threatens
- A fire releases toxic fumes
- A sudden health problem
- An active-shooter situation.

Many middle schools employ resource officers who serve to help prevent safety crises and maintain order. These officers are most useful when they do more than respond to rule infractions or act as police officers. Some coach sports, develop personal relationships with students, act as positive role models, and lend support when needed. Resource officers are typically members of the local police force assigned to school safety.

Schools may employ student concern specialists. These valuable individuals can serve as a second pair of eyes for a principal, concentrating on the physical well-being of the students. They can prevent acts of violence, intercept threats to student safety, and handle discipline problems. An effective student concern specialist listens carefully and watches constantly, interacting and intervening when appropriate. When physical safety is present, students will be more emotionally secure.

Emotional Safety

The sensitivity and vulnerability inherent in the emotional development of young adolescents should be acknowledged and addressed in middle school. Educators who understand and care about middle level students know the impact of an environment that provides **emotional safety**. Young adolescents need to be able to count on the school environment to provide a stable atmosphere where expressed emotions receive consistently caring responses. Unfortunately, homes and communities may not provide emotional safety.

Some critics of the middle level emphasis on affective issues and growth are quick to say that we should concentrate on academics and not on what they may call the "touchy-feely" aspects of early adolescence. In *What Every Middle School Teacher Should Know*, Brown and Knowles (2014) report on a number of research studies that have linked a caring environment (emotional safety) to cognitive growth. They make a case for positive student-teacher interpersonal relationships as vehicles for the improvement of the quality of learning. To help young adolescents preserve emotional safety, Redford (2018) suggests that we pause before assuming we know what's behind a student's disruptive behavior. In this way we take on the role of investigator rather than judge. We acknowledge that behaviors, and the reasons behind them, are quite complicated. "Disappointing behavior is no longer automatic evidence that a student is insensitive, doesn't care, or is not trying"(Redford, 2018). We preserve emotional safety.

Emotional safety entails minimizing stress for students. Teacher actions that may cause needless stress for young adolescents include:

- Yelling at one student or an entire class
- Applying punishment inappropriately
- Threatening students

- Making fun of students
- Establishing unrealistic academic demands or expectations
- Pushing students to learn abstract principles that are beyond their cognitive capabilities
- Assigning extensive homework that requires at least an hour or more of work each evening for each subject
- Embarrassing students in front of their most significant audience—their peers.

Brown and Knowles (2014) also say that we may disrupt the emotional stability needed for optimal student learning in subtle, and often unwitting, ways by:

- Refusing to lend a pencil, protractor, paper, or other supplies to students
- Caring more about completing the textbook than meeting each student's needs
- Treating each student the same regardless of differences in learning abilities or learning preferences
- Preventing students from interacting socially during class time
- Assessing student learning in only one way
- Designing lessons that are primarily teacher directed without hands-on opportunities for student learning
- Refusing to be flexible in curricular design, instructional processes, or scheduling
- Using quizzes to "catch" students who may not understand material
- Ignoring young adolescents' stages of cognitive, social, and emotional growth.

We see that making our classrooms less than emotionally safe can be quite inadvertent. It's pretty scary to know how much power a word, a look, a policy never intended to do harm, a withholding of support, and so on, may have in the life of a young adolescent. We must be very aware of our influence.

Perhaps one of the most proactive things we can do to promote emotional safety is to listen to our students without condemning them or even offering solutions. If they know we care about them, respect their absolutely natural fluctuations in mood, and are willing to allow them to grow, make mistakes, and begin again (and again!), they will tend to perceive emotional safety in our classrooms. Remember that emotional development and cognitive development are linked. So if students perceive emotional safety, they are likely to sense academic safety as well.

Academic Safety

Academic safety is a concept rarely discussed, and yet it is addressed regularly in practical ways by teachers intent on creating a positive and productive learning environment. What exactly does academic safety mean? It means, in the words of *Turning Points*, "Ensuring success for all students: All young adolescents should have the opportunity to succeed in every aspect of the middle grade program, regardless of previous achievement or the pace at which they learn" (Carnegie Council on Adolescent Development, 1989, p. 49). Success begets success. The corollary, unfortunately, is also true—lack of success begets lack of success.

When we succeed, we are willing to exert effort and take risks to attempt new and more challenging feats. Unfortunately, academic risk-taking is buried in many students before they even reach middle school; for others, it is a casualty of middle school. Our task as teachers is to minimize feelings of inadequacy by ensuring that every student succeeds at something.

One way to ensure some measure of success for each student is to internalize and act on our understanding of adolescent development by operationalizing the concept of differentiation. Using what we know about learning preferences and modalities, varying motivational levels, and maintenance of high expectations, we can create a learning environment that at once validates cognitive progress and raises the bar to preserve momentum.

The negative effect peers can have on the academic success of members of their social groups always surprises and dismays me when I witness it. In middle school awards assemblies, I have heard kids jeer as one of their own is called to the front to be recognized for an accomplishment. As adults we understand that underlying the jeers is a tender jealousy that hasn't matured enough to recognize it for what it is, much less lead to a comment of "Good job, my friend." The student being jeered could not care less about the psychological origins of "Geek," "Teacher's pet," or other taunts I have heard but am reluctant to put in print. This same kind of thing happens daily in many middle level settings.

The opposite kind of embarrassment is even more prevalent. Our students are afraid of failing in front of their peers. After feeling stupid in the eyes of their classmates, many will simply clam up and not participate. A sudden headache or need to go to the bathroom may occasionally work to get them out of the academic spotlight of perhaps reading aloud, going to the board to work a problem, or answering questions about an assignment. When headaches and bathroom breaks are exhausted, many turn to misbehavior as a refuge from the academic arena. We need to recognize these avoidance tactics as we find ways to move each student toward some measure of success.

To help ensure academic safety, teachers can do the following:

- Make sure no one laughs when students attempt to ask or answer a question.
- Establish realistic academic expectations and outcomes for each student.
- Recognize student efforts, as well as the products of those efforts.
- Eliminate competitive situations that create inequity among students.
- Develop cooperative grouping strategies that encourage students to collaborate in their learning and share their knowledge and expertise with one another.
- Use instructional strategies to address various learning preferences.
- Recognize and appreciate talents other than academic skills.

Physical, emotional, and academic safety are imperative for a positive and productive learning environment. When all three are attended to, our classrooms are healthier places for students. Let's look at ways to prevent problems in the classroom in order to maintain a positive and productive learning environment where students are physically, emotionally, and academically safe.

Self-Check 10.2

LO 10.3 Prevention Is a Worthy Goal

The old saying goes, "An ounce of prevention is worth a pound of cure." The more *proactively* we address classroom management, the less *reactive* we will have to be. Everything we do in our classrooms might be characterized as either preventing the bad by promoting the good or reacting to the bad and attempting to turn it into the good. I'd much rather spend time on the former than the latter.

The "70–20–10 principle" is applied in many contexts with differing meanings. When it comes to describing students in a classroom, it goes like this:

- Seventy percent of students behave and cooperate in the classroom. They rarely break rules.
- Twenty percent of students are unpredictable. Consequently, they need rules, structure, and consequences.

- Ten percent of students break rules repeatedly and may even be out of control much of the time. They have frequently experienced failure, either academically or behaviorally, or both.

Teachers must find ways to alter the behavior of the 20% and the 10% without power struggles and without spending so much time on classroom management that the 70% suffer. Given the 70–20–10 principle, we might expect a middle school class of 30 to have 21 or so students who pose no discipline problems, 5 or 6 who are behaviorally volatile, and maybe 3 who consistently challenge both our patience and resourcefulness.

Prevention through Engaging Instruction

Planning for instruction and implementing developmentally appropriate, engaging practices are key elements of effective management that result in learning and enjoyment for students and teachers. This is the number one thing teachers can control that has a major impact on maintaining a positive and productive learning environment. Students are less likely to misbehave when the work is interesting and challenging, when there are routines, when resources are sufficient, and when they know their teachers will grade their work and give feedback. These are all aspects of good instruction. *Motivating students through good instruction is the best preventive medicine.* Doing so requires our full attention. On the flip side, teachers who do not plan well may be distracted by unrelated matters, not have a clear notion of where the lesson is going, and communicate disorder to their students.

Be 100% Present

This is more difficult than you might imagine. Being physically present is one thing; being 100% mentally present is another. Teachers have personal lives just like anyone else, but in our profession it's extremely important to leave our worries in the car. This doesn't mean we don't share some of what concerns us, but we do so with the understanding that we are with young adolescents. We don't want to burden them or unnecessarily worry them. We can't let our problems spill over into the classroom environment.

Part of being 100% present is maintaining vigilant and responsive peripheral vision in the classroom. This means we purposefully watch and listen to everything that goes on inside and outside our classrooms, when kids are talking to one another in groups and during passing period. Erika Daniels tells us this "provides insights into our students' lives, minds, and emotions, which enables us to be more effective teachers" (2011, p. 33). Daniels gives an example that speaks volumes about why being 100% present can make a difference to vulnerable young adolescents when she overheard that Karina and Joaquin broke up. This information didn't change her lesson on fractions, but she didn't put the two of them in the same cooperative group that day. Unnecessary drama was prevented.

Standard 4

Middle Level Instruction and Assessment

Element d. Young Adolescent Motivation: Middle level teacher candidates demonstrate their ability to motivate all young adolescents and facilitate their learning through a wide variety of developmentally responsive materials and resources (e.g., technology, manipulative materials, information literacy skills, contemporary media). They establish equitable, caring, and productive learning environments for all young adolescents.

The wisdom of Jacob Kounin has been around for 50 years and it rings as true now as it did in 1970. When studying classroom management, he found that teachers differ little in how they handle problems once they arise. The differences were dramatic, however, when observing what successful classroom managers do to *prevent* classroom problems. Kounin concluded that the skills demonstrated by successful classroom managers could be termed **withitness**, or the ability to appear to have eyes in the back of their heads as they seem to see and hear everything. Teachers who practice withitness can juggle several situations at a time and still know when students are off-task or if there's a storm brewing. As you observe classrooms or reflect on scenarios, think about what withitness would look like and why it's an advantage.

Routines

Students occasionally get thirsty, need to use the restroom, forget supplies, are tardy or absent, need to see a counselor, or experience emotional crises. Each individual occurrence of this nature may have only a minor impact on the classroom. Collectively, these interruptions can significantly detract from the learning environment. Team and classroom routines are essential in minimizing the impact of relatively minor interruptions. **Routines** are expectations organized around a particular time, concept, or place that help guide students and teachers to accomplish tasks in the quickest and most efficient manner possible. Routines provide teachers more time to teach and students more time to learn.

Established routines are not meant to be restrictive. Rather, they free us to concentrate on curriculum, instruction, and assessment more fully with fewer distractions. We may want to establish routines to address taking/reporting attendance, changing seating arrangements, turning in late work, distributing and gathering materials, beginning and dismissing class, seeing the nurse, and going to lockers. Anticipating times, concepts, and places that may be better addressed through routines, as opposed to repeating instructions over and over, will waste less time and help our classrooms run more smoothly.

Before establishing classroom routines it's important to consider the full range of school policies that might relate to the areas to be addressed. For instance, the guidance counselor will likely have a procedure for students to follow who feel the need for counseling; the office will have mandatory ways for reporting attendance, although the method of taking attendance is usually up to individual teachers; there may be a general policy for time allowed to make up work following an absence; and students will likely need some sort of identification when in the hallways. Many routines can be established as a team. If all of a student's teachers do something in the same way, the likelihood of the student following the routine is increased.

Perhaps the most useful of all routines is one that allows us to get the attention of a group of students—the 30 or so in our classrooms, or the 100 or more in the cafeteria or on the field. The routine I have used for years is the hand-raising technique. Here's how it works. When you raise your hand, students raise theirs. During cooperative group work when many students are not facing you and are actively engaged, the few who may see your raised hand will raise theirs and other students will see them and follow suit. The key here is that when hands are raised, mouths are closed. When all hands are raised, all mouths are closed. You lower your hand and students do the same. Then you can speak, but the students can't. This technique works for 20 and for 200 if it's practiced from day one of school. It's most effective if whole teams consistently use it.

One routine that builds responsibility in students and saves needless repetition for teachers is the use of a "What did I miss?" notebook. This is a binder with a page designated for each school day. At the end of each day the teacher writes a description of what happened in class. You may have only one preparation per day as part of an interdisciplinary team, or two or three different preparations if you cross disciplines or teach on a two-person team. Regardless, keeping an updated "What did I miss?" notebook in your classroom is worth the time and effort.

A large calendar with important dates clearly indicated will help students stay organized. Insisting that students check the "What did I miss?" book and the calendar before asking about events/assignments is a routine that will save precious instructional time.

Designating baskets for each class period is a good idea. Students know they can turn in assignments or leave notes for you, and that they can pick up worksheets/handouts they may have missed from folders that are kept in their class basket.

Organizing materials and resources in a specific area and having a system for designated students to gather what's needed for themselves and others is an antichaos routine. Maybe one person per cooperative group, or the first person on each row in a more traditional classroom arrangement, is the material gatherer. Habits of picking up and putting away materials must be taught and practiced.

Classroom interruptions are inevitable. Late students, announcements, teachers and support staff at your door—the list could go on and on. Wise administrators do their best to protect instructional time, but schools, their occupants, and the public are unpredictable, and you can count on being interrupted on a regular basis. Teaching your students how to react to interruptions is a valuable lesson. For instance, when the public address (PA) system comes on, teach your students to instantly be silent. This doesn't mean the announcement is in any way more important than what's happening in class, but listening and dealing with the request or information quickly will get you back on track sooner. When someone appears at your door, teach your students to freeze if you're in a whole group activity, or to lower their voices if they are doing group work to free you to respond to the visitor.

Time spent actually teaching and practicing routines in the beginning of the school year will pay dividends throughout the year. Our students are going to form habits with or without us. How much better it is for all of us if the habits they form coincide with the efficient management of our classrooms. Don't overlook or minimize the role of well-established routines as part of maintaining a positive and productive classroom.

Wouldn't it be great if good instruction and productive routines actually prevented all classroom problems? Unfortunately, expectations (rules) and consequences are usually necessary to maintain a positive and productive learning environment. The combination of engaging instruction, effective routines, and appropriate expectations and consequences will go a long way toward prevention of classroom discipline problems.

Enhanced eText
Video Example 10.1

Traci Peters establishes valuable routines that help her classroom run smoothly.

Prevention through De-escalation

The **Crisis Prevention Institute (CPI)** is an international organization committed to best practices and safe behavior management methods that focus on prevention. They have developed very useful information and training for companies and others to help create safe and respectful environments. Of particular interest for teachers as we maintain positive and productive classroom environments are CPI's de-escalation tips (Eilers, 2018). I've taken a few of their tips and applied them briefly to interactions among teachers and students. You may only need one of the tips in preventive mode, or several at a time. Thinking through them will help prepare you for inevitable situations when your calming influence may prevent escalation.

- **Be empathetic and nonjudgmental:** Try to understand student points of view. We may not have had similar circumstances to allow for complete understanding, but we can withhold judgment, at least until all are calm and the bigger picture is discovered.

- **Respect personal space:** Give students room to breathe. Don't get in their faces or point at them in accusatory ways. Try to keep gesturing to a minimum because it can be seen as aggressive and intimidating. They will respond in kind.

- **Avoid overreacting:** Young adolescents can be quite impulsive; they often over-react. This is exactly why we can't! Unless there is immediate danger, our calm demeanor will do wonders for de-escalating a situation.

- **Focus on feelings:** We all have feelings, and sometimes we can't explain them because we don't understand them . . . and we're adults! Always validate that what kids are feeling are their feelings, plain and simple. They own them. To try to stop them from feeling whatever their feeling is fruitless. Acknowledge feelings and move forward.

- **Offer choices:** "Do you want to talk about this now? Or do you want time to think about it first?" There are situations that will de-escalate with a bit of silent reflection. Then there are situations when involving another student or someone else will help. Wait time is effective to allow nerves to calm and tempers to retreat.

Expectations

The word **expectations** is a more respectful name for what we have traditionally called **rules**. Students seem to respond more positively to expectations than to rules, in my experience. In this chapter I use both words. Expectations define what is and what is not acceptable in the classroom. Some expectations are dictated by school and/or district policies. Some middle schools have a prescriptive plan of very specific expectations that will directly affect your classroom. If so, the plan may have a sequence of consequences that all teachers are to follow for specific infractions. I have seen whole-school plans successfully administered, but I've also witnessed problems when school discipline policies conflict with what teams of teachers feel is best for their students. As a new teacher, you may sense that your hands are tied, and indeed they may be. Remember, however, that policies, agreeable or not, do not dictate your relationships with students.

As with routines, it's a good idea for teams to develop expectations and consequences together when possible. The team is a unit that should function smoothly in logical and consistent ways. It is my experience that teachers rarely agree on all the routines and expectations. Part of being a good team member is understanding the value of compromise and being willing to enforce some expectations that may seem relatively minor to you but are viewed by teammates to be of greater significance. We all have our "pet" procedures, likes, and dislikes when it comes to students and the classroom environment. Keep a sense of perspective in this area. For instance, if there is no school policy concerning gum chewing but your teammates are opposed, allowing students to chew gum in your classroom, even if you think it's fine, would undermine the other teachers. The gum would not always be spit out as they left your class, and students might unjustly label other teachers as "mean" for enforcing the "no gum" rule in their classrooms. If you think it's less than a big deal for shirts not to be tucked in but your teammates feel the expectation is important, it's not going to hurt you to notice and ask students to comply. I have found that vigilantly abiding by team rules is best for everyone, even when I am not personally convinced of their worth. By the way, wouldn't it be wonderful if gum chewing and untucked shirts were the worst of the issues we faced in schools?

GUIDELINES FOR ESTABLISHING EXPECTATIONS   There is no one single best set of expectations for classrooms. Burden and Byrd (2016) provide guidelines for establishing expectations, but they refer to them as rules that are straightforward and comprehensive. Their guidelines include the following:

1. Make classroom rules consistent with school rules.

2. Involve students in making the rules to the degree that you are comfortable.

3. Identify appropriate behaviors and translate them into positively stated classroom rules.

Sara Davis Powell

Requiring young adolescents to develop and follow their own sets of responsibility rules makes classroom conduct and learning personal.

4. Focus on important behavior.

5. Keep the number of rules to a minimum (four to six).

6. Identify incentives/rewards for students who follow the rules and consequences for students who break the rules.

TAKE A POSITIVE APPROACH It's important to state expectations in positive terms. Our goal is to promote appropriate behavior and, in doing so, curb inappropriate behavior. We want expectations to state what our students should do, not what they shouldn't do. For example, a positively written expectation would state "Be in your seats when the bell rings" as opposed to "Don't be out of your seat when the bell rings." Small differences in wording can have a real impact on how students respond. Positively stated expectations are clear to students and provide observable behaviors for teachers to praise. Negatively written rules focus on what's wrong and put our classrooms in punishment mode.

Examples of positive expectations that involve powerful "I" statements include:

- I will be the best student I can be.
- I will respect others and the environment.
- I will follow directions the first time they are given.

Using positive reinforcement simply means recognizing appropriate behavior, acknowledging it privately and publicly, and possibly rewarding it beyond acknowledgment. When expectations are stated in positive terms, we can simply say "Thank you for being in your seat when the bell rang." The acknowledgment carries with it a reinforcement because students hear the expectation repeated. For the 70% of our students who rarely break rules, positive reinforcement is generally enough to ensure appropriate behavior. For the 20% whose behavior vacillates between rule compliance and rule defiance, positive reinforcement stands a good chance of upsetting the balance between compliance and defiance in favor of appropriate behavior. For the 10% of our students who are chronic rule breakers, positive reinforcement (typically awarded the other 90%) allows them to hear and see what happens when rules are followed. Although not a common cure, finding occasions to positively reinforce this needy 10% will likely have an effect. It can't hurt. All of us seek attention at some point. *Disapproval* is attention and so is *approval*. We want our chronic misbehavers to experience the difference between positive attention and negative attention. Our goal is to make the

Making the Teaching and Learning Connection

Dear teacher candidates,

My journey to the classroom was through an alternative route. Teaching was not my ambition during or right out of college, but I'm so grateful life circumstances led me to this challenging and fun profession!

My classes are large and every desk is usually full. This makes me even more aware of potential management issues as the kids are close together and there are more chances of off-task behavior. But I have very few classroom management problems, mainly because there's almost no down-time. I keep the kids busy and productive. I also almost never insist on quiet. I learned my first year of teaching that making unreasonable (and developmentally inappropriate) demands only meant I had to be more of a policeman than a teacher. I expect my students to talk to each other, hopefully about the lesson, but a little socializing thrown in is OK, too.

Math requires modeling and dissecting of algorithms. I do most of this on the SMARTBoard, with kids following along using paper and pencil. To hold their attention, I often intentionally make mistakes. They love to call me out and we all have a good laugh. Humor brings us together and can even make math class fun!

I'm aware that I don't look like most teachers. I've had some tell me I don't have classroom management issues because the kids think I'm cool. Maybe they're right, to some extent. But I prefer to think my classes run smoothly because the kids know how much I care about them. If I didn't, I wouldn't be a teacher. The relationships get me up every morning and make my days worthwhile. What a great life!

I hope you find satisfaction and joy in the teaching profession!

Kadean

positive attention more enjoyable than the negative so "attention-getting" might be redirected by the student. Chronic misbehavers have so much room for improvement that we should have many opportunities to catch them doing better. Our responses to these students have much to do with their escalation or de-escalation. Let me repeat that: *Our responses to these students have much to do with their escalation or de-escalation.*

Teach Responsibility

Teaching students to be responsible is much more complex than teaching them to obey (Curwin, Mendler, & Mendler, 2018). Although we may be tempted to simply say "Just do what I say" to our students, Pavlov's experiments with food, bells, and salivating dogs is hardly an appropriate model to use when considering expectations and young adolescents. With our emphasis on developmental appropriateness and our quest to foster critical thinking, asking students to simply "obey or else" is incongruous. The work and time required to teach responsibility for actions is part of our job as teachers of young adolescents.

Teaching responsibility when it comes to compliance with expectations should be approached like any subject. We can use a variety of strategies based on Bloom's

Enhanced eText
Video Example 10.2

Math teacher Kadean Maddix uses humor to enhance his classroom learning environment.

taxonomy. Stopping at the knowledge level or simply posting the expectations or rules and expecting compliance will be very disappointing. We know learning that leads to any kind of action requires more of the taxonomy than the first level. Try this, and again we use the word *rules*:

1. Post the rules. (remembering/knowledge)
2. Discuss the rules. (understanding/comprehension)
3. Talk about reasons for rules. (analysis)
4. Practice the rules. (application)
5. Discuss rules as classroom governance. (evaluation)
6. Discuss how rules apply to different situations. (creating/synthesis)

Teaching responsibility entails promotion of decision-making skills. Making decisions about rule compliance happens on a conscious level. Teaching students that they have choices and how to make the choices that will be best for them and everyone else involved is teaching responsibility.

> *TWB* Goal 12. [Young adolescents] assume responsibility for his or her own actions and be cognizant of and ready to accept obligations for the welfare of others.

For the first week of school it's a good idea to spend five minutes or so each day discussing, modeling, and having students role-play expectations. We may ask them to write what compliance to a certain expectation might "look like," or perhaps what the classroom would be like without a particular expectation. For some classes, it may be helpful to do some expectation-related activity each Monday. After long holidays it's appropriate to emphasize expectations again.

Before leaving the topic of prevention of classroom problems, let's discuss a schoolwide initiative that has proved to be effective for some middle schools in helping create a positive and productive learning environment—school uniforms.

Uniforms

I'm a believer in uniforms for young adolescents. After some initial resistance, most schools that adopted uniforms in the 1980s and 1990s have stayed with the practice of requiring students to wear one of several variations on a clothing theme. Although the practice is started for different school-specific reasons, they mostly relate to middle school philosophy and student well-being.

Some of the benefits often associated with the initiation and continuance of uniforms in middle school include:

- The lessening of socioeconomic rifts among students
- Fashion becomes less important, with increased attention to learning
- Decreasing visible presence of gang identity and activity
- Decreased cost of school clothing
- Greater level of identity within the school.

One of the keys to successful development of a uniform policy is parental support. Parent-teacher committees generally select a variety of shirts, pants, or skirts from an easily accessible vendor. Most discount and department stores sell school uniforms. Because instituting a mandatory uniform policy is risky, in the beginning at least, when it comes to student morale, having a uniform fashion show with student models

Sara Davis Powell

Seventh-graders at STRIVE Prep West-wood Campus in Denver wear green shirts. Sixth-graders wear gold and 8th graders wear maroon.

and then allowing students to vote for colors and styles within the adult committee's parameters is a great idea. Given the choice, students would probably never initially say "yes" to uniforms. However, it is typical to hear comments such as "I don't have to decide what to wear" or "Everybody dresses alike, so we can think about other stuff" or "Now it's more fun to put on other clothes when I go places." If students are required to wear uniforms in elementary school, the requirement in middle school is a smoother transition. Many look forward to high school where uniform programs are less common.

For uniform policies to "stick," they must be mandatory. Dress codes are a matter of school policy and can be difficult to enforce because of the generally subjective nature of the rules and the time/attention required of teachers to be vigilant when there are so many instructionally important tasks to tend to. On the other hand, uniform violations are easy to spot. To avoid any legal questions that would be time consuming and costly to address, an "opt out" policy for parents who feel strongly about their students not wearing uniforms is advisable. In my experience, this option is rarely exercised. After the first year, schools may want to establish a uniform exchange program because kids tend to grow so quickly. When they outgrow a uniform that's still usable, they can exchange it for another size. New students can purchase uniforms at very reasonable prices at the uniform exchange store. Parent Teacher Associations usually have an interest in running such a program.

Self-Check 10.3

LO 10.4 Intervening When Prevention Isn't Enough

We must use prevention as our first line of defense—effective instruction that engages learners, well-established routines, and appropriate expectations. Although the prevention of misbehavior is our goal, there are times when **intervention**, or actions we take to curb or stop misbehavior, is necessary. It may be unobtrusive or involve implementation of consequences that require aggressive action on our part. Students can help other students with behavior improvement through peer mediation. Let's explore these methods of intervention after a brief discussion of restorative practices.

Restorative Practices

Restorative practices involve an approach to addressing behavioral issues that is unequivocally in sync with middle level philosophy. It is one that requires us to create and maintain positive relationships filled with respect and the building of personal responsibility. The hypothesis of restorative practices is that students "are more likely to make positive changes in their behavior when those in a position of authority do things *with* them, rather than *to* them or *for* them" (Oliver, 2016, p.31). This means that figuring out solutions to behavioral issues is a process of teacher and student working together to look at the issue, the reasons for the issue, the logical solutions, and then the plan moving forward.

We have repeatedly established that young adolescents are in the process of *becoming*, as we've discussed development, similarities and differences, curriculum, instruction, assessment, and more. Remembering every minute in your classroom that the kids are growing and learning how to be, and to be with others, will lead us to value restorative practices more than punitive ones and long-term progress rather than short-term compliance.

Unobtrusive Intervention

Effective classroom management involves the ever-vigilant peripheral vision (withitness) discussed earlier along with rational, calm decision making. We have to determine when to do what, as well as when to do nothing. This may sound contradictory, but it isn't. I'm not implying that we should do nothing when there is clearly an infraction. However, classrooms are plagued most days not with major rule infractions, but by small disruptions that require a dose of plain old common sense to know when and how to intervene. **Unobtrusive intervention** serves in many ways as a form of prevention. It's intervention because students do something that requires a response; it's prevention because it will likely prevent escalation that would result in the need to implement consequences.

Small disruptions include a student asking another for a pencil during individual silent work time; a normally on-time, ready-to-work student slipping into class just as the bell stops ringing; and two students suddenly laughing loudly while gathering materials. To stop class momentum to address these small things would waste more time than they're worth. Unobtrusive intervention doesn't disrupt the flow of classroom instruction. If you're conducting a class discussion of a reading passage and a student is just sitting with his book closed, publicly saying "Sean, open your book and sit up straight" will only alienate Sean and interrupt the thought processes of others. Casually walking toward Sean and opening his book, accompanied by a knowing look, may do the trick. This is an unobtrusive intervention.

Here are some unobtrusive things you might try to curb inattentiveness, annoying behavior, lack of participation, off-track distractions, and so on:

- Give "the look"—one your students recognize as disapproving.
- Move toward the student(s) in question.
- Pause and silently stare for a moment.
- Walk to the student's desk and put your hand on it.
- Use the student's name in an example.
- Ask the student to sum up what has been said or to repeat directions just given.

If necessary (and it often will be), you can be more assertive and still relatively unobtrusive by doing one of the following:

- Say "Sean, how should we be participating right now?"
- Ask the student to move to another part of the classroom.
- Ask the student to see you privately after class.

Sara Davis Powell

Silliness is common among young adolescents. Chances are unobtrusive intervention will curb most of it. However, if the class needs a brief break, a little laughter may do the trick.

When preventive measures are in place, simple unobtrusive intervention will keep most class periods running smoothly. Not using unobtrusive measures quickly and confidently will allow minor disruptions to escalate, requiring consequences.

Developing and Implementing Consequences

When disruptions and expectation violations interfere with your teaching and/or student learning, they require more than unobtrusive intervention. If appropriate, a reminder of a consequence may help. When the misbehavior occurs again, a warning might be given. If it occurs one more time, the next step is taken. Some misbehaviors don't begin benignly. They may burst into being blatantly enough to require implementation of predetermined consequences without warnings. A behavior may require instant action to curb the behavior or to remove the student from a situation.

Consequences define what will happen if expectations or rules are broken. If possible, consequences should follow behavior in natural and related ways. It's more likely a student will learn from a consequence than from a punishment. Punishment is done to someone by others, with the goal of unpleasantness that may prevent misbehavior in the future out of fear rather than understanding.

It's important that consequences fit the misbehavior, if not in type, at least in severity. For instance, writing on desks should have a consequence involving cleaning. If a student wastes class time, spending free time making up class work would be appropriate. It may work best for you and your team to have a menu of consequences, rather than a lockstep list—(1) warning; (2) phone call home; and (3) detention— because each situation is different. A phone call home may do it for one student, whereas for basically the same offense another may need detention. This is another reason to know our students well. Being fair doesn't always mean treating kids the same.

Rule violations actually provide opportunities for us to interact with students in ways that demonstrate maturity, restraint, concern for the overall good of the class, care for the misbehaver's well-being and growth, and wisdom. When we view instances of misbehavior as opportunities, we will address them in more positive ways. Now, let's look at some important factors affecting the implementation of consequences.

PARENTS AND FAMILIES   One of my favorite interventions, and one I included as often as possible as a classroom consequence, was parental and family contact. Some teachers report that there are an increasing number of situations when contacting a parent or guardian is less than effective. There are many students who, sadly, experience little support and/or guidance outside school. Unfortunately, these are often the very students who require the most intervention. They need and deserve our best efforts. There are many students, however, who respond with panic to the thought of a call home saying there is a behavior problem. For these kids, parental contact is an excellent motivator. For others, administrative intervention may be necessary.

ADMINISTRATIVE ASSISTANCE   When consequences are dictated by you or your team, implementing them without the assistance of administrators is preferable. The more office referrals you write, the more diminished your power will be as a classroom manager. However, there are times when it is appropriate to ask for administrative assistance. If a student reaches a consequence level that dictates an office referral, not giving one will send the message that you do not believe in the rule-consequence package that governs the classroom/team/school. Violent misbehaviors call for immediate administrative assistance. Verbal outrage, throwing objects in anger, instigating a fight, verbal abuse of a teacher or another student, physical abuse (or the threat of abuse), possession of contraband of any kind—these situations and others warrant calls for help. Read about one incident that involved focus student Darma in See How They Grow. Sometimes even students who are conscientious and well behaved are involved in potentially dangerous altercations. We hope these scenarios occur rarely, but we know that in some settings they are frequent. Students who repeatedly cause major disruptions are sometimes referred to as being out of control.

OUT OF CONTROL STUDENTS   Some students repeatedly challenge our classroom management skills. We all have them. I can still name the students who, over the years, have presented me with more challenge than I could handle with prevention

See How They Grow

Darma 8th grade
After more than eight years of a clean behavior record, Darma has a blot. Darma's last name, Suparman, won him a nickname among his friends of *Superman*. He liked it and grinned widely when his buddies would use the name. But, that was before Darma found himself in a heterogeneous class with kids he had never shared a class with before. A couple of the boys heard one of Darma's friends call him *Superman* and they began to taunt, "Hey, *Superman*, what are your powers?" and "Ladies, ladies, did you know *Superman* is in our class?" Lots of laughter, stares, and sarcasm by both boys and girls were focused on Darma. He was so stunned by the negative attention that he verbally lashed out and said, "Yes, I'm Superman with a brain, unlike you illiterate retards." At that a couple of boys jumped up, knocked over their desks, and started toward Darma, who stood up and started swinging at them. The teacher, who had been standing in the hall, ran in and called the office on the intercom. Within a minute a male assistant principal ran in, but not before there was an all-out fight going on.

The Lake Park zero tolerance for fighting meant that Darma and two other boys were suspended for three days. This was not only humiliating for Darma at school, it was considered shameful at home. Darma's first name means "doer of good deeds," as he was reminded by his dad. So Darma suffered at school because he had to be out and could not make up his work, and at home, because he knew he had disappointed his parents. Yes, he'll get past this and continue to be a successful student, but he'll never forget it. He is determined to not let incidents like this get to him in the future.

techniques or the occasional implementation of consequences. These are students who don't willingly become constructive members of our classrooms and who appear to enjoy disrupting the learning process, hopefully fewer than 10% in the 70–20–10 principle. They often become legends in the school. Sixth grade teachers will have heard about them before they hit middle school. If interventions have not had long-term positive effects, 8th grade teachers will have had years of warning.

The first step should be to seriously look at the student's history. Has she been referred for diagnostic testing? Are there home or family concerns? What interventions have been tried? Chances are the student has intellectual potential that isn't obvious from her behavior or grades. Helping her break out of the "I'm trouble" mode should be a group effort—the whole team plus the guidance counselor, school psychologist, administrators, and others. All may need to be involved to find in-school solutions.

Some students need more help than we are equipped to give. Chronic misbehavior, after interventions have failed, is a sign that alternative placement may be needed. The regular classroom is not the place for all students. The education of the vast majority of students should not be jeopardized by students who need more than we can give. Districts that provide a variety of school settings for these students are doing a real service for all students.

No doubt there will be occasions when two or three students misbehave at the same time. When this happens, you will be very glad you followed middle school philosophy that emphasizes the importance of understanding developmental processes and knowing your students well. Spending time analyzing the social dynamics of your classes pays off when faced with multiple behavior problems at once. If two or three students are involved, choose the one considered to be more of a leader. This could be the one who is most respected or considered funniest, or who, for whatever reason, wields the most power. Concentrate on correcting or controlling this student's behavior. This may take care of the behavior of the others. If not, continue intervention down the "power chain."

Dealing with misbehavior that appears to involve half or more of your class is cause for concern. The first step is to get their attention. Yelling is never the solution. If you use the hand-raising technique regularly, it will work in the majority of cases when there is more misbehavior than normal. Try turning off the lights. If you've never used this attention-getter, it may work. If you do it often, it will not be effective in getting the students quiet enough to hear your directions. Standing silently in the front of the room with your arms folded may get their attention once you are noticed. On a few occasions when students were excessively agitated, I closed my classroom door loudly to get attention. It worked, but I would use it only as a last resort. Once you have students' attention, you can proceed. At this point you must address the causes of the disruption. A class meeting is called for, as well as appropriate consequences. You are responsible for figuring out, with the help of your students, how to make changes to prevent similar behavior problems in the future. Displaying calm reasonableness will help ensure resolution and prevent a repeat performance. Never hesitate to ask other teachers how they would handle this, and other, situations.

Avoiding Power Struggles

When a teacher implements a consequence and the student refuses to comply, a **power struggle** is in the making. Power struggles, especially in a classroom, hallway, or cafeteria full of students, should be avoided. Quietly say to the student, "I feel a power struggle coming on and that's not the way I operate. Let's talk about this privately (or later or after class or . . .)." Some students have experienced "winning" a power struggle and have been viewed as tough by peers after succeeding in making the teacher angry or exhausting the teacher to the point of getting out of the consequence. These are students who take pride in initiating verbal struggles.

It's good to find a way to acknowledge a student's feelings by paraphrasing what the student expresses. For instance, you might respond to "It wasn't my fault and I'm not serving detention for it," with "I understand you feel it's not your fault and that you don't believe you deserve a detention. So we have a problem. Let's talk about a solution after class." Use of the pronoun *we* indicates that maybe there's a solution that can be reached that is not all about punishing him.

Stopping a power struggle before it starts is important, and so is the procedure we use to follow up. If a rule has been broken, then a resolution must occur. Ideally it will be the prescribed consequence, if one exists. If the student attempts to engage in a power struggle publicly, we can't expect an easy private conversation, but it will give us the opportunity to actively listen, acknowledge feelings, show understanding, and say things like, "I sure don't like our relationship to be like this. Work with me here." Most young adolescents want to be heard. Listening and being willing to engage in conversation goes a long way toward not only peacefully resolving a current behavior problem but also paving the way for future communication.

Many middle level students find themselves on the verge of, or in the midst of, a power struggle before they realize what's happening. The whole situation may be defused by a sense of humor on our part. Often students are secretly hoping we will have a way to lighten up the mood and clear the air when they're not quite sure how to back off.

Will you always be able to calmly resolve potential power struggles? Unfortunately, no. There will be times when administrative assistance will be called for. Students will be suspended, in and out of school. Consequences will be imposed that none of us particularly like, or even think best for individual kids who have complicated personal circumstances. In these situations it is extremely important for the teacher to show public support for the administration, even if we privately want to take issue with the consequence imposed.

We are responsible for doing the best we can, even in uncomfortable and difficult situations. Our students depend on us to be adults, to remain in control, and to keep them from crossing the line and getting into deeper trouble that causes consequences to become more and more severe.

Peer Mediation

As a supplement to teacher and administration classroom management procedures, some schools implement **peer mediation**. It may take many different forms, but basically peer mediation provides opportunities for students to problem solve concerning their disputes in the presence, and with the help, of a student acting as a mediator. If successful, peer mediation can lead to students taking increased responsibility for their actions as they learn socially acceptable ways of solving conflicts. It can lead to greater self-control and an understanding of alternatives to aggression, which almost always results in emotional or physical harm.

Peer mediation may be used to settle minor issues that arise among young adolescents such as arguments over everyday events, "having a bad day" dilemmas, harsh

For teachers, a level head and a sense of humor can diffuse would-be power struggles. Giving kids a chance to back down gracefully will often prevent behaviors that may lead to negative consequences.

Sara Davis Powell

Sara Davis Powell

words, hurt feelings, rumor spreading, temper flares, and more. To successfully help students settle disputes and acquire skills for handling future problems, a peer mediation program needs enthusiastic and dedicated teachers, counselors, and administrators to sustain the program's momentum. Resources include adult trainers who understand young adolescent development; curriculum that is developmentally appropriate and relevant to how kids process information; a plan that allows sessions to take place during the school day on an as-needed basis; a private, comfortable space to meet; and a system of deciding who will benefit and how they may access the program.

The only way a peer mediation program can hope to have an impact on the school environment is for it to be considered a valid alternative for **conflict resolution** by the kids themselves. This kind of validity does not come easily. The program must be presented to the whole student body as an attractive plan that may provide a way to not only peacefully coexist but also avoid consequences imposed by adults. Peer mediation will not be used if it is perceived as a "nerdy" or "lame" thing to do. The choice of peer mediators is crucial. They should be representative in terms of grade level, peer group identification, socioeconomic status, special program involvement, race, and gender. Recruitment and training of the right students in the school population is vital.

Not only do the students for whom disputes or problems are resolved benefit from peer mediation, but the students trained to be peer mediators reported that the training involved helped prepare them to solve their own conflicts. So, regardless of their efficacy with their peers' disputes, the mediator gains life skills because of the training. This implies that perhaps the whole school could benefit from peer mediator training. A valuable use of advisory time!

Now that we understand more about the prevention of inappropriate behavior, as well as what to do when disruptive and unproductive behavior occurs in our classrooms, let's examine some personal aspects of managing the learning environment.

Within Our Control

We influence, but cannot always control, students, colleagues, parents, and resources. However, we can control the key variable in effectively managing the classroom learning environment—ourselves. Consider this quote from renowned educator Haim Ginott:

> I've come to the frightening conclusion that I am the decisive element in the classroom. It's my personal approach that makes the climate. It's my mood that makes the weather. As a teacher I possess the tremendous power to make a child's life miserable or joyous. I can be a tool of torture or an instrument of inspiration. I can humiliate or humor, hurt or heal (Ginott, 1993, p. 15).

Frightening conclusion? Yes, the responsibility is tremendous. Whatever combination of strategies we choose, and in whatever set of circumstances we find ourselves, we are key to maintaining a positive, productive learning environment.

UNDERSTANDING OUR ROLE Understanding our students—their development, interests, concerns, and habits—is vital. Our ongoing purpose is to be with our students as they grow. We have already grown, at least out of adolescence. We are not, and should not attempt to be, like our students. Joining the student culture in an attempt to win their acceptance or popularity is a mistake. Read what Joey Huber has to say on this topic in Teachers Speak.

As a teacher, you are both the instructional leader and the classroom manager. Middle grades students don't need or want a teacher who at one moment is 13 and, in an instant, becomes the adult trying to control the classroom. The consistent message needs to be "I am the adult, you are the students. We will respect one another and learn from each other." To do otherwise is to send mixed messages. Joey learned this valuable lesson as a student teacher.

Teachers Speak

Joey Huber

Reflecting on my student teaching experience feels surreal because it seems like just a week or so ago I was trying to figure out how I would survive, and now I'm trying to figure out how to say good-bye. I learned so much. When I first started observing and working in my student teaching classroom, I think I stepped over the line and became too much of a buddy figure to the students. This eventually caught up with me when it was my turn to instruct the students. They were not prepared to take me seriously as an authority figure. This, in turn, led to many incidents in which students could not understand why I had to correct them. Students became frustrated, and it was tough to get them back on task. There was actually one point when a student said, "What's going on here, Mr. Huber? You used to be our friend and now you are one of *them*!" So, as you can see, the students were a bit confused and not

willing to accept me as their teacher because of my desire to be their buddy. I understand that now. My transition from observer/classroom helper to teacher would have been much smoother if I had drawn that proverbial teacher-student line from the beginning. We could have still had fun, but the kids would have understood our relationship more clearly.

My student teaching experience will always be part of who I am in the classroom. The lessons I learned and the relationships I made will make me a wiser and more effective teacher.

As adults we have a wide spectrum of personalities and life experiences. It's good to let students get to know us. Believe me, what we don't reveal, they'll make up! So be yourself—your adult self. An adult has emotions, hopes, problems, a sense of humor. Our students should see how thoughtful, mature people handle life. Remember, even if young adolescents appear to learn little else, they learn *us*.

GETTING OFF TO A GOOD START Students, as well as teachers, are often nervous about the first days and weeks of school. We can reassure our students and ourselves that the school year will bring positive experiences by doing some basic things such as:

- Making the classroom organized and inviting
- Greeting students warmly and sincerely
- Establishing and explaining classroom routines
- Establishing and clarifying rules and consequences
- Conducting a survey of students' interests and concerns
- Creating ways for students to get to know us and each other
- Forming cooperative groups and conducting an activity in which students will experience success
- Clarifying the major learning goals for the class
- Explaining grading criteria
- Attending extracurricular events.

It takes lots of preparation to begin a school year in a proactive and engaging style. It's serious business. I can honestly say that I have loved my students—all of them. I have cared deeply for them and always wanted the best for their lives. However, I also need to tell you there have been individual students I have had difficulty liking. Teachers are human. We are capable of loving the unlovable. However, liking the unlikable is much harder.

How can we make the most of a situation in which we feel the responsibility to address the needs of every student, even the one or two we like the least? The first step is to view the student as a "work in progress." Understanding both the developmental certainties and the possibilities of early adolescence will help us conjure up an attitude of excitement to see what a school year of maturing might do to make students more likable. Another tactic that helps is to purposefully spend time talking to the student you find hard to like about topics other than school. Finding a common interest will do wonders for a relationship. Try complimenting the student on a daily basis. Even the most unlikable middle level student will have some trait that can be viewed as positive. Finally, realize that if you find it this difficult to like a student, there's a chance you may be the only adult who is even trying to do so. It is within our control to at least treat each and every student with kindness and respect, regardless of the level of our personal affinity, and to do our best to appreciate them.

Being prepared for each new day, having common-sense expectations, possessing confidence that shows through in our relationships with colleagues and students—these actions are within our control. Managing the learning environment will become second nature to us when we recognize the personal power we possess to make a positive difference.

Self-Check 10.4

Why It Matters

Every concept and practice we have discussed in this chapter has as its ultimate goal the creation and maintenance of a classroom environment that supports learning. Managing the learning environment is a complex task. The part of the task that often receives the most attention is classroom management focusing on student behavior. We need to realize that student behavior is dependent on numerous variables, many of which are strongly influenced by our actions as teachers. Creating a positive and productive learning environment involves ensuring physical, emotional, and academic safety. Preventive measures include providing consistently engaging instruction; well-established and efficient routines; and appropriate and enforceable rules and consequences. When preventive measures are not sufficient, intervention becomes necessary. Deciding when and how to implement consequences, as well as wisely using resources such as parents, peer mediators, and other school personnel, is key to effective intervention.

Knowing ourselves, addressing our personal maturity, and thoroughly planning our initial and ongoing encounters with our students will lead us to, as Haim Ginott admonishes, "create the climate" and "make the weather" in our classrooms with the students for whom we are responsible.

Group Activities

1. In pairs, arrange to visit with a team of middle school teachers to find out how they:

   - Begin the school year in welcoming ways
   - Establish and maintain routines
   - Develop rules and enforce consequences

   Add these findings to your school files.

2. In groups of three or four, write a set of classroom rules you consider appropriate to post in a middle school classroom. Make a poster of the rules and be prepared to justify them.

3. As a class, brainstorm consequences for the rules posted in activity 2. Spend time discussing whether each item on the brainstormed list is a logical, related-to-the-rule consequence or if it more resembles punishment.

Individual Activities

1. In addition to the suggestions given for connecting with students, describe another way you might "win them over."

2. Did you ever feel physically threatened in school? If so, describe the circumstances. If not, tell about the factors that helped you perceive safety in your middle school.

3. Why is sarcasm an inappropriate form of humor to use in middle grades classrooms? Will you have trouble controlling your use of it?

Personal Journal

1. Did you feel accepted as a member of a caring community in your middle school? If so, what did being accepted feel like? If not, what made you feel like you were not accepted?

2. Do you recall your emotional safety being jeopardized by something a teacher may have said or done? Write about the memory.

3. Do you anticipate having difficulty knowing where and when to draw the teacher-student line because you want to identify with your students? Will your desire to be liked by them sometimes cloud your judgment? If you had a teacher for whom this was a dilemma, write a description of the circumstances.

Professional Practice

(It would be helpful to reread the description of Sadie Fox in Chapter 1 and her Teachers Speak feature in Chapter 5.)

Sadie Fox

Ms. Fox has never been a big "rule" person. When she was in school, she rarely caused a problem or got in trouble. But when she thought a rule was unfair or unreasonable, she found a way around it or removed herself from the situation that required the rule. When she began teaching at Valley View, Ms. Fox was pretty smug about classroom management. She has a lot to offer kids and figured that's all it would take for them to behave in class. She decided to have a classroom without rule signs. All she wanted was for the kids to respect her and each other, and to behave and learn. It didn't quite work out that way.

Because she was hired about a week after classes started when another teacher suddenly resigned, school was in full swing when she met the team teachers, was shown her classroom, and was given her books and materials. Word got out that Ms. Fox didn't believe in rules and, kind of like Las Vegas, what happens in Ms. Fox's room stays in Ms. Fox's room. For a while it all seemed to work. The kids were delighted with the non-teacher-like attitude. Ms. Fox's lessons were engaging and things were great for a few weeks.

Remember that for some items, more than one choice may be defensible. The purpose of the items is to stimulate thought and discussion.

1. The first sign of trouble for Ms. Fox was when five boys in her first period science class walked into second period social studies class with their uniform shirts untucked. It never occurred to Ms. Fox that this wasn't acceptable. After all, what's the big deal about a shirttail hanging out? When asked by the second period teacher, the boys said, "Oh, we forgot. Ms. Fox doesn't care." Because of this, the social studies teacher immediately found herself resenting Ms. Fox's apparent slackness. All of the following would have been appropriate ways of avoiding this scenario except:

   a. Even though they were busy, the team teachers should have spent time with Ms. Fox to fill her in on team rules.
   b. Ms. Fox could have asked about team expectations.
   c. The principal should have shared the team rules with Ms. Fox.
   d. Ms. Fox should have noticed by the time of this incident that the boys always had their shirttails tucked in.

2. After the shirttail incident, the other three team teachers decided they needed to meet with Ms. Fox specifically about the team rules they had developed. When Ms. Fox heard them and was given a chart that listed them, she

was surprised at how petty she considered them, including "No gum," "Walk on the right side of the hall during passing period," "Only one restroom pass per day," and "Even if the proper materials are not brought to class, students may not go to their lockers during class." What is the best way for Ms. Fox to respond to the teachers?

a. Ask for the reasons behind the rules and determine to enforce them as a team player.

b. Tell the teachers that as long as there are no problems in her classroom, she prefers to not enforce the team rules.

c. Choose the rules she will follow and ignore the rest.

d. Ask to join a different team.

3. Routines serve many purposes. All of the following are benefits of routines in the middle level classroom except:

a. Routines minimize the impact of relatively benign interruptions.

b. Routines give young adolescents more time to socialize.

c. Routines save instructional time.

d. Routines free teachers to concentrate on instruction.

4. Explain unobtrusive interventions and why they are important. Give at least two examples.

Chapter 11
Citizenship and Civility in the Middle Grades

Africa Studio/Shutterstock

The Association for Middle Level Education asserts that in order to become a fully functioning, self-actualized person, each young adolescent should understand local, national, and global civic responsibilities and demonstrate active citizenship through participation in endeavors that serve and benefit those larger communities.

THIS WE BELIEVE, PP. 11–12.

 Learning Outcomes

After studying this chapter, you will have knowledge and skills to:

11.1 Articulate the value of, and means for teaching, vital elements of citizenship through civic education.

11.2 Implement civic engagement in a middle level setting.

11.3 Promote civility in the classroom and beyond.

Dear Future Middle Level Teacher,

When Benjamin Franklin emerged from the Constitutional Convention in 1787, a woman approached him and asked, "What have we got, a republic or a monarchy?" He replied, "A republic, if you can keep it." Throughout our country's history, we've experienced challenges that have threatened in some measure our ability to keep our republic, and keep it strong. Now that we are almost two and a half centuries into this bold experiment of government of the people, by the people, and for the people, we continue to face challenges and grapple with our often-messy dilemmas in efforts to keep what we have and grow it into an even finer union.

With all the responsibilities teachers have, adding another may seem unreasonable. But promoting citizenship and civility is not necessarily a lesson plan or a formal subject to add to your day. Teaching and modeling citizenship and civility should, instead, permeate all our interactions with young adolescents. We've discussed the fact that we teach who we are, that it's inevitable. Adding citizenship and civility as part of the ongoing *us* lesson just brings greater awareness to what we say and do.

Yes, I'm adding to your responsibilities, and rightfully so. Our democratic way of life and perpetuation of our constitutional republic depend on the knowledge, skills, and dispositions of the people who live in the United States. This chapter skims the surface of citizenship and civility. My hope is that your interest will be piqued, and your determination strengthened, to do your part to promote citizenship and civility among young adolescents in varied and meaningful ways. And I thank you for that.

SDP

LO 11.1 Civic Education

Former Supreme Court Justice Louis Brandeis famously said, "The only title in our democracy superior to that of President is the title of *citizen*" (Foundation for Democracy & Justice, 2018). This bold statement places responsibility for the constitutional republic in our hands, and the future of the United States in the hands of the students in our classrooms. It's frightening to learn that civic education ranks last in terms of student knowledge as measured on the National Assessment of Educational Progress. In fact, only 23% of 8th graders scored proficient or higher in 2014 (National Assessment of Educational Progress, 2018). The National Council for the Social Studies defines **civic education**: "In a constitutional democracy, productive civic engagement requires knowledge of the history, principles, and foundations of our American democracy, and the ability to participate in civic and democratic processes" (2013a).

Each generation can point to a tumultuous time in the United States. Our political climate became increasingly polarized around political views and ideologies with the 2008 election of our first black president, Barack Obama. The coarseness of American politics intensified during the 2016 presidential campaign that pitted Hillary Clinton against Donald Trump. The **Southern Poverty Law Center** surveyed approximately 10,000 teachers during the 2016 presidential campaign and found that more than 50% of them said they saw an increase in less-than-civil discourse at the beginning of the 2016–2017 school year. In addition, more than 40% said they were hesitant to teach the election at all. Nine out of 10 teachers said they witnessed their school culture be negatively impacted, while 80% described heightened anxiety about the effect of the election on themselves and their families. Many teachers reported increases in verbal harassment, the use of racial slurs, derogatory language, incidents involving swastikas, Nazi salutes, and Confederate flags. More than 2500 of the 10,000 teachers described incidents of bigotry and harassment directly related to election rhetoric (Costello, 2016).

Kahlenberg and Janey (2016) called this deeply disturbing time in U.S. history as perhaps our "Sputnik moment"—comparing the role of Russia's launch of the first satellite in 1957 in the rethinking of math and science education to the 21st-century political upheaval and divisiveness—as a possible catalyst for the revitalization of civic education. Tripodo and Pondiscio explained "the citizen-making role of schools has become a forgotten purpose of public schools" (2017, p. 20). In addition, they reported—in a study of the 100 largest school districts in the United States—that very few districts even mention civics or citizenship in their mission statements. Civic education must be reinvigorated, now more than ever.

As depressing as all of this may be, there's a major glimmer of hope that shines as a result of tragedy. In the past two decades, the unprecedented number of school shootings has brought about a rising civic movement propelled by students who are fed up with what appears to be congressional stagnation. The students of Marjory Stoneman Douglas High School in Parkland, Florida, responded to the horrific slaughter of fellow students in 2018 with activism. They began a significant movement to encourage voter registration and participation in the choices available to all through both election of people to represent us and the privilege of voicing preferences on issues on ballots across the country. This momentum and the possibility of a "Sputnik moment" give us even more reason to reinvigorate robust civic education in middle level settings.

The **United Nations Educational, Scientific and Cultural Organization (UNESCO)** states that citizenship, or civic, education has three main objectives:

1. Educating people in citizenship and human rights through an understanding of the principles and institutions [which govern a state or nation];
2. Learning to exercise one's judgement; and
3. Acquiring a sense of individual and community responsibilities (UNESCO, 2010).

These three objectives align with (1) knowledge, (2) skills, and (3) dispositions critical to preserving our democratic way of life. Revisiting the *This We Believe* goals for young adolescents, we find that every one of the 13 goals is advanced by civic education. Let's explore the knowledge, skills, and dispositions of civic education through the lens of middle level teaching and learning.

Civic Knowledge

Former Supreme Court Justice Sandra Day O'Connor said, "Knowledge of our system of government is not handed down through the gene pool . . . The habits of citizenship must be learned" (Schiesel, 2008). And we must teach them. Remember that knowledge is power. Civic knowledge is empowering.

Why teach about the systems of government? Thomas Jefferson famously said in 1816, "If a nation expects to be ignorant and free, in a state of civilization, it expects what never was and never will be." Ignorance is the result of neglecting to teach our students the knowledge that provides context for how our democratic way of life was established, and what's required to perpetuate it.

Although social studies teachers are generally responsible for history and geography education in middle level schools, teaching the knowledge of our systems of government is the responsibility of all of us. When it comes to civic knowledge, we all bear responsibility. The National Assessment of Educational Progress (NAEP) civics assessment measures the civic knowledge that is critical to the responsibilities of citizenship in the United States's constitutional republic through categories of knowledge organized around these questions:

- What are civic life, politics, and government?
- What are the foundations in the U.S. political system?
- How does the government established by the U.S. Constitution embody the purpose, values, and principles of a democracy?
- What is the relationship of the United States to other nations and to world affairs?
- What are the roles of citizens in a democracy? (National Center for Education Statistics, 2018).

The concern that social studies education and the teaching of civic knowledge is being marginalized isn't new, but the reasons discussed in the rationale for civic education have contributed a sense of urgency. The adage that says what we test, we teach, continues to account for the lack of emphasis on social studies and, consequently, civics "Social studies occupies a unique place in our conversations about public schools. On the one hand, we acknowledge literacy about society, government, and the history that contextualizes our lives are critical elements of cultural knowledge for all citizens. Yet, at the same time, the country's accountability systems have generally placed social studies conspicuously lower in the hierarchy of academic achievement, superseded by math, literacy, and science" (Hansen & Quintero, 2017).

Most states' standards for social studies education, including civics, are guided by the standards of the National Council for the Social Studies (NCSS). The organizing principles of the NCSS standards are expressed in the C3 Framework (college, careers, and civic life) that creates explicit links to the Common Core State Standards for English Language Arts. The C3 Framework relies heavily on the skills of reading, writing, speaking, and listening, and includes these guiding principles:

- Social studies prepares the nation's young people for college, careers, and civic life.
- Inquiry is at the heart of social studies.
- Social studies involves interdisciplinary applications and welcomes integration of the arts and humanities.
- Social studies is composed of deep and enduring understandings, concepts, and skills from the disciplines (National Council for the Social Studies, 2013b).

These principles align in meaningful ways with the core principles of middle level education, don't they?

Most middle schools require social studies classes, but only eight states' civic education standards explicitly require that students learn about the two major political parties, or much of anything that involves controversy or disagreement. In fact, a comprehensive look at state social studies standards found that beyond an emphasis on the history of the United States and the Constitution, most states' standards don't go deeply enough to help students understand and engage in how American democracy works, an admittedly often-messy affair. Only 10 states lead students to consider controversial political or election-related issues, differences between the two major political parties, the reasons citizens should vote, or prompts for students to explore their own beliefs and opinions (McAvoy, Fine, & Ward, 2016).

We began this section with a quote by Justice O'Connor. Now, let's look at the free and accessible resources of iCivics, the user-friendly organization that presents civic education in engaging and effective ways, founded by Justice O'Connor in 2009. Justice O'Connor's vision is clear and ambitious: "To cultivate a new generation of students for thoughtful and active citizenship. Civic knowledge is a prerequisite for civic participation" (iCivics, 2018). The iCivics website includes units, lessons, games, WebQuests, teacher supports, and more, as described in Table 11.1.

TABLE 11.1 iCivics resources for teachers

Teacher Resource Categories	What's Included . . .
Curriculum units	sample units: foundations of government, road to the Constitution, civil rights, state and local government, Politics and public policy, media and influence, and international affairs.
Lesson plans	multiple lessons for each unit.
Games	innovative and interactive ways to engage students.
Drafting board	how to write an argumentative essay.
DBQuest	interactive document analysis tool.
WebQuests	readings and questions with links to specific web resources that help students see how the topic relates to the real world.
My iCivics	teacher tool for tracking and reporting student assignments.
Support materials	guides for pre-discussion and post-discussion questions, and classroom activities.

It is a great honor to include this chapter's *Making the Teaching and Learning Connection* feature written by iCivics Chief Development Office Molly Morrison. For the innumerable ways Justice O'Connor has served and continues to serve our nation, we thank her.

Making the Teaching and Learning Connection

When Justice O'Connor retired from the Supreme Court in 2006, after nearly 25 years on the bench, her exemplary career was already the embodiment of civic engagement and the U.S. pioneer spirit. An aspiring cattle rancher as a child, Justice O'Connor went on to forge a legal career at a time when few women did; she served in all three branches of Arizona state government; and she became the first woman to serve on the U.S. Supreme Court. But, she wasn't done yet.

Over the course of her career, Justice O'Connor grew concerned about a growing lack of understanding about our system of government and the disengagement that inevitably follows. She discovered that civic education had been disappearing from curricula across the country for decades. Where it was taught, it was often dry and uninspiring.

Justice O'Connor said, "Informed citizens are the lifeblood of democracy. As a citizen, you need to know how to be a part of it, how to express yourself—and not just by voting. Yet, barely a third of Americans can identify the three branches of government. Civic knowledge is not inherited through the gene pool, it must be taught to each generation."

In 2009, Justice O'Connor founded iCivics with the goal of transforming civic education for every student in America with innovative, truly engaging games and resources. Of all her accomplishments, Justice O'Connor considers iCivics to be her most important work and greatest legacy.

Justice O'Connor said, "Today's youth have developed extraordinary tools for communicating, for gathering information, and for organizing to get things done. I hope they will become effective citizens and leaders by using these tools to make their communities, their countries, and this world a better place."

Molly Morrison
Chief Development Officer, iCivics

CIVIC KNOWLEDGE ACROSS THE CURRICULUM   Helping grow our students into participating, responsible citizens is a worthy mission for middle level educators. Doing so as a team is ideal. Yes, the designated social studies teacher perhaps has the most time and opportunity to teach civic knowledge, but we should all contribute to ensure that civic knowledge is taught **across the curriculum**, meaning that it is embedded in our content areas and evident in our conversations with students. The following are a few ideas to help you get started.

Current Events   There are multiple reasons to include current events in classrooms, regardless of the subject area we teach. In terms of civic knowledge, an emphasis on current events is the perfect accompaniment to a more formal study of government and history. Current events can make foundational civic knowledge relevant and more interesting. Current events also allow for disagreements, giving us opportunities to help students engage in reasoned, informed debates about society's issues.

Individual teachers and teams of teachers can establish current events bulletin boards. If you are doing this alone, divide the board in sections: local, state, national, and international. Ask, or assign, the students to bring an article to class weekly—and be prepared to explain it. You can limit the task to government-related issues or include in the task the necessity of linking the article to civics. Students may print the articles from websites or actually cut them out of newspapers or magazines. If you are emphasizing current events as a team, each team member could pick a section for an individual bulletin board.

A timely and interesting current events article gives us an opportunity to talk with our kids about why something is important enough to be included in the newspaper or magazine. Is it the timeliness; the relevance to what's happening locally, nationally, or internationally; the conflict that's new or ongoing; the impact it may have on readers; or a combination of these reasons, or something else?

Try reading a current events article aloud and then ask students to answer questions you've written about the article. Doing this on a regular basis increases students' listening skills. Or give the questions first, have the students read them, and then listen for the answers.

The 5Ws—who, what, where, when, why—become like a scavenger hunt when applied to current events articles. Students can work in pairs to determine the 5Ws of articles and keep notebooks of the current events with 5W summaries.

We need to be ready for controversial topics to surface. In the United States, we are free to discuss, persuade, and change our minds. Make sure your students recognize this as a privilege—and a right—of our democratic way of life! For most class discussions, my first bit of advice would be to plan ahead. You may be able to think through some of the current issues; always check the board to see what's been posted. Here are some suggestions other than "plan ahead" to consider when controversy comes from sharing current events:

1. Have predetermined guidelines for all discussions in your classroom, including current events.
2. Determine how students may be recognized to speak.
3. Will everyone be required to speak? Is there a limit as to how many times someone may speak?
4. Agree to disagree agreeably.
5. Keep students focused on the issues in the article.
6. If time runs out and there are still students who want to speak, offer the option for them to write their opinions. If they do, they may have a chance to speak at a later time.
7. Don't give your opinion. Some students will feel that they must agree with you.

In addition to using current events to promote civic knowledge, introducing students to current events builds vocabulary, reading comprehension, problem solving abilities, and listening skills.

Hamilton   A recent phenomenon has increased interest in U.S history and government, particularly among teens and even preteens. Lin-Manuel Miranda wrote and produced *Hamilton,* an historically-based musical. Through his genius, our founding fathers have jumped from the pages of textbooks to the Broadway stage and beyond, including Hamilton Education Program, or EduHam, developed by the Gilder Lehrman Institute of American History. The president of the Institute tells us, "This project is transformative. 'Hamilton' has struck a chord with our nation's students because it embodies what great history education is all about: bringing the past to life and fostering connections with the exceptional individuals and moments that have made us who we are. This program empowers students to reclaim their own narrative and empowers teachers to bridge classroom learning with the stage" (Sutton, 2018). It would be great if each student could see the musical, but, even if that's not possible, the brilliant lyrics, the poetry, the beat, the infectious music can motivate learners. *History Now* on the Gilder Lehrman website provides resources and information, including YouTube and other media sources that provide many of the songs that have engaged us.

Teams can plan a *Hamilton Day* (or *Hamilton Week*) as a culmination of an emphasis on the American Revolution, the Constitution, the Federalist papers, or other related topics, even if U.S. history is not taught at a particular grade level. There are so many fun possibilities that will spark excitement that require as few as 5 minutes a day in each class, during advisory, or in homeroom. After exploring the resources and listening to the music, let your imagination take over!

Wall Space   As old-fashioned as it may seem in this digital age, students still notice what's on the walls of our classrooms. A math teacher can proudly display the Constitution; a science teacher can display the Bill of Rights. We should, at a minimum, all display the U.S. flag.

Hang posters around the classroom—branches of government, Declaration of Independence, presidents, maps, voter registration information, and so on. Even if you do nothing but hang them on your wall, the posters convey your belief that the information is important. If each teacher on a team, or just you if you aren't on a middle level team, takes a few minutes each week to read and discuss the posters, kids will learn.

Myrleen Pearson/Alamy Stock Photo

Pledging allegiance to the flag can be a meaningful expression of patriotism when young adolescents understand the meaning and history of the words.

Pledge of Allegiance   Many schools begin the day by reciting the Pledge of Allegiance. Others leave it up to individual teacher preference. The Pledge of Allegiance has become controversial in some states because of the words "under God," added in 1954 when Dwight Eisenhower became president. If your administrator says there's no problem, then begin your team's day by reciting the Pledge of Allegiance. Keep in mind that young adolescents may misunderstand some of the words. There are many YouTube videos that explain the words, with one of the best by a comedian of my childhood. Red Skelton's video about the Pledge of Allegiance is one of the most memorable. Look it up and see what you think. I've shown it many times and find that kids listen to it and remember. The 4 minutes it takes will likely have a meaningful impact.

Elections   Most of us give much more thought to civics and civic education as elections approach. Presidential elections provide discussion and assignment opportunities to read platforms of candidates, watch political news, analyze debates, learn about party history and beliefs, explore influences of media, and so on. Congressional elections provide the same opportunities, but to a lesser extent. Local races for county and city offices and school boards make it possible to attend campaign events; invite people running for office to our classrooms (be sure to balance speaker viewpoints to avoid undue influence); watch local political ads and dissect their verbal and visual messages; and more. School elections for student council and class officers gives students first-hand involvement. Asking students to nominate, campaign, and then vote for team colors, mottos, field trips, songs, mascot, and so on, are opportunities for learning about debate and the power of a vote. All these opportunities should carry the message that votes count, that we have a responsibility to exercise our right to make choices in our constitutional republic.

Civic Skills

In the previous section you read, "Knowledge is power. Civic knowledge is empowering." Let's explore what civic knowledge empowers us and our students to do. Knowledge plus **civic skills** equals empowerment to act, to make a positive difference in our homes, our schools, our communities, our nation, and our world. "We teach skills of citizenship as students learn lessons about community organization, the distribution of power and resources, rights, responsibilities, and, of course, injustice." Westheimer continues by eloquently stating, "Democracies make special demands on their citizens. Government of the people, by the people, and for the people requires the people to participate in decisions about laws and policies that affect us all" (Westheimer, 2017, p. 16).

NAEP ASSESSMENT FRAMEWORK   What are the civic skills essential for young adolescents to become informed, effective, and responsible citizens? The National Assessment of Educational Progress (2018), in their efforts to assess the civic knowledge and skills of 8th graders, refer to civic skills as intellectual skills and participatory skills. Intellectual skills include the categories of identifying and describing; explaining and analyzing; and evaluating, taking, and defending a stance. Participatory skills are categorized as interacting, monitoring, and influencing. The lists of individual skills for each category are long, with a brief summary in Table 11.2. Take time to read and consider the skills. When effectively taught and learned, the skills move young adolescents closer to the 13 goals of *This We Believe*.

Table 11.2   Intellectual and participatory skills of civic education

Intellectual Skills	Participatory Skills
Defining key terms and organizations of government	Listening, questioning, clarifying information or points of view
Identifying important individuals, symbols, institutions, ideas, and concepts	Discussing public affairs in a knowledgeable, responsible, and civil manner
Describing functions and processes, for example, legislative checks and balances, judicial review, foreign policy formation, and system of checks and balances	Managing conflicts through mediation, negotiation, compromise, consensus building, and adjudication
Describing historical origins—for example, of national holidays, sources of democracy, political authority	Following public issues in the media, using a variety of sources, such as television, radio, newspapers, journals, and magazines
Explaining the causes and effects of events and phenomena	Attending public meetings and hearings
Distinguishing between opinion and fact	Supporting or opposing candidates or positions on public issues
Clarifying responsibilities—for example, between personal and public responsibilities, between elected officials and citizens	Writing and speaking to support or oppose candidates and positions on public issues.
Evaluating the validity of arguments, analogies, and data	Voting

Based on *Civics Framework for the 2018 National Assessment of Educational Progress* by National Assessment Governing Board, U.S. Department of Education (pp. 25–33).

GLOBAL CITIZENSHIP SKILLS   The intellectual and participatory civic skills in Table 11.2 are vital to a strong democracy. They are also vital to positive **global citizenship**, or a way of living, that "recognizes" our world is an increasingly complex web of connections and interdependencies . . . [a world] in which our choices and actions may have repercussions for people and communities locally, nationally, and internationally" (Ideas for Global Citizenship, 2018).

UNESCO explained that there are three key components of global citizenship education:

- To acquire knowledge and understanding of local, national, and global issues and the interconnectedness of local and global concerns.
- To have a sense of belonging to a common humanity with shared values and responsibilities, while at the same time developing attitudes of empathy, solidarity, and respect for diversity.
- To act effectively and responsively at local, national, and global levels for a peaceful and sustainable world (UNESCO, 2015, p. 15).

The objectives of global citizenship education developed by UNESCO are similar to the intellectual and participatory skills of civic education, but with more emphasis on care, empathy, fairness, and social justice. In *Global Citizenship Education: Topics and Learning Objectives*, UNESCO provides specific objectives for global citizenship education for 12- to 15-year-olds in the categories of:

1. Local, national, and global systems and structures
2. Issues affecting interaction and connectedness of communities at local, national, and global levels
3. Underlying assumptions and power dynamics
4. Different levels of identity
5. Different communities people belong to and how these are connected
6. Difference and respect for diversity
7. Actions that can be taken individually and collectively
8. Ethically responsible behavior
9. Getting engaged and taking action (UNESCO, 2015, p. 31),

All nine of these categories support who we want young adolescents to become, mirroring perfectly *This We Believe* goal 10: "Respect and value the diverse ways people look, speak, think, and act within the immediate community and around the world," and *This We Believe* goal 13: "Understand local, national, and global civic responsibilities and demonstrate active citizenship through participation in endeavors that serve and benefit those larger communities" (National Middle School Association, 2010, p.12).

CIVIC SKILLS ACROSS THE CURRICULUM   Let's review the NAEP intellectual and participatory skills, each of which can be easily aligned with middle grades' content standards and skills we teach young adolescents in our content areas. Teaching the skills with citizenship in mind gives them increased meaning and context as we use materials and examples that show how they apply in very practical ways. Table 11.3 includes sample Common Core State Standards for English language arts that align with the civic skills.

DIGITAL CITIZENSHIP   Goal 4 in *This We Believe* states that we want young adolescents to "use digital tools to explore, communicate, and collaborate with the world and learn from the rich and varied resources available" (National Middle School Association, 2010, p.11). In other words, we want them to learn the skills of **digital citizenship**, or the skills to conduct themselves in responsible and effective ways in a digital world. Being a good digital citizen is more than knowing your way around the web. It's about connecting and collaborating in ways you didn't even know were possible (Common Sense Education, 2018).

Table 11.3 Civic skills and examples of alignment with ELA Common Core State Standards

Civic Skills from NAEP	Examples of Alignment with ELA Common Core State Standards
Identifying and describing	CCSS.ELA-LITERACY.W.5.9 Explain how an author uses reasons and evidence to support particular points in a text, identifying which reasons and evidence support which point[s]. CCSS.ELA-LITERACY.RST.6-8.6 Analyze the author's purpose in providing an explanation, describing a procedure, or discussing an experiment in a text.
Explaining and analyzing	CCSS.ELA-LITERACY.W.7.2 Write informative/explanatory texts to examine a topic and convey ideas, concepts, and information through the selection, organization, and analysis of relevant content. CCSS.ELA-LITERACY.RI.7.9 Analyze how two or more authors writing about the same topic shape their presentations of key information by emphasizing different evidence or advancing different interpretations of facts. CCSS.ELA-LITERACY.RI.7.7 Compare and contrast a text to an audio, video, or multimedia version of the text, analyzing each medium's portrayal of the subject (e.g., how the delivery of a speech affects the impact of the words).
Evaluating and defending	CCSS.ELA-LITERACY.W.6.1 Write arguments to support claims with clear reasons and relevant evidence. CCSS.ELA-LITERACY.SL.7.3 Delineate a speaker's argument and specific claims, evaluating the soundness of the reasoning and the relevance and sufficiency of the evidence. CCSS.ELA-LITERACY.SL.8.3 Delineate a speaker's argument and specific claims, evaluating the soundness of the reasoning and relevance and sufficiency of the evidence and identifying when irrelevant evidence is introduced.
Interacting	CCSS.ELA-LITERACY.RI.5.3 Explain the relationships or interactions between two or more individuals, events, ideas, or concepts in a historical, scientific, or technical text based on specific information in the text. CCSS.ELA-LITERACY.SL.8.1 Engage effectively in a range of collaborative discussions (one-on-one, in groups, and teacher-led) with diverse partners on grade 8 topics, texts, and issues, building on others' ideas and expressing their own clearly.
Monitoring	CCSS.ELA-LITERACY.RL.6.2 Determine a theme or central idea of a text and how it is conveyed through particular details; provide a summary of the text distinct from personal opinions or judgments. CCSS.ELA-LITERACY.SL.8.1 Acknowledge new information expressed by others, and, when warranted, qualify or justify their own views in light of the evidence presented.
Influencing	CCSS.ELA-LITERACY.SL.6.4 Present claims and findings, sequencing ideas logically and using pertinent descriptions, facts, and details to accentuate main ideas or themes; use appropriate eye contact, adequate volume, and clear pronunciation. CCSS.ELA-LITERACY.W.8.6 Use technology, including the Internet, to produce and publish writing and present the relationships between information and ideas efficiently as well as to interact and collaborate with others.

Based on Council of Chief State School Officers (2018). English language arts standards. www.corestandards.org/ELA

"Today, propaganda is everywhere and it takes new digital forms that blur the lines between entertainment, information, and persuasion" (Hobbs, 2017). We have many choices now to both consume and create media. This is positive in some regards, but negative in others. For young adolescents, the "blur" likely has more negative consequences than positive. They are, as we know, impressionable and often rash—not bad qualities, simply developmental traits. With so many messages flying at them, it's likely there's a lack of balance, making it difficult for kids to form their own opinions. They will often align with the last message they heard, what their parents say at home, what their peers talk about, and which memes or Instagram posts flood their consciousness. Hobbs provides five critical questions we should ask when analyzing digital messages:

- What information is being expressed?
- How is the message being presented to attract me?
- Through what method is the message communicated?
- What is the point of view?
- How might the audience of the message receive it?

Obviously, young adolescents are unlikely to think about these questions when they read, watch, or hear media opinions. We must teach them. It is undisputable that what we see and hear on television, Facebook, Instagram, and more, influence our political thoughts and actions. Sorting through it all is difficult for those of us who try very hard. For those who don't, being swayed by unbalanced exposure is inevitable.

With the proliferation of media and devices, teaching our students to be positive digital citizens requires that we allow the devices in schools. To ban the devices from school as a controlling strategy allows us to absolve ourselves of the responsibility to prepare kids to be 21st-century citizens (Krutka & Carpenter, 2017). No, you can't change district or school policies concerning digital devices in your school, but you and your team can certainly try. To do so is most likely to be on the right side of history.

CIVIC SKILLS ACROSS THE CURRICULUM The extensive and helpful organization, Common Sense Education, created *Digital Citizenship in Schools,* an initiative that provides free lessons to help students develop skills relevant to social media addressing Internet safety, privacy and security, relationships and communication, cyberbullying and digital drama, self-image and identity, and informational literacy. The comprehensive units and lessons are available for free. Each is aligned to the Common Core State Standards for grades 6, 7, and 8. Lesson 1 of Unit 1 is an excellent place to start: "Digital Life 101, What is the place of digital media in our lives?" Take a look on the *Digital Citizenship in Schools* website.

Table 11.4 provides a small sample of the resources available to teach civic knowledge and skills across the curriculum.

Table 11.4 Resources for teaching civic knowledge and skills

Organization	Brief Explanation	Website
Center for Civic Education	Partners with a network of 50 state civics, government, and law programs; sponsored by state bar associations and foundations, colleges and universities, and other civic and law nonprofit organizations to promote teaching and learning about the Constitution and Bill of Rights	www.civiced.org
The Gilder Lehrman Institute of American History	Leading U.S. history nonprofit organization dedicated to K–12 education while also serving the general public; mission is to promote the knowledge and understanding of U.S. history through educational programs and resources, including hundreds of lesson plans, essays, and videos free to use in the classroom	www.gilderlehrman.org/history-now
NAEP Civics Framework	Foundation for the 1998–2018 NAEP civics assessments, items were developed in accordance with it; items are administered to representative samples of students at grade 8 throughout the United States	https://nagb.gov/content/nagb/assets/documents/publications/frameworks/civics/2018-civics-framework.pdf
The Center for Information & Research on Civic Learning and Engagement (CIRCLE) Tufts University	Focuses on the political life of young people in the United States, especially those who are marginalized or disadvantaged; scholarly research informs policy and practice for healthier youth development and a better democracy	https://tischcollege.tufts.edu/research/circle
Share My Lesson	Thousands of free lessons dealing with civics, economics and history for middle level learners	https://sharemylesson.com/lessons/middle-school/social-studies
Civics Renewal Network	Consortium of nonpartisan, nonprofit organizations committed to strengthening civic life in the United States by increasing the quality of civics education in our nation's schools and by improving accessibility to high-quality, no-cost learning materials	www.civicsrenewalnetwork.org/
American Social History Project	Produces print, visual, and multimedia materials that explore the richly diverse social and cultural history of the United States	https://ashp.cuny.edu
Southern Poverty Law Center	Dedicated to fighting hate and bigotry and to seeking justice for the most vulnerable members of our society; uses litigation, education, and other forms of advocacy to work toward the day when the ideals of equal justice and equal opportunity will be a reality	www.splcenter.org
Facing History and Ourselves	Mission is to engage students of diverse backgrounds in an examination of racism, prejudice, and antisemitism in order to promote the development of a more humane and informed citizenry	www.facinghistory.org
Common Sense Media's Digital Citizenship in Schools	Nation's leading nonprofit organization dedicated to improving the lives of kids and families by providing the trustworthy information, education, and independent voice they need to thrive in the 21st century	www.commonsense.org/education/digital-citizenship
Character.org	Organization that promotes character education through sharing effective lessons, strategies, and best practices	http://character.org/lessons/lesson-plans/#ms

Civic Dispositions

Let's begin this section with a quote that you'll want to read several times before continuing: "I often wonder whether we do not rest our hopes too much upon constitutions, upon laws, and upon courts. These are false hopes . . . Liberty lies in the hearts of men and women . . . when it dies there, no constitution, no law, no court can save it." This statement is part of the "Spirit of Liberty" speech delivered in 1944 by Judge Leonard Hand during *I AM an American Day* held in New York City's Central Park, a swearing-in ceremony of more than 1000 new U.S. citizens during World War II. Remember what Judge Hand said to new citizens as you consider civic dispositions.

The framework for NAEP defines **civic dispositions** as "the traits of private and public character essential to the preservation and improvement of American constitutional democracy" (National Assessment of Educational Progress, 2018, p. 33). So, which came first, the civic dispositions or civic knowledge and skills? We typically think that actions follow beliefs. However, according to the National Assessment Governing Board that wrote the NAEP framework, "Civic dispositions develop slowly over time as a result of what one learns and experiences in the home, school, community, and organizations of civil society. From those experiences should come the understanding that American constitutional democracy requires the responsible self-governance of each individual; one cannot exist without the other" (National Assessment of Educational Progress, 2018, p. 33). This fact makes our responsibility to teach the knowledge and skills of citizenship even more urgent. We know kids forget some of the content of the classroom, but if the culminating effect is a set of dispositions described in this section, we will have helped mold productive, positive, engaged citizens!

The NAEP framework includes five civic dispositions necessary to preserve and improve our American constitutional republic:

- becoming an independent member of society;
- assuming the personal, political, and economic responsibilities of a citizen;
- respecting individual worth and human dignity;
- participating in civic affairs in an informed, thoughtful, and effective manner; and
- promoting the healthy functioning of American constitutional democracy.

The National Council for the Social Studies (2013a), in a position paper on moral and civic virtues, proposed that as a result of instruction and modeling, we want our students to be: "concerned for the rights and welfare of others, socially responsible, willing to listen to alternative perspectives, confident in their capacity to make a difference, . . . ready to contribute personally to civic and political action, . . . strike a reasonable balance between their own interests and the common good, [and] recognize the importance of and practice civic duties such as voting and respecting the rule of law." Let's consider one more list of dispositions. The Center for Civic Education, funded by the U.S. Department of Education, proposed that, "Students should be able to evaluate, take, and defend positions on the importance of certain dispositions or traits of character to themselves and American constitutional democracy" (Center for Civic Education, 2014). To achieve this standard, students should be able to explain the importance to the individual and society of the following dispositions or traits of character:

- Individual responsibility
- Self-discipline and self-governance
- Civility
- Courage
- Respect for the rights of other individuals
- Respect for law

- Honesty
- Open mindedness
- Critical mindedness
- Negotiation and compromise
- Persistence
- Civic mindedness
- Compassion
- Patriotism

Convinced of the importance of civic dispositions? These three lists from prominent organizations create lofty goals for teaching civic dispositions. Lofty, yes, but attainable. Remember that dispositions of citizenship rest on knowledge and skills, two very concrete aspects of civic education we can incorporate in our lessons.

Self-Check 11.1

LO 11.2 Civic Engagement

Operationalizing citizenship calls for active engagement. We've discussed civic knowledge, skill, and dispositions. We can know, know how, and believe, all without acting. But for citizenship to preserve and promote our democratic way of life, we must act. Before exploring ways to engage young adolescents, let's consider the need to balance engagement with civic education. Tripodo and Pondiscio (2017) explained that in our zeal to make civics relevant, we can't neglect to teach about history, government, politics, and the skills and dispositions of civics, elements that provide the foundation and context for civic engagement.

Civic engagement involves promoting the quality of life in a community, through both political and nonpolitical actions. Although civic engagement is usually considered working to make a difference in the civic life of one's own community, the concept also extends to state, nation, and the world. Young adolescents most often experience civic engagement through volunteering and service-learning. Both involve students interacting with their community in some way and, importantly, creating a sense of meaningful accomplishment. Regardless of the activity, it's vital that we help students equate their sense of helping others with addressing social or political issues. Developing a social consciousness is natural for young adolescents who value fairness and are seeking their role in the world.

Teaching for Social Consciousness and Responsibility

Social consciousness involves an awareness of society and the difficulties and hardships of others. Social consciousness precedes social responsibility. We must be aware before we are prompted to take actions that result from a sense of **social responsibility**, or personal investment in the welfare of others and our world. Teaching for social consciousness and responsibility is about relationships—specifically, relationships of our students with each other and humanity in general, with the world of living things, and with the environment. When we teach for social consciousness and responsibility, we cultivate students to be caring, community-involved citizens. The development of social consciousness can help young adolescents discover who they are and the abilities they possess. They realize that they can use their strengths to make a positive difference in a complex and diverse world.

When we consider the 13 goals for young adolescents in *This We Believe*, six speak directly to the concepts of social consciousness and social responsibility. You've seen them all within the preceding chapters. They are, however, rarely part of any planned curriculum. Because of this, we have to take the time and make the effort to purposefully include the goals in our classrooms and in our schools. Read the six goals in Figure 11.1. Then read them again.

Teaching for social consciousness and social responsibility is something we need to do across the curriculum. We understand that young adolescents are capable of empathy and compassion and are beginning to consider a broader world than their immediate community. Addressing topics of special interest to students, and teaching the standards through them, is engaging. We understand that interdisciplinary instruction provides opportunities to incorporate life lessons through instruction that revolves around a theme. Now that you are aware of the *This We Believe* goals that directly address social consciousness and social responsibility, I'm confident you will determine to include them in your classroom.

SKILLS TO ACT WITH SOCIAL CONSCIOUSNESS There are specific basic skills necessary for acting with social consciousness. We teach these skills throughout the curriculum. When we do, simply mentioning their broader application to local and global issues may spark the interest of our young adolescent learners. The skills include:

- Problem solving
- Communication
- Collaboration
- Conflict management
- Ability to see differing perspectives.

In addition, here are some concepts to consider when thinking about teaching social consciousness and social responsibility:

- Interdependence and interconnectedness

  Socially conscious individuals recognize that our world revolves around interdependence and interconnectedness. The prefix "inter" indicates *among*, as opposed to "intra," which indicates *within*. That's an important delineation to remember.

- Engaged citizenry

  Social responsibility creates an engaged citizenry, capable of working effectively toward the common good. We may not agree on issues, but the mere fact that we are engaged as citizens will lead to productive change.

- Practicing social responsibility

  The more opportunities we give students to actually practice social responsibility, the better. Engaging young adolescents in the practice of social responsibility is not

---

FIGURE 11.1 *This We Believe* goals that address social consciousness and responsibility

Goal 1: Become actively aware of the larger world, asking significant and relevant questions about the world and wrestling with big ideas and questions for which there may not be one right answer.

Goal 5: Be a good steward of the earth and its resources and a wise and intelligent consumer of the wide array of goods and services available.

Goal 8: Develop his or her strengths, particular skills, talents, or interests and have an emerging understanding of his or her potential contributions to society and to personal fulfillment.

Goal 10: Respect and value the diverse ways people look, speak, think, and act within the immediate community and around the world.

Goal 12: Assume responsibility for his or her own actions and be cognizant of and ready to accept obligations for the welfare of others.

Goal 13: Understand local, national, and global civic responsibilities and demonstrate active citizenship through participation in endeavors that serve and benefit those larger communities.

Based on National Middle School Association, *This We Believe*, 2010, pp. 11–12.

difficult. The needs abound. Debating the pros and cons of city and county initiatives, learning about bills before state legislatures and writing letters that express opinions to those in Congress, attending school board and county council meetings, interviewing people who work in government and for nonprofit organizations, all are simple and free ways for young adolescents to practice social responsibility.

IDENTIFYING PERTINENT SOCIAL AND GLOBAL ISSUES It's impossible to act on an issue that we've never heard about. As adults we often read newspapers and watch news reports. We tune into specials on global warming and water shortages. We are aware of homelessness and instances of inhumanity. We know the rain forest is disappearing and endangered species will be gone forever. That's part of our consciousness. Seldom is it part of the consciousness of young adolescents. It's not that they don't care. On the contrary, if they are aware, they generally care deeply and want to be part of solutions.

Not everyone is passionate about recycling. Many don't think the disappearance of millions of square miles of glaciers has any impact on their lives. There are people who think homelessness is a choice and the result of laziness. Others believe we are killing our planet because of what we discard, that climate change is real and threatening to human existence, and that economic realities are everyone's responsibility. Young adolescents are capable of becoming passionate about these and a multitude of other issues if they are part of their social consciousness. We can help students identify their social responsibilities and passions by raising their awareness. Regardless of the subject you teach, helping young adolescents increase their awareness may take as little as a 30-second mention or a 10-minute discussion. Bring up issues and ask for student opinions and solutions. Start conversations about the relationship of society to the environment. Assign projects and allow students to choose significant local or global issues. Ask students to consider big questions like these:

- How does my lifestyle affect others?
- What is my vision for the future of our planet?
- What can we accomplish together that will make a difference?

MODELING SOCIAL CONSCIOUSNESS AND RESPONSIBILITY Who we are and what we do impact students. We have tremendous influence over young adolescents by virtue of being teachers. Our attitudes shine through every day, and this incontrovertible fact puts the responsibility on us to live what we teach. If we are positive, caring, and concerned about society, all living things, and the environment, students learn that:

- Cooperation and empathy matter.
- Responsibility is personal and valuable.
- We can make a difference.

On the other hand, if we are negative, detached, or exhibit indifference toward social responsibility, students may mirror these non-productive qualities.

Most teachers believe that what they do makes a difference in the world. Modeling concern for others, peace, and justice offers us the opportunity to be an important part of the world we hope to create.

Service-Learning as Civic Engagement

Service-learning and volunteerism are not the same. **Volunteerism** has benefits to the volunteer and the person/group receiving the help. **Service-learning** takes the service connected to volunteerism and adds the dimension of learning, with components of preparation, service, and reflection. Let's add a fourth component . . . celebration! It's important to celebrate hard work and accomplishment. These four components of service-learning in Figure 11.2 are each vital and none should be omitted.

FIGURE 11.2 Service-learning components

1. Students prepare by:
   - Learning about issues
   - Building the skills they will need
   - Developing an action plan for service
2. Students act by:
   - Engaging in meaningful service
   - Making a difference in their community
   - Realizing connections to classroom curriculum
3. Students reflect by:
   - Analyzing and making sense of their experiences
   - Discussing, journaling, and presenting
4. Students celebrate by:
   - Collaboratively listing all the good they accomplished
   - Finding ways to share their accomplishments with their families and peers
   - Treating themselves to a fun gathering (with our help)

Some think of service-learning as a nice addition to what we do in middle school, if time permits. That's a very different approach compared to making service-learning an embedded part of a school's curriculum. These are two ends of the spectrum, with most middle schools somewhere in between. On the **National Youth Leadership Council's** website we find definitions, articles about service-learning experiences, and ideas and advice about beginning and sustaining varying levels of service-learning in our classrooms. (National Youth Leadership Council, 2018).

Service-learning projects may be completely locally based, depending on community needs. Some ideas for local projects are in Figure 11.3. In addition, service-learning projects may be conducted within the framework of an established organization or movement, with examples in Table 11.5. Let's give our students choices. Ask them what they care about. The payoff can be profound. Once the students have spoken concerning their priorities, the preparation part of the cycle can begin.

Collaboration, communication, and leadership are not only 21st-century knowledge and skills, but also have lifelong personal and academic benefits for the students who participate in service-learning. Through service-learning projects, accompanied by reflection and celebration, students learn how to meaningfully apply what they learn, respect themselves and others to a greater degree, understand community and global issues, and demonstrate leadership abilities as a collaborative team. When students see their actions positively affecting others, they want to continue to make a difference. This is what happens when service and learning intersect.

If you have opportunities to facilitate service-learning with your students, please do so. If your school doesn't already provide opportunities, creating the opportunities for service that lead to learning is a worthwhile mission. Young adolescents were not even born on the tragic day of September 11, 2001. It's a day that should never be forgotten. Figure 11.4 provides some background information. Read about a very meaningful service-learning emphasis at Chardon Middle School in Tim Bowens's own words.

Tetra Images/Alamy Stock Photo

There are many ways for students to engage in service-learning.

FIGURE 11.3 Ideas for local service-learning projects

- Mentoring and tutoring elementary students
- Advocating for change and social justice
- Restoring natural areas, parks, rivers, and beaches
- Teaching literacy or English through planned conversations and tutoring sessions
- Growing and harvesting food in a sustainable manner
- Collecting items for transitional housing and shelter organizations
- Enhancing health and well-being through food banks
- Providing companionship in nursing facilities
- Participating in an oral history project involving interviewing and writing about elderly people, members of the military, or family.

1. Students prepare
   - Every year in Chardon, Ohio, our middle level students learn about the horrific events of September 11, 2001. Annually our 6th graders visit the Flight 93 Memorial in Pennsylvania where they learn about the importance of the heroism of the passengers and crew of Flight 93 through presentations at the site by families of passengers and crew members, as well as students who were in nearby schools on 9/11.

2. Students act
   - After years of visiting temporary memorials for Flight 93, students and their community raised over $10,000 to help build the permanent memorial now at the site of the crash.
   - During the 2010–2011 school year, we worked with a local arts organization to create an oral history project. Nearly 30 individuals were interviewed concerning the events of 9/11, and specifically about Flight 93. The interviews were transcribed and made into a theater production.

Table 11.5 Sample established organizations as context for service-learning

Organization	About the Organization	Contact Information
Alex's Lemonade Stand Foundation (ALSF)	Alex (1996–2004) started a front yard lemonade stand to raise money for cancer research; now a national fundraising movement	www.alexslemonade.org
Project Learning Tree	Program of the American Forest Foundation; uses the forest to engage students in environmental concerns and solutions	www.plt.org
Veterans History Project	American Folklife Center collects, preserves, and makes accessible the personal accounts of American war veterans	www.loc.gov/vets
National Student Campaign Against Hunger and Homelessness (NSCAHH)	Largest student network fighting hunger and homelessness in the country	http://learningtogive.org/papers/paper199.html
Service for Peace	Established in 2002 by international youth volunteers from across the United States to help participants develop a sense of responsibility for others, confidence in their own ability to make a difference as they work together with people from backgrounds different from their own	www.serviceforpeace.org
PeaceJam	International education program originating in Colorado in 1993; purpose is to create young leaders committed to positive change in themselves, their communities, and the world through the inspiration of Nobel Peace Laureates	www.peacejam.org
Project Linus	Founded in 1996 to provide blankets for children who are seriously ill or have experienced trauma	www.projectlinus.org

Based on *Your Introduction to Education: Explorations in Teaching* by S. D. Powell, 2019, Upper Saddle River, NJ: Pearson.

FIGURE 11.4 Flight 93

On Tuesday morning, September 11, 2001, the United States came under attack as four commercial airplanes were hijacked. The unsuspecting airliner crews and passengers became victims of suicide missions carried out by 19 al-Qaeda terrorists, members of an Islamist militant group founded by Osama bin Laden in 1988. Three of the planes were used to strike targets on the ground, including the World Trade Center buildings in New York City and the U.S. Pentagon. Nearly 3000 people tragically lost their lives.

The fourth plane, United Airlines Flight 93, was en route from New Jersey to San Francisco when four al-Qaeda terrorists hijacked the plane by breaking into the cockpit and redirecting the flight toward Washington, DC, with the intent of crashing into the White House. Several passengers were able to call family and friends on the ground and learned of the hijacker's intentions. They courageously fought the hijackers and, in the process, Flight 93 crashed near Shanksville, Pennsylvania. Because of the actions of the 40 passengers and crew aboard the plane, the attack on the U.S. Capitol was thwarted.

- In 2012, teachers and students worked with artist Augusto Bordelois to create two murals made of thousands of pieces of colored mosaics. The murals are on permanent display on two staircases in Chardon Middle School. One represents 9/11 and the other is dedicated to Flight 93. Bordelois spent time preparing the students by showing how art and history are connected. He relayed examples of how important historical events (e.g., Washington crossing the Delaware) have been interpreted by artists. He also demonstrated the significance of monuments and memorials. This tied beautifully to our 6th-grade curriculum as we study ancient civilizations and their enduring impact/contributions. Look no further than the Egyptian pyramids for meaningful symbols and memorials.

3. Students reflect

- Since the murals are there for all to see (the artist feels they will stand even if the school was demolished-that's how well-constructed they are), students can take pride in them as they walk by in the years to come. They know that future generations of students will learn from their service-learning project.

- Teachers can use the murals as an introduction to 9/11 and for instruction prior to visiting Shanksville each spring.

- One of the more moving aspects of being at the Memorial occurs when we leave the site. We ask students to be silent and just quietly reflect on all they see. Now when students return to school, the murals bring that back.

Self-Check 11.2

LO 11.3 Civility

Civic education doesn't guarantee civility. Let's be clear about what civility means. Civility is more than just being nice to each other, although politeness is a word you'll find in the dictionary definition. Civility is speaking and listening with respect; it is allowing for disagreements while seeking commonalities that promote communication that neither degrades nor injures others.

Let's also be clear about what *incivility* is and what it looks like. **Incivility** is the absence of civility. It's both rudeness in actions and apathy when action is needed. Incivility leads to violence, hostile and unhealthy environments and political

Christine Ceraolo

Based on Personal communication with Tim Bowens, November 24, 2012.

divisiveness, while it robs all of us of our best efforts and our creativity. Incivility is modeled by peers and by adults who slip into the self-indulgence of yelling at one another, slamming doors, saying unkind things, screaming at other drivers, not having a cause to support, saying unkind things about people based on race or socioeconomic status . . . the list is one we can all add to. "Bad behavior flourishes when civility isn't the norm . . . Teaching civility walks companionably through life beside good decision-making and respecting others, strong interpersonal relationships and a sense of fairness" (Collins, 2017).

Teaching Civility

Teaching civility is another example of "We teach who we are. Students learn us." Civility rests on relationships, key among them being the teacher-student relationship. Modeling civility is the foundation for all efforts to teach it.

We teach math, science, social studies, and English language arts. We incorporate relevance and practice in the teaching and learning process. We look at examples, prompt inquiry, set expectations, and assess mastery. Yes, assessment of civility is subjective and difficult to measure in scientifically verifiable ways. But we know it when we see it in our classrooms. So let's teach it.

Character education programs abound. There's the "word of the day" approach, homeroom and advisory programs put together by both nonprofit and for-profit organizations, and resources developed locally or provided by the U.S department of Education. If your school implements a particular program, by all means, support it.

Eve Rifkin (2017), an experienced teacher in Arizona, explained it's not a lucky coincidence that the students in her classroom and school demonstrate civility. She and her colleagues make intentional decisions and create experiences that promote it every day. Collaborative groups are composed of students who are diverse. Norms of

Standard 5:
Middle Level Professional Roles

Middle level teacher candidates understand the complexity of teaching young adolescents, and they engage in practices and behaviors that develop their competence as professionals.

Marilyn Price-Mitchell, PhD (2015), is a developmental psychologist and researcher and the founder of *Roots of Action*. Among her suggestions for teaching civility include:

- Think about the impact of words on others before you use them.
- Apologize when you are wrong.
- Use respectful language when you disagree with someone.
- Don't let anger and emotion get in the way of listening to others.
- Lead by example.

These and other mottos need to become habitual for young adolescents. But we know that simply posting them won't be effective. We need to ask students to consider what they "look like" in practice, to role-play, to internalize, to hold each other to a standard that promotes civility. As teachers we have tremendous influence on the level of civility in our classrooms when we lead by example.

cooperation are set and expected. They periodically ask students to pause and reflect on their own comfort, and the comfort of others, in settings where there may be tension or disagreement.

When I was young and experienced hurt feelings, my mom would say, "Sticks and stones may break my bones, but words will never hurt me." Believing she would not mislead me, I would stop crying, stiffen my posture, and repeat the saying to myself over and over until, as is common with children, something else would catch my attention. But, Mom, you were wrong.

Words hurt. Words said to our face, said behind our back, written in a note to a supposed friend, or anonymously splashed on social media—regardless of the means, words hurt. In conversation and collaboration, carefully choosing our words is the civil thing to do.

There's a very practical reason for our students to learn about and practice civility. I propose that many jobs aren't lost because of a lack of skills or technical expertise to perform the work, but more often because of a lack of civility leading to the inability to collaborate. In 1756, Lady Mary Wortley Montagu famously said, "Civility costs nothing and buys everything." Personally and professionally, civility "buys everything."

Character.org is an organization providing free lesson plans middle level educators have found to be successful in teaching traits of civility. Take a look at their website and consider using lesson ideas in your classroom, regardless of the subject you teach. Remember: in middle level, we teach the whole child.

Enhanced eText
Video Example 11.1
Sixth-grade teacher Dani Ramsey leads by example in her classroom. She shows us what leading by example "looks like."

Self-Check 11.3

Why It Matters

Of all the topics we've explored in this book so far, perhaps citizenship and civility least require a wrap-up of why they matter. The entire chapter serves as a rationale for paying attention to the knowledge, skills, and dispositions of civic education, the reasons for incorporating civic engagement, and the value of cultivating civility. The words I leave you with at the end of this chapter are from *Your Introduction to Education* (Powell, 2019, p. 196).

> Some students come to school without a clear idea of what civility looks like because they don't live in the midst of it. Teachers must model civility, orchestrate an environment that fosters it, and then expect nothing less of students.

Group Activities

1. Discuss the current state of politics, what you hear, read, see about those involved. What civic knowledge, skills, and dispositions are important for young adolescents if they are to rise above any rancor and learn from adults' mistakes?

2. With your class, choose a theme from the Civic Knowledge section. Create a web showing how each subject area might address the theme that could become the basis for an interdisciplinary unit.

3. With your class, share instances of incivility you witnessed or experienced in middle school. List them on the board. When you have five or so, brainstorm how teachers might address the situations or issues involved with each.

Individual Activities

1. What do you lack in terms of civic education? Do you know as much as you should about government and history? Important documents? How Congress functions? Balance of powers? Current events?

2. We all have memories of hurtful things that have been said or done to us. Think back to when you were a young adolescent. Write about an instance you remember and how you now wish you had handled the situation.

Personal Journal

1. Hopefully you will be a part of a team of teachers that will plan together and support efforts to teach civic education. If you don't, how do you envision incorporating knowledge, skills, and dispositions of civics in your classroom?

2. Does service-learning appeal to you? What sort of project sparks your interest?

Professional Practice

Last October, the teachers on the 6th-grade Explorer team at Washington Middle School wrote a grant proposal to fund their attendance of the Association for Middle Level Education annual conference. It was the first national conference for any of them and they attended sessions with enthusiasm. One of the main points they wanted to take away from the conference was an idea for an interdisciplinary unit to implement in spring, one that would prove valuable and that could actually become a signature theme for their 6th-grade team. While they agreed to go to different sessions and then share what they learned, they would attend sessions on developing ID units together. Searching the conference program, they found three sessions to attend on unit development. Two sessions were general, and one was titled "Growing the Citizens We Need." The team knew they had found their theme, but the drawback of the session was that the unit only included social studies and ELA teachers and classrooms. *Remember that for some items, more than one choice may be defensible. The purpose of the items is to stimulate thought and discussion.*

1. The team's social studies teacher brought up the first concern. In 6th-grade students primarily study other nations rather than the United States. They studied the U.S. in 5th grade.

    How do you think the team should respond to this information and why?

    a. They should choose another theme that fits more closely with the prescribed social studies curriculum of their grade level.

    b. Because part of the 6th-grade guidelines indicate U.S. relationships with the developing world, they should decide to go ahead with the unit.

    c. Because the theme of citizenship is so very important, they should decide to go ahead with the unit.

    d. After further considering that they all have to develop lessons that address a theme in an interdisciplinary unit, the team should decide on a unit theme that lends itself more readily to the math and science classrooms.

2. The materials the team received at the conference session included a lengthy list of resources for developing the "Growing the Citizens We Need" unit. What would be the most effective and efficient way for the team to approach the resources?

    a. Just as they decided to experience the session together, they should set aside time after school for a few weeks to go through the resources to see what they find valuable.

    b. They should divide the resources, take a couple of weeks to go through them, and then get together to share what they've found.

    c. The 8th-grade social studies guidelines indicate that American history is the primary content for the year. The team should give the resource list to the three 8th-grade social studies teachers and ask them to determine if they use any of them to avoid overlap.

    d. Some of the resources require registration for a small fee. They should first eliminate these resources and then proceed to exploring the ones that are free.

3. At the very least, what could the three non-social studies teachers do to support the unit?

    a. They could arrange their flexible block schedule to accommodate more time in social studies for students over the course of the 3-week unit.

b. They could include a list of vocabulary words involved in the unit on their walls.

c. They could make phone calls to tell families that there will be a patriotic-themed picnic at the conclusion of the unit.

d. They could hang major government documents and posters about civics and citizenship in their classrooms and read them to the students and conduct discussions about their meaning and significance.

4. Pretend that you are the math teacher on the team. It's obvious that the social studies teacher will have lots of possibilities for her role in the unit. The ELA teacher is already selecting prose and poetry that address citizenship. The science teacher is going to think about ways to include responsibility for the environment as part of citizenship. What will you, as a math teacher, do to address citizenship in your classes?

Chapter 12
Relationships and Realities of Middle Level Education

Sara Davis Powell

> The importance of middle level education can never be overestimated. The future of individuals and, indeed, that of society is largely determined by the nature of the educational experiences of young adolescents during these formative years.
>
> THIS WE BELIEVE, P. 43.

 Learning Outcomes

After studying this chapter, you will have knowledge and skills to:

12.1 Explain the elements of teacher professionalism.

12.2 Examine ways to involve families and the community in the teaching and learning process.

12.3 Analyze relationships among teachers in schools.

12.4 Summarize ways to make transitions into and out of middle school smoother and more productive.

12.5 Recognize attributes of an exemplary middle level setting.

Dear Future Middle Level Teacher,

I hope you have enjoyed learning more about young adolescents and middle level education. Please know that we have only scratched the surface in this text. One of my favorite aspects of teaching is that every day brings new learning experiences. Every student presents both joy and challenge. Every lesson, no matter how carefully planned, includes some sort of surprise . . . unexpected student excitement, or the lack of it; unanticipated questions, or answers; the need for prior knowledge you thought already existed; the fire drill. There's never a dull moment!

We often hear that teachers in other countries are held in higher regard than in the United States. Although the reasons are complex, we never want one of them to be our lack of professionalism. When you teach, you represent the finest of all professions and the most dedicated of all people. Your charge is to be a professional in all your relationships: with students, their families, the community, and each other. Teaching is a profession that depends on our continual learning, sharing, supporting, and collaborating.

Deciding to be a middle level teacher incurs a few extra responsibilities. It's our job to spread the word that young adolescents are capable, interesting, and altruistic. Our students are middle level learners, not elementary and not high school, and therefore require specialized knowledge and preparation to bring out their tremendous potential. We have to recognize what works best, and then put into practice the philosophy that guides our interactions with curriculum, instruction, assessment, advisory, and, above all, the wonderful kids in the middle!

SDP

LO 12.1 Teacher Professionalism

Teacher **professionalism** involves attitudes and actions that consistently convey respect for learning and learners, as well as for the adults with whom we work. The Partnership for 21st Century Skills (P21) provides a list of characteristics of effective, professional teachers in Figure 12.1. Take a look at what professional teachers do.

Advocate for Students

Middle level educators must always **advocate** for students, putting their needs first. How do we become advocates for our students? Here are some ways to consider:

- In all conversations with colleagues and others, keep the focus on what's best for students.
- Be informed on issues that affect students and be proactive for their benefit.
- Support and involve families in ways that benefit young adolescents.

Every day teachers make big and small decisions that can affect learners in significant ways. Some decisions become second nature to us as we gain experience. Others require careful thought and large doses of common sense. Remember that all decisions have consequences and should be made from an advocacy perspective.

FIGURE 12.1 P21 characteristics of effective teachers

- Critical thinkers
- Problem solvers
- Innovators
- Effective communicators
- Effective collaborators
- Self-directed learners
- Information and media literate
- Globally aware
- Civically engaged
- Health conscious
- Financially and economically literate

Commit to Quality

Quality should characterize our knowledge of content and our relationships and interactions with students, colleagues, administrators, and families. Teacher professionalism in middle level education requires that developmental appropriateness and academic rigor are present in everything we do. We've discussed developmental appropriateness throughout this book. Academic rigor encompasses teaching meaningful content and maintaining high expectations for student learning. Academic rigor without developmental appropriateness will discourage, and often defeat, our students. Developmental appropriateness without academic rigor will accomplish little in terms of student learning. The concepts are interdependent in teaching and learning effectiveness.

Commit to Continual Growth

There's so much to learn about teaching, about our subject area fields and ways to make topics come alive for learners. Teachers should be lifelong learners. A commitment to continual growth provides a powerful model for students.

One way teachers grow is through reflection, or deliberately thinking about what we do with the intent of improving. We don't "turn off" our teaching commitment when we get in our cars to drive home. We should purposefully reflect on what went right, and what didn't, as we increase our knowledge and skills. John Dewey (1933) described reflection using words such as active, persistent, and careful. Being a reflective practitioner requires conscious effort. Here are some concepts to consider:

Enhanced eText
Video Example 12.1

New teachers watch classroom videos and then reflect on what they see and hear.

- Self-knowledge is vital to effective teaching and learning.
- Reading about and researching aspects of teaching grounds our practice and provides subject matter on which to reflect.
- Talking with other educators both informs and strengthens what we do and how we do it.
- Being deliberate—doing what we do for a reason—results in better decisions based on reflection (Powell, 2019, p. 18).

You'll have many opportunities to participate in professional development sessions and activities through your school and your district. Regardless of the topic or agenda, remember that when teachers gather, professional growth is possible, and perhaps inevitable. Through professional growth, leadership opportunities will present themselves. You will become a more effective teacher. You may become a team leader, a curriculum developer, an instructional coach, or fulfil other leadership roles while remaining in the classroom.

Develop Positive Dispositions

Our attitudes, values, and beliefs result in our dispositions; dispositions determine our approach to every aspect of teaching and learning. Some of the positive dispositions we want to develop include:

- I believe all students can learn.
- I respect and embrace student diversity.
- I value collaboration.
- I will demonstrate productive work habits and serve as a role model for students.
- I believe students are unique and deserve individual attention.
- I accept responsibility for student learning.
- I value life-long learning.

Enhanced eText
Video Example 12.2
Middle school principal Beth Thompson shares her school's leadership development opportunities.

Maintain Personal–Professional Healthy Balance

This section may strike you as premature. After all, you're just preparing to teach; you may have two or more years before you begin your first teaching position. But chances are you're struggling with balance right now as a college student, so you kind of get the concept. Let's talk a little about the importance of balancing professional and personal life. Doing so is part of teacher professionalism.

WHY BALANCE MATTERS There are certain aspects of our lives when balance isn't, or probably shouldn't be, an issue. Our love of family and friends, our spiritual beliefs, and our patriotism require all-in emotions and dedication. While we may feel and believe in uncompromising ways, our actions concerning these feelings and beliefs are restrained by time and good sense. When you are a teacher, the best-case-scenario is that you love what you do and are uncompromisingly dedicated to the profession and your students. But just like you don't spend every waking minute sending "I love you" texts or reading the Bible or other spiritual books or saluting the flag, so it should be for teaching, your chosen profession.

Enhanced eText
Video Example 12.3
Fifth-grade teacher Dee Lanier talks about dispositions necessary to be an effective teacher.

We are better professionals if we have personal joy and fulfillment. And to have personal joy we need time mentally, physically, emotionally, and socially to love our family and friends, to practice our faith, to support our country, and to do things that make us happy. Of course teaching can make us happy, too, but the time and energy we put into the classroom must be balanced with things we do just for ourselves and those we love. If you like to go out to dinner every week with friends, then do it. If you have three dogs and unwind by taking them to the park, then do it. If you play the piano or guitar for fun or for tips on Saturday nights, then keep on playing. You get the picture.

Yes, teaching can become overwhelming. But teachers should not have to give up their personal lives just because they spend their days with young adolescents who may have challenging issues. If we allow this to happen, it will diminish our personal joy and keep us from finding balance. Without balance our relationships and health can suffer, making us unhappy and, in a surprisingly short period of time, negatively impact our teaching effectiveness.

According to Sparks (2017) in *How Teachers' Stress Affects Students: A Research Roundup*, new research is helping to clarify how chronic teacher stress affects students' well-being and achievement. Sparks tells us that "teachers who reported higher levels of burnout had students with higher levels of the stress hormone cortisol each morning, suggesting classroom tensions could be 'contagious'." We can conclude from this that if we are stressed, often a result of lack of balance, our students can become stressed. What a vicious cycle this may cause. Taking care of ourselves is a win–win.

WAYS TO MAINTAIN BALANCE Not everyone has the privilege of loving their job. Teachers do. How many people get to surround themselves with things they love?

Science teachers get to play with rocks and minerals; they get to explain the life cycle with real animals; they get to excite kids with the laws of physics; they get to make **oobleck.** (Look it up!) Math teachers get to show how their favorite subject surrounds us, how patterns can be found everywhere. ELA teachers are surrounded by poetry, essays, novels, stories that activate imagination. Cool job. Through daily engagement, we change lives.

Because professionalism calls for personal and professional balance to be the best we can be, let's look at just a few of many concepts that may be useful to maintain this love of our jobs and have balanced lives.

1. **Be realistic.** As a caveat to what you just read, yes, we change lives, but very likely not every life we touch. We now know a lot about young adolescent development, diversity among students, and the societal context of teaching and learning. So many, many factors affect students in both negative and positive ways. Some of their challenges can be eased or eradicated by us; some we can only scratch the surface. We do what we can and shouldn't beat ourselves up when we can't seem to help much at all. One benefit of teaming is that if I can't get through to Ally or James, a teammate may be able to. There will be times when no matter what we do, bad things happen to kids for reasons completely out of our control. Celebrate even small successes and stay optimistic! Optimism is always more productive than pessimism.

2. **To stay mentally healthy, put other's opinions and comments in perspective.** Over the years I've had hundreds of people make off-hand comments like, "How can you stand to be around 13-year-olds all day?" or "Those kids would drive me nuts!" or "You have a degree in math and could do so many other things to make more money." or "I hated middle school. How can you go there every day?"

   And then there are comments like, "It must be nice to get three months off," "You can beat the traffic because you get to leave before 5 p.m.," or "You mean you get two weeks off at Christmas?"

   To the first set of comments, ask, "Have you ever thought about the fact that teachers make all other professions possible?" Let them think about that. To the second set of comments, it may be futile to tell them what we really do and the differences between giving your mind and heart and energy to kids all day, five days a week, and being a bank teller, a retail salesperson, a mechanic, an accountant, and so on. Perhaps a valid response might be, "Want to walk in my shoes for a day or a week?" Chances are you'll hear "Oh, no way. Never mind."

   I often tell my teacher candidates that no one understands what we do except other teachers—not significant others, parents, best friends—only teachers. And it's true.

   Along these same lines, I've often thought that every elected position should have as part of the congressional, mayoral, gubernatorial, and presidential orientation a mandatory week spent with a middle school team, planning, preparing, teaching, dealing with student and parent dilemmas, bus duty, and more. This might be the key to empathy, trust-building, respect engendering, and funding adequacy.

3. **Never take school work home.** You'll find some who disagree with this, but it's a key to my personal–professional balance. If that meant take-out for dinner, so be it. When I went home, I was home without one foot in school obligations. No paper grading, no lesson planning, no phone calls to make or emails to send. For me, this sometimes meant little socializing during the day other than during team meetings which are usually a mix of congenial talk and team business. I never left for the day without the next day planned, materials gathered, the next day's standard/objective on the board, and notes on things that should be done outside my classroom teaching. Some days I left school at 4 p.m., while I had some 6 p.m. check outs when most cars had left the parking lot.

   I often spend time in the evenings and on weekends reading journals and books about teaching and learning. With no papers to grade or plans to make, this is enjoyable and helps me grow professionally. Try it!

4. **Plan something to look forward to.** Think about the pleasure of anticipation. Looking forward to a trip or party doesn't at all diminish our care for our students and our devotion to our profession. Instead, it creates balance!

5. **Understand that teachers have multiple roles and we do our best to relish the challenge.** We are confidants, antibullying guardians, lenders of supplies, psychologists, mediators, and much more. If we are joyful adults with satisfying personal lives, we are up to the challenge. We can walk into our classrooms each day knowing we are not perfect, but also knowing that any mistakes we make are not intentional because our decisions and actions come from genuine, caring hearts. That's a lot to be grateful for. We may go home worried about a student or a situation, but this only shows that we take our responsibilities seriously and are good people.

A quick search of the Internet will yield many articles about decreasing stress and avoiding burn out. But the articles and blogs don't stop there. Many bemoan the harried life of teachers, the supposed impossibility of weaving family life and effective teaching together, the huge bags of papers lugged home, the sleepless nights of planning and preparing . . . there's considerable whining and that's unfortunate. We can teach in smart and efficient ways. Recently a college sophomore who wasted most of his freshman year in a mess of late work, ditching class, enduring parental displeasure, and continual stress, rushed into my office and proclaimed, "You know what, Dr. Powell?"

Me: "What, Jamie?"

Jamie: "I discovered this semester that if I do what I'm supposed to do when I'm supposed to do it, I'm not stressed!"

I stood up, hugged him, and congratulated him on learning a life lesson that will serve him well for his entire career, not just his junior and senior years of teacher preparation.

Self-Check 12.1

LO 12.2 Involving Family and Community

Professionalism dictates that we welcome families and the community to be our partners in the education of young adolescents. The more people actively involved in appropriate ways with our students, the more they learn and grow. Although most books and articles discuss parent involvement, I choose to use the word **family** to encompass biological parents, stepparents, grandparents, aunts/uncles, older siblings, and others who either live in the home or share guardianship of our students. So while the word *family* in this chapter is still synonymous with the word *parent* for many of our students, the implications should be stretched to more realistically encompass all our students and their individual circumstances. The principles are the same, even if the players are changing.

No matter how we define family, involving those closest to our students in the life of the school, and specifically in their students' schoolwork and relationships at school, has a positive impact on learning. A discouraging fact of life in most middle schools is decreasing family involvement compared with elementary schools. Most middle schools experience sharp decreases in family involvement between grades 6 and 8 because parents and others often think they are promoting independence. Another reason for withdrawal of involvement stems from many young adolescents' negative view of their families being part of their school experiences, or in any aspect of their lives outside the home. Families and teachers can tell humorous, and not so humorous, stories of students ignoring family members who attempt involvement. After a couple of "funny" instances, families decide to back off and give their students the space they appear to want.

For some families, *academic intimidation* is a reason for decreasing involvement. When homework becomes too difficult for family members, they shy away from school. Perhaps they dropped out before high school graduation or were never successful academically. Immigrant families often experience intimidation due to *language barriers*. English learners are increasing in numbers; finding ways to involve their families is becoming a dilemma of growing magnitude. Along with language barriers, *cultural differences* can create misunderstandings and reluctance. Some immigrant families don't realize that direct contact with schools and teachers is desirable, and that asking questions and giving input with regard to teaching and learning are sure to improve the process. Understanding reticent families and approaching them in sensitive and appropriate ways about a variety of opportunities for their involvement will benefit all of us.

Getting to Know Families

A commitment to involving families means making efforts to get to know them. Inviting families to get involved needs to be guided not only by what schools have to offer them, but what they have to offer schools. Matching potential family contributions to school needs, and then being sensitive to what families expect of schools, will foster positive and productive relationships.

There are many questions we can ask families to find out what they want and expect from us, as well as what they have to offer the home-school partnership. A questionnaire can be an excellent before-school contact. This is an ideal initiative for teams. Each teacher takes responsibility for a homeroom or advisory group. The questionnaire can be sent with a welcome letter or in a packet of materials to be signed and returned. A contest to see which homeroom or advisory group has the highest return rate may help get information back from a larger percentage of students. Figure 12.2 shows a sample form. If you communicate electronically with families, email is an excellent option.

Familiarizing Families with Middle Level Education

If families understand middle level philosophy with its student-centered focus on developmental appropriateness, their apprehensions about sending their children to middle school may be at least partially allayed. A 2001 study found that "[p]arents reporting high familiarity with middle level practices were more likely to report positive attitudes and engagement at their child's school" (Mulhall, Mertens, & Flowers, 2001, p. 60). The study also showed that some common middle level practices are a mystery to the majority of parents:

- Only about half were "somewhat familiar" or "very familiar" with cooperative learning.
- Fewer than half had any familiarity with interdisciplinary teaming.
- Only about 30% had any level of familiarity with advisory.

Communicating the value of the practices of middle level education, including interdisciplinary teaming, advisory, integrated lessons, and cooperative learning, is an ongoing process. These practices, after all, permeate what we do.

Communication

Getting to know families and familiarizing them with middle level philosophy and practices happens through effective communication. Ongoing communication with families enlists them as partners as long as the communication includes listening, as well as giving information. Some communication vehicles are schoolwide such as open house and report cards. Others are initiated by teams and individual teachers, with face-to-face, phone, print, and electronic options.

FIGURE 12.2 Sample questions for getting to know families

1. Who lives in your household?
   Name _____ Age _____ Relationship to student _____

2. What do you think your student's greatest strengths are?

3. What is your goal for your student during this school year?

4. Are there certain concerns, home situations, or medical problems we should be aware of in order to work more effectively with your student?

5. What activities does your student enjoy?

6. What one subject area do you think your student will struggle most with this year?

7. What does your student do afterschool? Is someone home when he/she arrives? Does he/she have regular activities?

8. Would your student benefit from regular afterschool sessions designed to help with homework? Would transportation be needed to take him/her home?

9. One of our team goals is to expand opportunities for our students to explore many interests. What special interest do you have that you would share with us this year (e.g., occupation, hobby, talent, etc.)?

10. Because we believe that education is a home-school partnership, we ask that you participate in ways in which you are comfortable. Here are some possibilities.

    Please check ways you would like to be involved occasionally.

    Bake for events _____ Field trip chaperone _____

    Collect project supplies _____ Homeroom parent _____

    Tutor after school _____ Big brother/sister program _____

    Organize fundraisers _____ Field day volunteer _____

    Assist in classroom _____ Materials preparation _____

    "Phone tree" leader _____ Career day speaker _____

    How would you prefer we communicate with you?

    Mail address: _____

    Email address: _____

    Phone number: _____ Best times: _____

    Notes sent with student addressed to: _____

A very real barrier to school–home communication may be language. The English learners in your classroom will likely live in homes in which English is not spoken fluently, nor read with comprehension. You need to know this. Many schools have translators available, perhaps even a teacher on staff. Talk with your principal and other teachers about how best to communicate with families if there are language barriers. Be very aware of this challenge, regardless of the means of communication you choose.

FACE-TO-FACE Most middle schools have an open house at the beginning of the school year that many call **back-to-school night**. Typically, families are given their students' schedules that they follow through each of the class periods, which are shortened to 10 to 15 minutes. This allows them to meet teachers and get a feel for the paths the student walks each day. Back-to-school night provides a wonderful opportunity to make a positive first impression on families. Here are some guidelines for success:

• Make your classroom as neat and attractive as possible. Even though it's the beginning of the year, be sure you already have some student work displayed.

Sara Davis Powell

Even though focus student Darma speaks English fluently, his parents have difficulty at times with school communications.

- Greet families at the door with a smile and a firm handshake.
- Give families a handout that may include your background, a brief statement about the importance of your subject area, a list of needed materials/supplies, classroom management policies, grading policies, and so forth.
- Pass around a sign-in sheet asking for student name and family member name(s), as well as how they prefer to communicate.
- Prepare to speak for about five minutes and then welcome questions.
- Offer a clipboard on which families can request individual conferences. Back-to-school night is not the time to discuss individual students.
- Thank families for attending and express the need and desire for their participation throughout the year.

Family-Teacher Conference A critically important face-to-face communication is the **family-teacher conference**. Often the skills and tactics for these potentially stressful meetings are learned on the job through trial and error. Most schools have organized times when families are invited to sign up for 15- to 30-minute conference times with either individual teachers or teams of teachers. Some schools have half days or evenings when teachers are available to talk with families. These conferences may be for exchange of information with mostly positive, affirming dialogue, or they may entail the necessity of corrective plans dealing with academics or behavior. Some schools designate a day following report card distribution when families are invited to the school. Three to four opportunities may be scheduled for conferences of this nature each school year. Up-to-date student folders with sample work and any notes about the student should be readily available along with an accurate and complete list of assignments and grades.

Conferences that are initiated for specific reasons require another level of preparation. If you are conferencing as an individual teacher, you will want to have the same resources listed in the previous paragraph. Make some notes to organize the information you want to convey as well as the questions you want to ask. Some tentative action plan ideas are helpful. If you are conferencing as a team, each teacher needs to be ready, with one of you leading the conference. This person is responsible for stating the main purpose of the conference, keeping the discussion focused, and summarizing the agreed-upon strategies to be implemented. Another teacher needs to take notes during the conference and complete a form similar to the one in Figure 12.3. Make sure at least one teacher can open the conference on a positive note to help put the family more at ease. You can see how efficient a team conference can be. As an individual teacher conferencing with a family, the whole responsibility falls on you. You still must document the conference fully and file your conference form.

Family conferences may be initiated either by teachers or by families because of specific concerns. These may occur anytime during the year. I strongly recommend that teams of teachers meet with families. I have seen the positive dynamics, the cohesive solutions, and the growth of empathy that is possible when a group of adults share information and formulate proactive strategies to benefit an individual student. Here's a fairly common scenario.

FIGURE 12.3 Sample family conference form

Student name: _____ Date: _____

Family attending: _____

_____

Teachers attending: _____

_____

Others: _____

_____

Notes (continue on back as needed):

Summary of concerns:

Plan of action:

Follow-up communication plan:

Maurice's grades are slipping and it's only the sixth week of school. He has been referred to the office several times for behavior problems. He became very angry in fourth block yesterday and loudly called an 8th grade girl a derogatory word during social studies. He was sent to the Behavior Improvement Room (BIR) for the rest of the day and his mom was called. She agreed to meet with Maurice's team of teachers at 7:30 the next morning. The team got together after school the day before the conference to talk about Maurice. They discovered, as almost always happens, that one or more teachers had not seen the dramatic grade drop, nor had they regularly seen any misbehavior.

When the conference begins, the teachers who are having relatively more success with Maurice speak first and give the positive side. Then a designated teacher explains the problems the other teachers are observing as well as the office referrals and BIR incidents. Teachers express their desire for Maurice to succeed and ask his mom to talk about anything she has observed, to ask questions, to give insights, etc. The conversation then becomes one about planning ways to help Maurice find both academic and behavioral success.

The resulting value of the whole team and the family meeting together depends in large measure on the attitude and demeanor of the teachers. There is a very real chance that Maurice's mom could have been intimidated and overwhelmed by four or five teachers sitting in desks where they are very comfortable and confident. Friendliness and the offer of coffee or a soft drink go a long way toward making the conference one of honest, sincere communication. The bottom line is that we all have the same goal—Maurice's success. Say it often, and mean it.

Room arrangement is important for conferences. A circle of chairs works best. Using all student desks may prove embarrassing. Provide at least two sturdy, armless chairs so that all sizes of family members and teachers can be seated comfortably. Teachers should never sit behind a teacher desk with family members on the other side.

Another consideration is our choice of words. We are the experts in education, but most families are the experts on their kids. We would not expect them to spout adolescent development theory, but rather to use straightforward language to convey their concerns and descriptions of circumstances. So should we. Education jargon should be eliminated as much as possible. For instance, saying "Jennifer sometimes doesn't respond to what pedagogical research tells us is most aligned to the content" is journal talk, not family talk. Instead, try, "Jennifer doesn't seem to understand what we're talking about in class. I need your help to find ways of teaching that will help her 'get it.'"

Always have at least two positive things to say about a student with whose family you are meeting. This allows you to employ what teachers sometimes call the "sandwich formula." You place negative slices between layers of positive comments at the beginning and end of the conference. The "sandwich" will be much more palatable than a steady diet of negative information!

Whether or not students attend family-teacher conferences depends on individual circumstances. It's true that we want students to learn and practice responsibility. Participating in a family conference allows all parties to hear the same things at the same time while actively involving the student in the specified improvement plan. However, there are times when families may have information to share with teachers that they prefer not to discuss in front of their students. There are also cultural considerations.

Enhanced eText

Video Example 12.4

Middle school teacher Dani Ramsey gives advice about family communication.

Student-Led Conferences Growing in popularity for a wide array of reasons, **student-led conferences** have the potential to bring more families into the teaching and learning process. Students plan and lead the conversation. Schools implementing this innovative way of informing families of student progress and goals report very favorable results. It's clear that the most vital elements of a student-led conference are the student and the family, with the teacher there to consult and encourage. Here are some reasons for having student-led conferences:

- Student ownership of the quality of academic work
- Provision for student-family interactions based on student effort and accomplishment
- Focal point that is academic rather than behavioral
- Process of organizing portfolio that gives student a sense of "wholeness" and connectedness of work
- Student acquisition and practice of communication skills
- Student goal-setting for academic progress
- Greater family participation (families usually show up in larger numbers when their students are involved).

Students need guidance as they begin to prepare for student-led conferences. Students should be asked to outline, if not script, what they will say to their families. If time permits, they benefit from practicing with peers. It's a great idea to choose a student to work with privately on his presentation. Then role-play as the family member of the student to demonstrate what a conference might look and sound like. Few strategies teach more efficiently and effectively than modeling. This is also an ideal time for students to learn communication skills, as well as basic manners. Dressing appropriately, opening doors for families, and introducing families to teachers are appropriate life skills for conferences. Speaking clearly, asking for and answering questions, and communicating organized points are skills that can benefit students for a lifetime. Of course, the students willing to lead family conferences are likely the ones who need it least. In any event, it's a positive thing to do.

Families also need to be prepared for the student-led conference. Sending a letter home informing parents about what to expect in a student-led conference is advisable. We know how important it is to evaluate new or different efforts from several perspectives. Figure 12.4 contains samples of evaluations that can be completed by families and students.

FIGURE 12.4 Student-led conference evaluations

Student Evaluation

1. What was the best thing about your family conference?

   _____

   _____

2. What would you change about the conference?

   _____

   _____

3. Were your family's reactions what you expected? Explain.

   _____

   _____

4. How will you prepare for the next conference?

   _____

   _____

Family Evaluation

Thank you for joining us today for your student-led conference. Please take a minute to give us some feedback about your experience by circling the response closest to your opinion.

1. The student-led conference was:

   very worthwhile.

   Worthwhile.

   not worthwhile.

2. The time we spent in conferencing was:

   too short.

   the right amount.

   too long.

3. The amount and nature of what our student presented was:

   revealing and informative.

   adequate, but still leaves questions.

   Inadequate.

4. Access to team teachers before, during, and after our conference was:

   Satisfactory.

   Unsatisfactory.

If you have comments you would like to share with us, please write them below or call: us. Thank you for participating in this important event with us!

PHONE COMMUNICATION   That dreaded "call from the teacher" has given this form of communication a bad rap. However, calls can and should be made for positive reasons as well as for problem situations.

Reaching families by phone during the day can be difficult. Leaving messages makes our phone etiquette important. Never just hang up. With caller ID, the family will know someone from school called. If you are calling with a student compliment, you may want to cheerfully deliver the positive message and say that if the family would like to hear more good things they can feel free to reach you during your planning period. Be sure you are readily available if the family member returns the call during the times you specify. If the subject is less than positive, always let them know that the student is fine, but that there is a matter you'd like to discuss at their convenience. Ask the family to call you the following day during your planning period or to leave a message in the office, giving a time and number where they can be reached later in the day. If the situation warrants a more immediate response or definitely requires a conference, your message should indicate the appropriate sense of urgency and let the family know you will keep trying to reach them in the evening.

If you call a family and discover that the home phone number has changed or been disconnected or the cell phone is no longer in service, let your administrators know immediately. They will follow up to get the most current information.

PRINT COMMUNICATION   Probably the most frequently used form of communication is print. Often it's one-way communication and, if we rely on students to deliver the message, it's likely to be "no-way" communication. Written communication is by far the easiest way to relay information. Because it seems easy, it often has a tendency to become sloppy. I can't overemphasize the need to proofread everything that is sent to families. Educational jargon and obscure vocabulary are neither necessary nor desirable. Plain, to the point, informative writing is called for—with no grammatical or spelling errors.

Print communication can take many forms: progress reports, report card comments, general school information typically sent in the beginning of the year, announcements of meetings/events, letters about school picture day, fundraising information—the list is long. Your team will send a welcome letter with multiple bits of information; you'll send your own letter about your subject area, expectations, grading, and behavior policies; and your team may opt to send home periodic newsletters featuring student activities, outlining projects, recognizing accomplishments, and announcing future events.

Sending individual less-than-positive notes home with students and expecting them to be promptly delivered is unrealistic. On the other hand, complimentary notes almost always end up under a refrigerator magnet. The yearlong benefits of occasional "happy notes" cannot be overstated. Family appreciation and support will likely be yours for just a few minutes of your time in recognizing a positive trait or action. All students have them. It may not be for outstanding academic progress, but all young adolescents have something to their credit that can be praised. Find that something and be proactive about developing family relationships.

ELECTRONIC COMMUNICATION   Using free sites such as schoolnotes.com and blackboard.com to electronically communicate with home may prove very successful in some communities. Most schools have websites and many allow individual teachers to have their own pages. If you decide to post periodically, make sure it's current. You don't want families accessing the site in February only to see wishes for a fun winter break.

Email is another option to investigate. For families who work in places with computer access and those who habitually check their email on their phones, this is a time efficient, and usually "kid proof," way to communicate. Texting may be an option, but having your cell number available to families and students is a personal decision. I would not do this unless I had a phone solely dedicated to my classroom. Remember that balancing our school and personal lives is important.

WHY WE HESITATE TO COMMUNICATE   It's one thing to say school-home communication is important, or hear it said in a teacher workshop, and quite another to regularly practice it. Why? Let's take a minute to consider this.

New teachers often say that the thought of talking to families is terrifying. And why shouldn't it be? Many of the parents of middle level students are old enough to be the parents of some new teachers. Talking with them with confidence and authority takes practice and time. Listening as experienced teachers communicate with families is a great way to pick up tips and phrases, and a sense of composure. However, actually talking with parents is the only way to acquire the skill. It gets easier with time, but the butterflies in the stomach will probably never stop fluttering entirely. Timidity is one of those challenges of teaching we should work diligently to overcome.

Time constraints often pose problems. There are only so many hours in a day and, yes, we do have lives—hopefully rich, full ones—outside the classroom. In terms of positive communication, set some goals. I found it very reasonable to make five "happy calls" a week along with sending at least five "happy notes" home. These are nonconfrontational, even fun, communications that take surprisingly little time, but often go undone solely for lack of resolve.

Letting problems fester because we are either too nervous or too short on time to communicate with families is detrimental to the student and the learning environment in our classrooms. Lack of academic progress needs to be addressed early in order to be remediated, or at least improved, with family help. Although families should keep a close watch on student progress, and many do try, weaker students rapidly become experts in communicating only good news about school while concealing the less positive aspects of their actual performance. Calling home the week before the end of a grading period is not using communication effectively. It's very frustrating for families to realize that it's almost too late to have any real effect. When behavioral problems are allowed to fester because of our reluctance to communicate, not only will the student's misbehavior escalate, but chances are other students will be affected and our effectiveness will be diminished.

In some cases, families may be seen as part of the problem rather than partners in seeking solutions. This view may or may not be justified. Jumping to the conclusion that families contribute to whatever the problem may be is dangerous. Every option of involving families in solution paths should be explored and utilized.

There are experienced teachers who, in some situations, have become jaded when it comes to encouraging family involvement. They live with a history of unsuccessful attempts to positively involve families in the education of young adolescents. A succession of ignored attempts, and even blatant refusals to work toward solutions, have colored their view of the value, or even the feasibility, of families being part of the process. They may be justified in their skepticism, but you may hold the key to reaching families by merit of tenacity, untried strategies, or the strength of your personality. Although I generally hesitate to advise new teachers to pay little heed to experienced teachers, in this case my hope is that you will consistently communicate with families, even those with reputations of reticence, and extend multiple invitations for them to participate in their students' education.

Opportunities for Family Involvement

Rarely do families of young adolescents eagerly approach the school and ask to be part of the activities. It is usually up to us to initiate and organize opportunities. Families have a wealth of knowledge, experiences, talents, hobbies, and special skills that can be used to enrich the lives of your students. The form in Figure 12.5 asks families to volunteer for a number of service needs. If a family member checks an area, by all means find a way to invite him to participate in that area at some point during the year.

It's helpful to compile and organize responses as a team. There will be "natural fits" that can be easily incorporated into the planned curriculum. If the topic of driving an 18-wheeler doesn't leap out as a curricular bright spot, it may fit nicely into an afternoon "buffet of exploration" in which students sign up to attend four 20-minute sessions according to their interests. Clogging, fly tying, kite building, a day in the life of a CPA, baseball card collecting—what an interesting assortment you're likely to find. I've found that families greatly appreciate an acknowledgment when they are open enough to say, "Here's what I do and I'm willing to share it with the kids." A postcard, phone call, or email note will complete the communication loop and let you express your appreciation.

FIGURE 12.5 Family interests survey

Because we strongly believe that middle school is an ideal time for students to explore and discover their own interests and talents, we'd like to invite you to share yours with us. From time to time we organize opportunities for family members to tell about and/or demonstrate what they do professionally or how they enjoy their leisure or hobby time. Your special skills and training may fit perfectly into an area of study or be appropriate for a "buffet of exploration" involving many adults and their areas of expertise. Sound like fun? You bet! We'd love to hear from you.

Name:_____

Student:_____

I would like to share my interest in:

_____

You may contact me at (phone or email):

_____

Thanks for your time. You are our partners in learning here at Lincoln Middle School!

Here are some more volunteer opportunities to offer families. Those who are not comfortable in the spotlight of a career day or an afternoon of interest sharing may, if asked, be willing and often pleased to help out in other ways.

- Participating in school "spruce up" days including grounds work, cleanup, painting, fixing, and so forth
- Translating to help language minority families communicate with teachers and school
- Participating in service-learning ventures
- Sponsoring clubs and special events
- Performing clerical duties related to a special event
- Setting up and monitoring "phone tree" communication
- Assisting in the school office or library.

Family volunteers should be treated with respect and courtesy. They should not have to wonder what to do or how to do it. Specific directions and time frames provide the structure to keep everyone in a comfort zone. Always acknowledge the value of volunteerism in whatever ways you can.

Community Involvement

The word *community* to this point has been used to describe the goal for our classroom, team, grade level, and even our entire school. However, community in this chapter simply means people who live in the same geographical area. Our schools function within communities of people of all ages who inevitably have different lifestyles. Finding ways to draw them into the teaching and learning cycle of our middle schools is a challenge worth pursuing. The community is involved with public education in one way, like it or not, and that is financial. The federal government funds about 12% of public education costs, while state and local taxes share close to equally, in most cases, the remaining 88%. With or without children of school age, and whether they approve or disapprove of school board decisions, are bothered by the noise of P.E. classes on the field, or comforted by the enthusiasm of youth, the public still funds the overwhelming portion of public education. Our schools run the gamut from sources of pride for the community to sources of embarrassment. Pride and embarrassment, and everything in between, stem from perceptions of what we do and the results of our efforts. Sometimes the perceptions are based on accurate information, but many times they are not. If a school is perceived negatively, getting the positive word out when things are going well is difficult, but doable.

COMMUNITIES MATTER   I have known many young adolescents over whom I wish only our school teams had influence. These are the kids who have to grow up way too early in an attempt to cope with the cards of life they have been dealt. They're the ones for whom we may say, "If I only had the money to run a great big happy home for dozens of kids, this one I could help." No matter how physically, emotionally, and academically safe we make our learning environment, when the school is locked up for the evening, our kids go out into the community and away from our protection and influence.

Some communities have qualities that enhance, or at least don't appear to hinder, our teaching and learning efforts. They offer physical comfort and relative safety, family participation, recreational and cultural options, and at least give lip service to the value of education. What generally distinguishes these communities from those in the previous paragraph? You guessed it—socioeconomic status. Statistics will bear this out, but just because it seems to be so doesn't mean it can't be changed. The school, the children, and the community are, for better or worse, inextricably linked. We can't expect 10- to 15-year-olds to lead the way and, without passionate leadership, communities by themselves seldom bring about school (and thereby student) reform. The school is in a position to make a difference for 7 to 10 hours a day. In partnership, the community and the school can grow together in claiming all the children as their own.

Some schools have formed partnerships with local businesses. **Business partners** support the school in whatever fashion suits their expertise. For instance, a pizza restaurant may occasionally donate pizzas for some special student recognition or event. An industry may offer field trip tours to explain how a business operates. A dry-cleaning business might clean school curtains or band uniforms. A catering business might contribute goodies to a back-to-school gathering. And of course cash donations are seldom refused! Besides tangible contributions, employees may volunteer their time to tutor or mentor individuals and be part of an after-school program. Recognition is vitally important. The school should publicize the fact that a particular business has agreed to be a partner in education through newsletters and signs in and around the school. Teachers and staff should always welcome volunteers and be overtly appreciative of those willing to partner with us.

WAYS TO INVOLVE COMMUNITY   To accomplish widespread community initiatives, the involvement of entire schools or school districts is required. However, there are ways that we, as individual teachers and teams, can promote positive perceptions and relationships within the community. Here are 10 suggestions to consider.

1. **Be informed.** Information is power. There's a lot to understand about public education. As the adults closest to the "action," we should not only know what's going on but also be aware of the influences that determine the who, what, when, and where of education locally, state wide, and nationally.

2. **Be positive public relations agents.** To people who do not have students in school or are not at all involved in schooling, we *are* the school. We may provide the only portrayal of education some people see, aside from an occasional news story, and these are often negative. The overriding image of what we do in schools should be positively portrayed.

3. **Acknowledge problems, suggest solutions.** If we are informed, and if we determine to be positive public relations agents, we can and should acknowledge problems in a forum that allows for more than cursory discussion. It is also our

responsibility to seek solutions and offer them publicly. If there are glaring achievement gaps at your school, you should admit to it and be able to facilitate discussions within the community about solution paths.

4. **Don't overemphasize the need for funding.** You probably have heard community members make a blanket statement similar to "Throwing money at schools won't fix anything." No, blindly throwing money won't do much for us. However, additional funding could make huge differences in upgraded facilities, salaries to attract the best and the brightest to our profession, ongoing professional development opportunities, fully funded afterschool programs available to all students, appropriate technology for all schools, and more. An adequately funded and well-managed budget *will* make a difference. When we propose greater funding, let's be able to back up the request with how it will make a difference.

5. **Use the media proactively.** The influence of television and newspapers is tremendous. Part of being informed involves watching news reports and reading articles about education. If you are infuriated by negative publicity to the exclusion of what's happening that's positive, do something about it. Call the media about positive events, and write intelligent letters to the editor while encouraging students to do the same.

6. **Spotlight students.** Search for ways to get student work in front of the community. From artwork in galleries to ideas on public issues, our students are so very capable of contributing to the community good.

7. **Invite the community in.** When the community feels welcome and has positive reasons to walk through the school doors, they are likely to feel a sense of identification and ownership.

8. **Actively participate in the community.** We can be positive ambassadors for our schools in the community by being actively involved in things that interest us, including civic, religious, service, and social groups. The wider our sphere of influence, the more opportunities we have to promote community awareness and involvement in our schools.

9. **Promote community service.** We have discussed the impact service-learning has on our students. Let's not underestimate the impact of service-learning on the community. Not only do the deeds involved make a difference, but the community perception of our students can be greatly enhanced when they know about or see firsthand the services our students perform.

10. **Know about community resources.** There are times when it is beneficial to extend our classrooms into the community to take advantage of the wealth of knowledge and facilities available. In addition, community resources provide family counseling, medical assistance, legal advocacy, and a tremendous number of services to assist students and their families. We may not know the extent of these services, but we should be able to point those who trust us in the right direction so that they can take advantage of community resources.

Self-Check 12.2

LO 12.3 Professional Relationships with Colleagues

"One incontrovertible finding emerges from my career spent working in and around schools: The nature of relationships among the adults within a school has a greater influence on the character and quality of that school and on student accomplishment than anything else" (Barth, 2006, p. 9). Roland Barth, highly respected former teacher and principal, continues by saying, "In short, the relationships among the educators in a school define all relationships within the school's culture" (Barth, 2006 p. 9). The four basic relationships among teachers as defined by Barth are parallel play, adversarial relationships, congenial relationships, and collegial relationships.

Parallel Play

Normal development for 1- and 2-year-olds involves parallel play. They sit on the floor just inches from one another and play with their own toys. They may not acknowledge each other's presence or play together in any way; they are engaged in **parallel play**. Although this is normal for young children, when teachers involve themselves in a kind of adult parallel play, it's unfortunate. Teachers may close their doors and choose not to share lessons or materials, and may only reluctantly share information, denying themselves and other teachers opportunities for individual and collective growth.

Adversarial Relationships

As detrimental as parallel play among teachers can be, even worse is when there are **adversarial relationships** within a school. These destructive relationships involve gossip, avoidance, criticism, talking behind the backs of others, and destructive competition. Not only is this behavior unprofessional, it is counterproductive to learning because the nature of relationships has a tremendous impact on student accomplishments.

Congenial Relationships

Being polite and enjoying each other's company are signs of **congenial relationships**. In many schools, and on many teams, there's a sense of camaraderie in which the adults seem to respect one another and enjoy being together. You will have congenial relationships with many of the adults in your school. Teachers of different ages, personality types, interests, cultures, and races will be part of your school. You'll find friendships and people to interact with socially, as well as others very different from yourself. Developing congenial relationships makes school more fun. Students can sense when their teachers enjoy the people around them. That's being a role model in a most practical way.

Collegial Relationships

Relationships with other teachers that promote growth through **collaboration** and sharing of professional expertise are **collegial**. The famous baseball manager Casey Stengel said, "Getting good players is easy. Getting 'em to play together is the hard part" (Barth, 2006, p. 11). There are lots of "good players" in schools, teachers who positively affect student learning. Developing collegiality means getting teachers to "play" together. Barth tells us he looks for three signs of collegiality when he visits schools:

- Educators talking with one another about practice and sharing craft knowledge
- Educators observing one another while they are engaged in practice
- Educators rooting for one another's success.

Courtesy of Barbara Hairfield

Teacher congeniality and collegiality make days at school more enjoyable!

These three components are possible when the adults in a school understand that all the young adolescents are their responsibility, not just the kids in their classes or on their team. This realization leads to collaboration rather than competition. Collegial teachers talk with each other about students, curriculum, instruction, assessment, developmental appropriateness, and all the other aspects of the profession. They observe each other with the goal of improving instruction. Collegiality leads us to be happy for the successes of others because this means students are learning and growing in productive ways.

Self-Check 12.3

LO 12.4 Transitions

The journey into and out of a middle level setting can be intimidating. Our responsibility extends to the **transitions** of students who are about to enter a middle level setting and those who are completing their middle level years. These transitions can be the stuff of both exhilaration and nightmares! Understanding young adolescent development issues prompts us to want to do everything we can to make transitions into and out of "the middle" as smooth and painless as possible.

Young adolescents want to feel as though they know what to expect concerning the concrete aspects of their upcoming new settings, like schedules and transportation, so they can concentrate on the less than clear-cut issues revolving around relationships. These relationships form connections among peers and the adults in the building.

The **Boomerang Project** is an organization that provides helpful information and resources to ease the important transitions for young adolescents. Where Everyone Belongs (WEB) involves 8th graders forming relationships with 6th graders to welcome them and keep them emotionally safe. Link Crew is a high school orientation and transition program for high school freshmen. Juniors and seniors act as Link Crew Leaders, serving as positive role models, motivators, and student mentors. Take a look.

Entering a Middle Level Setting

The fear of the unknown can be daunting for 10- and 11-year-olds. They have been in an elementary setting for years and are typically comfortable with how things work there. In fact, they are the "big kids." Now it's time to go to a middle school or middle level setting—usually a larger, more adultlike facility; as many as seven different teachers and classes a day; multiple books and supplies to put in and take out of lockers; much older and more mature 8th graders to possibly fear and avoid; new kids in classes from other elementary schools—so many unknowns.

Media can heighten preteen apprehensions, while masquerading as humor. *Middle School: The Worst Years of My Life* by James Patterson portrays a lonely 6th grader with a "dragon-lady" teacher. *The Diary of a Wimpy Kid* series presents numerous situations where a middle school boy is tormented by domineering adults and bullying kids. Other books such as *The Drama Years: Real Girls Talk about Surviving Middle School— Bullies, Brands, Body Image, and More* (Kilpatrick & Joiner, 2012) may be helpful, especially if read together with family or close friends.

A major study published in 2015 in *Research in Middle Level Education Online* asked young adolescents to reveal gender, race, and age as they responded "very concerned," "somewhat concerned," "a little concerned," or "not concerned" for the prompts in Figure 12.6. Authors Bailey, Giles, and Rogers (2015) recommend that more studies be conducted that look more closely at the concerns of students based on race and gender,

FIGURE 12.6 Transitioning to middle school concerns from major study

Getting lost

Having enough time to eat lunch

Using my locker

Undressing in front of others for PE

Making new friends

Being bullied by older students

Peer pressure to drink or smoke

Having harder subjects and tests

Meeting students of the opposite sex

Belonging to the right clubs or groups

Going to the restroom

New school rules

Other

Based on An Investigation of the Concerns of Fifth Graders Transitioning to Middle School (2015). Bailey, Giles, and Rogers. *Research in Middle Level Education Online*, *38*(5).

since they saw marked differences, and by setting, rural, suburban, and urban. Important information for middle level teachers and administrators resulted, including:

- Girls, in general, have more concerns about transitioning from a 5th grade setting to middle school.

- Concern about undressing in front of others for PE class was most frequently rated the highest, especially for girls. We know that puberty brings so many physical changes and young adolescents are so self-consciousness.

- Girls were significantly more concerned about getting lost, being pressured by peers to drink and smoke, being bullied, and meeting academic challenges.

- Students who self-identified as black or other race were more concerned with using a locker in middle school than white students.

- There were significant differences concerning time to eat lunch for both race and school type. Black students and inner-city students were more concerned about having enough time to eat lunch. More than 90% of these students attended schools with very high percentages of students receiving free or reduced-price lunches. Concern for lunch time may have stemmed from unstable food sources outside school or longer lunch lines.

- Students at the inner-city schools were more concerned about many things than students in other schools, including: restroom use, making new friends, belonging to the right clubs, learning and following new rules.

- Here's one we can all help remedy. Eleven percent of the students in the study wrote in the other category that they were concerned with having "mean" or "bad" teachers.

Articulation among adults in both elementary and middle schools to ease the transition makes sense. "Unfortunately, some teachers might make such statements as, 'You won't be able to get away with this in middle school' or 'If you think this is tough, just wait until you get to middle school.' Such comments can create misconceptions and misunderstandings as well as negative attitudes toward middle level schools" (King, 2017). Elementary teachers may make these statements not out of malice, but simply out of lack of awareness of how harmful they can be to the transition process.

All of us must recognize the need and choose to make a difference in easing the transition. This conscious choice on the part of principals, elementary and middle level teachers, counselors, and families, coupled with commitment, precedes the formation of a plan. Here are some strategies to help ease the transition into a middle level setting.

1. Perhaps the most important thing we can do to smooth at least some of the angst associated with transitioning to middle school is to find ways to create a sense of familiarity for the new setting. Sixth grade teachers, counselors, and the middle level principal visit elementary schools to talk with 5th graders and answer their questions.

2. Sixth grade students visit elementary schools to talk about "kid stuff," including the things they may remember worrying about a year earlier. It's very encouraging to hear survival stories.

3. Make a video of the middle school to be shown to rising middle level kids, typically 5th graders. I have organized several of these, with students carrying the camera and narrating the tour. It's great fun for the kids who make the video and equally so for the ones who watch. The young adolescent sense of humor shines through, putting everyone more at ease.

4. Offer tours of the middle school for transitioning students to take as a group. They have the security of their buddies with them as they walk around the new environment, listen in on classes, meet teachers and students, and see where they will enjoy the next three years. Include a "walk through" of a typical schedule and a demonstration of how to open and secure lockers. If possible, let the 5th graders try opening a locker, preferably with success. As silly as it may seem to us, there is an inordinate amount of fear linked to lockers, both how to use them appropriately and how to avoid being stuffed into one. Another source of anxiety is changing clothes for PE. On the tour the students can see that there are some provisions for privacy.

5. Send information to families and students about class scheduling, team assignments, books and supplies, school hours, transportation, and dates of special open houses for rising 6th graders and families. This information might also be published in the local newspaper.

Figure 12.7 is a survey you may want to give the first week of 6th grade to gauge the fears of the middle school "newbies." Add or delete items based on teacher experiences or the information from *An Investigation of the Concerns of Fifth Graders Transitioning to Middle School.*

Moving On

There is an abundance of research that points to 9th grade as the year of unprecedented absenteeism, academic failure, and excessively high student dropout rates. Communities and high schools are recognizing the dire need to help young adolescents as they move from middle school to high school. Some high schools have 9th grade academies in which students are set apart from the rest of the high school. They have their own administrators and elements that help them create identity, like separate facilities for classes and lunch. Continuing middle level practices into 9th grade such as teaming to whatever degree possible is advisable. If 8th graders know they will be eased into high school, their fears can be at least partially allayed. Remember that transition is a process, not an event.

Workload is a concern for many students as they leave middle school. Encourage 8th graders to continue to use a planner to keep up with assignments. Talk with them in realistic ways about time management. If they participate in extracurricular activities, even more of their time will be consumed by these activities in high school. Homework will no doubt increase. If students have six or seven classes a day, the demands will be much greater. If they will have a block schedule and four classes a semester, they can anticipate more homework per class.

Some of the same transition strategies in the previous section are also appropriate for the transition into high school. Figure 12.8 is a survey you may want to give during the last semester of 8th grade to gauge the fears of young adolescents as they transition to high school. In addition to the suggestions for transitioning into middle school, use the surveys to

- Guide 8th grade teachers and counselor to initiate advisory or other gatherings to specifically address concerns.
- Display survey results graphically to let students know they are not alone in their apprehensions. Let students form groups and discuss survey results.
- Ask current 9th graders to be available to answer pressing questions and give advice.

There is one overriding theme in this book that by now should be second nature in your thoughts about teaching. The message is that the diversity of background, ability, motivation, and life circumstances of our students must be considered in everything we do in and out of our classrooms. Middle school may be the last, best hope of

FIGURE 12.7 What I worry about when I think about going to middle school

WHAT WORRIES ME ABOUT GOING TO MIDDLE SCHOOL

Name: _____

Put an X in the Box That Best Describes Your Level of Concern	Not Worried at All	A Little Worried	Pretty Worried	Very Worried
Moving from class to class				
Getting lost				
Finding the bathroom				
Making new friends				
Work will be hard				
Changing in front of others in PE				
Locking and unlocking my locker				
Who to sit with in the cafeteria				
Learning new rules and routines				
School is bigger				
Older kids in the hallway				
Being made fun of				
Looking different from other kids				
Being bullied				

Other things that worry me about going to middle school:

_____

FIGURE 12.8 What I worry about when I think about going to high school

WHAT WORRIES ME ABOUT GOING TO HIGH SCHOOL

Name: _____

Put an X in the Box that Best Describes Your Level of Concern.	Not Worried at All	A Little Worried	Pretty Worried	Very Worried
Deciding which classes to take each year				
Getting lost				
Finding the bathroom				
Making new friends				
Work will be hard				
Knowing which clubs/ activities to join				
Playing on a sports team				
Who to sit with in the cafeteria				
Learning new rules and routines				
School is bigger				
Older kids in the hallway				
Knowing how to act like I'm not a freshman				
Looking different from other kids				
Being bullied				
Not having a driver's license				
Finding (or not) a boyfriend or girlfriend				
Pressure to do things that make me uncomfortable				

Other things that worry me about going to high school:

_____

incorporating enough differentiation to reach learners in ways that will bring out their potential and give them hope and confidence for the future.

Our Focus Students Transition to High School

We have gotten to know nine young adolescents and followed them from 6th grade to 8th grade. Take a last look at our nine students as they approach high school where the complexity of the program, the size of the institution, and the potential for "slipping through the cracks" may make a strong middle level foundation even more important.

Self-Check 12.4

Zach • 8th grade

Zach had his share of ups and downs in middle school but seems to be doing all right as 8th grade ends. As you can see by comparing his 8th grade picture to his 6th grade one in Chapter 2, he has gravitated toward individualism a bit. Mom is not too pleased with his long hair, but Zach takes his Ritalin regularly and makes decent grades, so she's happy. She has just signed the papers to buy a home in the suburbs for herself, Zach, and her parents. This will mean that Zach won't go to the urban high school next year. He's unhappy about leaving his friends but will try to stay in touch with them. Zach doesn't make friends easily and will probably be uncomfortable for a while in his new school, but he has a good support system at home and an acceptable level of interest in doing well in school. He should be fine.

DeVante • 8th grade

DeVante still lives in the same apartment with his granny, but he no longer hangs around after school and in the evening with the guys who are gang-related. Through Jefferson Middle School, Mr. Joyner and other teachers who saw his potential, and Kim's family, DeVante has become a high-achieving student and is showing emerging leadership skills. He was granted admission to the district's technology high school. He's very excited and is looking forward to school next year. He's disappointed that Kim won't be joining him at Ravenwood Technology Academy but understands that her interests are in broadcasting, and possibly drama. They promised each other that they will talk every day. DeVante could very possibly earn a college scholarship. He will need someone, possibly a guidance counselor, to help him channel his interests and skills to make the most of high school, and into a college that matches his ambitions.

Emily • 8th grade

Emily entered 8th grade with a new sense of confidence. Her grades were good, she enjoyed a growing group of friends, and found that boys were noticing her. In 8th grade she actually started feeling popular as she was included in lots of activities. Her parents decided to find a private speech therapist for her, and she has made significant progress. One of her boyfriends told her he thinks her slight lisp is sexy. Her earlier embarrassment due to speech difficulties is mainly a memory now. Emily is excited about going to high school. She has friends and is eager to meet more kids from other middle schools that feed into the one large high school in her district. She's even thinking about trying out for the 9th grade cheerleading squad. Emily has flourished since we first met her in 6th grade.

Kim • 8th grade

Kim has blossomed throughout middle school. She is comfortable in social settings, has made all As and Bs in her classes, and is eager to move on to Washington High School for the Performing Arts. Her parents are very happy with Kim because she worked hard to make good grades even in subjects she doesn't particularly care for. Kim still wants to be a broadcaster but has expanded her ambitions to possibly include drama. She's still crazy about DeVante and will miss him next year. Kim's challenge in high school will be to study enough to continue to achieve good grades, even if she doesn't particularly see the point of some of the required courses, so that she can get into a college of her choice. She's looking that far forward primarily because college is a nonnegotiable in her family.

Gabe • 8th grade

Gabe is ending his middle school experience in a much better place than when he began. His grades and standardized test scores allowed him to pass from 6th to 7th to 8th grade, but just barely. This last year in middle school was one of progress. His interest in robotics and Ms. Fox's encouragement kept him gladly showing up each day. His confidence improved, and he ended the year with no grades lower than C. But even with this progress, Gabe is going to have some challenges in high school. The work will be harder and the teachers and students aren't teamed. One key to Gabe's success as he progresses through school will be a teacher who will show a special interest in him. He has the potential to be the first in his family to graduate from high school. There will probably be some discouraging moments when the work will be difficult for him and extra encouragement will be needed to get him through.

Janie • 8th grade

Janie changed so much between 6th and 7th grade that her parents worried about her. After meeting with her teachers, they felt better but still kept her close to them and were watchful. Comparing Janie's 7th grade picture in Chapter 9 to her 8th grade picture tells the story of how she matured. Janie's circle of friends changed some in middle school, as it expanded beyond her immediate neighborhood. For a while she gravitated to kids and families her parents considered outside the mainstream, but by the fall of 8th grade the purple streak in her hair went away and hasn't returned. Now at the end of 8th grade she continues to read a lot and has started writing a novel. She's even eager to take English courses in high school and learn about writing. She will enter high school with a 3.1 GPA and is determined to do well.

(Continued)

Andy • 8th grade

Andy isn't faring well as his middle school experience ends. In 6th grade he began bullying several smaller boys. By the end of 7th grade his reputation was known throughout Hamilton Middle School as someone to be avoided. In 8th grade he was suspended three times for verbal abuse of teachers and expelled once for fighting. After Andy spent a month out of school, his dad went to the school board and asked that he be reinstated and promised to keep a close watch on him. He finished 8th grade with all Cs, Ds, and an F, but he passed the state standardized tests and was promoted to high school. Andy is often seen driving his dad's truck without a license, and the other kids say he drinks large quantities of beer each evening. He's only 14, and the smile in his 8th grade picture masks his undesirable behavior. Andy will need a very strong mentor teacher in high school who will call him on his behavior toward others, try to teach him about personal responsibility, and insist that he do his schoolwork. That's a lot to expect of a teacher, but this is likely Andy's only hope of successfully completing high school.

Darma • 8th grade

Darma determined to not let anything stand in the way of his success. His sudden loss of temper during the behavior incident in 8th grade shocked him, and he has given the whole situation a great deal of thought. Math and science continue to be his favorite subjects. He will enter high school with a perfect 4.0 GPA. He and his parents expect nothing less. Darma and his friends remain close and are excited about going to high school. Their local school offers a wide array of interesting electives, including engineering, astronomy, and a sequence of advanced math courses. The future is bright for Darma.

Maria • 8th grade

Maria's English is improving with Ms. Esparza's help. In fact, Ms. Esparza is the only teacher at MLK Middle School that Maria has warmed to, partially because of the language they share. As she leaves 8th grade with mostly Cs, Maria is still hanging out with older teenagers who have dropped out of school. She has become the girlfriend of an 18-year-old who works at odd jobs occasionally and lives with his older brother near Maria's apartment. Ms. Esparza is apprehensive about Maria going to high school. Although there is a bilingual program there, the school is much larger, and she fears Maria will get lost in the crowd and drop out without anyone even noticing. Ms. Esparza plans to meet with the high school bilingual teachers, as she does every year, to talk with them about how to possibly shepherd some of her students who have little support outside school.

Now that we know these nine students, each with his or her own gifts and challenges, each with a future so dependent on the adults who influence them, we see even more clearly our responsibilities.

LO 12.5 Recognizing Attributes of an Exemplary Middle Level Setting

Enhanced eText

Video Example 12.5

Principal Beth Thompson tells us about her experiences with hiring new teachers for her Title I middle school, along with advice for teachers.

I wish I could say that recognizing an exemplary middle level setting is as easy as compiling a master list of characteristics from *This We Believe, Turning Points,* and the many other sources available, and then checking off, say, 75%, and *voila!,* you've found an exemplary school! However, defining a successful or "true" middle school or middle level setting is, like most things in life, complex. There are middle schools I would term exemplary that exhibit only some of the tenets that have been discussed. There are combinations of characteristics that "work" for different reasons in different settings.

There is no one best prescription for success. Yes, there are some basics without which it is more difficult to create and maintain a developmentally responsive middle level school. For instance, teaming carries with it so many possibilities for success that it is considered by most educators to be an absolute for middle schools. But teams can take a variety of forms. An advisory program is so important to young adolescent growth; however, advisory is more of an attitude than a specific practice, so it's difficult to quantify. Heterogeneous grouping is desirable in many instances, but not in all. Connecting elements of the curriculum using active learning strategies and measuring knowledge and skills with authentic and varied assessments leads to more effective teaching and learning.

It's almost impossible for a school to thrive under weak or apathetic leadership. It's particularly important for new teachers to have supportive and wise administrators, the sort of folks who diligently push themselves and the adults in the school to consistently put students first. The ideal scenario is one in which you have choices about where you feel comfortable and which school environment aligns with your developing philosophy of teaching.

The concept of balance makes sense when we examine individual tenets of middle level philosophy and practice. Most have the potential to lose effectiveness, and perhaps even be detrimental, if carried to extremes. For instance, if we emphasize "flexible organizational structures" from *This We Believe* to an extreme and lose the basic concepts of consistency and routine (valuable elements in the education of young adolescents), we are not providing the best environment for our students. The key to creating balance is equipping ourselves with options and the judgment to know when and how to implement them. This has everything to do with recognizing (and creating!) exemplary middle level settings. The better we know our students and the broader our grasp of practices that reflect middle level philosophy, the more likely it is that who we are and what we do will bring us closer to a school environment that works for young adolescents. We must use our knowledge, skills, creativity, and energy as teachers "[i]f we want our children to be smart but not arrogant, flexible but not easily deterred from their hopes and dreams, compassionate toward others but not overly accommodating, self-confident but not too preoccupied with themselves, proud but not exclusive" (San Antonio, 2006, p. 12).

Let's revisit the *This We Believe* descriptors of a successful school for young adolescents from Chapter 1. Some practices will come and go, but these 16 guidelines continue to be applicable.

Curriculum, Instruction, and Assessment

- Educators value young adolescents and are prepared to teach them.
- Students and teachers are engaged in active, purposeful learning.
- Curriculum is challenging, exploratory, integrative, and relevant.
- Educators use multiple learning and teaching approaches.
- Varied and ongoing assessments advance learning as well as measure it.

Leadership and Organization

- A shared vision developed by all stakeholders guides every decision.
- Leaders are committed to and knowledgeable about this age group, educational research, and best practices.
- Leaders demonstrate courage and collaboration.
- Ongoing professional development reflects best educational practices.
- Organizational structures foster purposeful learning and meaningful relationships.

Culture and Community

- The school environment is inviting, safe, inclusive, and supportive of all.
- Every student's academic and personal development is guided by an adult advocate.
- Comprehensive guidance and support services meet the needs of young adolescents.
- Health and wellness are supported in curricula, schoolwide programs, and related policies.
- The school actively involves families in the education of their children.
- The school includes community and business partners.

This chapter's *Making the Teaching and Learning Connection* features a champion in the promotion of best practices for young adolescents, Dr. Nancy Ruppert, a professor at the University of North Carolina, Asheville and my dear friend. Nancy has spent her entire career advocating for young adolescents and quality middle level education. As a professor continually active in middle school issues and challenges, she has returned to the middle grades math classroom as a teacher on several occasions to put into practice what her research has told her is effective in making positive differences for kids. From 2017 to 2019 Nancy served as president of the Association for Middle Level Education, taking her expertise and passion to national and international levels.

Making the Teaching and Learning Connection

Becoming . . .
What does it mean for you as an educator?

Your journey, your whole journey, has prepared you for the day you begin teaching young adolescents. Jobs you love, and some you don't; relationships you experience, endure, celebrate; challenges you meet, fail, change, aspire to; courses, blogs, social media you learn from or drop; positive and negative experiences in classrooms, schools, life; mentors who inspire and disappoint . . . all influence who you are and provide insight to who you will become. Experiences, opportunities, and events are tools and insights that help you grow and learn. Embrace your past and choose your future as an educator. Become a great teacher.

What does it mean for your students?

At the core of any learning is the value and power of relationships. Successful teams and schools begin with strong relationships. In your classroom, remember that the young adolescents need to know you care about them. They, too, are becoming. They and you will make mistakes. Have the courage and insight to recognize their needs, celebrate their growth, forgive, and create an environment that values every student. Your classroom, your team, your school must be safe from ridicule, with the freedom to make mistakes and learn from them. Let mistakes and successes be equally valuable. Become their advocate.

What does it mean for the future?

View young adolescents as tomorrow's leaders, connect content to their lives, and give them opportunities to dream and create. Collaborate with families, the community, and colleagues to develop challenging experiences and tasks for them. Together, consider ways to prepare your students to lead. Take care of those with whom you teach; reach out, communicate, and serve those who also love young adolescents. Live in a spirit of hope for tomorrow. Become empowered.

Becoming never ends!

Take care of yourself,
Nancy

It's been half a century since the words *middle school* were proposed as an alternative structure within which to educate young adolescent learners. Middle level education grew out of both dissatisfaction with the junior high philosophy and a realization that the middle years, typically 10 to 15, are unique and require a developmentally responsive philosophy to effectively bridge the gap between childhood and full-blown adolescence/young adulthood. Recognition of the legitimacy of early adolescence as a life stage needing and deserving its own special educational experience has garnered the attention of more and more educators and researchers. What has evolved over more than five decades is a middle level teaching and learning philosophy that is coherent in its unwavering dedication to developmental responsiveness and academic rigor. Perpetuation of these two basic tenets depends in large measure on you, the future generation of middle level leaders.

"If middle school leaders expect to soon cross the finish line now that the 21st century has dawned, maybe they have not set their goals as high as they should" (George & Alexander, 2003, p. 584). These are Paul George's final words in *The Exemplary Middle School*. He reminds us that when we see our goals almost fulfilled, it's time to raise the bar. Some middle schools have implemented all the tenets of *Turning Points* and embraced the philosophy of *This We Believe*. For these schools, and the teachers who are the backbone, heart, and head of the organizations, the challenge is to continue serving young adolescents in developmentally responsive ways that promote even greater academic rigor through appropriate practice. They should look toward modifying and adding tenets to our guiding documents as learners, society, subject matter, and political realities evolve.

For many schools and teachers, George's "finish line" is so far away on the cluttered landscape of their circumstances that the danger lies in losing sight of the ideals needed to guide their efforts. If in your first years of teaching you find yourself in such a situation, perhaps your greatest gifts to the school and students will be your optimism for the possibilities of middle level education.

It's just as difficult for me to end this fourth edition of *Introduction to Middle Level Education* as it was to end the original text. My head and heart are still in the content. I love my career in education, and specifically middle level education. Teachers are my heroes. There is no finer profession. One of my mantras is "Teachers make all other professions possible." What a privilege and what a joy. I congratulate you on your choice to teach, and learn with, young adolescents. You will never be bored. You will always be challenged. And you will have fun along the way. Welcome to the adventure!

Self-Check 12.5

Group Activities

1. Visit a school in your class file and ask the following questions:

   a. How is back-to-school night orchestrated in your school or by your team?

   b. Do you send an individual and/or team "welcome to school" letter? (Ask for a copy.)

   c. How do you/your team use community resources such as business partners, service organizations, mentors, and others?

   d. How do you/your team conduct family conferences? Have you tried student-led conferences? (Be ready to explain how they work.)

2. Divide the nine focus students among your class members. Each of you will write a paragraph describing what you might have done as one of the students' teachers to make his/her middle school experience more successful than indicated in the Professional Practice sections. Be prepared to share your ideas.

Individual Activities

1. Write a brief narrative that you might use on back-to-school night to introduce yourself and your philosophy of teaching young adolescents.

2. While in the mall you run into a parent who is quite angry about a decision her student's teacher team made. The team is on your grade level. You are well aware of the situation and disagree with the decision that was made. Write a narrative of how you would handle the situation.

Personal Journal

1. Do you remember when you entered middle school/junior high? Write about how you felt and your first impressions.

2. Was your family involved in your school while you were in middle school? If so, in what ways? If not, did you want them to be?

3. When it was time for you to go to high school, what were your main concerns? Was it a difficult or pleasant transition?

Glossary

ability grouping: assigning a student to classes based on academic ability and achievement

abstract thinking: adultlike thinking characterized by ability to generalize and visualize

academic language: the vocabulary used for academic purposes; the language of a particular discipline

academic rigor: involves challenging students to think, perform, and grow to a level that they were not at previously

academic safety: an environment that ensures opportunities for success for all students regardless of previous achievement or pace of learning

academic self-esteem: the belief that one has the ability to be academically successful

accountability: being held responsible for student progress and effective use of resources

across the curriculum: content and skills embedded in multiple subject areas

advance organizer: an attention-grabbing opening for a lesson

adversarial relationships: destructive relationships involving gossip, avoidance, criticism, talking behind the backs of others, and destructive competition

advisory: a special time regularly set aside for a small group of students to meet with a specific school staff member

advocate: teachers who consistently promote the well-being of students

affective dimension: learning that considers emotions, feelings, dispositions, and attitudes

affiliates: organizations officially attached to a larger body

alternative assessment: generally, any assessment that is not a traditional pencil-and-paper test

amygdala: emotional portion of the brain

assessment: methods to gather evidence of student learning

assimilation: process of bringing all races and ethnicities into the mainstream by encouraging them to behave in ways that align with the dominant culture

Association for Middle Level Education (AMLE):   formerly National Middle School Association; largest organization advocating for young adolescents

Attention Deficit Disorder (ADD):   often characterized by an inability to focus for a sufficient length of time

Attention Deficit Hyperactivity Disorder (ADHD):   ADD often accompanied by a lack of impulse control

authentic assessment: assessment that involves, and occurs within, a meaningful and/or real-life context

Autism Speaks: a national organization dedicated to promoting solutions for the children and adults diagnosed with ASD

autism spectrum disorder (ASD):   a complex developmental disorder that affects how a person behaves, interacts with others, communicates, and learns

back-to-school night: an event designed to introduce families to the middle school environment

backward design: planning for curriculum and instruction by first making decisions about the desired learning results and methods of assessment

bilingual education: education option for English learners delivered in two languages

bisexual: people who have sexual or romantic feelings for both men and women

block schedule: any schedule that allows for more time to be spent in a given class than the traditional 50 minutes

Bloom's taxonomy: presents the classic six levels of thinking: knowledge, comprehension, application, analysis, synthesis, and evaluation

Boomerang Project: an organization that provides helpful information and resources to ease the important transitions for young adolescents

brain-based learning: using what we know about how the brain functions to guide decisions concerning curriculum content and instructional strategies

bullied: kids who are targets of bullies; the bullied may be passive, physically weak, or unattractive, have low self-concepts, be socially unskilled, cognitively or academically gifted, lesbian, gay

bully: a person seeking power he or she may not feel exists in other parts of life; bullies may exert power by harming others, by intimidating and being dominant

bullying: aggression with intent to harm; use of power in a relationship to hurt or humiliate

business partners: businesses that agree to support schools in a variety of ways, depending on their expertise and/or interest levels

bystander: with regard to bullying, those who watch it take place

Character.org: an organization providing free lesson plans middle level educators have found to be successful in teaching traits of civility

charter school: a public school that is freed in specific ways from the typical regulations required of other public schools

Council of Chief State School Officers: non-partisan, non-profit organization of public officials who head departments of elementary and secondary education in the United States

childhood gender nonconformity: children act in ways, and have preferences, that more closely match the opposite sex; often resolves by age 12

circadian rhythms: a 24-hour internal clock that is running in the background of your brain and cycles between sleepiness and alertness at regular intervals; also known as your sleep/wake cycle

citizen: a native or naturalized member of a state or nation who owes allegiance to its government and is entitled to its protection

civic dispositions: beliefs and values that foster productive citizenship and civility

civic education: in a constitutional democracy, productive civic engagement requires knowledge of the history, principles, and foundations of our American democracy, and the ability to participate in civic and democratic processes

civic engagement: working to make a difference in the civic life of our communities and developing the combination of knowledge, skills, values and motivation to make that difference

civic knowledge: information necessary for engaged citizenship through respectful and productive participation in the democratic process

civic skills: lead to empowerment to act, to make a positive difference in our homes, our schools, our communities, our nation, and our world

civility: disagreeing without disrespect, seeking common ground as a starting point for dialogue about differences, listening past one's preconceptions, and teaching others to do the same

classroom assessment: any form of assessment that occurs as a direct part of classroom teaching and learning

classroom management: maintaining an ordered environment in which learning may be accomplished

collaboration: working together to accomplish a task or goal

collaborative planning: planning for instruction with other teachers, typically team members (interdisciplinary) or those who teach the same subject

collegial relationships: promoting growth through collaboration and sharing of professional expertise

Collegiate Middle Level Association (CMLA): organization for college students interested in middle level teacher preparation; affiliate of the Association for Middle Level Education

Common Core State Standards Initiative: details what K–12 students throughout the United States should know in English language arts and mathematics at the conclusion of each school grade

common planning time: time set aside during the instructional day when teams of teachers meet

community of learners: close, trusting school-based relationships that encourage both personal and intellectual growth

complementary content and skills: content and skills that relate to one another in ways that enhance meaning and relevance

concrete thinking: childlike thinking characterized by the organization of experiences and information around what's visible and familiar

conflict resolution: the settling of student disputes

congenial relationships: being polite and enjoying each other's company

consequences: define what will happen if rules are broken

constructive correcting: taking advantage of the teachable moments brought about by mis-behavior

constructivism: students using higher-order thinking skills to construct or discover their own learning

convergent question: question with one correct answer

cooperative learning: students working together in small groups to accomplish a learning task or a learning objective

core subjects: subject areas generally considered basic for middle school: language arts, math, science, and social studies

Council for Exceptional Children (CEC): a professional association of educators dedicated to advancing the success of children with exceptionalities.

Crisis Prevention Institute (CPI): an international organization committed to best practices and safe behavior management methods that focus on prevention

criterion-referenced assessment: assessing what students know and are able to do according to stated learning goals

critical thinking: higher-order thinking requiring purposeful objectivity and consistency

cultural pluralism: recognition that our country's people consist of varying cultures, ethnicities, and races that all contribute to a common goal of freedom and productivity

cultural responsiveness: an approach to education that crosses disciplines and cultures to engage learners by incorporating their ways of being, knowing, and doing

culture: specific shared values, beliefs, and attitudes

curriculum: planned and unplanned aspects of what students experience in school; typically thought of as the "what" of teaching

curriculum mapping: making calendar-based plans for the sequence of what is taught

cyberbullying: bullying accomplished through technology

cybercitizenship: characterized by conscientiousness in the cyberworld

demonstration: strategy involving showing students something that would be difficult to convey through words alone

developmental appropriateness: actions and attitudes attuned to developmental needs and interests of students

developmental responsiveness: understanding the unique nature of young adolescents and continually considering how we can use that knowledge to build a supportive learning environment

diagnostic assessment: assessment that determines existence and level of mastery for purposes of planning curriculum and instruction

dispositions: attitudes and beliefs that guide and determine behavior

differentiation of instruction: providing differing learning opportunities in terms of content, process, and product based on students' levels of readiness, interests, and learning profiles

digital citizenship: requires skills to conduct ourselves in responsible and effective ways in a digital world

divergent question: open-ended question, often with many possible responses

diversity: differences among students that may include, but are not limited to, gender, learning style, interest, family structure, race, culture, socioeconomics, and multiple intelligences

early adolescence: period of life typically considered ages 10 to 15

edTPA: a performance-based, subject-specific assessment and support system used by teacher preparation programs throughout the United States to emphasize, measure and support the skills and knowledge that all teachers need

Education for All Handicapped Children Act (PL 94–142): mandated, among other things, that all children with handicaps be given the right to a free and appropriate public education in the least restrictive environment (LRE) guided by an Individualized Education Program

Education World: a large site loaded with practical information and strategies to assist teachers with lesson planning

educational technology: any technology-based device or program that enhances teaching and learning

emotional intelligence: consists of five dimensions: self-awareness, handling emotions, motivation, empathy, and social skills

emotional safety: an environment that provides a stable atmosphere where expressed emotions receive consistently caring responses

empathy: the capacity to see situations from another's point of view

empowerment: the process of becoming stronger and more confident; the knowledge and skills young adolescents need to take responsibility for their lives

encore courses: refers to related arts courses

English learners (ELs): people for whom English is not the first language and who have little or no proficiency using the English language; also referred to as English language learners (ELLs)

equity: the quality of being fair and impartial

English as a Second Language (ESL): students receive individual-ized assistance once or twice a week for about an hour each session, with little or no emphasis placed on preserving native language or culture

ethnicity: sense of group identification, political and economic inter-ests, and behavioral patterns

ETS: Educational Testing Service

evaluation: making judgments about the quality of work or prod-ucts of work

exceptionalities: abilities and disabilities that set students apart from other students

executive skills: a set of mental qualities that help us get things done. We all have many to lesser or greater degrees, with some skills perhaps still weak even for adults

executive function: see executive skills

expectations: define what is and what is not acceptable in the classroom

expenditure per pupil: funding from all sources given to the public school a student attends

exploratory class: course that encourages students to take a broad, overview-oriented look at a subject or interest area; typically six to nine weeks in length but may last an entire school year

family: encompasses biological parents, stepparents, grandparents, aunts, uncles, older siblings, and others who either live in the home or share guardianship of our students

family-teacher conference: conferences that involve family members and teachers

flexible ability grouping: calls for grouping and regrouping that meets individual learning needs

flexible block: schedule that allows teachers to divide class time in a variety of ways as appropriate to best address specific academic plans

flipped classroom: entails using technology to digitally deliver a mini-lecture or provide content that's accessible on electronic devic-es, freeing classroom time for engaging in discussion and activities that may have been formerly reserved for homework

forced-choice assessment: common type of both classroom and standardized assessment with students simply choosing a correct response from the choices provided; for example, matching, true or false, multiple-choice, and fill-in-the-blank

formal curriculum: subjects mandated by district and state, and guided by standards

formative assessment: ways of monitoring learning and providing feedback to students and teachers on progress toward mastery

gay: homosexual; term usually applied to males

gender identity: an individual's concept of self as male or female

generalization: a statement based on specific details or facts, but does not necessarily apply to all in a certain group; often begins with "tend to"

gifted and talented students: students who may excel in intellec-tual, creative, artistic, and/or leadership abilities

global citizenship: a way of living that recognizes our world is an increasingly complex web of connections and interdependencies; realization that choices and actions may have repercussions for people and communities locally, nationally, and internationally

goals: broad statements of intent without specific steps to fulfillment and often lacking in means of measuring success

grade: number or letter representation; score of evaluation received over time and reported to students and adults

gradual release model: teaching and learning framework that shifts responsibility for learning to the learner through a series of steps that rely on us knowing both our students and our content very well

graphic organizers: visual representation of knowledge that empha-sizes relationships

guidance counselor: professional who addresses students' affective needs and concerns that affect personal and academic growth

heterogeneous ability grouping: grouping of students without consideration of academic abilities or achievements

heterosexual: romantic or sexual attraction to the opposite sex

homogeneous ability grouping: see *ability grouping* and *tracking*

homosexual: romantic or sexual attraction to the same sex

house: a word that designates a "school-within-a-school"

hovering: a term describing a philosophy of closely monitoring young adolescents as they mature

hyperactivity: defined as age-inappropriate increased activity in multiple settings

IDEA: Individuals with Disabilities Education Act

IEP: Individualized Education Program

iCivics: user-friendly organization that presents civic education in engaging and effective ways, founded by Justice O'Connor in 2009

idiosyncratic: occurring in stops and starts, seldom predictable; no two students develop in the same ways at the same time

impulsivity: refers to the tendency to act rashly and without judgment or consideration

incivility: absence of civility; both rudeness in actions and apathy when action is needed

inclusion: assignment of students with special needs to regular classrooms; sometimes referred to as *mainstreaming*

individualized education program (IEP): a detailed plan by which we want students with exceptionalities to reach specific goals; typically developed by educators, the family, and others as appropriate

Individuals with Disabilities Education Act (IDEA): reauthoriza-tion of PL94142

informal curriculum: refers to what students learn that isn't written in a lesson plan or necessarily intentionally transmitted to students

inquiry-based learning: learning by questioning and investigating

integrative curriculum: subject areas are interwoven around a conceptual theme chosen as a result of student needs and interests

intelligence quotient (IQ): total score derived from several stand-ardized tests designed to assess human intelligence

interdisciplinary instruction: subject areas are related and blended, often blurring subject boundaries; also referred to as thematic instruction

interdisciplinary teaming: see *teaming*; interdisciplinary because different subjects, or disciplines, are represented

interdisciplinary unit: a unit of study addressing a theme with individual subject areas contributing and sometimes blending, and with subject boundaries often blurring

International Association for the Evaluation of Educational Achievement: an independent cooperative of national research institutions and governmental research agencies

International Society for Technology in Education (ISTE): gives detailed descriptions of the knowledge and skills related to technology use appropriate for young adolescents and other K–12 students

intervention: actions taken to curb or stop misbehavior

item analysis: a way of looking at general patterns of what an entire class knows, doesn't know, or partially knows; accomplished by tallying how many students answer each item incorrectly. In this way, a picture emerges of patterns of knowledge.

jigsaw: cooperative learning strategy that involves students teaching students

Jing: a program that allows you to capture your brief lesson and make it available to your students through screencasts, or specifically designed videos

junior high: a precursor to middle school, with departmentalized organization much like a high school, typically encompassing grades 7 through 9

K-W-L chart: way of organizing brainstorming or the beginning of a unit of study; K stands for "what we Know," W stands for "what we Want to learn," and L stands for "what we Learned"

LGBTQ: a common way of referring to those who identify as lesbian, gay, bisexual, transgender, and questioning

learning centers: designated places in a classroom with information and activities to promote independent or small group learning using a variety of modalities; sometimes called *learning stations*

learning disabled (LD): a designated special-needs category, manifested in many forms

learning objective: states the learning that is intended to take place as a result of instruction; objectives are measurable

learning outcomes: similar to learning objectives in that the stated learning is measurable

least restrictive environment (LRE): the setting that has the fewest restrictions within which a student can function at capacity

lecture: strategy involving teacher talking and students listening

lesbian: term used for homosexual females

lesson launch: a distinct beginning of the lesson that helps learners focus on what's ahead

Link Crew: a high school orientation and transition program for high school freshmen

long-range plan: comprehensive guide for facilitating learning involving student profiles, content and sequencing, classroom management philosophy, instructional strategies, and overall organizational factors

looping: a team of teachers and students who stay together for more than one academic year

LRE: Least Restrictive Environment, an environment in which students with special needs function that incorporates the fewest possible restrictions; for many of these students, the LRE is the regular classroom setting

magnet school: public school that offers a different focus involving curriculum, instruction, or both

mainstreaming: policy of blending students with special needs with the general student population; sometimes referred to as *inclusion*

manipulatives: objects designed so that learners can perceive a concept by manipulating it, providing ways for learners to learn concepts through developmentally appropriate hands-on experience

metacognition: the process of thinking about one's own thinking

middle school: a school specifically structured to meet the developmental needs of young adolescents, typically 10- to 15-year-olds

mini-lecture: a brief lecture used to introduce a topic or provide concise information

Mind, Brain, Education (MBE): a dynamic area of science researching how the brain works

modalities: refer to how students use their senses in the learning process

multiage grouping: students of two or more grade levels intentionally placed together as ability and/or interests dictate

multicultural education: purposeful process of incorporating opportunities for students to gain insights about cultural differences locally and globally with the goal of increased acceptance and appreciation

multidisciplinary instruction: instruction in which subjects remain distinct but are linked together by a common theme

National Assessment of Educational Progress (NAEP): compares states to states; known as the nation's report card

National Forum to Accelerate Middle-Grades Reform: an organization of researchers, educators, leaders, and officers of professional organizations, all committed to advocating for young adolescents to improve academic performance and health

National Governors Association: organization of all U.S. governors

National Middle School Association (NMSA): now Association for Middle Level Education (AMLE)

NCATE: National Council for the Accreditation of Teacher Educators

NCLB: No Child Left Behind federal legislation

NCSS: National Council for the Social Studies

NCTE: National Council of Teachers of English

NCTM: National Council of Teachers of Mathematics

neuroscience: science concerned with nervous system and brain functioning

Next Generation Science Standards: outline what students need to know and be able to do to be scientifically literate, grade level by grade level, and promote excellence and equity for all students in science; state that science should be an active process for students

norm-referenced assessment: compares individual student performances relative to the overall performance of a group of students using percentile rankings

nurture: everything that affects a person other than gene make-up

objectives: statements of measurable learning that results from instruction; more specific than goals

oobleck: easy-to-make substance that's an example of a non-Newtonian fluid, meaning it can be both a liquid and a solid

parallel play: teachers may close their doors and choose to not share lessons or materials, and may only reluctantly share information, denying themselves and other teachers opportunities for individual and collective growth

parent/family-teacher conference: an opportunity for family members to meet with teacher(s) to discuss student progress in work, performance, understanding, and/or behavior

peer mediation: opportunity for students to problem solve concerning their disputes in the presence, and with the help, of a student acting as mediator

performance assessment: involves tasks that require students to apply knowledge

physical safety: the elimination of threatening and/or real scenarios such as theft, verbal abuse, weapons, and unwanted horseplay

plasticity: the brain's ability to stretch and grow or replace some brain loss due to injury

portfolio: collection of student work that may show progress over time or may be limited to the students' best-quality products

power struggle: when a teacher implements a consequence and the student refuses to comply

Praxis: series of tests developed by the Educational Testing Service to assess the knowledge and skills of preservice and practicing teachers

prefrontal cortex: rational part of the brain

principal: oversees every aspect of school life and answers to the district for all that occurs at the school

privilege gap: gap between haves and have-nots based on socioeconomic status

professionalism: involves attitudes and actions that consistently convey respect for learning and learners, as well as for the adults with whom we work

Progress in International Reading Literacy Study (PIRLS): compares countries worldwide in two specific types of reading: literary and informational

project-based learning (PBL): students work on a project over an extended period of time that engages them in solving a real-world problem or answering a complex question

proximity: the accessibility of teacher to students

puberty: biological transition between childhood and young adulthood

race: categorizes individuals based on certain outward physical characteristics

racism: prejudice based on the belief that one race is superior to another

reflection: purposeful analysis of actions and/or experiences with the goal of altering and improving future actions and/or experiences

reflective practitioner: deliberately thinking about what we do with the intent of improving; purposefully reflecting on what went right, and what didn't, as we increase our knowledge and skills

related arts: courses other than core (language arts, math, science, and social studies); also known as exploratory or encore courses

relational bullying: most often practiced by girls, is the systematic diminishment of a bullied child's sense of self through ignoring, isolating, excluding, or shunning behaviors

reliability: refers to the consistency with which assessment measures what it is meant to measure

restorative practices: an approach to addressing behavioral issues that calls for teacher to work with students to look at an issue, the reasons for the issue, the logical solutions, and then develop the plan for moving forward

results orientation: philosophy that says a practice may appear to be ideal for young adolescents, but if, in a particular circumstance, it doesn't result in increased learning or positive growth physically, intellectually, emotionally, socially, or morally, it should not be implemented

rigor: teaching meaningful content and maintaining high expectations for student learning

role-play: assuming another person's perspective and mimicking circumstances when given specific parameters

routines: expectations organized around a particular time, concept, or place that help guide students and teachers to accomplish tasks in the quickest and most efficient manner possible

rubric: scoring guide that provides the criteria for assessing the quality of a performance or product and includes a gradation for each criterion, generally from poor to excellent, with quality often indicated by numbers

rules: see *expectations*

rural settings: communities with lots of open spaces and limited retail

scaffolding: providing appropriate supports for students as they learn a concept and then move toward acquisition of another

Schools to Watch: designated exemplary middle schools with criteria established by the National Forum to Accelerate Middle-Grades Reform

school-within-a-school: a segment of teachers and students of a large school population who function as a unit with regard to organization, use of space, and scheduling

score: number given to student work to indicate evaluation

self-compassion: encourages us to face our flaws and our weaknesses and view ourselves realistically; treating ourselves with the same kindness and understanding we show others

self-concept: a person's sum total of what he knows about himself, including gender, name, personality, physical characteristics, likes and dislikes, beliefs, and family

self-discipline: monitoring our own behavior and making adjustments to actions and attitudes when needed

self-esteem: how one values or sees worth of self-concept traits (see self-concept)

service-learning: students providing services to individuals and groups with volunteerism accompanied by academic learning

sex: biologically assigned at birth as male or female; the act of procreation

sexism: the belief that one sex is superior to another; most often used as male superiority to females

sexting: sending text messages about sex

sexual harassment: a form of sex discrimination involving unwanted and unwelcome sexual behavior

sexual orientation: the sex to which one is sexually and romantically attracted – heterosexuality, bisexuality, and homosexuality

Sheltered Instruction Observation Protocol (SIOP): an approach to lesson planning that adds a specific language component to address the needs of English learners

single-subject planning: planning lessons within one specific subject

site-based management: school administrators and teachers make most of the decisions

Six Seconds: non-profit organization that helps individuals, parents, and educators navigate emotional issues in ways that increase emotional intelligence

social consciousness: involves an awareness of society and the difficulties and hardships of others

social media: communication through texting or instant messaging or any form of personal communication utilizing technology

social responsibility: personal investment in the welfare of others and our world

socioeconomic status (SES): a measurement of economic conditions using several criteria including income, occupation, and education; most often thought of as a measure of wealth

soft bigotry: showing bias by adjusting expectations based on race

Southern Poverty Law Center: organization dedicated to fighting hate and bigotry and to seeking justice for the most vulnerable members of our society

standard: a benchmark against which progress is measured; what a student should know and be able to do

standardized assessment: assessment with content typically representing a broad base of knowledge and administered to many segments of a general population, usually either nationwide or statewide

stereotyping: assuming a statement (see *generalization*) applies to everyone in a particular group

structured English immersion (SEI): delivery of education to English learners with English instruction involving the majority of the school time, with other subjects secondary

student-focused instruction: creating opportunities that empower students to be self-directed learners

student-led conference: event during which families and teachers focus on, and are led by, the student in discussions and displays of classroom accomplishments

suburban setting: generally small to medium-sized towns, or on the outskirts of cities, typically with distinct neighborhoods or subdivisions

summative assessment: means of making judgments about the quality of a process or product; typically administered at the end of a unit of study and used as a basis for assigning grades

teaming: a specific group of teachers (usually two to five) representing different subject areas and responsible for collaboratively facilitating the academic and social growth of a designated group of students

think-aloud: strategy involving modeling thinking skills to show students how they might go about solving problems, approaching a task, or processing new information

thinking skills: cognitive acts that may simply involve awareness of surroundings or may be as complex as making judgments that lead to actions

think-pair-share (TPS): versatile strategy that poses a question, asks students to think about it, then pair with another to discuss it, then share with the larger group

This We Believe: position statement of the Association for Middle Level Education, formerly the National Middle School Association

Title I: federal funding given to public schools where more than 50% of the students qualify for free or reduced-price meals; used to supplement regular school funding

toxic stress: possible result of living in poverty, can lead to impaired memory, making it harder to learn, solve problems, follow rules, pay attention, and control impulses

tracking: placing and keeping students in specific ability groups (see *ability grouping*)

transgender: refers to people who persistently identify with a gender that is different from their birth sex and may surgically alter their bodies to reflect their new identity

transitions: moving from grade to grade for middle school, and the time when students leave elementary school and the passage into high school; in the classroom, the process of going from activity to activity

Trends in International Math and Science Study (TIMSS): compares countries in math and science worldwide through randomized assessment every four years

Turning Points: 1989 publication by the Carnegie Council on Adolescent Development that outlines middle level education philosophy

Turning Points 2000: written in 2000 by Jackson and Davis, it serves as an update of the 1989 *Turning Points* document, with strategies for implementation of middle level philosophy based in part on the experiences of schools that have attempted to implement the original *Turning Points* tenets

unconditional teaching: occurs when we accept students for who they are, not for what they do; an attitude that lets students know that they matter to us, even when they mess up, don't achieve, or misbehave

United Nations Educational, Scientific and Cultural Organization (UNESCO): an agency of the United Nations that encourages international peace and universal respect for human rights by promoting collaboration among nations

unobtrusive intervention: serves as a form of prevention that doesn't disrupt the flow of classroom instruction

urban settings: large cities with downtowns

validity: refers to the degree to which an assessment measures what it is designed to measure

vertical articulation: communication with teachers in other grade levels

volunteerism: giving time to assist with a cause

wait-time: time, and perhaps extended time, that gives all students opportunities to formulate and clarify responses

wayside teaching: opportunities to teach for which there are no official lesson plans, such as encounters with students in the hallway or cafeteria, or at the bus stop

webbing: a graphic way of connecting subject areas to a common theme

weight: value given to specific student work relative to other assignments

weighting grades: counting some grades more heavily than others based on relative importance

wheel courses: another term for related arts classes, referring to the fact that they are rotated

Where Everyone Belongs (WEB): involves 8th graders forming relationships with 6th graders to welcome them and keep them emotionally safe

whole language: learning to read and write within an authentic context as opposed to learning skills in isolation

withitness: in Kounin, a teacher's ability to overlap activities; the competent and confident management of classroom movement

young adolescents: generally considered 10- to 15-year-olds

zone of proximal development: the level at which a student can almost, but not completely, grasp a concept or perform a skill

References

American Academy of Pediatrics. (2015a). Gender identity development in children. Retrieved January 1, 2018, from www.healthychildren.org/English/ages-stages/gradeschool/pages/Gender-Identity-and-Gender-Confusion-In-Children.aspx

American Academy of Pediatrics. (2015b). Gender non-conforming & transgender children. Retrieved January 1, 2018, from www.healthychildren.org/English/ages-stages/gradeschool/Pages/Gender-Non-Conforming-Transgender-Children.aspx

American Academy of Pediatrics. (2016). Gay, lesbian, and bisexual teens: Facts for teens and their parents. Retrieved January 2, 2018, from www.healthychildren.org/English/ages-stages/teen/dating-sex/Pages/Gay-Lesbian-and-Bisexual-Teens-Facts-for-Teens-and-Their-Parents.aspx

Anderson, L. W., & Krathwohl, D. R. (Ed.). (2001). *A taxonomy for learning, teaching, and assessing.* New York, NY: Longman.

Anderson, M. (2016). *Learning to choose, choosing to learn.* Alexandria, VA: ASCD Learn. Teach. Lead.

Anfara, V. A., & Waks, L. (2000). Resolving the tension between academic rigor and develop-mental appropriateness. *Middle School Journal, 32*(2), 46–51.

Annie E. Casey Foundation. (2017). *Kids count data book: State trends in child well-being.* Retrieved January 7, 2018, from www.aecf.org/m/resourcedoc/aecf-2017kidscountdatabook.pdf#page=25

Arth, A. E., Lounsbury, J. H., McEwin, C. K., & Swaim, J. H. (1995). *Middle level teachers: Portraits of excellence.* Columbus, OH: National Middle School Association and National Association of Secondary School Principals.

Asp, K. (2016). 10 proven tips to make your sleep deprived teen sleep better. Retrieved January 26, 2018, from www.aastweb.org/blog/10-proven-tips-to-get-your-sleep-deprived-teen-sleep-better

Association for Middle Level Education. (n.d.). Organizing the middle school curriculum. Retrieved from www.amle.org/Publications/Web-Exclusive/Organizing/tabid/651/Default.aspx

Autism Society. (2016). Medical diagnosis. Retrieved July 20, 2016, from www.autism-society.org/what-is/diagnosis/medical-diagosis/

Autism Speaks. (2016). Learn the signs of autism. Retrieved July 20, 2016, from www.autismspeaks.org/what-autism/learn-signs

Bailey, G., Giles, R. M., & Rogers, S. E. (2015). An investigation of the concerns of fifth graders transitioning to middle school. *Research in Middle Level Education Online, 38*(5). Retrieved April 8, 2018, from https://files.eric.ed.gov/fulltext/EJ1059740.pdf

Bailey, N. J. (2011). Break the silence and make school safe for all kids! Part 1: Awareness and strategies for teachers. *Middle Ground, 15*(2), 10–12.

Barker, E. (2016). *Barking up the wrong tree.* New York, NY: Harper Collins Publishers.

Barth, R. S. (2006). Improving relationships within the schoolhouse. *Educational Leadership, 63*(6), 9–13.

Beane, J. A. (1993). *A middle school curriculum: From rhetoric to reality* (2nd ed.). Columbus, OH: National Middle School Association.

Bennett, C. I. (2015). *Comprehensive multicultural education: Theory and practice* (8th ed.). Upper Saddle River, NJ: Pearson Education, Inc.

Bergmann, J. (2016). Flipped learning. Retrieved June 8, 2018, from www.jonbergmann.com/

Bloom, B. S. (1956). *Taxonomy of educational objectives, handbook I: Cognitive domain.* New York, NY: Longmans, Green.

Boghani, P. (2017). How poverty can follow children into adulthood. Retrieved January 22, 2018, from www.pbs.org/wgbh/frontline/article/how-poverty-can-follow-children-into-adulthood/

Brown, D. F., & Knowles, T. (2014). *What every middle school teacher should know* (3rd ed.). Portsmouth, NH: Heinemann.

Budge, K. M., & Parrett, W. H. (2018). *Disrupting poverty: Five powerful classroom practices.* Alexandria, VA: ASCD.

Burden, P. R., & Byrd, D. M. (2016). *Methods for effective teaching: Meeting the needs of all students* (7th ed.). Upper Saddle River, NJ: Pearson.

Burns, M. (2015). The five key ingredients in quality neuroscience-based learning programs. *ASCD Express, 10*(16).

Caputo, J. (December, 2017). Should transgender persons serve? Annapolis, MD: *Proceedings, U.S. Naval Institute.*

Carnegie Council on Adolescent Development. (1989). *Turning points: Preparing American youth for the 21st century.* Washington, DC: Author.

Caskey, M. M., & Carpenter, J. (2012). Organizational models for teacher learning. *Middle School Journal, 43*(5), 52–62.

Caskey, M. M., Anfara, V. A., Mertens, S. B., & Flowers, N. (2013). CPT project: Findings, implications, and recommendations. In *Common planning time in middle level schools: Research studies from the MLER SIG's national project.* Charlotte, NC: Information Age Publishing, Inc.

Center for Civic Education. (2014). National standards for civics and government, 5–8 content standards. Retrieved May 18, 2018, from www.civiced.org/standards?page=58erica

Centers for Disease Control and Prevention (CDC). (2017). Childhood obesity facts. Atlanta, GA: Author. Retrieved January 15, 2018, from www.cdc.gov/healthyschools/obesity/facts.htm

Chandler, A. (2017). How can I help students develop the essential skills needed in the decision-making process? *AMLE Magazine, 5*(3), 41.

Child Trends. (2013). Parental involvement in schools. Retrieved January 10, 2018, from www.childtrends.org/?indicators=parental-involvement-in-schools

Child Trends. (2015). Percentage of All Births That Were to Unmarried Women, by Race and Hispanic Origin and Age: Selected Years, 1960–2014. Retrieved January 5, 2018, from www.childtrends.org/wp-content/uploads/2015/03/75_appendix1.pdf

Cohen, S., & Brugar, K. (2013). I want that … flipping the classroom. *Middle Ground, 16*(4), 12–13.

Collaborative for Academic, Social, and Emotional Learning. (2018). Retrieved March 12, 2018, from https://casel.org/core-competencies/

Collins, L. M. (2017). Teaching civility a crucial step in helping a child build a future. Retrieved May 23, 2018, from www.deseretnews.com/article/765590535/Teaching-civility-a-crucial-step-in-helping-a-child-build-a-future.html

Common Sense. (2015). The common sense consensus: Media use by tweens and teens. Retrieved January 20, 2018, from www.commonsensemedia.org/sites/default/files/uploads/research/census_executivesummary.pdf

Common Sense Education. (2018). Digital citizenship. Retrieved May 20, 2018, from www.commonsense.org/education/digital-citizenship

Costello, M. (2016). The Trump effect: The impact of the presidential election on our nation's schools. Southern Poverty Law Center. Retrieved May 23, 2018, from www.splcenter.org/20161128/trump-effect-impact-2016-presidential-election-our-nations-schools

Council of Chief State School Officers. (2018). English language arts standards. Retrieved May 25, 2018, from www.corestandards.org/ELA

Cruz, S., & Padilla, R. (2011). The value of routines and rituals. *Middle Ground, 14*(4), 16–17.

Curwin, R. L., Mendler, A. N., & Mendler, B. D. (2018). *Discipline with dignity* (4th ed.). Alexandria, VA: Association for Supervision and Curriculum Development.

Daniels, E. (2011). Creating motivating learning environments: Teachers matter. *Middle School Journal, 43*(2), 32–37.

Dewey, J. (1933). *How we think: A restatement of the relation of reflective thinking to the educative process.* Boston, MA: D.C. Heath.

Eilers, E. (2018). CPI's top 10 de-escalation tips. Retrieved March 31, 2018, from www.crisisprevention.com/Blog/October-2017/CPI-s-Top-10-De-Escalation-Tips-Revisited

Eisenbach, B. B., Clark, S., & Gooden, A. (2016). Cultivating connections with diverse families. *AMLE Magazine, 4*(2), 18–20.

Elliot, L. (2012). *Pink brain, blue brain: How small differences grow into troublesome gaps— And what we can do about it.* Oxford, UK: One World Publications.

Ernst, J. (1996). *Middle school study skills.* Huntington Beach, CA: Teacher Created Materials.

Estes, T. H., & Mintz, S. L. (2016). *Instruction: A models approach* (7th ed.). Boston, MA: Pearson Allyn & Bacon.

Faulkner, S. A., & Cook, C. M. (2013). Components of school culture that enhance the effective use of common planning time in two high performing middle schools. In *Common planning time in middle level schools: Research studies from the MLER SIG's national project.* Charlotte, NC: Information Age Publishing, Inc.

Fenter, R. C. (2009). The power of looping and long-term relationships. *Middle Ground, 12*(3), 29.

Fernandez-Alonso, R., Suarez-Alvarez, J., & Muniz, J. (2015). Adolescents' homework performance in mathematics and science: personal factors and teaching practices. *Journal of Educational Psychology, 107*(4), 1075–1085. Retrieved March 23, 2018, from www.apa.org/pubs/journals/releases/edu-0000032.pdf

Flowers, N., Begum, S., Carpenter, D. M. H., & Mulhall, P. F. (2017). Turnaround success: An exploratory study of three middle grades schools that achieved positive contextual and achievement outcomes using the schools to watch i3 project. *Research in Middle Level Education 40.* Retrieved December 26, 2017, from file:///C:/Users/1/Desktop/IMLE%204e%20chapters/IMLE%204e%20Ch.1/Turnaround%20Success_%20An%20Exploratory%20Study%20of%20Three%20Middle%20Grades%20Schools%20that%20Achieved%20Positive%20Contextual%20and%20Achievement%20Outcomes%20Using%20the%20Schools%20to%20Watch%20i3%20Project_%20RMLE%20Online_%20Vol%2040,%20No%208.html

Garfinkle, J. (2018). 5 qualities of emotionally intelligent leaders. Retrieved January 17, 2018, from www.smartbrief.com/original/2018/01/5-qualities-emotionally-intelligent-leaders?utm_source=brief

Gay, Lesbian, and Straight Network. (2016). National school climate survey. Retrieved February 9, 2018, from www.glsen.org/article/lgbtq-secondary-students-still-face-hostility-school-considerable-improvements-show-progress

George, P. S., & Alexander, W. M. (2003). *The exemplary middle school.* Belmont, CA: Wadsworth/Thomson Learning.

Ginott, H. G. (1993). *Teacher and child.* New York, NY: Collier Books, MacMillan.

Goleman, D. (1995). *Emotional intelligence.* New York, NY: Bantam Books.

Gollnick, D. M., & Chinn, P. C. (2017). *Multicultural education in a pluralistic society* (10th ed.). Upper Saddle River, NJ: Pearson.

Grissom, J., & Redding, C. (2016). Discretion and disproportionality: Explaining the underrepresentation of high-achieving students of color in gifted programs. *American Educational Research Association 2*(1), 1–25.

Guare, R., Dawson, P., & Guare, C. (2013). *Smart but scattered teens.* New York, NY: Guilford Press.

Gurian, M. (2017). *Saving our sons: A new path for raising healthy and resilient boys.* Spokane, WA: Gurian Institute Press.

Hansen, M., & Quintero, D. (2017). The state of the nation's social studies educators. Retrieved May 20, 2018, from www.brookings.edu/blog/brown-center-chalkboard/2017/07/03/the-state-of-the-nations-social-studies-educators/

Heward, W. L. (2013). *Exceptional children: An introduction to special education* (10th ed.). Upper Saddle River, NJ: Merrill/Prentice Hall.

Hobbs, R. (2017). Teaching and learning in a post-truth world. *Educational leadership, 75*(3), 26–31.

iCivics. (2018). Our story. Retrieved May 22, 2018, from www.icivics.org/our-story

Ideas for Global Citizenship. (2018). What is global citizenship? Retrieved May 23, 2018, from www.ideas-forum.org.uk/about-us/global-citizenship

Institute for Civility in Government. (2018). What is civility? Retrieved May 28, 2018, from www.instituteforcivility.org/who-we-are/what-is-civility/

Jackson, A. W., & Davis, G. A. (2000). *Turning points 2000: Educating adolescents in the 21st century.* New York, NY: Carnegie Corporation of New York.

Jensen, E. (2016). Understanding brain-based learning. Retrieved March 16, 2018, from www.jensenlearning.com/news/what-is-brain-based-teaching/brain-based-teaching

Jones, S.M., & Kahn, J. (2017). The evidence base for how we learn: Supporting students' social, emotional, and academic development. Retrieved December 27, 2017, from https://casel.org/wp-content/uploads/2017/09/SEAD-Research-Brief-9-12-web.pdf

Juvonen, J., Wang, Y., & Espinoza, G. (2012, December). Physical aggression, spreading of rumors, and social prominence in early adolescence: Reciprocal effects supporting gender similarities? *Journal of Youth and Adolescence.* Retrieved from http://link. springer.com/article/10.1007%2Fs10964-012-9894-0

Kahlenberg, R. D., & Janey, C. (2016, November 10). Is Trump's victory the jump-start civics education needed? *The Atlantic.*

Kids Health. (2017). Overweight and obesity. Retrieved January 15, 2018, from http://kidshealth.org/en/parents/overweight-obesity.html

King, S. (2017). Transitions with the brain in mind. *AMLE Magazine, 5*(2), 22–24.

Knowledge Is Power Program. (2018). Retrieved March 10, 2018, from www.kipp.org

Kohn, A. (2005). Unconditional teaching. *Educational Leadership, 63*(1), 20–24.

Kounin, J. (1970). *Discipline and group management in classrooms.* New York, NY: Holt, Rinehart, and Winston.

Krutka, D., & Carpenter, J. P. (2017). Digital citizenship in the curriculum. *Educational leadership, 75*(3), 51–55.

Levin, D. M., & Mee, M. (2016). How middle schools can meet the essential attributes of middle level education. *AMLE Magazine, 3*(7), 6–8.

Lounsbury, J. H. (1991). *As I see it.* Columbus, OH: National Middle School Association.

Malefyt, T. (2016). Learning centers in the secondary classroom. Retrieved March 14, 2018, from www.edutopia.org/blog/learning-centers-in-secondary-classroom-ted-malefyt

Marx, R., & Kettrey, H. H. (2016). Could gay-straight alliances reduce school bullying? Retrieved January 20, 2018, from https://apnews.com/b693ad66b99f4acc82a9b9ae52a7fbf1/could-gay-straight-alliances-reduce-school-bullying

Marzano, R. J., Pickering, D. J., & Pollock, J. E. (2012). *Classroom instruction that works: Research-based strategies for increasing student achievement* (2nd ed.). Alexandria, VA: ASCD Learn. Teach. Lead.

Marzano, R. J. (2016). *The Marzano compendium of instructional strategies.* Retrieved March 21, 2018, from file:///C:/Users/1/Downloads/FormalAssessmentsofIndividualStudents-1.pdf

McAvoy, P., Fine, R., & Ward, A. H. (2016). State standards scratch the surface of learning about political parties and ideology working paper #81. Retrieved May 5, 2018, from https://civicyouth.org/wp-content/uploads/2016/09/State-Standards-and-Political-Ideology.pdf

McEwin, C. K., & Greene, M. W. (2010). Results and recommendations from the 2009 national surveys of randomly selected and highly successful middle level schools. *Middle School Journal, 42*(1), 49–63.

McEwin, C. K., & Greene, M. W. (2011). *The status of programs and practices in America's middle schools: Results from two national studies.* Westerville, OH: Association for Middle Level Education.

McKay, T., Misra, S., & Lindquist, C. (2017). Violence and LGBTQ+ Communities: What do we know, and what do we need to know? Retrieved January 16, 2018, from www.rti.org/sites/default/files/rti_violence_and_lgbtq_communities.pdf

Mertens, S. B., Anfara, V. A., Caskey, M. M., & Flowers, N. (Eds). (2013). *Common planning time in middle level schools: Research studies from the MLER SIG's national project*. Charlotte, NC: Information Age Publishing, Inc.

Mertens, S. B., Hurd, E., & Tilford, K. (2013). The implementation and use of common planning time. In *Common planning time in middle level schools: Research studies from the MLER SIG's national project*. Charlotte, NC: Information Age Publishing, Inc.

Mulhall, P. F., Mertens, S. B., & Flowers, N. (2001). How familiar are parents with middle level practices? *Middle School Journal, 33*(2), 57–61.

National Alliance for Public Charter Schools. (2016). Charter school data dashboard. Retrieved March 4, 2018, from http://dashboard2.publiccharters.org/National/

National Assessment of Educational Progress. (2018). 2014 civics assessment. Retrieved May 12, 2018, from www.nationsreportcard.gov/hgc_2014/#civics

National Assessment Governing Board. (2018). *Civics Framework for the 2018 National Assessment of Educational Progress*. U.S. Department of Education.

National Association for Gifted Children, (n.d.). NAGC position statements & white papers. Retrieved January 3, 2018, from www.nagc.org/about-nagc/nagc-position-statements-white-papers

National Center for Education Statistics. (2015a). English language learners. Retrieved January 6, 2018, from https://nces.ed.gov/fastfacts/display.asp?id=96

National Center for Education Statistics. (2015b). What does the NAEP civics assessment measure? Retrieved May 2, 2018, from https://nces.ed.gov/nationsreportcard/civics/whatmeasure.aspx

National Center for Education Statistics. (2017). The middle grades longitudinal study of 2017–2018. Retrieved June 6, 2018, from https://nces.ed.gov/surveys/mgls/

National Center for Children in Poverty. (2017). Child poverty. Retrieved June 2, 2018, from www.nccp.org/topics/childpoverty.html

National Center for Homeless Education. (2016). *Education for homeless children and youths program*. Retrieved January 8, 2018, from https://nche.ed.gov/downloads/data-comp-1213-1415.pdf

National Council for the Social Studies. (2013a). *The college, career, and civic life (C3) framework for social studies state standards: Guidance for enhancing the rigor of K–12 civics, economics, geography, and history*. Silver Spring, MD: NCSS. Retrieved May 12, 2018, from www.socialstudies.org/c3

National Council for the Social Studies. (2013b). Revitalizing civic learning in our schools. Retrieved May 28, 2018, from www.socialstudies.org/positions/revitalizing_civic_learning

National Council of Teachers of Mathematics. (1995). *Assessment standards for school mathematics*. Reston, VA: Author.

National Crime Prevention Council. (2017). Cyberbullying. Retrieved January 18, 2018, from www.ncpc.org/resources/cyberbullying/what-parents-can-do-about-cyberbullying/

National Institute on Drug Abuse. (2017). Overdose death rates. Retrieved January 13, 2018, from www.drugabuse.gov/related-topics/trends-statistics/overdose-death-rates

National Institutes for Health (2013). Autism spectrum disorder: Uncovering clues to a complicated condition. Retrieved June 7, 2018, from https://search.nih.gov/search?utf8=%E2%9C%93&affiliate=hip&dc=940&query=autism&commit=Go

National Middle School Association. (2010). *This we believe: Keys to educating young adolescents*. Westerville, OH: Author.

National Sleep Foundation. (2018). Teens and sleep. Retrieved January 28, 2018, from https://sleepfoundation.org/sleep-topics/teens-and-sleep

National Youth Leadership Council. (2018). National service-learning conference. Retrieved May 22, 2018, from https://nylc.org/conference/

Newman, T. (2016). Sex and Gender: What Is the Difference? Medical News Today. Retrieved January 2, 2018, from www.medicalnewstoday.com/articles/232363.php

O'Connor, K. (2009). *How to grade for learning* (3rd ed.). Arlington Heights, IL: Skylight Professional Development.

Olszewski-Kubilius, P. (2013). Setting the record straight on ability grouping. *TeacherMagazine. org*. Retrieved from www.edweek.org/tm/articles/2013/05/20/fp_olszewski.html?tkn=OTUFmqJ5WF0iISbCBlLIytMENN0Uj8BcK2nq&cmp=ENL-TU-NEWS1

Padawer, R. (2012). What's so bad about a boy who wants to wear a dress? Retrieved January 6, 2018, from www.nytimes.com/2012/08/12/magazine/whats-so-bad-about-a-boy-who-wants-to-wear-a-dress.html

Pearsall, M. (2017). Successful advisory programs can have significant positive impacts on student engagement. *AMLE Magazine, 5*(4), 19–21.

Pew Hispanic Center. (2017). U.S. population growth has levelled off. Retrieved January 4, 2018, from www.pewresearch.org/fact-tank/2017/08/03/u-s-hispanic-population-growth-has-leveled-off/

Pinto, L. (2013). *From Discipline to Culturally Responsive Engagement*. Thousand Oaks, CA: Corwin.

Powell, S. D. (2010). *Wayside teaching: Connecting with students to support learning*. Thousand Oaks, CA: Corwin.

Powell, S. D. (2019). *Your introduction to education: Explorations in teaching* (4th ed.). Upper Saddle River, NJ: Pearson, Inc.

Price-Mitchell, M. (2015). Civility 101: Who's teaching the class? Retrieved May 22, 2018, from www.rootsofaction.com/civility-101-whos-teaching-the-class/

Project HOME. (2017). Facts on homelessness. Retrieved January 9, 2018, from https://projecthome.org/about/facts-homelessness

Radcliffe, C., & Kalish, E. C. (2017). Predictors of persistently poor children's economic success. Retrieved January 21, 2018, from www.mobilitypartnership.org/publications/escaping-poverty

Reinberg, S. (2018). Sleepy U.S. teens are running on empty. Retrieved January 26, 2018, from https://consumer.healthday.com/kids-health-information-23/adolescents-and-teen-health-news-719/sleepy-u-s-teens-are-running-on-empty-730521.html

Rifkin, E. (2017, November 17). Yes, kids need more civics education—but they need to be taught civility at least as much. *The Washington Post*. Retrieved May 29, 2018, from www.washingtonpost.com/news/answer-sheet/wp/2017/11/17/yes-kids-need-more-civics-education-but-they-need-to-be-taught-civility-at-least-as-much/?utm_term=.3289859ddf1f

Ruiz, E. C. (2012). Setting higher expectations: Motivating middle graders to succeed. Retrieved January 9, 2018, from www.amle.org/BrowsebyTopic/WhatsNew/WNDet/TabId/270/ArtMID/888/ArticleID/307/Setting-Higher-Expectations-Motivating-Middle-Graders-to-Succeed.aspx

Sadowski, M. (2016). *Safe is not enough: Better schools for LGBTQ students*. Boston, MA: Harvard Education Press.

San Antonio, D. M. (2006). Broadening the world of early adolescence. *Educational Leadership, 63*(7), 8–13.

Schaefer, M. B., Malu, K. F., & Yoon, B. (2016). An historical overview of the middle school movement, 1963–2015. *Research in Middle Level Education, 39*(5).

Schiesel, S. (2008). Former Justice promotes web-based civics lessons. Retrieved May 14, 2018, from www.nytimes.com/2008/06/09/arts/09sand.html

Schneider, J. (2017). The urban-school stigma. *The Atlantic*. Retrieved January 11, 2018, from www.theatlantic.com/education/archive/2017/08/the-urban-school-stigma/537966/

Slavin, R. E. (2015). *Educational psychology: Theory and practice* (11th ed.). Upper Saddle River, NJ: Pearson, Inc.

Snider, T. Z. (2014). Let kids sleep later. Retrieved January 26, 2018, from www.cnn.com/2014/08/28/opinion/snider-school-later-start-times/index.html

Sparks, S. (2017). How teachers' stress affects students: A research roundup. *Education Week*. Retrieved April 6, 2018, from www.edweek.org/tm/articles/2017/06/07/how-teachers-stress-affects-students-a-research.html

Stigler, J. W., & Hiebert, J. (2009). *The teaching gap*. New York: Simon & Schuster, Inc.

Stop Bullying Now. (2004). Retrieved from http://stopbullyingnow.hrsa.gov/index.asp?area=effects

STRIVE Preparatory Schools. (2018). Retrieved March 11, 2018, from www.striveprep.org/

Substance Abuse and Mental Health Services Administration (SAMHSA). (2016). Key substance use and mental health indicators in the United States: Results from the 2016 national survey on drug use and health. Retrieved January 14, 2018, from www.samhsa.gov/data/sites/default/files/NSDUH-FFR1-2016/NSDUH-FFR1-2016.htm#illicit1

Sutton, M. (2018). Education matters: The Hamilton effect on education may make classrooms of the future "The room where it happens." Retrieved May 22, 2018, from www.delmartimes.net/our-columns/sd-cm-nc-education-matters-20180116-story.html

Terada, Y. (2018). What's the right amount of homework? Retrieved March 26, 2018, from www.edutopia.org/article/whats-right-amount-homework

The Recovery Village. (2017). Drug use in middle school. Retrieved January 14, 2018, from www.therecoveryvillage.com/teen-addiction/middle-school-drug-use/#gref

The University of Rochester Medical Center. (2017). Health encyclopedia: Understanding the teen brain. Retrieved December 27, 2017, from www.urmc.rochester.edu/encyclopedia/content.aspx?ContentTypeID=1&ContentID=3051

Tokuhama-Espinosa, T. (2012). What neuroscience says about personalized learning. *Educational Leadership, 69*(5), retrieved March 12, 2018, from www.ascd.org/publications/educational-leadership/feb12/vol69/num05/What-Neuroscience-Says-About-Personalized-Learning.aspx

Tripodo, A., & Pondiscio, R. (2017). Seizing the civic education moment. *Educational Leadership, 75*(3), 20–25.

Turnbull, R., Turnbull, A., Wehmeyer, M., & Shogren, K. A. (2016). *Exceptional lives: Special education in today's schools* (8th ed.). Upper Saddle River, NJ: Pearson, Inc.

UNESCO. (2010). Citizenship education for the 21st century. Retrieved May 21, 2018, from www.unesco.org/education/tlsf/mods/theme_b/interact/mod07task03/appendix.htm

UNESCO. (2015). Global citizenship education: Topics and learning objectives. Retrieved May 22, 2018, from http://unesdoc.unesco.org/images/0023/002329/232993e.pdf

U.S. Census Bureau. (2016). Defining Rural at the U.S. Census Bureau. Retrieved January 14, 2018, from www2.census.gov/geo/pdfs/reference/ua/Defining_Rural.pdf

U.S. Department of Health and Human Services. (2018). Stopbullying.gov. Retrieved January 14, 2018, from www.stopbullying.gov/what-is-bullying/index.html

Vaughn, S. R., Bos, C.S., & Schumm, J. S. (2014). *Teaching students who are exceptional, diverse, and at risk in the general education classroom* (6th ed.). Upper Saddle River, NJ: Pearson, Inc.

Westheimer, J. (2017). What kind of citizens do we need? *Educational Leadership, 75*(3), 12–18.

Wiggins, G. P., & McTighe, J. (1998). *Understanding by design*. Alexandria, VA: Association for Supervision and Curriculum Development.

Wiggins, G. P., & McTighe, J. (2012). *The understanding by design guide to advanced concepts in creating and reviewing units*. Alexandria, VA: Association for Supervision and Curriculum Development.

Wiggins, G. P., & McTighe, J. (2013). *Essential questions: Opening doors to student understanding*. Alexandria, VA: Association for Supervision and Curriculum Development.

Willis, J. (2018). Aiding reading comprehension with post-its. Retrieved March 15, 2018, from www.edutopia.org/article/aiding-reading-comprehension-post-its

Wlassoff, V. (2015). Sex—Is it all in the brain? Retrieved January 2, 2018, from http://brainblogger.com/2015/11/28/sex-is-it-all-in-the-brain/

Woolfolk, A. (2016). *Educational psychology* (13th ed.). Upper Saddle River, NJ: Pearson, Inc.

Wormeli, R. (2013). Looking at executive function. *AMLE Magazine 1*(1).

Subject Index

Page numbers followed by f or t indicate figures or tables, respectively.